Yamaha
YFZ350 Banshee & YFM350X Warrior ATVs
Owners Workshop Manual

**by Mike Stubblefield
and John H Haynes**

Member of the Guild of Motoring Writers

Models covered:

YFZ350 Banshee, 1987 through 2003

YFM350X Warrior, 1987 through 2003

(7F1 - 2314)

ABCDE
FGHIJ
KLMNO
PQ

Haynes Publishing

Sparkford Nr Yeovil
Somerset BA22 7JJ England

Haynes North America, Inc

861 Lawrence Drive
Newbury Park
California 91320 USA

Acknowledgments

Our thanks to G. P. Sports, Santa Clara, California, for providing the facilities used for these photographs; to Chris Campbell, service manager, for arranging the facilities and fitting the mechanical work into his shop's busy schedule; and to Craig Wardner, service technician, for doing the mechanical work and providing valuable technical information.

© **Haynes North America, Inc. 1999, 2003**

With permission from J.H. Haynes & Co. Ltd.

A book in the Haynes Owners Workshop Manual Series

Printed in the U.S.A.

ISBN 1 56392 515 X

Library of Congress Control Number 2003110304

British Library Cataloguing in Publication Data
A catalogue record for this book is available from the British Library

We take great pride in the accuracy of information given in this manual, but motorcycle manufacturers make alterations and design changes during the production run of a particular motorcycle of which they do not inform us. No liability can be accepted by the authors or publishers for loss, damage or injury caused by any errors in, or omissions from, the information given.

03-208

Contents

1992 Yamaha Banshee

About this manual

Its purpose

The purpose of this manual is to help you get the best value from your motorcycle. It can do so in several ways. It can help you decide what work must be done, even if you choose to have it done by a dealer service department or a repair shop; it provides information and procedures for routine maintenance and servicing; and it offers diagnostic and repair procedures to follow when trouble occurs.

We hope you use the manual to tackle the work yourself. For many simpler jobs, doing it yourself may be quicker than arranging an appointment to get the vehicle into a shop and making the trips to leave it and pick it up. More importantly, a lot of money can be saved by avoiding the expense the shop must pass on to you to cover its labor and overhead costs. An added benefit is the sense of satisfaction and accomplishment that you feel after doing the job yourself.

Using the manual

The manual is divided into Chapters. Each Chapter is divided into numbered Sections, which are headed in bold type between horizontal lines. Each Section consists of consecutively numbered paragraphs or steps.

At the beginning of each numbered Section you will be referred to any illustrations which apply to the procedures in that Section. The reference numbers used in illustration captions pinpoint the pertinent Section and the Step within that Section. That is, illustration 3.2 means the illustration refers to Section 3 and Step (or paragraph) 2 within that Section.

Procedures, once described in the text, are not normally repeated. When it's necessary to refer to another Chapter, the reference will be given as Chapter and Section number. Cross references given without use of the word 'Chapter' apply to Sections and/or paragraphs in the same Chapter. For example, 'see Section 8' means in the same Chapter.

References to the left or right side of the vehicle assume you are sitting on the seat, facing forward.

Motorcycle manufacturers continually make changes to specifications and recommendations, and these, when notified, are incorporated into our manuals at the earliest opportunity.

Even though we have prepared this manual with extreme care, neither the publisher nor the authors can accept responsibility for any errors in, or omissions from, the information given.

NOTE

A **Note** provides information necessary to properly complete a procedure or information which will make the procedure easier to understand.

CAUTION

A **Caution** provides a special procedure or special steps which must be taken while completing the procedure where the Caution is found. Not heeding a Caution can result in damage to the assembly being worked on.

WARNING

A **Warning** provides a special procedure or special steps which must be taken while completing the procedure where the Warning is found. Not heeding a Warning can result in personal injury.

Introduction to the Yamaha YFM350X Warrior and YFZ350 Banshee

The Yamaha YFM350X Warrior and YFZ350 Banshee are highly successful and popular sport all-terrain vehicles.

The engine on Warrior models is an air-cooled single-cylinder four-stroke with a single overhead camshaft. Fuel is delivered to the cylinder by a single Mikuni carburetor. The engine on Banshee models is a liquid-cooled parallel twin-cylinder two-stroke. Fuel is delivered to the cylinders by a pair of Mikuni carburetors.

The front suspension is a double wishbone design with a coil spring/shock absorber unit; the rear suspension consists of a swingarm, a shock absorber and the links that connect the two.

The braking system consists of a disc brake at each front wheel and a single disc on the rear axle. All three brakes are hydraulically actuated.

All models are chain driven.

Identification numbers

The frame serial number is stamped into the left side of the frame (see illustration). The engine number is stamped into a pad which is located on the right side of the crankcase on earlier models and on left side on later models (see illustration). Both of these numbers should be recorded and kept in a safe place so they can be furnished to law enforcement officials in the event of a theft.

The frame serial number, engine serial number and carburetor identification number should also be kept in a handy place (such as with your driver's license) so they are always available when purchasing or ordering parts for your machine.

The models covered by this manual are as follows:
YFM350X Warrior, 1987 through 2003
YFZ350 Banshee, 1987 through 2003

Identifying model years

The procedures in this manual identify the vehicles by model year. The model year is included in a decal on the frame, but in case the decal is missing or obscured, the following table identifies the initial frame number of each model year.

Warrior

Year	Initial frame number, VIN or production code
1987	JY41UY*HC000101
1988	JY42XKWO*JC000101
1989	JY43GDWO*KC000101
1990	3GD-0010101
1991	3GD-063101
1992	3GD-080101
1993	JY43GDAO*PA095101
1994	3GD-108101
1995	3GD-124101
1996	3GD-140101
1997	JY43GDAO*VA176953
1998	3GDM
1999	3GDS (YFM350XLC) or 3GDR (YFM350XL)
2000	3GDU or 3GDV
2001	Not available
2002	5NF4 or 5NF5
2003	Not available

Banshee

Year	Initial frame number, VIN or production code
1987	2GU-000101
1988	2GU-030101
1989	3GC-000101
1990	3GC-010101 or 3GC-024101
1991	3GC-025101
1992	3GC-036101
1993	JV42GGAO*PA049101
1994	JY43GGAO*RA059101
1995	3GC-096101
1996	3GC-082101
1997	JY33GGAO*VA111026
1998	JY43GGAO*VA111026
1999	5FK2
2000	5FK6
2001	Not available
2002	5FKE
2003	Not available

The engine serial number is located on the crankcase

The frame serial number is located on the left side of the frame

Buying parts

Once you have found all the identification numbers, record them for reference when buying parts. Since the manufacturers change specifications, parts and vendors (companies that manufacture various components on the machine), providing the ID numbers is the only way to be reasonably sure that you are buying the correct parts.

Whenever possible, take the worn part to the dealer so direct comparison with the new component can be made. Along the trail from the manufacturer to the parts shelf, there are numerous places that the part can end up with the wrong number or be listed incorrectly.

The two places to purchase new parts for your motorcycle - the accessory store and the franchised dealer - differ in the type of parts they carry. While dealers can obtain virtually every part for your motor-cycle, the accessory dealer is usually limited to normal high wear items such as shock absorbers, tune-up parts, various engine gaskets, cables, chains, brake parts, etc. Rarely will an accessory outlet have major suspension components, cylinders, transmission gears, or cases.

Used parts can be obtained for roughly half the price of new ones, but you can't always be sure of what you're getting. Once again, take your worn part to the wrecking yard (breaker) for direct comparison.

Whether buying new, used or rebuilt parts, the best course is to deal directly with someone who specializes in parts for your particular make.

General specifications

Wheelbase	
YFM350X	1200 mm (47.2 inches)
YFZ350	1280 mm (50.4 inches)
Overall length	
YFM350X	1840 mm (72.4 inches)
YFZ350	1855 mm (73.0 inches)
Overall width	
YFM350X	1080 mm (42.5 inches)
YFZ350	1100 mm (43.3 inches)
Overall height	
YFM350X	1080 mm (42.5 inches)
YFZ350	1080 mm (42.5 inches)
Seat height	
YFM350X	765 mm (30.1 inches)
YFZ350	8700 mm (31.5 inches)
Ground clearance	
YFM350X	125 mm (4.92 inches)
YFZ350	135 mm (5.31 inches)
Weight with oil and full fuel tank	
YFM350X	191 kg (421 lbs)
YFZ350	
1987 through 1989	182 kg (401 lbs)
1990	185 kg (408 lbs)
1991	186 kg (410 lbs)
1992 on	187 kg (412 lbs)

Maintenance techniques, tools and working facilities

Basic maintenance techniques

There are a number of techniques involved in maintenance and repair that will be referred to throughout this manual. Application of these techniques will enable the amateur mechanic to be more efficient, better organized and capable of performing the various tasks properly, which will ensure that the repair job is thorough and complete.

Fastening systems

Fasteners, basically, are nuts, bolts and screws used to hold two or more parts together. There are a few things to keep in mind when working with fasteners. Almost all of them use a locking device of some type (either a lock washer, locknut, locking tab or thread adhesive). All threaded fasteners should be clean, straight, have undamaged threads and undamaged corners on the hex head where the wrench fits. Develop the habit of replacing all damaged nuts and bolts with new ones.

Rusted nuts and bolts should be treated with a penetrating oil to ease removal and prevent breakage. Some mechanics use turpentine in a spout type oil can, which works quite well. After applying the rust penetrant, let it -work for a few minutes before trying to loosen the nut or bolt. Badly rusted fasteners may have to be chiseled off or removed with a special nut breaker, available at tool stores.

If a bolt or stud breaks off in an assembly, it can be drilled out and removed with a special tool called an E-Z out (or screw extractor). Most dealer service departments and motorcycle repair shops can perform this task, as well as others (such as the repair of threaded holes that have been stripped out).

Flat washers and lock washers, when removed from an assembly, should always be replaced exactly as removed. Replace any damaged washers with new ones. Always use a flat washer between a lock washer and any soft metal surface (such as aluminum), thin sheet metal or plastic. Special locknuts can only be used once or twice before they lose their locking ability and must be replaced.

Tightening sequences and procedures

When threaded fasteners are tightened, they are often tightened to a specific torque value (torque is basically a twisting force). Overtightening the fastener can weaken it and cause it to break, while under-tightening can cause it to eventually come loose. Each bolt, depending on the material it's made of, the diameter of its shank and the material it is threaded into, has a specific torque value, which is noted in the Specifications. Be sure to follow the torque recommendations closely.

Fasteners laid out in a pattern (i.e. cylinder head bolts, engine case bolts, etc.) must be loosened or tightened in a sequence to avoid warping the component. Initially, the bolts/nuts should go on finger tight only. Next, they should be tightened one full turn each, in a criss-cross or diagonal pattern. After each one has been tightened one full turn, return to the first one tightened and tighten them all one half turn, following the same pattern. Finally, tighten each of them one quarter turn at a time until each fastener has been tightened to the proper torque. To loosen and remove the fasteners the procedure would be reversed.

Disassembly sequence

Component disassembly should be done with care and purpose to help ensure that the parts go back together properly during reassembly. Always keep track of the sequence in which parts are removed. Take note of special characteristics or marks on parts that can be installed more than one way (such as a grooved thrust washer on a shaft). It's a good idea to lay the disassembled parts out on a clean surface in the order that they were removed. It may also be helpful to make sketches or take instant photos of components before removal.

When removing fasteners from a component, keep track of their locations. Sometimes threading a bolt back in a part, or putting the washers and nut back on a stud, can prevent mix-ups later. If nuts and bolts can't be returned to their original locations, they should be kept in a compartmented box or a series of small boxes. A cupcake or muffin tin is ideal for this purpose, since each cavity can hold the bolts and nuts from a particular area (i.e. engine case bolts, valve cover bolts, engine mount bolts, etc.). A pan of this type is especially helpful when working on assemblies with very small parts (such as the carburetors and the valve train). The cavities can be marked with paint or tape to identify the contents.

Whenever wiring looms, harnesses or connectors are separated, it's a good idea to identify the two halves with numbered pieces of masking tape so they can be easily reconnected.

Gasket sealing surfaces

Throughout any motorcycle, gaskets are used to seal the mating surfaces between components and keep lubricants, fluids, vacuum or pressure contained in an assembly.

Many times these gaskets are coated with a liquid or paste type gasket sealing compound before assembly. Age, heat and pressure can sometimes cause the two parts to stick together so tightly that they are very difficult to separate. In most cases, the part can be loosened by striking it with a soft-faced hammer near the mating surfaces. A regular hammer can be used if a block of wood is placed between the hammer and the part. Do not hammer on cast parts or parts that could be easily damaged. With any particularly stubborn part, always recheck to make sure that every fastener has been removed.

Avoid using a screwdriver or bar to pry apart components, as they can easily mar the gasket sealing surfaces of the parts (which must remain smooth). If prying is absolutely necessary, use a piece of wood, but keep in mind that extra clean-up will be necessary if the wood splinters.

After the parts are separated, the old gasket must be carefully scraped off and the gasket surfaces cleaned. Stubborn gasket material can be soaked with a gasket remover (available in aerosol cans) to soften it so it can be easily scraped off. A scraper can be fashioned from a piece of copper tubing by flattening and sharpening one end. Copper is recommended because it is usually softer than the surfaces to be scraped, which reduces the chance of gouging the part. Some gaskets can be removed with a wire brush, but regardless of the method used, the mating surfaces must be left clean and smooth. If for some reason the gasket surface is gouged, then a gasket sealer thick enough to fill scratches will have to be used during reassembly of the components. For most applications, a non-drying (or semi-drying) gasket sealer is best.

Hose removal tips

Hose removal precautions closely parallel gasket removal precautions. Avoid scratching or gouging the surface that the hose mates against or the connection may leak. Because of various chemical reactions, the rubber in hoses can bond itself to the metal spigot that the hose fits over. To remove a hose, first loosen the hose clamps that secure it to the spigot. Then, with slip joint pliers, grab the hose at the clamp and rotate it around the spigot. Work it back and forth until it is completely free, then pull it off (silicone or other lubricants will ease removal if they can be applied between the hose and the outside of the spigot). Apply the same lubricant to the inside of the hose and the outside of the spigot to simplify installation.

If a hose clamp is broken or damaged, do not reuse it. Also, do not reuse hoses that are cracked, split or torn.

Spark plug gap adjusting tool

Feeler gauge set

Control cable pressure luber

Hand impact screwdriver and bits

Tools

A selection of good tools is a basic requirement for anyone who plans to maintain and repair a motorcycle. For the owner who has few tools, if any, the initial investment might seem high, but when compared to the spiraling costs of routine maintenance and repair, it is a wise one.

To help the owner decide which tools are needed to perform the tasks detailed in this manual, the following tool lists are offered: *Maintenance and minor repair*, *Repair and overhaul* and *Special*. The newcomer to practical mechanics should start off with the *Maintenance and minor repair* tool kit, which is adequate for the simpler jobs. Then, as confidence and experience grow, the owner can tackle more difficult tasks, buying additional tools as they are needed. Eventually the basic kit will be built into the *Repair and overhaul* tool set. Over a period of time, the experienced do-it-yourselfer will assemble a tool set complete enough for most repair and overhaul procedures and will add tools from the *Special* category when it is felt that the expense is justified by the frequency of use.

Maintenance and minor repair tool kit

The tools in this list should be considered the minimum required for performance of routine maintenance, servicing and minor repair work. We recommend the purchase of combination wrenches (box end and open end combined in one wrench); while more expensive than

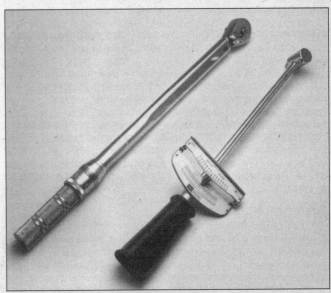

Torque wrenches (left - click; right - beam type)

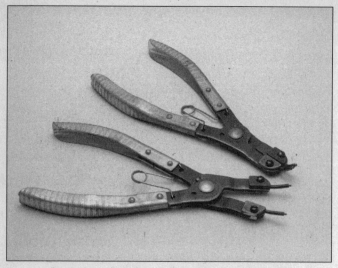

Snap-ring pliers (top - external; bottom - internal)

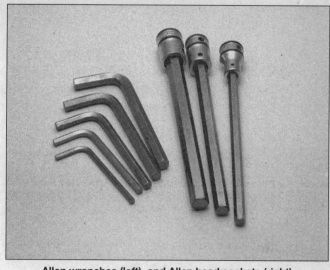

Allen wrenches (left), and Allen head sockets (right)

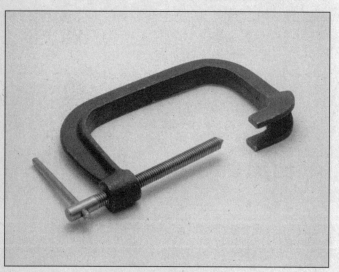

Valve spring compressor

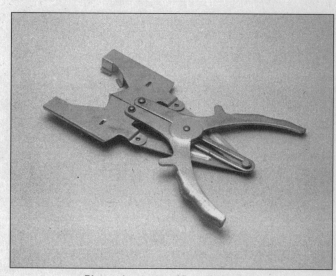

Piston ring removal/installation tool

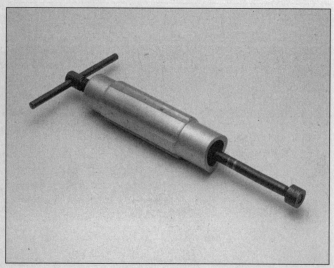

Piston pin puller

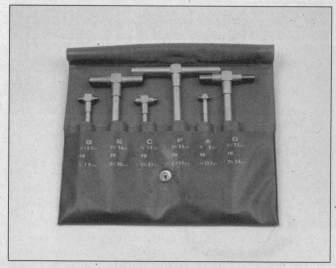

Telescoping gauges

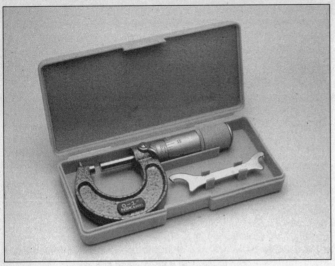

0-to-1 inch micrometer

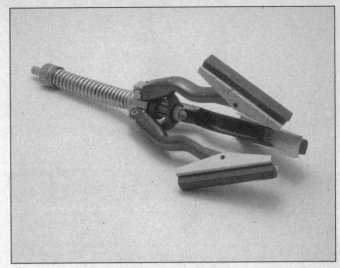

Cylinder surfacing hone

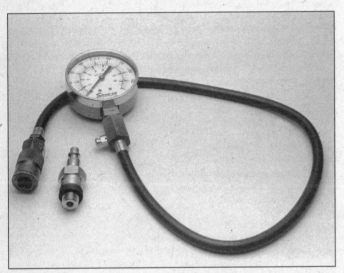

Cylinder compression gauge

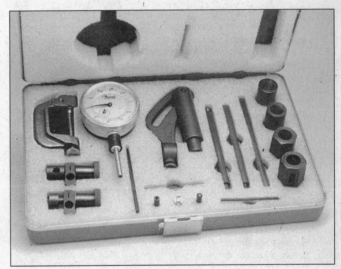

Dial indicator set

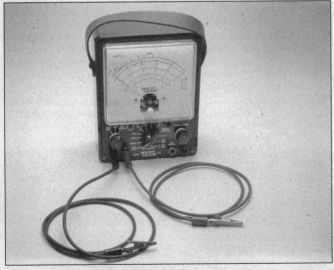

Multimeter (volt/ohm/ammeter)

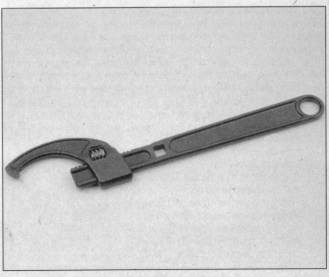

Adjustable spanner

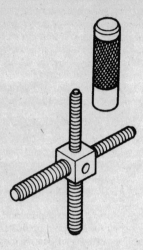

Alternator rotor puller

open-ended ones, they offer the advantages of both types of wrench.

Combination wrench set (6 mm to 22 mm)
Adjustable wrench - 8 in
Spark plug socket (with rubber insert)
Spark plug gap adjusting tool
Feeler gauge set
Standard screwdriver (5/16 in x 6 in)
Phillips screwdriver (No. 2 x 6 in)
Allen (hex) wrench set (4 mm to 12 mm)
Combination (slip-joint) pliers - 6 in
Hacksaw and assortment of blades
Tire pressure gauge
Control cable pressure luber
Grease gun
Oil can
Fine emery cloth
Wire brush
Hand impact screwdriver and bits
Funnel (medium size)
Safety goggles
Drain pan
Work light with extension cord

Repair and overhaul tool set

These tools are essential for anyone who plans to perform major repairs and are intended to supplement those in the Maintenance and minor repair tool kit. Included is a comprehensive set of sockets which, though expensive, are invaluable because of their versatility (especially when various extensions and drives are available). We recommend the 3/8 inch drive over the 1/2 inch drive for general motorcycle maintenance and repair (ideally, the mechanic would have a 3/8 inch drive set and a 1/2 inch drive set).

Alternator rotor removal tool
Socket set(s)
Reversible ratchet
Extension - 6 in
Universal joint
Torque wrench (same size drive as sockets)
Ball pein hammer - 8 oz
Soft-faced hammer (plastic/rubber)
Standard screwdriver (1/4 in x 6 in)
Standard screwdriver (stubby - 5/16 in)
Phillips screwdriver (No. 3 x 8 in)
Phillips screwdriver (stubby - No. 2)
Pliers - locking
Pliers - lineman's

Pliers - needle nose
Pliers - snap-ring (internal and external)
Cold chisel - 1/2 in
Scriber
Scraper (made from flattened copper tubing)
Center punch
Pin punches (1/16, 1/8, 3/16 in)
Steel rule/straightedge - 12 in
Pin-type spanner wrench
A selection of files
Wire brush (large)

Note: *Another tool which is often useful is an electric drill with a chuck capacity of 3/8 inch (and a set of good quality drill bits).*

Special tools

The tools in this list include those which are not used regularly, are expensive to buy, or which need to be used in accordance with their manufacturer's instructions. Unless these tools will be used frequently, it is not very economical to purchase many of them. A consideration would be to split the cost and use between yourself and a friend or friends (i.e. members of a motorcycle club).

This list primarily contains tools and instruments widely available to the public, as well as some special tools produced by the vehicle manufacturer for distribution to dealer service departments. As a result, references to the manufacturer's special tools are occasionally included in the text of this manual. Generally, an alternative method of doing the job without the special tool is offered. However, sometimes there is no alternative to their use. Where this is the case, and the tool can't be purchased or borrowed, the work should be turned over to the dealer service department or a motorcycle repair shop.

Paddock stand (for models not fitted with a centerstand)
Valve spring compressor
Piston ring removal and installation tool
Piston pin puller
Telescoping gauges
Micrometer(s) and/or dial/Vernier calipers
Cylinder surfacing hone
Cylinder compression gauge
Dial indicator set
Multimeter
Adjustable spanner
Manometer or vacuum gauge set
Small air compressor with blow gun and tire chuck

Buying tools

For the do-it-yourselfer who is just starting to get involved in motorcycle maintenance and repair, there are a number of options available when purchasing tools. If maintenance and minor repair is the extent of the work to be done, the purchase of individual tools is satisfactory. If, on the other hand, extensive work is planned, it would be a good idea to purchase a modest tool set from one of the large retail chain stores. A set can usually be bought at a substantial savings over the individual tool prices (and they often come with a tool box). As additional tools are needed, add-on sets, individual tools and a larger tool box can be purchased to expand the tool selection. Building a tool set gradually allows the cost of the tools to be spread over a longer period of time and gives the mechanic the freedom to choose only those tools that will actually be used.

Tool stores and motorcycle dealers will often be the only source of some of the special tools that are needed, but regardless of where tools are bought, try to avoid cheap ones (especially when buying screwdrivers and sockets) because they won't last very long. There are plenty of tools around at reasonable prices, but always aim to purchase items which meet the relevant national safety standards. The expense involved in replacing cheap tools will eventually be greater than the initial cost of quality tools.

It is obviously not possible to cover the subject of tools fully here. For those who wish to learn more about tools and their use, there is a book entitled *Motorcycle Workshop Practice Manual* (Book no. 1454) available from the publishers of this manual. It also provides an introduction to basic workshop practice which will be of interest to a home mechanic working on any type of motorcycle.

Care and maintenance of tools

Good tools are expensive, so it makes sense to treat them with respect. Keep them clean and in usable condition and store them properly when not in use. Always wipe off any dirt, grease or metal chips before putting them away. Never leave tools lying around in the work area.

Some tools, such as screwdrivers, pliers, wrenches and sockets, can be hung on a panel mounted on the garage or workshop wall, while others should be kept in a tool box or tray. Measuring instruments, gauges, meters, etc. must be carefully stored where they can't be damaged by weather or impact from other tools.

When tools are used with care and stored properly, they will last a very long time. Even with the best of care, tools will wear out if used frequently. When a tool is damaged or worn out, replace it; subsequent jobs will be safer and more enjoyable if you do.

Working facilities

Not to be overlooked when discussing tools is the workshop. If anything more than routine maintenance is to be carried out, some sort of suitable work area is essential.

It is understood, and appreciated, that many home mechanics do not have a good workshop or garage available and end up removing an engine or doing major repairs outside (it is recommended, however, that the overhaul or repair be completed under the cover of a roof).

A clean, flat workbench or table of comfortable working height is an absolute necessity. The workbench should be equipped with a vise that has a jaw opening of at least four inches.

As mentioned previously, some clean, dry storage space is also required for tools, as well as the lubricants, fluids, cleaning solvents, etc. which soon become necessary.

Sometimes waste oil and fluids, drained from the engine or cooling system during normal maintenance or repairs, present a disposal problem. To avoid pouring them on the ground or into a sewage system, simply pour the used fluids into large containers, seal them with caps and take them to an authorized disposal site or service station. Plastic jugs (such as old antifreeze containers) are ideal for this purpose.

Always keep a supply of old newspapers and clean rags available. Old towels are excellent for mopping up spills. Many mechanics use rolls of paper towels for most work because they are readily available and disposable. To help keep the area under the motorcycle clean, a large cardboard box can be cut open and flattened to protect the garage or shop floor.

Whenever working over a painted surface (such as the fuel tank) cover it with an old blanket or bedspread to protect the finish.

Safety first!

Professional mechanics are trained in safe working procedures. However enthusiastic you may be about getting on with the job at hand, take the time to ensure that your safety is not put at risk. A moment's lack of attention can result in an accident, as can failure to observe simple precautions.

There will always be new ways of having accidents, and the following is not a comprehensive list of all dangers; it is intended rather to make you aware of the risks and to encourage a safe approach to all work you carry out on your bike.

Essential DOs and DON'Ts

DON'T start the engine without first ascertaining that the transmission is in neutral.

DON'T suddenly remove the pressure cap from a hot cooling system - cover it with a cloth and release the pressure gradually first, or you may get scalded by escaping coolant.

DON'T attempt to drain oil until you are sure it has cooled sufficiently to avoid scalding you.

DON'T grasp any part of the engine or exhaust system without first ascertaining that it is cool enough not to burn you.

DON'T allow brake fluid or antifreeze to contact the machine's paint work or plastic components.

DON'T siphon toxic liquids such as fuel, hydraulic fluid or antifreeze by mouth, or allow them to remain on your skin.

DON'T inhale dust - it may be injurious to health (see *Asbestos* heading).

DON'T allow any spilled oil or grease to remain on the floor - wipe it up right away, before someone slips on it.

DON'T use ill fitting wrenches or other tools which may slip and cause injury.

DON'T attempt to lift a heavy component which may be beyond your capability - get assistance.

DON'T rush to finish a job or take unverified short cuts.

DON'T allow children or animals in or around an unattended vehicle.

DON'T inflate a tire to a pressure above the recommended maximum. Apart from over stressing the carcase and wheel rim, in extreme cases the tire may blow off forcibly.

DO ensure that the machine is supported securely at all times. This is especially important when the machine is blocked up to aid wheel or fork removal.

DO take care when attempting to loosen a stubborn nut or bolt. It is generally better to pull on a wrench, rather than push, so that if you slip, you fall away from the machine rather than onto it.

DO wear eye protection when using power tools such as drill, sander, bench grinder etc.

DO use a barrier cream on your hands prior to undertaking dirty jobs - it will protect your skin from infection as well as making the dirt easier to remove afterwards; but make sure your hands aren't left slippery. Note that long-term contact with used engine oil can be a health hazard.

DO keep loose clothing (cuffs, ties etc. and long hair) well out of the way of moving mechanical parts.

DO remove rings, wristwatch etc., before working on the vehicle - especially the electrical system.

DO keep your work area tidy - it is only too easy to fall over articles left lying around.

DO exercise caution when compressing springs for removal or installation. Ensure that the tension is applied and released in a controlled manner, using suitable tools which preclude the possibility of the spring escaping violently.

DO ensure that any lifting tackle used has a safe working load rating adequate for the job.

DO get someone to check periodically that all is well, when working alone on the vehicle.

DO carry out work in a logical sequence and check that everything is correctly assembled and tightened afterwards.

DO remember that your vehicle's safety affects that of yourself and others. If in doubt on any point, get professional advice.

IF, in spite of following these precautions, you are unfortunate enough to injure yourself, seek medical attention as soon as possible.

Asbestos

Certain friction, insulating, sealing and other products - such as brake pads, clutch linings, gaskets, etc. - contain asbestos. *Extreme care must be taken to avoid inhalation of dust from such products since it is hazardous to health*. If in doubt, assume that they *do* contain asbestos.

Fire

Remember at all times that gasoline (petrol) is highly flammable. Never smoke or have any kind of naked flame around, when working on the vehicle. But the risk does not end there - a spark caused by an electrical short-circuit, by two metal surfaces contacting each other, by careless use of tools, or even by static electricity built up in your body under certain conditions, can ignite gasoline (petrol) vapor, which in a confined space is highly explosive. Never use gasoline (petrol) as a cleaning solvent. Use an approved safety solvent.

Always disconnect the battery ground (earth) terminal before working on any part of the fuel or electrical system, and never risk spilling fuel on to a hot engine or exhaust.

It is recommended that a fire extinguisher of a type suitable for fuel and electrical fires is kept handy in the garage or workplace at all times. Never try to extinguish a fuel or electrical fire with water.

Fumes

Certain fumes are highly toxic and can quickly cause unconsciousness and even death if inhaled to any extent. Gasoline (petrol) vapor comes into this category, as do the vapors from certain solvents such as trichloroethylene. Any draining or pouring of such volatile fluids should be done in a well ventilated area.

When using cleaning fluids and solvents, read the instructions carefully. Never use materials from unmarked containers - they may give off poisonous vapors.

Never run the engine of a motor vehicle in an enclosed space such as a garage. Exhaust fumes contain carbon monoxide which is extremely poisonous; if you need to run the engine, always do so in the open air or at least have the rear of the vehicle outside the workplace.

The battery

Never cause a spark, or allow a naked light near the vehicle's battery. It will normally be giving off a certain amount of hydrogen gas, which is highly explosive.

Always disconnect the battery ground (earth) terminal before working on the fuel or electrical systems (except where noted).

If possible, loosen the filler plugs or cover when charging the battery from an external source. Do not charge at an excessive rate or the battery may burst.

Take care when topping up, cleaning or carrying the battery. The acid electrolyte, even when diluted, is very corrosive and should not be allowed to contact the eyes or skin. Always wear rubber gloves and goggles or a face shield. If you ever need to prepare electrolyte yourself, always add the acid slowly to the water; never add the water to the acid.

Electricity

When using an electric power tool, inspection light etc., always ensure that the appliance is correctly connected to its plug and that, where necessary, it is properly grounded (earthed). Do not use such appliances in damp conditions and, again, beware of creating a spark or applying excessive heat in the vicinity of fuel or fuel vapor. Also ensure that the appliances meet national safety standards.

A severe electric shock can result from touching certain parts of the electrical system, such as the spark plug wires (HT leads), when the engine is running or being cranked, particularly if components are damp or the insulation is defective. Where an electronic ignition system is used, the secondary (HT) voltage is much higher and could prove fatal.

ATV chemicals and lubricants

A number of chemicals and lubricants are available for use in vehicle maintenance and repair. They include a wide variety of products ranging from cleaning solvents and degreasers to lubricants and protective sprays for rubber, plastic and vinyl.

Contact point/spark plug cleaner is a solvent used to clean oily film and dirt from points, grime from electrical connectors and oil deposits from spark plugs. It is oil free and leaves no residue. It can also be used to remove gum and varnish from carburetor jets and other orifices.

Carburetor cleaner is similar to contact point/spark plug cleaner but it usually has a stronger solvent and may leave a slight oily residue. It is not recommended for cleaning electrical components or connections.

Brake system cleaner is used to remove grease or brake fluid from brake system components (where clean surfaces are absolutely necessary and petroleum-based solvents cannot be used); it also leaves no residue.

Silicone-based lubricants are used to protect rubber parts such as hoses and grommets, and are used as lubricants for hinges and locks.

Multi-purpose grease is an all purpose lubricant used wherever grease is more practical than a liquid lubricant such as oil. Some multi-purpose grease is colored white and specially formulated to be more resistant to water than ordinary grease.

Gear oil (sometimes called gear lube) is a specially designed oil used in transmissions and final drive units, as well as other areas where high friction, high temperature lubrication is required. It is available in a number of viscosities (weights) for various applications. The transmission on Banshee models is lubricated by four-stroke motor oil.

Motor oil, of course, is the lubricant specially formulated for use in the engine. It normally contains a wide variety of additives to prevent corrosion and reduce foaming and wear. Motor oil comes in various weights (viscosity ratings) of from 5 to 80. The recommended weight of the oil depends on the seasonal temperature and the demands on the engine. Light oil is used in cold climates and under light load conditions; heavy oil is used in hot climates and where high loads are encountered. Multi-viscosity oils are designed to have characteristics of both light and heavy oils and are available in a number of weights from 5W-20 to 20W-50. On Banshees, the engine oil is premixed with the gasoline. On Warriors, the same oil supply is shared by the engine and transmission.

Gas additives perform several functions, depending on their chemical makeup. They usually contain solvents that help dissolve gum and varnish that build up on carburetor and intake parts. They also serve to break down carbon deposits that form on the inside surfaces of the combustion chambers. Some additives contain upper cylinder lubricants for valves and piston rings.

Brake fluid is a specially formulated hydraulic fluid that can withstand the heat and pressure encountered in brake systems. Care must be taken that this fluid does not come in contact with painted surfaces or plastics. An opened container should always be resealed to prevent contamination by water or dirt.

Chain lubricants are formulated especially for use on the final drive chains of vehicles so equipped. A good chain lube should adhere well and have good penetrating qualities to be effective as a lubricant inside the chain and on the side plates, pins and rollers. Most chain lubes are either the foaming type or quick drying type and are usually marketed as sprays.

Degreasers are heavy duty solvents used to remove grease and grime that may accumulate on engine and frame components. They can be sprayed or brushed on and, depending on the type, are rinsed with either water or solvent.

Solvents are used alone or in combination with degreasers to clean parts and assemblies during repair and overhaul. The home mechanic should use only solvents that are non-flammable and that do not produce irritating fumes.

Gasket sealing compounds may be used in conjunction with gaskets, to improve their sealing capabilities, or alone, to seal metal-to-metal joints. Many gasket sealers can withstand extreme heat, some are impervious to gasoline and lubricants, while others are capable of filling and sealing large cavities. Depending on the intended use, gasket sealers either dry hard or stay relatively soft and pliable. They are usually applied by hand, with a brush, or are sprayed on the gasket sealing surfaces.

Thread cement is an adhesive locking compound that prevents threaded fasteners from loosening because of vibration. It is available in a variety of types for different applications.

Moisture dispersants are usually sprays that can be used to dry out electrical components such as the fuse block and wiring connectors. Some types can also be used as treatment for rubber and as a lubricant for hinges, cables and locks.

Waxes and polishes are used to help protect painted and plated surfaces from the weather. Different types of paint may require the use of different types of wax polish. Some polishes utilize a chemical or abrasive cleaner to help remove the top layer of oxidized (dull) paint on older vehicles. In recent years, many non-wax polishes (that contain a wide variety of chemicals such as polymers and silicones) have been introduced. These non-wax polishes are usually easier to apply and last longer than conventional waxes and polishes.

Troubleshooting

Contents

1   Starter motor does not rotate (YFM350X models)

1   Engine kill switch Off.
2   Fuse blown. Check fuse (Chapter 9).
3   Battery voltage low. Check and recharge battery (Chapter 9).
4   Starter motor defective. Make sure the wiring to the starter is secure. Test starter relay (Chapter 9). If the relay is good, then the fault is in the wiring or motor.
5   Starter relay faulty. Check it according to the procedure in Chapter 8.
6   Starter switch not contacting. The contacts could be wet, corroded or dirty. Disassemble and clean the switch (Chapter 9).
7   Wiring open or shorted. Check all wiring connections and harnesses to make sure that they are dry, tight and not corroded. Also check for broken or frayed wires that can cause a short to ground (see wiring diagrams, Chapter 9).
8   Ignition (main) switch defective. Check the switch according to the procedure in Chapter 9. Replace the switch with a new one if it is defective.
9   Engine kill switch defective. Check for wet, dirty or corroded contacts. Clean or replace the switch as necessary (Chapter 9).
10   Starting circuit cut-off relay, neutral switch, reverse switch or front brake switch defective. Check the relay and switches according to the procedure in Chapter 9. Replace the switch with a new one if it is defective.

2   Starter motor rotates but engine does not turn over (YFM350X models)

1   Starter motor clutch defective. Inspect and repair or replace (Chapter 9).
2   Damaged starter idle or wheel gears. Inspect and replace the damaged parts (Chapter 9).

3   Starter works but engine won't turn over (seized) (YFM350X models)

Seized engine caused by one or more internally damaged components. Failure due to wear, abuse or lack of lubrication. Damage can include seized valves, rocker arms, camshaft, piston, crankshaft, connecting rod bearings, or transmission gears or bearings. Refer to Chapter 2 for engine disassembly.

4   No fuel flow

1   No fuel in tank.
2   Tank cap air vent obstructed. Usually caused by dirt or water. Remove it and clean the cap vent hole.
3   Clogged strainer in fuel tap. Remove and clean the strainer (Chapter 1).
4   Fuel line clogged. Pull the fuel line loose and carefully blow through it.
5   Inlet needle valve clogged. A very bad batch of fuel with an unusual additive may have been used, or some other foreign material has entered the tank. Many times after a machine has been stored for many months without running, the fuel turns to a varnish-like liquid and forms deposits on the inlet needle valve and jets. The carburetor should be removed and overhauled if draining the float chamber does not solve the problem.

5   Engine flooded

1   Float level too high. Check as described in Chapter 4 and replace the float if necessary.
2   Inlet needle valve worn or stuck open. A piece of dirt, rust or other debris can cause the inlet needle to seat improperly, causing excess fuel to be admitted to the float bowl. In this case, the float chamber should be cleaned and the needle and seat inspected. If the needle and seat are worn, then the leaking will persist and the parts should be replaced with new ones (Chapter 4).
3   Starting technique incorrect. Under normal circumstances (i.e., if all the carburetor functions are sound) the machine should start with little or no throttle. When the engine is cold, the choke should be operated and the engine started without opening the throttle. When the engine is at operating temperature, only a very slight amount of throttle should be necessary. If the engine is flooded, turn the fuel tap off and hold the throttle open while cranking the engine. This will allow additional air to reach the cylinder. Remember to turn the fuel tap back on after the engine starts.

6   No spark or weak spark

1   Ignition switch Off.
2   Engine kill switch turned to the Off position.
3   Spark plug dirty, defective or worn out. Locate reason for fouled plug using spark plug condition chart and follow the plug maintenance procedures in Chapter 1.
4   Spark plug cap or secondary wiring faulty. Check condition. Replace either or both components if cracks or deterioration are evident (Chapter 5).
5   Spark plug cap not making good contact. Make sure that the plug cap fits snugly over the plug end.
6   CDI magneto defective. Check the unit, referring to Chapter 5 for details.
7   CDI unit defective. Check the unit, referring to Chapter 5 for details.
8   Ignition coil defective. Check the coil, referring to Chapter 5.
9   Ignition or kill switch shorted. This is usually caused by water, corrosion, damage or excessive wear. The kill switch can be disassembled and cleaned with electrical contact cleaner. If cleaning does not help, replace the switches (Chapter 9).
10   Wiring shorted or broken between:
  a) Ignition switch and engine kill switch (or blown fuse)
  b) CDI unit and engine kill switch
  c) CDI and ignition coil
  d) Ignition coil and plug
  e) CDI unit and CDI magneto
    Make sure that all wiring connections are clean, dry and tight. Look for chafed and broken wires (Chapters 5 and 9).

7   Compression low

1   Spark plug loose. Remove the plug and inspect the threads. Reinstall and tighten to the specified torque (Chapter 1).
2   Cylinder head not sufficiently tightened down. If the cylinder head is suspected of being loose, then there's a chance that the gasket or head is damaged if the problem has persisted for any length of time. The head nuts and bolts should be tightened to the proper torque in the correct sequence (Chapter 2).
3   Incorrect valve clearance (Warrior). This means that the valve is not closing completely and compression pressure is leaking past the valve. Check and adjust the valve clearances (Chapter 1).
4   Cylinder and/or piston worn. Excessive wear will cause compression pressure to leak past the rings. This is usually accompanied by worn rings as well. A top end overhaul is necessary (Chapter 2).
5   Piston rings worn, weak, broken, or sticking. Broken or sticking piston rings usually indicate a lubrication or carburetion problem that causes excess carbon deposits or seizures to form on the pistons and rings. Top end overhaul is necessary (Chapter 2).
6   Piston ring-to-groove clearance excessive. This is caused by

excessive wear of the piston ring lands. Piston replacement is necessary (Chapter 2).

7 Cylinder head gasket damaged. If the head is allowed to become loose, or if excessive carbon build-up on a piston crown and combustion chamber causes extremely high compression, the head gasket may leak. Retorquing the head is not always sufficient to restore the seal, so gasket replacement is necessary (Chapter 2).

8 Cylinder head warped. This is caused by overheating or incorrectly tightened head nuts and bolts. Machine shop resurfacing or head replacement is necessary (Chapter 2).

9 Valve spring broken or weak (Warrior). Caused by component failure or wear; the spring(s) must be replaced (Chapter 2).

10 Valve not seating correctly (Warrior). This is caused by a bent valve (from over-revving or incorrect valve adjustment), burned valve or seat (incorrect carburetion) or an accumulation of carbon deposits on the seat (from carburetion or lubrication problems). The valves must be cleaned and/or replaced and the seats serviced if possible (Chapter 2).

8 Stalls after starting

1 Incorrect choke action. Make sure the choke knob or lever is getting a full stroke and staying in the out position.

2 Ignition malfunction (Chapter 5).

3 Carburetor malfunction (Chapter 4).

4 Fuel contaminated. The fuel can be contaminated with either dirt or water, or can change chemically if the machine is allowed to sit for several months or more. Drain the tank and float bowl and refill with fresh fuel (Chapter 4).

5 Intake air leak. Check for loose carburetor-to-intake joint connections or loose carburetor top (Chapter 4).

6 Engine idle speed incorrect. Turn throttle stop screw until the engine idles at the specified rpm (Chapter 1).

9 Rough idle

1 Ignition malfunction (Chapter 5).

2 Idle speed incorrect (Chapter 1).

3 Carburetor malfunction (Chapter 4).

4 Idle fuel/air mixture incorrect (Chapter 4).

5 Fuel contaminated. The fuel can be contaminated with either dirt or water, or can change chemically if the machine is allowed to sit for several months or more. Drain the tank and float bowl (Chapter 4).

6 Intake air leak. Check for loose carburetor-to-intake joint connections, loose or missing vacuum gauge access port cap or hose, or loose carburetor top (Chapter 4).

7 Air cleaner clogged. Service or replace air cleaner element (Chapter 1).

Poor running at low speed

10 Spark weak

1 Battery voltage low. Check and recharge battery (Chapter 9).

2 Spark plug fouled, defective or worn out. Refer to Chapter 1 for spark plug maintenance.

3 Spark plug cap or secondary (HT) wiring defective. Refer to Chapters 1 and 5 for details on the ignition system.

4 Spark plug cap not making contact.

5 Incorrect spark plug. Wrong type, heat range or cap configuration. Check and install correct plug listed in Chapter 1. A cold plug or one with a recessed firing electrode will not operate at low speeds without fouling.

6 CDI unit defective (Chapter 5).

7 CDI magneto defective (Chapter 5).

8 Ignition coil defective (Chapter 5).

11 Air/fuel mixture incorrect

1 .Pilot screw out of adjustment (Chapter 4).

2 Pilot jet or air passage clogged. Remove and overhaul the carburetor (Chapter 4).

3 Air bleed holes clogged. Remove carburetor and blow out all passages (Chapter 4).

4 Air cleaner clogged, poorly sealed or missing.

5 Air cleaner-to-carburetor boot poorly sealed. Look for cracks, holes or loose clamps and replace or repair defective parts.

6 Float level too high or too low. Check and replace the float if necessary (Chapter 4).

7 Fuel tank air vent obstructed. Make sure that the air vent passage in the filler cap is open.

8 Carburetor intake joint loose. Check for cracks, breaks, tears or loose clamps or bolts. Repair or replace the rubber boot and its O-ring.

12 Compression low

1 Spark plug loose. Remove the plug and inspect the threads. Reinstall and tighten to the specified torque (Chapter 1).

2 Cylinder head not sufficiently tightened down. If the cylinder head is suspected of being loose, then there's a chance that the gasket and head are damaged if the problem has persisted for any length of time. The head nuts and bolts should be tightened to the proper torque in the correct sequence (Chapter 2).

3 Improper valve clearance (Warrior). This means that the valve is not closing completely and compression pressure is leaking past the valve. Check and adjust the valve clearances (Chapter 1).

4 Cylinder and/or piston worn. Excessive wear will cause compression pressure to leak past the rings. This is usually accompanied by worn rings as well. A top end overhaul is necessary (Chapter 2).

5 Piston rings worn, weak, broken, or sticking. Broken or sticking piston rings usually indicate a lubrication or carburetion problem that causes excess carbon deposits or seizures to form on the pistons and rings. Top end overhaul is necessary (Chapter 2).

6 Piston ring-to-groove clearance excessive. This is caused by excessive wear of the piston ring lands. Piston replacement is necessary (Chapter 2).

7 Cylinder head gasket damaged. If the head is allowed to become loose, or if excessive carbon build-up on the piston crown and combustion chamber causes extremely high compression, the head gasket may leak. Retorquing the head is not always sufficient to restore the seal, so gasket replacement is necessary (Chapter 2).

8 Cylinder head warped. This is caused by overheating or improperly tightened head nuts and bolts. Machine shop resurfacing or head replacement is necessary (Chapter 2).

9 Valve spring broken or weak (Warrior). Caused by component failure or wear; the spring(s) must be replaced (Chapter 2).

10 Valve not seating properly. This is caused by a bent valve (from over-revving or improper valve adjustment), burned valve or seat (improper carburetion) or an accumulation of carbon deposits on the seat (from carburetion, lubrication problems). The valves must be cleaned and/or replaced and the seats serviced if possible (Chapter 2).

13 Poor acceleration

1 Carburetor leaking or dirty. Overhaul the carburetor (Chapter 4).

2 Timing not advancing. The CDI magneto or the CDI unit may be defective. If so, they must be replaced with new ones, as they can't be repaired.

3 Engine oil viscosity too high (Warrior). Using a heavier oil than that recommended in Chapter 1 can damage the oil pump or lubrication system and cause drag on the engine.

4 Brakes dragging. Usually caused by a sticking brake caliper piston, warped disc or bent spindle. Repair as necessary (Chapter 7).

Poor running or no power at high speed

14   Firing incorrect

1   Air cleaner restricted. Clean or replace element (Chapter 1).
2   Spark plug fouled, defective or worn out. See Chapter 1 for spark plug maintenance.
3   Spark plug cap or secondary wiring defective. See Chapters 1 and 5 for details of the ignition system.
4   Spark plug cap not in good contact (Chapter 5).
5   Incorrect spark plug. Wrong type, heat range or cap configuration. Check and install correct plugs listed in Chapter 1. A cold plug or one with a recessed firing electrode will not operate at low speeds without fouling.
6   CDI unit or CDI magneto defective (Chapter 5).
7   Ignition coil defective (Chapter 5).

15   Fuel/air mixture incorrect

1   Pilot screw out of adjustment. See Chapter 4 for adjustment procedures.
2   Main jet clogged. Dirt, water or other contaminants can clog the main jets. Clean the fuel tap strainer and in-tank strainer, the float bowl area, and the jets and carburetor orifices (Chapter 4).
3   Main jet wrong size (Chapter 4).
4   Throttle shaft-to-carburetor body clearance excessive. Refer to Chapter 4 for inspection and part replacement procedures.
5   Air bleed holes clogged. Remove and overhaul carburetor (Chapter 4).
6   Air cleaner clogged, poorly sealed, or missing.
7   Air cleaner-to-carburetor boot poorly sealed. Look for cracks, holes or loose clamps, and replace or repair defective parts.
8   Float level too high or too low. Check float level and replace the float if necessary (Chapter 4).
9   Fuel tank air vent obstructed. Make sure the air vent passage in the filler cap is open.
10   Carburetor intake joint loose. Check for cracks, breaks, tears or loose clamps or bolts. Repair or replace the rubber boots (Chapter 4).
11   Fuel tap clogged. Remove the tap and clean it (Chapter 1).
12   Fuel line clogged. Pull the fuel line loose and carefully blow through it.

16   Compression low

1   Spark plug loose. Remove the plug and inspect the threads. Reinstall and tighten to the specified torque (Chapter 1).
2   Cylinder head not sufficiently tightened down. If the cylinder head is suspected of being loose, then there's a chance that the gasket and head are damaged if the problem has persisted for any length of time. The head nuts and bolts should be tightened to the proper torque in the correct sequence (Chapter 2).
3   Improper valve clearance (Warrior). This means that the valve is not closing completely and compression pressure is leaking past the valve. Check and adjust the valve clearances (Chapter 1).
4   Cylinder and/or piston worn. Excessive wear will cause compression pressure to leak past the rings. This is usually accompanied by worn rings as well. A top end overhaul is necessary (Chapter 2).
5   Piston rings worn, weak, broken, or sticking. Broken or sticking piston rings usually indicate a lubrication or carburetion problem that causes excess carbon deposits or seizures to form on the pistons and rings. Top end overhaul is necessary (Chapter 2).
6   Piston ring-to-groove clearance excessive. This is caused by excessive wear of the piston ring lands. Piston replacement is necessary (Chapter 2).
7   Cylinder head gasket damaged. If a head is allowed to become loose, or if excessive carbon build-up on the piston crown and com-

bustion chamber causes extremely high compression, the head gasket may leak. Retorquing the head is not always sufficient to restore the seal, so gasket replacement is necessary (Chapter 2).
8   Cylinder head warped. This is caused by overheating or improperly tightened head nuts and bolts. Machine shop resurfacing or head replacement is necessary (Chapter 2).
9   Valve spring broken or weak. Caused by component failure or wear; the spring(s) must be replaced (Chapter 2).
10   Valve not seating properly. This is caused by a bent valve (from over-revving or improper valve adjustment), burned valve or seat (improper carburetion) or an accumulation of carbon deposits on the seat (from carburetion or lubrication problems). The valves must be cleaned and/or replaced and the seats serviced if possible (Chapter 2).

17   Knocking or pinging

1   Carbon build-up in combustion chamber. Use of a fuel additive that will dissolve the adhesive bonding the carbon particles to the crown and chamber is the easiest way to remove the build-up. Otherwise, the cylinder head will have to be removed and decarbonized (Chapter 2).
2   Incorrect or poor quality fuel. Old or improper grades of fuel can cause detonation. This causes the piston to rattle, thus the knocking or pinging sound. Drain old fuel and always use the recommended fuel grade.
3   Spark plug heat range incorrect. Uncontrolled detonation indicates the plug heat range is too hot. The plug in effect becomes a glow plug, raising cylinder temperatures. Install the proper heat range plug (Chapter 1).
4   Improper air/fuel mixture. This will cause the cylinder to run hot, which leads to detonation. Clogged jets or an air leak can cause this imbalance (Chapter 4).

18   Miscellaneous causes

1   Throttle valve doesn't open fully. Adjust the cable slack (Chapter 1).
2   Clutch slipping. May be caused by improper adjustment or loose or worn clutch components. Refer to Chapter 1 for adjustment or Chapter 2 for clutch overhaul procedures.
3   Timing not advancing.
4   Engine oil viscosity too high. Using a heavier oil than the one recommended in Chapter 1 can damage the oil pump or lubrication system and cause drag on the engine.
5   Brakes dragging. Usually caused by a sticking brake caliper piston, warped disc or bent spindle. Repair as necessary.

Overheating

19   Cooling system malfunction (Banshee)

1   Coolant level low. Check coolant level as described in Chapter 1. If coolant level is low, the engine will overheat.
2   Leak in cooling system. Check cooling system hoses and radiator for leaks and other damage. Repair or replace parts as necessary (Chapter 3).
3   Thermostat sticking open or closed. Check and replace as described in Chapter 3.
4   Faulty radiator cap. Remove the cap and have it pressure checked at a service station.
5   Coolant passages clogged. Have the entire system drained and flushed, then refill with new coolant.
6   Water pump defective. Remove the pump and check the components.
7   Clogged radiator fins. Clean them by blowing compressed air or high-pressure water through the fins from the back side.

20 Engine overheats

1   Engine oil level low. Check and add oil (Chapter 1).
2   Wrong type of oil (Warrior). If you're not sure what type of oil is in the engine, drain it and fill with the correct type (Chapter 1).
3   Air leak at carburetor intake joint. Check and tighten or replace as necessary (Chapter 4).
4   Fuel level low. Check and adjust if necessary (Chapter 4).
5   Worn oil pump or clogged oil passages (Warrior). Replace pump or clean passages as necessary.
6   Clogged external oil line (Warrior). Remove and check for foreign material (see Chapter 2).
7   Carbon build-up in combustion chambers. Use of a fuel additive that will dissolve the adhesive bonding the carbon particles to the piston crown and chambers is the easiest way to remove the build-up. Otherwise, the cylinder head will have to be removed and decarbonized (Chapter 2).
8   Operation in high ambient temperatures.

21 Firing incorrect

1   Spark plug fouled, defective or worn out. See Chapter 1 for spark plug maintenance.
2   Incorrect spark plug (Chapter 1).
3   Faulty ignition coil(s) (Chapter 5).

22 Air/fuel mixture incorrect

1   Pilot screw out of adjustment (Chapter 4).
2   Main jet clogged. Dirt, water and other contaminants can clog the main jet. Clean the fuel tap strainer, the float bowl area and the jets and carburetor orifices (Chapter 4).
3   Main jet wrong size. The standard jetting is for sea level atmospheric pressure and oxygen content.
4   Air cleaner poorly sealed or missing.
5   Air cleaner-to-carburetor boot poorly sealed. Look for cracks, holes or loose clamps and replace or repair.
6   Fuel level too low. Check fuel level and float level and adjust or replace the float if necessary (Chapter 4).
7   Fuel tank air vent obstructed. Make sure that the air vent passage in the filler cap is open.
8   Carburetor intake manifold loose. Check for cracks or loose clamps or bolts. Check the carburetor-to-manifold gasket and the manifold-to-cylinder head O-ring (Chapter 4).

23 Compression too high

1   Carbon build-up in combustion chamber. Use of a fuel additive that will dissolve the adhesive bonding the carbon particles to the piston crown and chamber is the easiest way to remove the build-up. Otherwise, the cylinder head will have to be removed and decarbonized (Chapter 2).
2   Improperly machined head surface or installation of incorrect gasket during engine assembly.

24 Engine load excessive

1   Clutch slipping. Can be caused by damaged, loose or worn clutch components. Refer to Chapter 2 for overhaul procedures.
2   Engine oil level too high (Warrior). The addition of too much oil will cause pressurization of the crankcase and inefficient engine operation. Check Specifications and drain to proper level (Chapter 1).
3   Engine oil viscosity too high (Warrior). Using a heavier oil than the one recommended in Chapter 1 can damage the oil pump or lubrication system as well as cause drag on the engine.
4   Brakes dragging. Usually caused by a sticking brake caliper piston, warped disc or bent spindle. Repair as necessary (Chapter 7).

25 Lubrication inadequate

1   Engine oil level too low (Warrior) or premix too lean (Banshee). Friction caused by intermittent lack of lubrication or from oil that is overworked can cause overheating. The oil provides a definite cooling function in the engine. Check the oil level (Chapter 1).
2   Poor quality engine oil or incorrect viscosity or type. Oil is rated not only according to viscosity but also according to type. Some oils are not rated high enough for use in this engine. Check the Specifications Section and change to the correct oil (Chapter 1).
3   Camshaft or journals worn (Warrior). Excessive wear causing drop in oil pressure. Replace cam or cylinder head. Abnormal wear could be caused by oil starvation at high rpm from low oil level or improper viscosity or type of oil (Chapter 1).
4   Crankshaft and/or bearings worn. Same problems as paragraph 3. Check and replace crankshaft assembly if necessary (Chapter 2).

Clutch problems

26 Clutch slipping

1   Clutch friction plates worn or warped. Overhaul the clutch assembly (Chapter 2).
2   Clutch metal plates worn or warped (Chapter 2).
3   Clutch spring(s) broken or weak. Old or heat-damaged spring(s) (from slipping clutch) should be replaced with new ones (Chapter 2).
4   Clutch release mechanism defective. Replace any defective parts (Chapter 2).
5   Clutch housing unevenly worn. This causes improper engagement of the plates. Replace the damaged or worn parts (Chapter 2).

27 Clutch not disengaging completely

1   Clutch cable incorrectly adjusted (see Chapter 1).
2   Clutch plates warped or damaged. This will cause clutch drag, which in turn will cause the machine to creep. Overhaul the clutch assembly (Chapter 2).
3   Sagged or broken clutch spring(s). Check and replace the spring(s) (Chapter 2).
4   Engine/transmission oil deteriorated. Old, thin, worn out oil will not provide proper lubrication for the discs, causing the secondary clutch to drag. Replace the oil and filter (Chapter 1).
5   Engine/transmission oil viscosity too high. Using a thicker oil than recommended in Chapter 1 can cause the clutch plates to stick together, putting a drag on the engine. Change to the correct viscosity oil (Chapter 1).
6   Clutch housing seized on shaft. Lack of lubrication, severe wear or damage can cause the housing to seize on the shaft. Overhaul of the clutch, and perhaps transmission, may be necessary to repair the damage (Chapter 2).
7   Clutch release mechanism defective. Worn or damaged release mechanism parts can stick and fail to apply force to the pressure plate. Overhaul the release mechanism (Chapter 2).
8   Loose clutch center nut. Causes housing and center misalignment putting a drag on the engine. Engagement adjustment continually varies. Overhaul the clutch assembly (Chapter 2).
9   Weak or broken clutch springs (Chapter 2).

Gear shifting problems

28 Doesn't go into gear or lever doesn't return

1   Clutch not disengaging. See Section 27.
2   Shift fork(s) bent or seized. May be caused by lack of lubrication. Overhaul the transmission (Chapter 2).
3   Gear(s) stuck on shaft. Most often caused by a lack of lubrication or excessive wear in transmission bearings and bushings. Overhaul the transmission (Chapter 2).
4   Shift drum binding. Caused by lubrication failure or excessive wear. Replace the drum and bearing (Chapter 2).
5   Shift lever return spring weak or broken (Chapter 2).
6   Shift lever broken. Splines stripped out of lever or shaft, caused by allowing the lever to get loose. Replace necessary parts (Chapter 2).
7   Shift mechanism pawl broken or worn. Full engagement and rotary movement of shift drum results. Replace shaft assembly (Chapter 2).
8   Pawl spring broken. Allows pawl to float, causing sporadic shift operation. Replace spring (Chapter 2).

29 Jumps out of gear

1   Shift fork(s) worn. Overhaul the transmission (Chapter 2).
2   Gear groove(s) worn. Overhaul the transmission (Chapter 2).
3   Gear dogs or dog slots worn or damaged. The gears should be inspected and replaced. No attempt should be made to service the worn parts.

30 Overshifts

1   Pawl spring weak or broken (Chapter 2).
2   Shift cam stopper lever not functioning (Chapter 2).

Abnormal engine noise

31 Knocking or pinging

1   Carbon build-up in combustion chamber. Use of a fuel additive that will dissolve the adhesive bonding the carbon particles to the piston crown and chamber is the easiest way to remove the build-up. Otherwise, the cylinder head will have to be removed and decarbonized (Chapter 2).
2   Incorrect or poor quality fuel. Old or improper fuel can cause detonation. This causes the piston(s) to rattle, thus the knocking or pinging sound. Drain the old fuel (Chapter 4) and always use the recommended grade fuel (Chapter 1).
3   Spark plug heat range incorrect. Uncontrolled detonation indicates that the plug heat range is too hot. The plug in effect becomes a glow plug, raising cylinder temperatures. Install the proper heat range plug (Chapter 1).
4   Improper air/fuel mixture. This will cause the cylinder to run hot and lead to detonation. Clogged jets or an air leak can cause this imbalance. See Chapter 3.

32 Piston slap or rattling

1   Cylinder-to-piston clearance excessive. Caused by improper assembly. Inspect and overhaul top end parts (Chapter 2).
2   Connecting rod bent. Caused by over-revving, trying to start a badly flooded engine or from ingesting a foreign object into the combustion chamber. Replace the damaged parts (Chapter 2).

3   Piston pin or piston pin bore worn or seized from wear or lack of lubrication. Replace damaged parts (Chapter 2).
4   Piston ring(s) worn, broken or sticking. Overhaul the top end (Chapter 2).
5   Piston seizure damage. Usually from lack of lubrication or overheating. Replace the pistons and bore the cylinder, as necessary (Chapter 2).
6   Connecting rod upper or lower end clearance excessive. Caused by excessive wear or lack of lubrication. Replace worn parts.

33 Valve noise (Warrior)

1   Incorrect valve clearances. Adjust the clearances by referring to Chapter 1.
2   Valve spring broken or weak. Check and replace weak valve springs (Chapter 2).
3   Camshaft or cylinder head worn or damaged. Lack of lubrication at high rpm is usually the cause of damage. Insufficient oil or failure to change the oil at the recommended intervals are the chief causes.

34 Other noise

1   Cylinder head gasket leaking.
2   Exhaust pipe leaking at cylinder head connection. Caused by improper fit of pipe, damaged gasket or loose exhaust flange. All exhaust fasteners should be tightened evenly and carefully. Failure to do this will lead to a leak.
3   Crankshaft runout excessive. Caused by a bent crankshaft (from over-revving) or damage from an upper cylinder component failure.
4   Engine mounting bolts or nuts loose. Tighten all engine mounting bolts and nuts to the specified torque (Chapter 2).
5   Crankshaft bearings worn (Chapter 2).
6   Camshaft chain tensioner defective. Replace according to the procedure in Chapter 2.
7   Camshaft chain, sprockets or guides worn (Chapter 2).

Abnormal driveline noise

35 Clutch noise

1   Clutch housing/friction plate clearance excessive (Chapter 2).
2   Loose or damaged clutch pressure plate and/or bolts (Chapter 2).
3   Broken clutch springs (Chapter 2).

36 Transmission noise

1   Bearings worn. Also includes the possibility that the shafts are worn. Overhaul the transmission (Chapter 2).
2   Gears worn or chipped (Chapter 2).
3   Metal chips jammed in gear teeth. Probably pieces from a broken gear or shift mechanism that were picked up by the gears. This will cause early bearing failure (Chapter 2).
4   Engine oil level too low. Causes a howl from transmission. Also affects engine power and clutch operation (Chapter 1).

37 Final drive noise

1   Dry or dirty chain. Inspect, clean and lubricate (see Chapter 1).
2   Chain out of adjustment. Adjust chain slack (see Chapter 1).
3   Chain and sprockets damaged or worn. Inspect the chain and sprockets and replace them as necessary (Chapter 6).
4   Sprockets loose (Chapter 6).

Abnormal chassis noise

38 Suspension noise

1   Spring weak or broken. Makes a clicking or scraping sound.
2   Steering shaft bearings worn or damaged. Clicks when braking. Check and replace as necessary (Chapter 6).
3   Shock absorber fluid level incorrect. Indicates a leak caused by defective seal. Shock will be covered with oil. Replace shock (Chapter 6).
4   Defective shock absorber with internal damage. This is in the body of the shock and can't be remedied. The shock must be replaced with a new one (Chapter 6).
5   Bent or damaged shock body. Replace the shock with a new one (Chapter 6).

39 Brake noise

1   Squeal caused by dust on brake pads. Usually found in combination with glazed pads. Clean using brake cleaning solvent (Chapter 7).
2   Contamination of brake pads. Grease, water or dirt causing pads to chatter or squeal. Clean or replace pads (Chapter 7).
3   Pads glazed. Caused by excessive heat from prolonged use or from contamination. Do not use sandpaper, emery cloth or carborundum cloth or any other abrasives to roughen pad surface; abrasives will stay in the pad material and damage the disc. A very fine flat file can be used, but pad replacement is suggested as a cure (Chapter 7).
4   Disc warped. Can cause chattering, clicking or intermittent squeal. Usually accompanied by a pulsating lever and uneven braking. Replace the disc (Chapter 7).
5   Loose or worn wheel bearings. Check and replace as necessary (Chapter 7).

Excessive exhaust smoke

40 White smoke

1   Piston oil ring worn (Warrior). The ring may be broken or damaged, causing oil from the crankcase to be pulled past the piston into the combustion chamber. Replace the rings with new ones (Chapter 2).
2   Cylinder worn, cracked, or scored. Caused by overheating or oil starvation. If worn or scored, the cylinder will have to be rebored and a new piston installed. If cracked, the cylinder will have to be replaced (see Chapter 2).
3   Valve oil seal damaged or worn (Warrior). Replace oil seals with new ones (Chapter 2).
4   Valve guide worn (Warrior). Perform a complete valve job (Chapter 2).
5   Engine oil level too high, which causes the oil to be forced past the rings (Warrior). Drain oil to the proper level (Chapter 1).
6   Head gasket broken between oil return and cylinder (Warrior). Causes oil to be pulled into the combustion chamber. Replace the head gasket and check the head for warpage (Chapter 2).
7   Abnormal crankcase pressurization, which forces oil past the rings. Clogged breather or hoses usually the cause (Chapter 2).

41 Black smoke

1   Air cleaner clogged. Clean or replace the element (Chapter 1).
2   Main jet too large or loose. Compare the jet size to the Specifications (Chapter 4).

3   Choke stuck, causing fuel to be pulled through choke circuit (Chapter 4).
4   Fuel level too high. Check the fuel level and float level and adjust if necessary (Chapter 4).
5   Inlet needle held off needle seat. Clean the float chamber and fuel line and replace the needle and seat if necessary (Chapter 4).

42 Brown smoke

1   Main jet too small or clogged. Lean condition caused by wrong size main jet or by a restricted orifice. Clean float chamber and jets and compare jet size to Specifications (Chapter 4).
2   Fuel flow insufficient. Fuel inlet needle valve stuck closed due to chemical reaction with old fuel. Float level incorrect; check and replace float if necessary. Restricted fuel line. Clean line and float chamber.
3   Carburetor intake tube loose (Chapter 4).
4   Air cleaner poorly sealed or not installed (Chapter 1).

Poor handling or stability

43 Handlebar hard to turn

1   Steering shaft nut too tight (Chapter 6).
2   Lower bearing or upper bushing damaged. Roughness can be felt as the bars are turned from side-to-side. Replace bearing and bushing (Chapter 6).
3   Steering shaft bearing lubrication inadequate. Causes are grease getting hard from age or being washed out by high pressure car washes. Remove steering shaft and replace bearing (Chapter 6).
4   Steering shaft bent. Caused by a collision, hitting a pothole or by rolling the machine. Replace damaged part. Don't try to straighten the steering shaft (Chapter 6).
5   Front tire air pressure too low (Chapter 1).

44 Handlebar shakes or vibrates excessively

1   Tires worn or out of balance (Chapter 1 or 7).
2   Swingarm bearings worn. Replace worn bearings by referring to Chapter 6.
3   Wheel rim(s) warped or damaged. Inspect wheels (Chapter 7).
4   Wheel bearings worn. Worn front or rear wheel bearings can cause poor tracking. Worn front bearings will cause wobble (Chapter 7).
5   Wheel hubs installed incorrectly (Chapter 7).
6   Handlebar clamp bolts or bracket nuts loose (Chapter 6).
7   Steering shaft nut or bolts loose. Tighten them to the specified torque (Chapter 6).
8   Motor mount bolts loose. Will cause excessive vibration with increased engine rpm (Chapter 2).

45 Handlebar pulls to one side

1   Uneven tire pressures (Chapter 1).
2   Frame bent. Definitely suspect this if the machine has been rolled. May or may not be accompanied by cracking near the bend. Replace the frame.
3   Wheel out of alignment. Caused by incorrect toe-in adjustment (Chapter 1) or bent tie-rod (Chapter 6).
4   Swingarm bent or twisted. Caused by age (metal fatigue) or impact damage. Replace the swingarm (Chapter 6).

5   Steering stem bent. Caused by impact damage or by rolling the vehicle. Replace the steering stem (Chapter 6).

46   Poor shock absorbing qualities

1   Too hard:
  a) *Shock internal damage.*
  b) *Tire pressure too high (Chapters 1 and 7).*
2   Too soft:
  a) *Shock oil insufficient and/or leaking (Chapter 6).*
  d) *Springs weak or broken (Chapter 6).*

Braking problems

47   Brakes are spongy, don't hold

1   Disc brake pads worn (Chapters 1 and 7).
2   Disc brake pads contaminated by oil, grease, etc. Clean or replace pads (Chapter 7).
3   Disc warped. Replace disc (Chapter 7).

48   Brake lever or pedal pulsates

1   Disc warped. Replace disc (Chapter 7).
2   Axle bent. Replace axle (Chapter 7).
3   Brake caliper bolts loose (see Chapter 7).
4   Brake caliper shafts damaged or sticking, causing caliper to bind. Lube the shafts or replace them if they're corroded or bent (Chapter 7).
5   Wheel warped or otherwise damaged (Chapter 7).
6   Wheel hub or axle bearings damaged or worn (Chapter 7).

49   Brakes drag

1   Lever or pedal balky or stuck. Check pivot and lubricate (Chapter 7).
2   Brake caliper binds. Caused by inadequate lubrication or damage to caliper shafts (Chapter 7).
3   Brake caliper piston seized in bore. Caused by wear or ingestion of dirt getting past deteriorated seal (Chapter 7).
4   Brake pad(s) damaged. Pad material separated from backing plate. Usually caused by faulty manufacturing process or contact with chemicals. Replace pads (Chapter 7).
5   Pads incorrectly installed (Chapter 7).
6   Brake pedal or lever freeplay insufficient (Chapter 1).

Chapter 1
Tune-up and routine maintenance

Contents

Specifications

Engine

Spark plugs
  Warrior
    1987 through 2000
      Type.. NGK D8EA or ND X24ES-U
      Gap... 0.6 to 0.7 mm (0.024 to 0.028 inch)
    2001 and later
      Type.. NGKDR8EA
      Gap... 0.6 to 0.7 mm (0.024 to to 0.028 inch)
  Banshee
    1987 through 2000
      Type.. NGK B8ES or ND W24ES
      Gap... 0.7 to 0.8 mm (0.028 to 0.031 inch)
    2001 and later
      Type.. NGKBR8ES
      Gap... 0.7 to 0.8 mm (0.028 to 0.031 inch)
Valve clearance (Warrior)
  Intake... 0.06 to 0.10 mm (0.002 to 0.004 inch)
  Exhaust... 0.16 to 0.20 mm (0.006 to 0.008 inch)
Engine idle speed... 1450 to 1550 rpm
Pilot air screw opening (Banshee)................................. Two turns out
Compression (Warrior)
  Standard... 850 kPa (121 psi)
  Minimum... 800 kPa (114 psi)
  Maximum... 900 kPa (128 psi)

Chassis

Brake pad thickness (limit)
    Front
        1987 through 1989... 0.8 mm (0.03 inch)
        1990 on.. 1.0 mm (0.03 inch)
    Rear .... 1.0 mm (0.04 inch)
Front brake lever freeplay
    1987 through 2000 .... 4 to 8 mm (0.16 to 0.31 inch) (at lever tip)
    2001 and later .... zero
Rear brake pedal height .... 10 mm (0.39 inch) below footpeg
Throttle lever freeplay
    Warrior.. 3 to 5 mm (0.12 to 0.20 inch)
    Banshee
        1987 .... 3 to 5 mm (0.12 to 0.20 inch)
        1988 on .... 4 to 6 mm (0.16 to 0.24 inch)
Clutch lever freeplay... 5 to 10 mm (0.20 to 0.39 inch)
Drive chain slack
    Warrior.. 30 to 40 mm (1.18 to 1.57 inches)
    Banshee .... 15 to 20 mm (0.59 to 0.79 inch)
Speed limiter screw setting .... Do not back out more than 12 mm (0.47 inch)
Minimum tire tread depth .... 3 mm (1/8 inch)
Tire pressures (cold)
Warrior
    1987 through 1991
        Front
            Standard.. 4.3 psi
            Maximum.. 4.7 psi
            Minimum.. 3.8 psi
        Rear
            Standard.. 3.6 psi
            Maximum.. 4.0 psi
            Minimum.. 3.1 psi
    1992 and 1993
        Front
            Standard.. 4.4 psi
            Maximum.. 4.7 psi
            Minimum.. 3.9 psi
        Rear
            Standard.. 3.6 psi
            Maximum.. 4.0 psi
            Minimum.. 3.2 psi
    1994 on
        Front
            Standard.. 3.6 psi
            Maximum.. 4.0 psi
            Minimum.. 3.2 psi
        Rear
            Standard.. 3.6 psi
            Maximum.. 4.0 psi
            Minimum.. 3.2 psi
Banshee
    1987 through 1989
        Front
            Standard.. 4.3 psi
            Maximum.. 4.7 psi
            Minimum.. 3.8 psi
        Rear
            Standard.. 3.6 psi
            Maximum.. 4.0 psi
            Minimum.. 3.1 psi
    1990
        Front
            Standard.. 4.4 psi
            Maximum.. 4.7 psi
            Minimum.. 3.9 psi
        Rear
            Standard.. 3.6 psi
            Maximum.. 4.0 psi
            Minimum.. 3.2 psi

Banshee (continued)
  1991 on
    Front
      Standard .... 4.4 psi
      Maximum .... 4.7 psi
      Minimum .... 3.9 psi
    Rear
      Standard .... 4.4 psi
      Maximum .... 4.7 psi
      Minimum .... 3.9 psi
Front wheel toe-in .... 0 to 10 mm (0 to 0.4 inch)

Torque specifications

Coolant drain plugs (Banshee) .... 14 Nm (120 in-lbs)
Oil filter cover bolts (Warrior) .... 10 Nm (84 in-lbs)
Oil drain plugs
  Engine (Warrior) .... 32 Nm (23 ft-lbs)
  Transmission (Banshee) .... 20 Nm (168 in-lbs)
Clutch adjusting screw locknut .... 15 Nm (11 ft-lbs)
Spark plugs .... 17.5 Nm (12.5 ft-lbs)
Tie rod locknuts .... 30 Nm (22 ft-lbs)*

Apply non-permanent thread locking agent to the locknut threads.

Recommended lubricants and fluids

Engine oil
  Warrior
    Type .... Yamalube or equivalent 10W40 SE
    Capacity
      At oil change .... 2.5 liters (2.6 quarts)
      After engine overhaul .... 3.2 liters (3.4 quarts)
  Banshee
    Type .... Yamalube "R" 2-stroke racing oil (if Yamalube R is not available, use
Castrol R30, A545 or A747)
  Mixing ratio
    Yamalube R 24:1
    Castrol R30, A545 and A747 .... 20:1
Transmission oil capacity (Banshee)
  Type .... Yamalube 4 or equivalent API SE or SF grade oil
  Viscosity .... SAE 10W-30
  Capacity
    At oil change .... 1.5 liters (1.6 quarts)
    After engine overhaul .... 1.7 liters (1.8 quarts)
Air filter oil .... Yamaha foam air filter oil, or 10W-30 engine oil
Cooling system (Banshee)
  System capacity
    1987 through 1989 .... 2.5 liters (2.6 quarts)
    1990 on .... 1.5 liters (1.6 quarts)
    Reservoir tank capacity .... 0.28 liter (0.30 quart)
Miscellaneous
  Wheel bearings .... Medium weight, lithium-based multi-purpose grease
  Swingarm pivot bearings .... Medium weight, lithium-based multi-purpose grease
  Steering shaft bushings .... Medium weight, lithium-based multi-purpose grease
  Cables and lever pivots .... Medium weight, lithium-based multi-purpose grease
  Brake pedal/shift lever/throttle lever pivots .... Medium weight, lithium-based multi-purpose grease

1

1 Yamaha Warrior and Banshee Routine maintenance intervals

Note: *The pre-ride inspection outlined in the owner's manual covers checks and maintenance that should be carried out on a daily basis. It's condensed and included here to remind you of its importance. Always perform the pre-ride inspection at every maintenance interval (in addition to the procedures listed). The intervals listed below are the shortest intervals recommended by the manufacturer for each particular operation during the model years covered in this manual. Your owner's manual may have different intervals for your model.*

Daily or before riding

Check the operation of both brakes - check the brake lever and pedal for correct freeplay
Check the throttle for smooth operation and correct freeplay
Make sure the engine kill switch works correctly
Check the tires for damage, the presence of foreign objects and correct air pressure
Check the engine oil level (Warrior) or transmission oil level (Banshee)
Check the fuel level and inspect for leaks
Check the air cleaner drain tube and clean it if necessary
If the drain tube is clogged, clean the air filter element
Inspect the drive chain
Make sure the steering operates smoothly
Verify that the headlight and taillight are operating satisfactorily
Check all fasteners, including wheel nuts and axle nuts, for tightness
Check the underbody for mud or debris that could start a fire or interfere with vehicle operation

Every 20 to 40 hours

Clean the air filter element and replace it if necessary*
*More often in dusty or wet conditions.

Every six months

Change the engine oil (Warrior) or the transmission oil (Banshee)
Clean and gap and, if necessary, replace the spark plug(s)
Inspect the fuel tap, fuel line(s) and, on Banshee models, the oil line
Check the throttle for smooth operation and correct freeplay
Check choke operation
Check idle speed and adjust it if necessary
Inspect the front and rear brake discs
Check brake operation and brake lever and pedal freeplay
Check the clutch for smooth operation and correct lever freeplay
Lubricate the steering shaft and front suspension
Lubricate and inspect the drive chain, sprockets and rollers
Check steering system operation and freeplay
Inspect the wheels and tires
Check the wheel bearings for looseness or damage
Inspect the front and rear suspension
Check all chassis fasteners for tightness
Check the skid plates for looseness or damage
Check the exhaust system for leaks and check fastener tightness

---

2 Introduction to tune-up and routine maintenance

Refer to illustration 1.1

This Chapter covers in detail the checks and procedures necessary for the tune-up and routine maintenance of your vehicle. Section 1 includes the routine maintenance schedule, which is designed to keep the machine in proper running condition and prevent possible problems. The remaining Sections contain detailed procedures for carrying out the items listed on the maintenance schedule, as well as additional maintenance information designed to increase reliability. Maintenance information is also printed on decals, which are mounted in various locations on the vehicle **(see illustration)**. Where information on the decals differs from that presented in this Chapter, use the decal information.

Since routine maintenance plays such an important role in the safe and efficient operation of your vehicle, it is presented here as a comprehensive check list. These lists outline the procedures and checks that should be done on a routine basis.

Deciding where to start or plug into the routine maintenance schedule depends on several factors. If you have a vehicle whose warranty has recently expired, and if it has been maintained according to the warranty standards, you may want to pick up routine maintenance as it coincides with the next mileage or calendar interval. If you have

owned the machine for some time but have never performed any maintenance on it, then you may want to start at the nearest interval and include some additional procedures to ensure that nothing important is overlooked. If you have just had a major engine overhaul, then you may

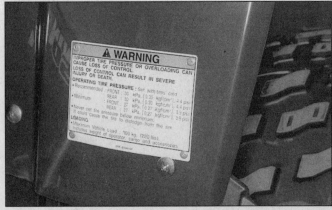

1.1 Decals on the vehicle include maintenance and safety information

3.2a Make sure that the brake fluid level in the front brake master cylinder reservoir is above the LOWER mark

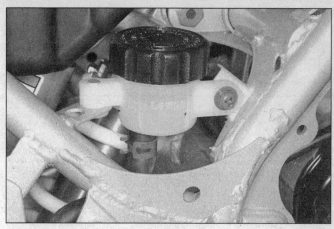

3.2b Make sure that the brake fluid level in the rear brake master cylinder reservoir is above the LOWER mark

want to start the maintenance routine from the beginning. If you have a used machine and have no knowledge of its history or maintenance record, you may desire to combine all the checks into one large service initially and then settle into the maintenance schedule prescribed.

The Sections that describe the inspection and maintenance procedures are written as step-by-step comprehensive guides to the actual performance of the work. They explain in detail each of the routine inspections and maintenance procedures on the check list. References to additional information in applicable Chapters is also included and should not be overlooked.

Before beginning any actual maintenance or repair, the machine should be cleaned thoroughly, especially around the oil filler plug, spark plug, engine covers, carburetor, etc. Cleaning will help ensure that dirt does not contaminate the engine and will allow you to detect wear and damage that could otherwise easily go unnoticed.

3   Fluid levels - check

Brake fluid

Refer to illustrations 3.2a and 3.2b

1   With the vehicle in a level position, turn the handlebars until the top of the front brake master cylinder is as level as possible.

2   The fluid level is visible through the master cylinder reservoir. Make sure that the fluid level is above the Lower mark on the reservoir **(see illustrations)**.

3   If the level is low, the brake fluid must be replenished. Before uncovering the master cylinder, place rags beneath the reservoir (to protect the paint from brake fluid spills) and remove all dust and dirt

from the area around the master cylinder.

4   To remove the cover from the front brake master cylinder, remove the cover screws, then lift off the cover, rubber diaphragm and float (if equipped). **Caution:** *Don't operate the brake lever with the cover removed.* To remove the cap from the rear brake master cylinder, simply unscrew it.

5   Add new, clean brake fluid of the recommended type to bring the level above the Lower mark. Don't mix different brands of brake fluid in the reservoir, as they may not be compatible. Also, don't mix different specifications (DOT 3 with DOT 4).

6   Reinstall the float (if equipped), rubber diaphragm and cover. Tighten the cover screws securely (don't overtighten them, or you'll strip the threads).

7   Wipe any spilled fluid off the reservoir body.

8   If the brake fluid level was low, inspect the front brake system for leaks (see Section 4).

Engine oil (Warrior models)

Refer to illustrations 3.11a and 3.11b

9   Support the vehicle in a level position, then start the engine and allow it to reach normal operating temperature. **Warning:** *Do not run the engine in an enclosed space such as a garage or shop.*

10   Stop the engine and allow the machine to sit undisturbed in a level position for about five minutes.

11   To check the engine oil, unscrew the dipstick from the right side of the crankcase **(see illustration)**. Pull it out, wipe it off with a clean rag, and reinsert it (let the dipstick rest on the threads; don't screw it back in). Pull the dipstick out and check the oil level on the dipstick scale **(see illustration)**. The oil level should be between the Maximum and Minimum level marks on the scale.

3.11a On Warrior models, unscrew the engine oil filler cap . . .

3.11b . . . and pull out the dipstick; the oil level must be between the upper and lower marks

3.15a On Banshee models, unscrew the transmission oil filler cap and pull out the dipstick . . .

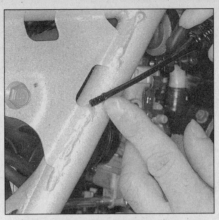

3.15b . . . the oil level must be between the upper and lower marks

3.18 On Banshee models, make sure that the coolant level is between the FULL and LOW marks

12   If the level is below the Minimum mark, add oil through the dipstick hole. Add enough oil of the recommended grade and type to bring the level up to the Maximum mark. Do not overfill.

Clutch and transmission oil (Banshee models)

Refer to illustrations 3.15a and 3.15b

13   The transmission and clutch share a common oil supply separate from the engine oil.

14   Park the vehicle in a level position, then start the engine and allow it to reach normal operating temperature. **Warning:** *Do not run the engine in an enclosed space such as a garage or shop.*

15   Stop the engine, unscrew the dipstick cap and note the oil level on the dipstick **(see illustrations)**. It should be between the upper and lower marks.

16   If the level is below the lower mark, add enough oil of the recommended grade and type to bring the level up to the upper mark. Do not overfill.

17   Inspect the filler cap O-ring and replace it if it's cracked, cut or deteriorated.

Coolant (Banshee models)

Refer to illustration 3.18

Note: *Check the coolant level in the reservoir tank when the engine is cold.*

18   With the vehicle on level ground, note the coolant level in the coolant reservoir tank **(see illustration)**.

19   The coolant level should be between the FULL and LOW marks

on the reservoir (the level varies with the temperature of the coolant).

20   If the coolant level is below the LOW mark, flip open the access door above the reservoir, remove the reservoir cap and add soft water to bring the level between the FULL and LOW marks. **Caution:** *If soft water is unavailable, use distilled water; do NOT use hard water or salt water, both of which will damage the engine.*

4   Brake system - general check

Refer to illustrations 4.4a, 4.4b and 4.8

1   Always inspect the brakes before riding! A routine pre-ride general check will ensure that problems are discovered and remedied before they become dangerous.

2   Inspect the brake lever and pedal for loose pivots, excessive play, bending, cracking and other damage. Replace any damaged parts (see Chapter 7). Make sure all brake fasteners are tight.

4   Squeeze the front brake lever so that the brake pads protrude from the calipers and look at the wear indicator. **Note:** *On some early calipers, there's an inspection plug in the back of the caliper.* On early pads, there's a groove formed in the friction material, next to the backing plate **(see illustration)**. When the pads are worn enough to expose the groove, replace them. On later pads, there's a wear line running along the edge of each pad, parallel to the backing plate **(see illustration)**. If the pad material has been worn down to the wear lines - or is getting close to the lines - it's time for new pads (see Chapter 7).

5   Depress the rear brake pedal so that the pads protrude from the

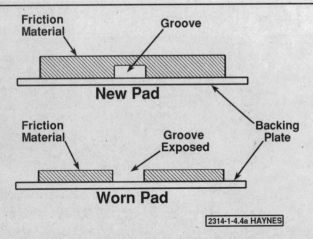

4.4a Replace early pads if the groove in the friction material is exposed by pad wear

4.4b Replace later pads If the friction material is worn to or near the indicator lines (arrow)

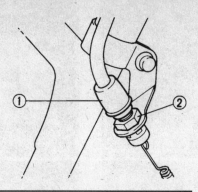

4.8 The brake light switch (if equipped) is mounted near the brake pedal

1 *Brake light switch*
2 *Adjusting nut*

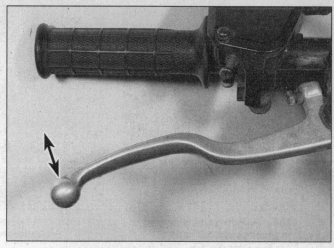

5.1 Measure brake lever freeplay at the lever tip . . .

caliper and look at the wear grooves. Again, if the pad material is worn down to the lines, install new pads (see Chapter 7).

6   If you have difficulty determining whether the pads are excessively worn because the wear indicator is hard to see (or the aftermarket pads don't have any kind of indicator), remove the pads (see Chapter 7), measure the thickness of the pads and compare your measurements to the pad thickness limits listed in this Chapter's Specifications.

7   Verify that the parking brake system will hold the vehicle on an incline. If it won't, adjust the parking brake (see Chapter 7).

8   Some Maine and New Hampshire models are equipped with a brake light which is activated by a brake light switch **(see illustration)** at the rear brake pedal. If you own one of these models, make sure that the brake light works when the rear brake pedal is applied (it should come on just before the brake light begins to work). If it doesn't, hold the body of the brake light switch so that it doesn't turn, and rotate the switch adjusting nut as necessary.

5   Front brake lever freeplay and rear brake pedal height - check and adjustment

Front brake lever freeplay

Refer to illustrations 5.1 and 5.2

1   Operate the brake lever and measure freeplay at the tip of the lever **(see illustration)**. If it's not within the range listed in this Chapter's Specifications, adjust it as described below.

2   Loosen the adjuster locknut **(see illustration)** and turn the adjuster in or out to obtain the correct freeplay.

3   Tighten the adjuster locknut securely and recheck the lever freeplay.

Rear brake pedal height

Refer to illustration 5.4

4   The upper side of the rear brake pedal should be the specified distance (listed in this Chapter's Specifications) below the top of the footpeg **(see illustration)**.

5   If the pedal height is incorrect, inspect the rear brake pads (see Section 4). If the pads are okay, inspect the rear brake master cylinder, brake hose and caliper for a leak (see Chapter 7). Pedal height is not adjustable.

6   Steering system - inspection and toe-in adjustment

Inspection

1   This vehicle is equipped with bearings at the upper and lower ends of the steering shaft. These can become dented, rough or loose during normal use of the machine. In extreme cases, worn or loose parts can cause steering wobble that is potentially dangerous.

2   To check, block the rear wheels so the vehicle can't roll, jack up the front end and support it securely on jackstands.

3   Point the wheel straight ahead and slowly move the handlebar from side-to-side. Dents or roughness in the bearing will be felt and the bars will not move smoothly. **Note:** *Make sure any hesitation in movement is not being caused by the cables and wiring harnesses that run to the handlebar.*

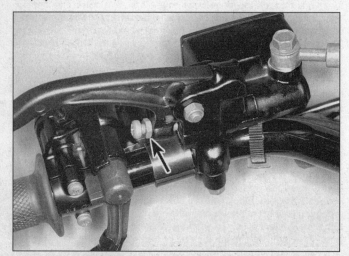

5.2 . . . if it's incorrect, loosen the adjuster locknut (arrow), turn the adjuster screw to change it and tighten the locknut

5.4 Measure brake pedal height from the top of the footpeg to the top of the pedal (arrows)

1

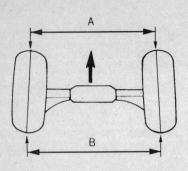

6.10 Toe-in measurement
(B minus A = toe-in)

6.11a Loosen the locknuts (arrows) at the tie rod inner ends . . .

6.11b . . . and at the outer ends (left arrow); use a wrench on the flat (right arrow) to hold and turn the tie rod

4   If the handlebar doesn't move smoothly, or if it has excessive lateral play, remove and inspect the steering shaft bushings (see Chapter 6).

5   Look at the tie-rod ends (inner and outer) while slowly turning the handlebar from side-to-side. If there's any vertical movement in the tie-rod balljoints, replace them (see Chapter 6).

Toe-in adjustment

Refer to illustrations 6.10, 6.11a and 6.11b

6   Roll the vehicle forward onto a level surface and stop it with the front wheels pointing straight ahead.

7   Make a mark at the front and center of each tire, even with the centerline of the front hub.

8   Measure the distance between the marks with a toe-in gauge or steel tape measure.

9   Have an assistant push the vehicle backward while you watch the marks on the tires. Stop pushing when the tires have rotated exactly one-half turn, so the marks are at the backs of the tires.

10   Again, measure the distance between the marks. Subtract the front measurement from the rear measurement to get toe-in **(see illustration)**.

11   If toe-in is not as specified in this Chapter's Specifications, hold each tie-rod with a wrench on the flats and loosen the locknuts **(see illustrations)**. Turn the tie-rods an equal amount to change toe-in. When toe-in is set correctly, tighten the locknuts to the torque listed in this Chapter's Specifications.

7   Suspension - check

1   The suspension components must be maintained in top operating condition to ensure rider safety. Loose, worn or damaged suspension parts decrease the vehicle's stability and control.

2   Lock the front brake and push on the handlebars to compress the front shock absorbers several times. See if they move up-and-down smoothly without binding. If binding is felt, the shocks should be inspected as described in Chapter 5.

3   Check the tightness of all front suspension nuts and bolts to be sure none have worked loose.

4   Inspect the rear shock absorber for fluid leakage and tightness of the mounting nuts and bolts. If leakage is found, the shock should be replaced.

5   Raise the rear of the vehicle and support it securely on jackstands. Grab the swingarm on each side, just ahead of the axle. Rock the swingarm from side to side - there should be no discernible movement at the rear. If there's a little movement or a slight clicking can be heard, make sure the swingarm pivot shaft is tight. If the pivot shaft is tight but movement is still noticeable, the swingarm will have to be removed and the bearings replaced as described in Chapter 5.

6   Inspect the tightness of the rear suspension nuts and bolts.

8   Drive chain and sprockets - check, adjustment and lubrication

Refer to illustrations 8.3, 8.5, 8.6a, 8.6b and 8.6c

1   A neglected drive chain won't last long and can quickly damage the sprockets. Routine chain adjustment isn't difficult and will ensure maximum chain and sprocket life.

2   To check the chain, support the vehicle securely on jackstands with the rear wheels off the ground. Place the transmission in neutral.

3   Push down and pull up on the top run of the chain and measure the slack midway between the two sprockets **(see illustration)**, then compare the measurements to the value listed in this Chapter's Specifications. As wear occurs, the chain will actually stretch, which means adjustment is necessary to remove some slack from the chain. In some cases where lubrication has been neglected, corrosion and galling may cause the links to bind and kink, which effectively shortens the chain's length. If the chain is tight between the sprockets, rusty or kinked, it's time to replace it with a new one. **Note:** *Repeat the chain slack measurement along the length of the chain - ideally, every inch or so. If you find a tight area, mark it with felt pen or paint and repeat the measurement after the machine has been ridden. If the chain's still tight in the same areas, it may be damaged or worn. Because a tight or kinked chain can damage the transmission countershaft bearing, it's a good idea to replace it.*

4   Check the entire length of the chain for damaged rollers or O-rings, loose links and loose pins.

5   Look through the slots in the engine sprocket cover and inspect the engine sprocket **(see illustration)**. Check the teeth on the engine sprocket and the rear sprocket for wear (see Chapter 7). Refer to Chapter 7 for the sprocket replacement procedure if the sprockets appear to be worn excessively. **Note:** *Never install a new chain on old sprockets and never use the old chain if you install new sprockets - replace the chain and sprockets as a set.*

6   Check the chain rollers and slider **(see illustrations)**. If a roller or slider is worn, replace it (see Chapter 7).

Adjustment

Refer to illustrations 8.8a, 8.8b and 8.8c

7   Rotate the rear wheels until the chain is positioned with the least amount of slack present.

8   Loosen the upper and lower rear hub bolts **(see illustrations)**. Loosen the adjuster locknuts and turn the adjuster on each side of the swingarm evenly until the proper chain tension is obtained. Be sure to turn the adjusters evenly to keep the wheel in alignment **(see illustration)**. If the adjusters reach the end of their travel, the chain is excessively worn and should be replaced with a new one (see Chapter 7).

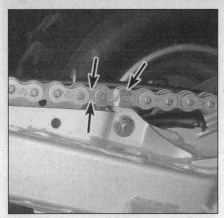

8.3 Measure drive chain slack along the upper chain run; make sure the master link clip (arrow) is secure

8.5 Inspect the front sprocket teeth for excessive wear; make sure there's no play in the sprocket

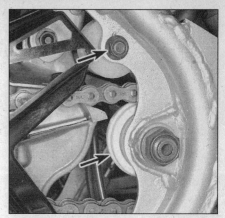

8.6a Check the upper chain roller (upper arrow), the front chain guide (lower arrow) . . .

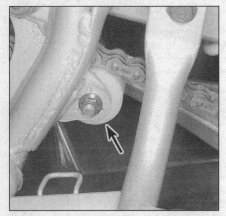

8.6b . . . the lower chain roller (arrow) . . .

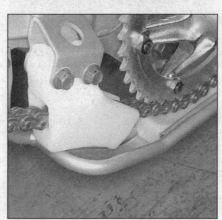

8.6c . . . and the rear chain guide for excessive wear; replace if they're worn or if the rollers turn roughly

8.8a Loosen the upper hub nut and bolt . . .

Lubrication

Note: If the chain is dirty, it should be removed and cleaned before it's lubricated (see Chapter 7).

9   The best time to lubricate the chain is after the vehicle has been ridden. When the chain is warm, the lubricant will penetrate the joints between the side plates to provide lubrication. Yamaha specifies SAE 30 to 50 engine oil only; do not use chain lube, which may contain sol-vents that can damage the chain's rubber O-rings. Apply the oil to the area where the side plates overlap - not to the middle of the rollers.

10   Apply the lubricant along the top of the lower chain run, so that when the machine is ridden centrifugal force will move the lubricant into the chain, rather than throwing it off.

11   After applying the lubricant, let it soak in a few minutes before wiping off any excess.

8.8b . . . the lower hub bolts, chain adjuster locknuts and adjusters (arrows)

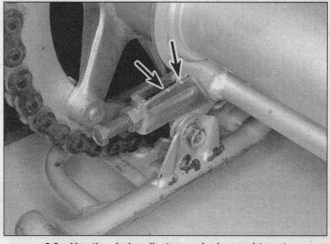

8.8c Use the chain adjuster marks (arrows) to set the adjusters evenly

9.4 Check tire pressure with a gauge that will read accurately at the low pressures used in ATV tires

9.5 Be sure the directional arrow points in the forward rotating direction of the tire

10.3 Rock the wheel and tire from side-to-side to check wheel bearing play

9 Tires/wheels - general check

Refer to illustrations 9.4 and 9.5

1   Routine tire and wheel checks should be made with the realization that your safety depends to a great extent on their condition.
2   Check the tires carefully for cuts, tears, embedded nails or other sharp objects and excessive wear. Operation of the vehicle with excessively worn tires is extremely hazardous, as traction and handling are directly affected. Measure the tread depth at the center of the tire and replace worn tires with new ones when the tread depth is less than that listed in this Chapter's Specifications.
3   Repair or replace punctured tires as soon as damage is noted. Do not try to patch a torn tire, as wheel balance and tire reliability may be impaired.
4   Check the tire pressures when the tires are cold and keep them properly inflated **(see illustration)**. Proper air pressure will increase tire life and provide maximum stability and ride comfort. Keep in mind that low tire pressures may cause the tire to slip on the rim or come off, while high tire pressures will cause abnormal tread wear and unsafe handling. **Caution:** *ATV tires operate at very low pressures. Overinflation may rupture them.*
5   Make sure the tires are installed on the correct side of the vehicle. ATV tires are directional; that is, they are designed to rotate in only one forward direction. The direction of forward rotation is indicated by an arrow molded into the tire sidewall **(see illustration)**.
6   The steel wheels used on this machine are virtually maintenance free, but they should be kept clean and checked periodically for cracks, bending and rust. Never attempt to repair damaged wheels; they must be replaced with new ones.
7   Check the valve stem locknuts to make sure they're tight. Also, make sure the valve stem cap is in place and tight. If it is missing, install a new one made of metal or hard plastic.

10 Front wheel bearings - check

Refer to illustration 10.3

1   Raise the front of the vehicle and support it securely on jackstands.
2   Spin the front wheels by hand. Listen for noise, which indicates dry or worn wheel bearings.
3   Grasp the top and bottom of the tire and try to rock it back-and-forth **(see illustration)**. If there's more than a very small amount of play, the wheel bearings are in need of adjustment or replacement. Refer to Chapter 7 for service procedures.

11 Lubrication - general

Refer to illustrations 11.3, 11.7a and 11.7b

1   Since the controls, cables and various other components of an ATV are exposed to the elements, they should be lubricated periodically to ensure safe and trouble-free operation.
2   The throttle lever, brake levers and brake pedal should be lubricated frequently. Yamaha recommends 10W-30 motor oil inside cables and for the pivot points of levers and pedals. Multi-purpose lithium grease is recommended for cable ends and other lubrication points, such as suspension and steering bushings. In order for the lubricant to be applied where it will do the most good, the component should be disassembled. However, if chain and cable lubricant is being used, it can be applied to the pivot joint gaps and will usually work its way into the areas where friction occurs. If motor oil or light grease is being used, apply it sparingly as it may attract dirt (which could cause the controls to bind or wear at an accelerated rate). **Note:** *One of the best lubricants for the control lever pivots is a dry-film lubricant (available from many sources by different names).*
3   The throttle and clutch cables should be removed and treated with a commercially available cable lubricant which is specially formulated for use on ATV control cables. Small adapters for pressure lubricating the cables with spray can lubricants are available and ensure that the cable is lubricated along its entire length **(see illustration)**. When attaching a cable to its handlebar lever, be sure to lubricate the barrel-shaped fitting at the end with multi-purpose grease.
4   To lubricate the cables, disconnect one end, then lubricate the cable with a pressure lube adapter **(see illustration 11.3)** (clutch cable, see Chapter 2; throttle cable, see Chapter 4).
5   Refer to Chapter 6 for the following lubrication procedures:
   a) *Upper steering shaft bushing*
   b) *Swingarm bearings and dust seals*
6   Refer to Chapter 7 for the following lubrication procedures:
   a) *Rear brake pedal pivot*
   b) *Front wheel bearings*
7   Using a grease gun, lubricate the front suspension and lower steering column bushings through the grease nipples **(see illustrations)**.

12 Fasteners - check

1   Since vibration of the machine tends to loosen fasteners, all nuts, bolts, screws, etc. should be periodically checked for proper tightness. Also make sure all cotter pins or other safety fasteners are correctly installed.

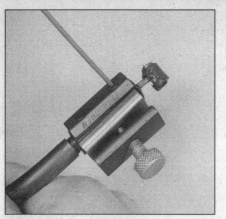

11.3 Lubricating a cable with a pressure lube adapter (make sure the tool seats around the inner cable)

11.7a There are three grease fittings (arrows) on each pair of front suspension arms . . .

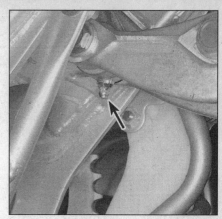

11.7b . . . and a grease fitting (arrow) on the underside of the rear suspension connecting rod

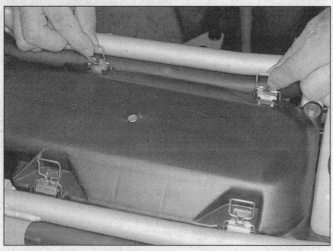

14.2a To remove a Banshee air cleaner cover, release these clips (arrows)

2   Pay particular attention to the following:
Spark plug(s)
Transmission oil drain plug
Gearshift pedal
Brake pedal
Footpegs
Engine mount bolts

Shock absorber mount bolts
Front axle nuts
Rear axle nuts
Skid plate bolts

3   If a torque wrench is available, use it along with the torque specifications at the beginning of this, or other, Chapters.

13   Skid plates - check

1   Check the skid plates under the vehicle for damage (see Chapter 8). The front skid plate also includes the front bumper. Have damaged plates repaired, or else replace them.
2   Make sure the skid plate fasteners are all in position and tightly secured.

14   Air filter element and drain tube - cleaning

Element cleaning
Refer to illustrations 14.2a, 14.2b, 14.3a, 14.3b, 14.3c and 14.3d
1   Remove the seat (see Chapter 8).
2   Remove the cover from the air filter housing. On Warrior models, the cover is secured by five screws; on Banshee models, it's secured by four hooks **(see illustrations)**.
3   Remove the air filter element **(see illustration)** and separate the element from the element guide **(see illustrations)**.

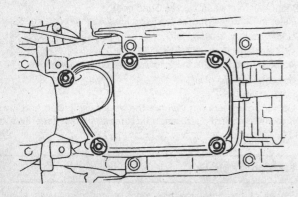

14.2b To remove a Warrior air cleaner cover, remove these screws (arrows)

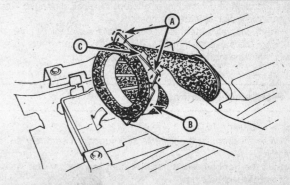

14.3a Lift the air filter out of the air cleaner housing (Banshee shown; Warrior similar)

| A | Arrows (point upward) | C | Tab on band (to rear of |
| B | Arrows (point forward) | | vehicle) |

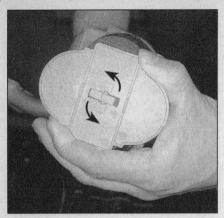

14.3b To disassemble the filter element and guide, rotate the element endplate 90 degrees and pull it off

14.3c Separate the filter element from the plastic guide (Banshee)

14.3d Separate the filter element from the metal guide (Warrior)

4   Clean the element and guide in a high flash point solvent, squeeze the solvent out of the foam and let the guide and element dry completely.

5   Soak the foam element in the foam filter oil listed in this Chapter's Specifications, then squeeze it firmly to remove the excess oil. Don't wring it out or the foam may be damaged. The element should be thoroughly oil-soaked, but not dripping.

6   Reassemble the element and guide.

7   Installation is the reverse of removal.

Drain tube cleaning

Refer to illustration 14.8

8   Check the drain tube **(see illustration)** for accumulated water and oil. If oil or water has built up in the tube, squeeze its clamp, remove the tube from the air cleaner housing and clean it out. Install the drain tube on the housing and secure it with the clamp. **Note:** *A drain tube that's full indicates the need to clean the filter element and the inside of the case.*

15   Fuel system - inspection

Refer to illustrations 15.1, 15.5a, 15.5b, 15.9a and 15.9b

Warning: *Gasoline is extremely flammable, so take extra precautions when you work on any part of the fuel system. Don't smoke or allow open flames or bare light bulbs near the work area, and don't work in a garage where a natural gas-type appliance (such as a water heater or clothes dryer) is present. Since gasoline is carcinogenic, wear latex gloves when there's a possibility of being exposed to fuel, and if you spill any fuel on your skin, rinse it off immediately with soap and water. Mop up any fuel spills immediately and do not store fuel-soaked rags where they could ignite. When you perform any kind of work on the fuel system, wear safety glasses and have a fire extinguisher suitable for class B type fires (flammable liquids) on hand.*

1   Check the fuel tank, the fuel tap, the fuel line and the carburetor for leaks and evidence of damage **(Banshee models, see illustration; Warrior models, see illustration 25.1b)**.

2   If carburetor gaskets are leaking, the carburetor should be disassembled and rebuilt (see Chapter 4).

3   If the fuel tap is leaking, tightening the screws may help. If leakage persists, the tap should be disassembled and repaired or replaced with a new one.

4   If the fuel line is cracked or otherwise deteriorated, replace it with a new one.

5   Place the fuel tap lever in the Off position. Remove and drain the fuel tank. Remove the screws and detach the tap from the tank **(see illustrations)**.

6   Clean the strainer with solvent and let it dry.

7   Installation is the reverse of removal. Be sure to use a new O-ring. Hand-tighten the screws firmly, but don't overtighten them. If you do, the O-ring will be distorted, which will result in fuel leaks.

8   After installation, run the engine and check for fuel leaks.

9   Anytime the vehicle is going to be stored for a month or more, remove and drain the fuel tank. Also loosen the float chamber drain screw and drain the fuel from the carburetor **(see illustrations)**.

10   Inspect the condition of the crankcase breather hose. Replace it if it's cracked, torn or deteriorated.

14.8 Check the drain tube (arrow) for accumulated water and oil

15.1 Inspect the fuel tap, the fuel line and the float chamber seam (arrows) for leaks (Banshee)

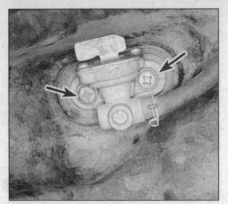

15.5a Remove the fuel tap screws (arrows) . . .

15.5b . . . and separate the tap and strainer from the tank

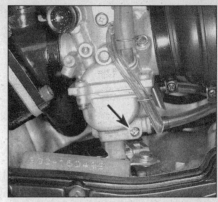

15.9a Float chamber drain screw (arrow) (Banshee)

15.9b Float chamber drain screw (A) and idle speed adjustment screw (B) (Warrior)

16.1a Banshee spark plugs are in the top of the cylinder head

16 Spark plug(s) - inspection, cleaning and gapping

Refer to illustrations 16.1a, 16.1b, 16.1c, 16.5a and 16.5b

1   Twist the spark plug cap **(see illustrations)** to break it free from the plug, then pull it off. If available, use compressed air to blow any accumulated debris from around the spark plug. Remove the plug with a spark plug socket **(see illustration)**.

2   Inspect the electrodes for wear. Both the center and side electrodes should have square edges and the side electrode should be of uniform thickness. Look for excessive deposits and evidence of a cracked or chipped insulator around the center electrode. Compare your spark plugs to the color spark plug reading chart on the inside back cover. Check the threads, the washer and the ceramic insulator body for cracks and other damage.

3   If the electrodes are not excessively worn, and if the deposits can be easily removed with a wire brush, the plug can be regapped and reused (if no cracks or chips are visible in the insulator). If in doubt concerning the condition of the plug, replace it with a new one, as the expense is minimal.

4   Cleaning the spark plug by sandblasting is permitted, provided you clean the plug with a high flash-point solvent afterwards.

16.1b The Warrior spark plug is on the side of the cylinder head

16.1c Unscrew the plug with a spark plug socket

16.5a Spark plug manufacturers recommend using a wire type gauge when checking the gap - if the wire doesn't slide between the electrodes with a slight drag, adjustment is required

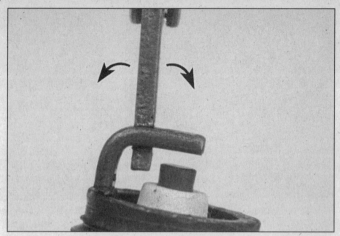

16.5b To change the gap, bend the side electrode only, as indicated by the arrows, and be very careful not to crack or chip the ceramic insulator surrounding the center electrode

5   Before installing a new plug, make sure it is the correct type and heat range. Check the gap between the electrodes, as it is not preset. For best results, use a wire-type gauge rather than a flat gauge to check the gap **(see illustration)**. If the gap must be adjusted, bend the side electrode only and be very careful not to chip or crack the insulator nose **(see illustration)**. Make sure the washer is in place before installing the plug.

6   Since the cylinder head is made of aluminum, which is soft and easily damaged, thread the plug into the head by hand. Slip a short length of hose over the end of the plug to use as a tool to thread it into place. The hose will grip the plug well enough to turn it, but will start to slip if the plug begins to cross-thread in the hole - this will prevent damaged threads and the accompanying repair costs.

7   Once the plug is finger tight, the job can be finished with a socket. If a torque wrench is available, tighten the spark plug to the torque listed in this Chapter's Specifications. If you do not have a torque wrench, tighten the plug finger tight (until the washer bottoms on the cylinder head) then use a spark plug socket to tighten it an additional 1/4 turn. Regardless of the method used, do not over-tighten it.

8   Reconnect the spark plug cap.

17 Engine oil and filter (Warrior models) - change

Refer to illustrations 17.5a, 17.5b, 17.6 and 17.16

1   Consistent routine oil and filter changes are the single most important maintenance procedure you can perform on a vehicle. The oil not only lubricates the internal parts of the engine, transmission and clutch, but it also acts as a coolant, a cleaner, a sealant and a protectant. Because of these demands, the oil takes a terrific amount of abuse and should be replaced often with new oil of the recommended grade and type.

2   Before changing the oil and filter, warm up the engine so the oil will drain easily. Be careful when draining the oil, as the exhaust pipe, the engine and the oil itself can cause severe burns.

3   Park the vehicle over a clean drain pan.

4   Remove the dipstick/oil filler cap to vent the crankcase and act as a reminder that there is no oil in the engine.

5   Remove the drain plug from the engine **(see illustration)** and allow the oil to drain into the pan. The O-ring, spring and strainer will probably fall as out as the plug is removed, so be careful not to lose them **(see illustration)**.

6   Remove the oil filter cover bolts, then remove the cover, O-ring and filter element **(see illustration)**. If additional maintenance is planned for this time period, check or service another component while the oil is allowed to drain completely.

7   Wipe any remaining oil out of the filter housing area of the

17.5a Unscrew the oil drain plug (arrow) and remove the O-ring, spring and strainer

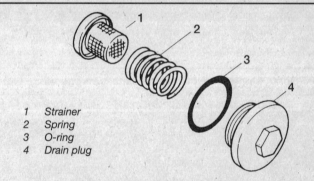

1   Strainer
2   Spring
3   O-ring
4   Drain plug

17.5b Engine oil drain plug details

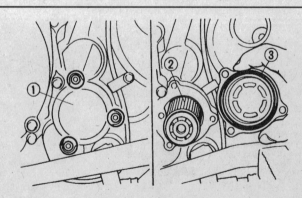

17.6 Oil filter details (Warrior); be sure the open end of the filter faces into the engine

1   Oil filter cover   3   Cover O-ring
2   Filter element

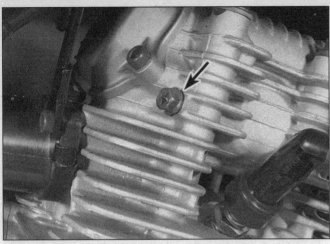

17.16 Loosen the oil gallery plug (arrow) slightly; if oil doesn't seep from the plug within one minute of idling, stop the engine and find out why

crankcase and make sure the oil passage is clear. Clean the drain plug's oil strainer with solvent and let it dry completely.

8   Check the condition of the drain plug threads and the O-rings.

9   Install the filter element with its open end facing into the engine **(see illustration 16.6b). Caution:** *The filter must be installed facing the correct direction or oil starvation may cause severe engine damage.*

10   Install the cover with a new O-ring and tighten the bolts to the torque listed in this Chapter's Specifications.

11   Install the oil strainer, spring and engine drain plug, using a new O-ring if the old one is worn or damaged. Tighten the plug to the torque listed in this Chapter's Specifications. Avoid overtightening, as damage to the engine case will result.

12   Before refilling the engine, check the old oil carefully. If the oil was drained into a clean pan, small pieces of metal or other material can be easily detected. If the oil is very metallic colored, then the engine is experiencing wear from break-in (new engine) or from insufficient lubrication. If there are flakes or chips of metal in the oil, then something is drastically wrong internally and the engine will have to be disassembled for inspection and repair.

13   If there are pieces of fiber-like material in the oil, the clutch is experiencing excessive wear and should be checked.

14   If the inspection of the oil turns up nothing unusual, refill the crankcase to the proper level with the recommended oil and install the dipstick/filler cap.

15   Start the engine and let it run for two or three minutes. Shut it off, wait a few minutes, then check the oil level. If necessary, add more oil to bring the level up to the upper level mark on the dipstick. Check around the drain plug(s) and filter cover for leaks.

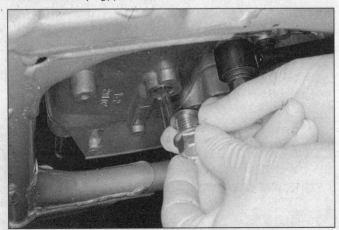

18.2 Transmission oil drain plug (Banshee)

16   Loosen the oil gallery plug on the cylinder head slightly **(see illustration)**. Start the engine and let it idle. Oil should seep from the plug within one minute. If not, oil is not flowing properly. Shut the engine off and find the problem before running it further. Make sure the oil filter is installed in the proper direction.

17   The old oil drained from the engine cannot be reused in its present state and should be disposed of. Check with your local refuse disposal company, disposal facility or environmental agency to see if they will accept the oil for recycling. Don't pour used oil into drains or onto the ground. After the oil has cooled, it can be drained into a suitable container (capped plastic jugs, topped bottles, milk cartons, etc.) for transport to one of these disposal sites.

18   Transmission oil (Banshee models) - change

Refer to illustration 18.2

1   Park the vehicle in a level position, then start the engine and allow it to reach normal operating temperature. **Warning:** *Do not run the engine in an enclosed space such as a garage or shop.*

2   Place a clean pan under the transmission drain plug. Remove the plug and drain the transmission oil **(see illustration)**. While the oil is draining, check the condition of the drain plug threads and the sealing washer.

3   After all the old oil has drained, install the drain plug with its sealing washer and tighten it to the torque listed in this Chapter's Specifications.

4   Before refilling the transmission, check the old oil carefully. If the oil was drained into a clean pan, small pieces of metal or other material can be easily detected. If the oil is very metallic colored, then the transmission is experiencing wear from break-in (new parts) or from insufficient lubrication. If there are flakes or chips of metal in the oil, then something is drastically wrong internally and the engine will have to be disassembled for inspection and repair.

5   If there are pieces of fiber-like material in the oil, the clutch friction discs are worn excessively and should be replaced.

6   If the inspection of the oil turns up nothing unusual, refill the transmission to the proper level with the recommended oil and install the filler cap.

7   Start the engine and let it run for two or three minutes. Shut it off, wait a few minutes, then check the oil level in the inspection window. If necessary, add more oil to bring the level up to the upper level mark on the window. Check around the drain plug for leaks.

19   Cooling system (Banshee models) - check

Refer to illustration 19.7

1   The cooling system should be carefully inspected at the recommended intervals. Look for evidence of leaks, check the condition of the coolant, check the radiator for clogged fins and damage and make sure the fan operates when required.

2   Examine each of the rubber coolant hoses along its entire length. Look for cracks, abrasions and other damage. Squeeze each hose at various points. They should feel firm, yet pliable, and return to their original shape when released. If they are dried out or hard, replace them.

3   Look for leaks at each cooling system joint. Tighten the hose clamps carefully to halt minor leaks. If a hose is seriously cracked or torn at a hose clamp, tightening the clamp won't stop the leak; it might even accelerate it. If a hose leaks after tightening the hose clamp, drain the coolant (see Section 20), loosen the clamp, pull off the hose and inspect it closely. If the damage is close to the end of the hose, cut off the damaged end and reattach the hose. If the damage is too far from the end of the hose, cutting off the end of the hose is not an option; replace the hose.

4   Inspect the radiator for evidence of leaks and other damage. Radiator leaks usually produce tell-tale deposits or stains on the surface of the core below the leak. If the radiator is leaking, remove it (see Chapter 3) and have it repaired by a radiator shop or replace it. **Caution:** *Do NOT use a liquid leak-stopping compound to try to repair leaks.*

1

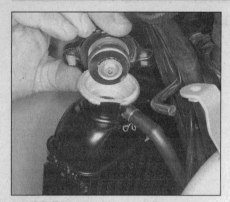

19.7 To prevent burns, follow safety precautions in the text when removing the Banshee radiator cap

20.4a Left cylinder coolant drain plug (arrow) (Banshee)

20.4b Right cylinder coolant drain plug (Banshee)

5   Inspect the radiator cooling fins for mud, dirt and insects. Debris stuck in the fins can impede the flow of air through the radiator. If the fins are dirty, force water or low-pressure compressed air through the fins from the backside of the radiator. If any of the fins are bent or distorted, straighten them carefully with a screwdriver.

6   Remove the radiator cover.

7   Remove the radiator cap **(see illustration)** as follows: Turn it counterclockwise until it reaches the first detent. If you hear a hissing sound (indicating there is still pressure in the system), wait until it stops. Then press down on the cap and continue turning it counterclockwise until it's free.

8   Inspect the condition of the coolant in the radiator. If it's rust-colored, or if accumulations of scale are visible in the radiator, drain, flush and refill the system with new coolant. Inspect the cap gaskets for cracks and other damage. Have the cap tested by a dealer service department or replace it with a new one. Install the cap by turning it clockwise until it reaches the first detent, then push down on the cap and continue turning it until it stops.

9   Analyze the condition of the antifreeze in the coolant with an antifreeze hydrometer. Sometimes coolant may look like it's in good condition, but might be too weak to offer adequate protection. If the hydrometer indicates a weak mixture, flush and refill the cooling system (see Section 20).

10   Start the engine and let it reach normal operating temperature, then check for leaks again. As the coolant temperature increases, the fan should come on automatically and the temperature should begin to drop. If it doesn't, check the fan and fan circuit (see Chapter 3).

11   If the coolant level is constantly low, but there is no evidence of leaks, have the system pressure checked by a Yamaha dealer service department, motorcycle repair shop or service station.

20   Cooling system (Banshee models) - draining, flushing and refilling

Warning 1: *Don't allow antifreeze to come into contact with your skin or with painted surfaces of the vehicle. Rinse off spills immediately with plenty of water. Antifreeze is highly toxic if ingested. Never leave antifreeze in an open container or in puddles on the floor; children and pets are attracted by its sweet odor and may drink it. Check with local authorities regarding the proper disposal of used antifreeze. Many communities have collection centers that can dispose of antifreeze safely. Finally, antifreeze is combustible, so don't store it or put it near open flames.*

Warning 2: *Let the engine cool completely before performing this Step. Opening the radiator cap while the engine is hot will allow scalding coolant to spray out.*

Draining

Refer to illustrations 20.4a and 20.4b

1   Remove the radiator cover (see Chapter 8).

2   Put a shop rag over the radiator cap. Slowly rotate the cap counterclockwise to the first detent and allow any residual pressure to escape. When the hissing sound ceases, push down on the cap, turn it counterclockwise again and remove it.

3   Remove the seat (see Chapter 8) and remove the coolant reservoir cap.

4   Place a large, clean drain pan under the engine, remove the drain plugs **(see illustrations)** and drain the coolant into the container. **Note:** *The coolant will rush out with considerable force, so be prepared to quickly readjust the position of the drain pan.*

5   Remove the coolant reservoir (see Chapter 3) and drain it. Wash out the reservoir with clean water. Install the reservoir.

Flushing

6   Flush the system with clean tap water by inserting a garden hose into the radiator filler neck. Allow the water to run through the system until it is clear when it exits the drain bolt holes. If the radiator is extremely corroded, remove it (see Chapter 3) and have it cleaned by a radiator shop.

7   Using new gaskets, install the drain bolts and tighten them to the torque listed in this Chapter's Specifications.

8   Fill the cooling system with clean water mixed with a flushing compound. Make sure the flushing compound is compatible with aluminum, and follow the manufacturer's instructions carefully.

9   Start the engine and allow it to reach normal operating temperature. Let it run for about ten minutes.

10   Stop the engine. Let the machine cool for awhile, then cover the radiator cap with a heavy rag and turn it counterclockwise to the first stop, releasing any pressure that may be present in the system. Once the hissing stops, push down on the cap and remove it completely.

11   Drain the system.

12   Fill the system with clean water, then repeat Steps 9, 10 and 11.

Refilling

13   Fill the system with the correct coolant mixture (listed in this Chapter's Specifications). Fill the system to the top of the radiator cap filler neck and install the radiator cap. Fill the reservoir to the FULL mark and install the reservoir cap.

14   Inspect the system for leaks.

21   Clutch lever freeplay - check and adjustment

1   The clutch cable is adjusted at the clutch lever. On Banshee models, clutch freeplay can also be adjusted at the crankcase end of the clutch cable, but this is normally unnecessary.

21.2 Measure clutch lever freeplay at the lever tip

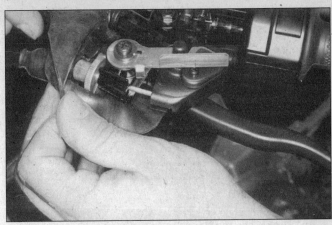

21.3a To adjust clutch lever freeplay, pull back the rubber dust cover . . .

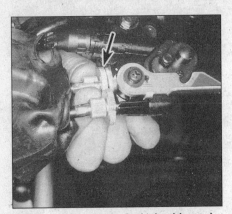

21.3b . . . loosen the lockwheel (arrow) and turn the adjuster nut

21.6a Banshee clutch freeplay can also be adjusted at the clutch: hold the adjuster screw and back off its locknut . . .

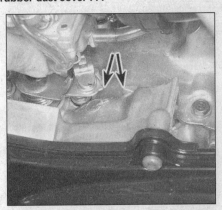

21.6b . . . then turn the screw in or out to align the pointer on the clutch push lever with the index mark on the crankcase (arrows)

22.1 The synchronizing mark on each carburetor's throttle valve should be visible through these windows with the throttle wide open (Banshee)

Adjusting clutch freeplay at the crankcase (Banshee models only)

Refer to illustrations 21.6a and 21.6b

4   Drain the transmission oil (see Section 18).

5   Remove the right crankcase cover (see Chapter 2).

6   Loosen the adjuster screw locknut at the clutch pressure plate **(see illustration)**. Rotate the clutch push lever in a counterclockwise direction until the lever stops, then turn the adjuster screw in or out until the pointer on the push lever is aligned with the pointer on the crankcase **(see illustration)**.

7   Tighten the adjuster screw locknut to the torque listed in this Chapter's Specifications.

8   Install the right crankcase cover (see Chapter 2).

9   Fill the transmission with the recommended oil (see Section 18).

10   Adjust clutch lever freeplay at the handlebar.

22 Carburetor synchronization (Banshee models) - check and adjustment

Refer to illustrations 22.1, 22.5a and 22.5b

1   With the engine off, move the throttle lever several times and verify that it's operating smoothly. Push the throttle lever forward until it stops and, holding it in this position, look through the window in each carburetor **(see illustration)** and verify that the punch mark on each throttle valve is visible and centered in the window.

2   If the punch mark on either throttle valve is either not visible or is visible but not centered in the window, the carburetors must be synchronized.

Adjusting clutch lever freeplay at the handlebar (all models)

Refer to illustrations 21.2, 21.3a and 21.3b

2   Operate the clutch lever and check freeplay at the lever tip **(see illustration)**.

3   If freeplay isn't within the range listed in this Chapter's Specifications, pull the cover off the clutch lever freeplay adjuster **(see illustration)**, loosen the adjuster locknut, turn the adjuster nut to set freeplay **(see illustration)** and tighten the locknut.

3   Remove the seat, the radiator cover, the fuel tank cover, the front fender and the front fender stay (see Chapter 8).
4   Remove the fuel tank (see Chapter 4).
5   Remove the dust boot from the throttle cable adjuster **(see illustration)**. Loosen the locknut **(see illustration)** and turn the adjuster in or out until the punch mark is centered in the window. Tighten the locknut and slide the dust boot back over the cable adjuster.
6   Install the fuel tank (see Chapter 4).
7   Install the front fender stay, front fender, fuel tank cover, radiator cover and seat (see Chapter 8).

23   Idle speed - check and adjustment

Refer to illustrations 23.2 and 23.4
1   Before adjusting the idle speed, make sure the spark plug gap is correct (see Section 16). Also, turn the handlebars back-and-forth and note whether the idle speed changes. If it does, the throttle cable may be incorrectly routed. Be sure to correct this problem before proceeding.
2   On Banshee models, the carburetors must be synchronized (see Section 22) and the pilot air screws **(see illustration)** must be correctly adjusted before adjusting the idle speed. Turn in each pilot air screw until it bottoms lightly, then turn it back out the number of turns listed in this Chapter's Specifications.
3   Start the engine and warm it up to its normal operating temperature. Make sure the transmission is in Neutral, then hook up an inductive-type tachometer.
4   Turn the idle speed adjustment screw(s) **(Banshee models, see illustration; Warrior models, see illustration 15.9b)** to bring the idle speed within the range listed in this Chapter's Specifications. Turning the screw in increases the idle speed; backing it out decreases the idle speed.
5   Snap the throttle open and shut a few times, then recheck the idle speed. If necessary, repeat the adjustment procedure.
6   If a smooth, steady idle can't be achieved, the fuel/air mixture may be incorrect. Refer to Chapter 3 for additional carburetor information.

24   Throttle cable and speed limiter - check and adjustment

Throttle cable

Refer to illustrations 24.3 and 24.5
1   Before proceeding, check and, if necessary, adjust the idle speed (see Section 23).
2   Make sure the throttle lever moves easily from fully closed to fully open with the front wheel turned at various angles. The lever should return automatically from fully open to fully closed when released. If

23.2 To adjust the pilot air screws on Banshee models, turn in each screw (arrow) until it seats lightly, then back it out two turns

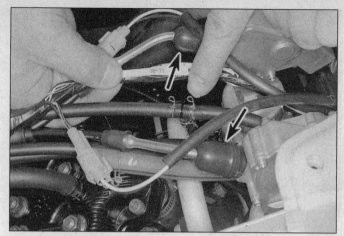

22.5a To synchronize Banshee carburetors, pull back the dust boot (arrows) for the carburetor that's out of sync . . .

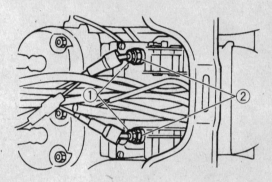

22.5b . . . loosen the locknut (1) and turn the adjuster (2) until the synchronizing mark is centered in the carburetor window (with the throttle lever wide open)

the throttle sticks, check the throttle cable for cracks or kinks in the housing. Also, make sure the inner cable is clean and well-lubricated.
3   Measure freeplay at the throttle lever **(see illustration)**. If it's within the range listed in this Chapter's Specifications, no adjustment is necessary. If not, adjust it as follows.
4   Pull back the rubber boot from the adjuster at the handlebar end of the throttle cable.
5   Loosen the adjuster lockwheel **(see illustration)**. Turn the adjuster to set freeplay, then tighten the lockwheel.

23.4 Idle speed adjustment screws (Banshee)

24.3 Check throttle lever freeplay at the lever tip

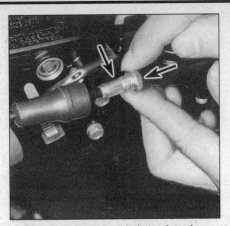

24.5 To adjust throttle lever freeplay, loosen the lockwheel (right arrow) and turn the adjuster (left arrow) in or out

24.6 Measure limiter screw length from the throttle housing to the underside of the screw head

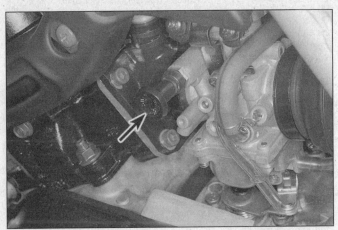

25.1a Slide the choke knob (arrow) in and out and check for smooth operation (Banshee models)

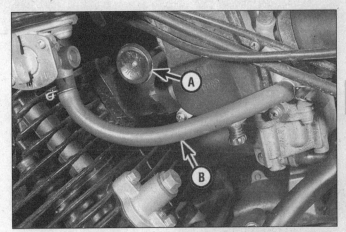

25.1b Slide the choke knob in and out and check for smooth operation (Warrior models)

A   Choke knob   B   Fuel line

Speed limiter

Refer to illustration 24.6

6   The speed limiter (**see illustration**) can be used to restrict maximum throttle opening. Turning the screw in reduces the maximum throttle opening; backing it out increases maximum throttle opening.

7   To change the speed limiter screw setting, loosen the locknut, turn the screw in or out as necessary and tighten the locknut. Screw length is measured from the underside of the screw head to the throttle housing. **Warning:** *Do NOT back out the speed limiter screw farther than the maximum setting listed in this Chapter's Specifications; doing so will affect throttle lever operation.*

25   Choke - operation check

Refer to illustrations 25.1a and 25.1b

1   Operate the choke knob (**see illustrations**) and note whether it operates smoothly.

2   If the choke knob doesn't operate smoothly, inspect the choke system (see Chapter 4).

26   Battery (Warrior models) - check

Refer to illustrations 26.3, 26.6, 26.12a and 26.12b

Warning: *Be extremely careful when handling or working around the battery. The electrolyte is very caustic and an explosive gas (hydrogen) is given off when the battery is charging.*

1   This procedure applies to batteries that have removable filler caps, which can be removed to add water to the battery. If the original equipment battery has been replaced by a sealed maintenance-free battery, the electrolyte can't be topped up.

2   Remove the seat (see Chapter 8).

3   Unhook the battery retainer strap and lift the battery up partially (**see illustration**). The electrolyte level is visible through the translucent battery case - it should be between the Upper and Lower level marks.

26.3 Remove this cover for access to the battery (Warrior)

26.6 Check the battery's specific gravity with a hydrometer

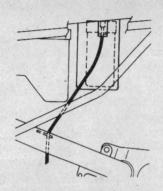

26.12a Battery breather hose routing (1987 and 1988 Warrior)

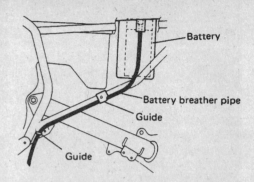

26.12b Battery breather hose routing (1989 and later Warrior)

4   If the electrolyte is low, remove the cell caps and fill each cell to the upper level mark with distilled water. Do not use tap water (except in an emergency) and do not overfill. The cell holes are quite small, so it may help to use a plastic squeeze bottle with a small spout to add the water. If the level is within the marks on the case, additional water is not necessary.

5   Next, check the specific gravity of the electrolyte in each cell with a small hydrometer made especially for motorcycle batteries. These are available from most dealer parts departments or motorcycle accessory stores.

6   Remove the caps, draw some electrolyte from the first cell into the hydrometer **(see illustration)**, then note the specific gravity. Compare the reading to the value listed in this Chapter's Specifications. **Note:** *Add 0.004 points to the reading for every 10-degrees F above 68-degrees F (20-degrees C) - subtract 0.004 points from the reading for every 10-degrees below 68-degrees F (20-degrees C).*

7   Return the electrolyte to the appropriate cell and repeat the check for the remaining cells. When the check is complete, rinse the hydrometer thoroughly with clean water.

8   If the specific gravity of the electrolyte in each cell is as specified, the battery is in good condition and is apparently being charged by the machine's charging system.

9   If the specific gravity is low, the battery is not fully charged. This may be due to corroded battery terminals, a dirty battery case, a malfunctioning charging system, or loose or corroded wiring connections. On the other hand, it may be that the battery is worn out, especially if the machine is old, or that infrequent use of the machine prevents normal charging from taking place.

10   Be sure to correct any problems and charge the battery if neces-

sary. Refer to Chapter 8 for additional battery maintenance and charging procedures.

11   Install the battery cell caps, tightening them securely. Reconnect the cables to the battery, attaching the positive cable first and the negative cable last. Make sure to install the insulating boot over the positive terminal.

12   Install all components removed for access and make sure the battery vent tube is routed correctly **(see illustrations)**. Be very careful not to pinch or otherwise restrict the tube, as the battery may build up enough internal pressure during normal charging system operation to explode.

13   If the vehicle will be stored for an extended time, fully charge the battery, then remove it. Disconnect the negative cable and remove the battery retainer strap. Disconnect the positive cable and vent tube and lift the battery out. **Warning:** *Always disconnect the negative cable first and reconnect it last to avoid sparks which could cause a battery explosion.*

14   Store the battery in a cool dark place. Check specific gravity at least once a month and recharge the battery if it's low.

27 Valve clearance (Warrior models) - check and adjustment

Refer to illustrations 27.6a, 27.6b, 27.7, 27.8, 27.10 and 27.11

1   The engine must be cool to the touch for this maintenance procedure, so if possible let the machine sit overnight before beginning.

2   Remove the seat (see Chapter 8).

27.6a Remove the Allen bolts (arrows) and remove the adjusting hole cover (the exhaust cover has three bolts; the intake cover has two)

27.6b Replace the cover O-ring if it's cracked, torn or deteriorated; the ridge inside the cover must be at the top when reinstalling the cover

27.7 Remove the timing hole plug

27.8 Align the notch in the crankcase cover with the TDC line on the alternator rotor inside the hole - the TDC has a T next to it (right arrow); the line next to the F mark (left arrow) is the advance timing mark, used to check ignition timing (cover removed for clarity)

3   Disconnect the cable from the negative terminal of the battery (see Section 26).
4   Remove the fuel tank (see Chapter 4), the handlebar (see Chapter 6) and the front fender (see Chapter 8).
5   Remove the spark plug (see Section 16). This will make it easier to turn the crankshaft.
6   Remove the valve adjusting hole covers **(see illustrations)**.
7   Remove the timing hole plug **(see illustration)**.
8   Position the piston at Top Dead Center (TDC) on the compression stroke as follows: Turn the crankshaft until the mark on the rotor is aligned with the timing notch on the crankcase **(see illustration)**. Wiggle the rocker arms - there should be some play. If the rocker arms are tight, the engine is at TDC on the exhaust stroke. Rotate it one full turn, until the timing mark and notch are aligned again. Recheck to make sure the rocker arms are now loose.
9   With the engine in this position, both of the valves can be checked.
10   To check, insert a feeler gauge of the thickness listed in this Chapter's Specifications between the valve stem and rocker arm **(see illustration)**. Pull the feeler gauge out slowly - you should feel a slight drag. If there's no drag, the clearance is too loose. If there's a heavy drag, the clearance is too tight.
11   If the clearance is incorrect, loosen the adjuster locknut with a box-end wrench (ring spanner). Turn the adjusting screw with a wrench or special valve adjusting tool until the correct clearance is achieved, then tighten the locknut **(see illustration)**.

12   After adjusting, recheck the clearance with the feeler gauge to make sure it wasn't changed when the locknut was tightened.
13   Now measure the other valve, following the same procedure you used for the first valve. Make sure to use a feeler gauge of the specified thickness.
14   With both of the clearances within the Specifications, install the valve adjusting hole covers with their internal ridges up **(see illustration 27.6b)**. Use new O-rings on the covers if the old ones are hardened, deteriorated or damaged.
15   Apply silicone sealant to the threads of the timing hole plug and install it.
16   The remainder of installation is the reverse of removal.

28   Cylinder compression (Warrior models) - check

Refer to illustration 28.5

1   Among other things, poor engine performance may be caused by leaking valves, incorrect valve clearances, a leaking head gasket, or worn piston, rings and/or cylinder wall. A cylinder compression check will help pinpoint these conditions and can also indicate the presence of excessive carbon deposits in the cylinder head.

1

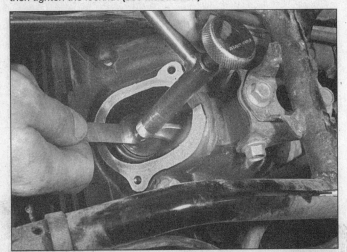

27.10 Measure valve clearance with a feeler gauge; to adjust it, loosen the locknut and turn the adjusting screw; this Yamaha special tool is convenient . . .

27.11 . . . but you can also use a box wrench on the locknut (left arrow) and an open wrench on the square head of the adjusting screw (right arrow)

28.5 A compression gauge with a threaded fitting for the spark plug hole is preferable to the type that requires hand pressure to maintain the seal

2   The only tools required are a compression gauge and a spark plug wrench. Depending on the outcome of the initial test, a squirt-type oil can may also be needed.

3   Check valve clearances and adjust if necessary (see Section 27). Start the engine and allow it to reach normal operating temperature, then remove the spark plug (see Section 16). Work carefully - don't strip the spark plug hole threads and don't burn your hands.

4   Disable the ignition by disconnecting the primary (low tension) wires from the coil (see Chapter 5). Be sure to mark the locations of the wires before detaching them.

5   Install the compression gauge in the spark plug hole **(see illustration)**. Hold or block the throttle wide open.

6   Crank the engine over a minimum of four or five revolutions (or until the gauge reading stops increasing) and observe the initial movement of the compression gauge needle as well as the final total gauge reading. Compare the results to the value listed in this Chapter's Specifications.

7   If the compression built up quickly and evenly to the specified amount, you can assume the engine upper end is in reasonably good mechanical condition. Worn or sticking piston rings and a worn cylinder will produce very little initial movement of the gauge needle, but compression will tend to build up gradually as the engine spins over. Valve and valve seat leakage, or head gasket leakage, is indicated by low initial compression which does not tend to build up.

8   To further confirm your findings, add a small amount of engine oil to the cylinder by inserting the nozzle of a squirt-type oil can through the spark plug hole. The oil will tend to seal the piston rings if they are leaking.

9   If the compression increases significantly after the addition of the oil, the piston rings and/or cylinder are definitely worn. If the compression does not increase, the pressure is leaking past the valves or the head gasket. Leakage past the valves may be due to insufficient valve clearances, burned, warped or cracked valves or valve seats or valves that are hanging up in the guides.

10   If compression readings are considerably higher than specified, the combustion chamber is probably coated with excessive carbon deposits. It is possible (but not very likely) for carbon deposits to raise the compression enough to compensate for the effects of leakage past rings or valves. Refer to Chapter 2, remove the cylinder head and carefully decarbonize the combustion chamber.

29 Exhaust system - inspection

1   Periodically, inspect the exhaust system for leaks and loose fasteners.

2   On Banshee models, make sure that all the springs are correctly installed (see Chapter 4).

3   On Warrior models, the exhaust pipe flange nuts at the cylinder head are especially prone to loosening, which could cause damage to the head (see Chapter 4). Check them frequently and keep them tight. If tightening the flange nuts fails to stop the leak, replace the gasket (see Chapter 4).

Chapter 2 Part A
Engine, clutch and transmission (Banshee)

Contents

Specifications

Cylinder head
Warpage limit ... 0.03 mm (0.0012 inch)

Reed valve
Thickness ... 0.37 to 0.47 mm (0.0146 to 0.0185 inch)
Valve stopper height ... 10.3 to 10.7 mm (0.406 to 0.421 inch)
Valve bending limit ... 0.5 mm (0.02 inch)

Cylinder
Bore
    Standard ... 64.00 to 64.02 mm (2.520 to 2.521 inches)
    Limit ... 64.1 mm (2.524 inches)
Taper limit ... 0.05 mm (0.002 inch)
Out-of-round limit ... 0.01 mm (0.004 inch)
Surface warpage limit ... Not specified

Piston and rings

Diameter	
Standard..	63.94 to 64.00 mm (2.517 to 2.520 inches)
First oversize	64.25 mm (2.53 inches)
Second oversize	64.50 mm (2.54 inches)
Piston diameter measuring point (above bottom of piston)	10 mm (0.39 inch)
Piston-to-cylinder clearance...	0.060 to 0.065 mm (0.0024 to 0.0026 inch)
Piston pin bore in piston...	Not specified
Piston pin outer diameter	Not specified
Ring end gap (both rings)	0.30 to 0.45 mm (0.012 to 0.018 inch)
Ring side clearance (both rings)	0.02 to 0.06 mm (0.0008 to 0.0024 inch)

Clutch

Spring free length	
Standard..	36.4 mm (1.43 inches)
Limit..	34.4 mm (1.35 inches)
Friction plate thickness	
Standard..	3 mm (0.118 inch)
Limit..	2.7 mm (0.106 inch)
Metal plate	
Thickness	1.2 mm (0.047 inch)
Warpage limit	0.05 mm (0.002 inch)
Clutch pushrod bend limit (long rod)	0.2 mm (0.008 inch)

Kickstarter

Kick clip friction force	0.8 to 1.3 kg (1.8 to 2.9 lbs)

Transmission

Shaft runout limit	0.08 mm (0.003 inch)

Crankshaft and connecting rods

Crankshaft assembly width (from outer face of left flywheel to outer face of right flywheel)..	155.90 to 156.05 mm (6.138 to 6.144 inches)
Width across each pair of flywheels and connecting rod small end	53.95 to 54.00 mm (2.124 to 2.126 inches)
Runout limit...	0.05 mm (0.0021 inch)
Connecting rod big end side clearance..	0.25 to 0.75 mm (0.0098 to 0.0295 inch)
Connecting rod small end side play	
Standard..	0.36 to 0.98 mm (0.0142 to 0.0386 inch)
Limit..	2.0 mm (0.08 inch)

Torque specifications

Engine mounting bolts (front and rear)	45 Nm (32 ft-lbs)
Front engine stay bolts	30 Nm (22 ft-lbs)
Tension rod bolts..	25 Nm (32 ft-lbs)
Tension rod stay bolts	45 Nm (32 ft-lbs)
Tension rod-to-tension stay bolts	45 Nm (32 ft-lbs)
Cylinder head-to-coolant hose adapter bolts....................................	12 Nm (96 in-lbs)
Cylinder head nuts	28 Nm (20 ft-lbs)
Cylinder base nuts	28 Nm (20 ft-lbs)
Carburetor intake joint Allen bolts	10 Nm (86 inch-lbs)
Reed valve screws..	1 Nm (8 inch-lbs)*
Crankcase cover screws	7 Nm (61 inch-lbs)
Clutch spring bolts	10 Nm (86 inch-lbs)
Clutch center nut	90 Nm (65 ft-lbs)
Water pump/primary drive gear nut...	65 Nm (47 ft-lbs)
Kickstarter pedal pinch bolt	25 Nm (18 ft-lbs)
Shift cam plate to shift drum Torx screw.......................................	Not specified*
Shift cam stopper lever bolt	10 Nm (86 inch-lbs)
Shift cam guide bar screws	14 Nm (120 in-lbs)
Crankcase bolts (must be torqued in four steps, as follows)	
Step 1, tighten the upper bolts to	5 Nm (43 in-lbs)
Step 2, tighten the lower bolts to	10 Nm (86 in-lbs)
Step 3, tighten the lower bolts to	25 Nm (18 ft-lbs)
Step 4, tighten the upper bolts to	10 Nm (86 in-lbs)

Apply non-permanent thread locking agent to the threads.

1 General information

The engine on Banshee models is a liquid-cooled, twin-cylinder two-stroke. The engine/transmission assembly is constructed from aluminum alloy. The crankcase is divided horizontally.

The cylinder, piston, crankshaft bearings and connecting rod lower end bearing are lubricated by the fuel, which is a mixture of gasoline and two-stroke oil. The two-stroke oil is mixed into the fuel each time fuel is added to the tank. The transmission and clutch are lubricated by four-stroke engine oil, which is contained in a sump within the crankcase. Power from the crankshaft is routed to the transmission via a wet, multi-plate type clutch. The transmission has six forward gears.

2 Operations possible with the engine in the frame

The components and assemblies listed below can be removed without having to remove the engine from the frame. If, however, a number of areas require attention at the same time, removal of the engine is recommended.

Cylinder head
Cylinders and pistons
Water pump (see Chapter 3)
External shift mechanism
Clutch
Water pump gear and primary drive gear
Kickstarter and idler gear
CDI magneto (see Chapter 9)

3 Operations requiring engine removal

It is necessary to remove the engine/transmission assembly from the frame and separate the crankcase halves to gain access to the following components:

Crankshaft and connecting rods
Transmission shafts
Internal shift mechanism (shift drum and forks)
Crankcase bearings

4 Major engine repair - general note

1   It is not always easy to determine when or if an engine should be completely overhauled, as a number of factors must be considered.
2   High mileage is not necessarily an indication that an overhaul is needed, while low mileage, on the other hand, does not preclude the need for an overhaul. Regular maintenance is probably the single most important consideration. An engine that has regular and frequent transmission oil changes, as well as other required maintenance, will most likely give many hours of reliable service. Conversely, a neglected engine, or one which has not been broken in properly, may require an overhaul very early in its life.
3   Poor running that can't be accounted for by seemingly obvious causes (fouled spark plug, leaking head gasket or cylinder base gasket, worn piston rings, carburetor problems) may be due to leaking crankshaft seals. In two-stroke engines, the crankcase acts as a suction pump to draw in fuel mixture and as a compressor to force it into the cylinder. If the crankshaft seals are leaking, the pressure drop will cause a loss of performance.
4   If the engine is making obvious knocking or rumbling noises, the connecting rod and/or main bearings are probably at fault. The upper connecting rod bearing should be replaced at the maintenance interval listed in Chapter 1.
5   A top-end overhaul consists of replacing the piston and rings and inspecting the cylinder bore. The cylinder can be bored for an oversize piston if necessary.
6   A lower-end engine overhaul generally involves inspecting the crankshaft, transmission and crankcase bearings and seals. Unlike four-

stroke engines equipped with plain main and connecting rod bearings, there isn't much in the way of machine work that can be done to refurbish existing parts. Worn bearings, gears, seals and shift mechanism parts should be replaced with new ones. The crankshaft and connecting rod components are available separately, but rebuilding a crankshaft is a specialized operation which should be done by a qualified shop. While the engine is being overhauled, other components such as the carburetor can be rebuilt also. The end result should be a like-new engine that will give as many trouble-free hours as the original.
7   Before beginning the engine overhaul, read through all of the related procedures to familiarize yourself with the scope and requirements of the job. Overhauling an engine is not all that difficult, but it is time consuming. Plan on the vehicle being tied up for a minimum of two (2) weeks. Check on the availability of parts and make sure that any necessary special tools, equipment and supplies are obtained in advance.
8   Most work can be done with typical shop hand tools, although a number of precision measuring tools are required for inspecting parts to determine if they must be replaced. Often a dealer service department or other repair shop will handle the inspection of parts and offer advice concerning reconditioning and replacement. As a general rule, time is the primary cost of an overhaul so it doesn't pay to install worn or substandard parts.
9   As a final note, to ensure maximum life and minimum trouble from a rebuilt engine, everything must be assembled with care in a spotlessly clean environment.

5 Crankcase pressure and vacuum - check

This test can pinpoint the cause of otherwise unexplained poor running. It can also prevent piston seizures by detecting air leaks that can cause a lean mixture. It requires special equipment, but can easily be done by a Yamaha dealer or other ATV shop. If you regularly work on two-stroke engines, you might want to consider purchasing the tester for yourself (or with a group of other riders). You may also be able to fabricate the tester.

The test involves sealing off the intake and exhaust ports, then applying vacuum and pressure to each spark plug hole with a hand vacuum/pressure pump, similar to the type used for brake bleeding and automotive vacuum testing.

First, remove the carburetors and the exhaust system (see Chapter 4). Block off the carburetor openings with rubber plugs, clamped securely in position. Place rubber sheet (cut from a tire tube or similar material) over each exhaust port and secure it with a metal plate.

Apply air pressure to each spark plug hole with the vacuum/pressure pump. Check for leaks at the crankcase gasket, intake manifold, reed valve gasket, cylinder base gasket and head gasket. If the crankcase mating surface leaks between the transmission sump and the crankcase (the area where the crankshaft spins), transmission oil will be sucked into the crankcase, causing the fuel mixture to be oil-rich. Also check the seals at the ends of the crankshaft. If the leaks are large, air will hiss as it passes through them. Small leaks can be detected by pouring soapy water over the suspected area and looking for bubbles.

After checking for air leaks, apply vacuum with the pump. If vacuum leaks down quickly, the crankshaft seals are leaking.

6 Engine - removal and installation

Warning: *Engine removal and installation should be done with the aid of an assistant to avoid damage or injury that could occur if the engine is dropped.*

Removal

Refer to illustrations 6.8a, 6.8b, 6.11, 6.12, 6.14a and 6.14b
1   Drain the engine coolant and the transmission oil (see Chapter 1).
2   Remove the seat, the radiator cover, the fuel tank cover, the front fender, the front fender stays and the rear fender (see Chapter 8).

2A

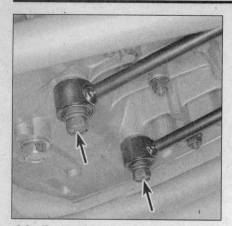

6.8a To detach the tension rods, remove these bolts (arrows) . . .

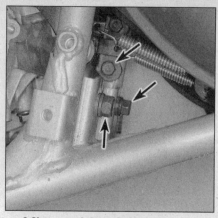

6.8b . . . and these bolts (two lower arrows); upper arrow indicates the left engine stay

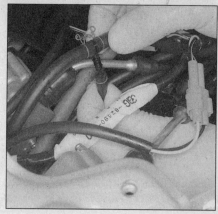

6.11 Disconnect the breather hose

3   Remove the fuel tank, the carburetors and the exhaust system (see Chapter 4). Clearly label and disconnect all breather hoses (see hose routing diagrams at the end of Chapter 12).
4   Remove the footrests (see Chapter 8).
5   Remove the gearshift lever (see Section 16).
6   Unplug the electrical connector for the CDI magneto (see Chapter 9). If you're going to replace the CDI magneto, or if you're going to separate the crankcase halves, it's easier to remove the magneto assembly now, while the engine is still bolted into the frame.
7   Remove the drive chain and sprocket (see Chapter 7).
8   Remove the tension rods **(see illustrations)**.
9   Disconnect the clutch cable (see Section 12).
10   Remove the rear brake master cylinder (see Chapter 7). (It's not necessary to disconnect the brake hose from the master cylinder; simply unbolt the master cylinder and hang it out of the way with a cable tie.)
11   Disconnect the crankcase breather hose **(see illustration)**.
12   Disconnect the coolant inlet hose **(see illustration 3.3b in Chapter 3)**, and the outlet and bypass hoses **(see illustration)**, from the engine.
13   Wipe off any spilled coolant from the cylinder head, then disconnect the spark plug wires from the spark plugs and remove the spark plugs (see Chapter 1).
14   Remove the engine mounting bolts and nuts at the front and rear **(see illustrations)**. Remove the engine stay bolts **(see illustration 6.8b)**.
15   Have an assistant help you lift the engine out of the frame from the right side of the vehicle.

6.12 Loosen the clamps (arrows) and disconnect the coolant outlet and bypass hoses from the head

Installation

16   Have an assistant help lift the engine into the frame. Align the mounting bolt holes, then install the bolts and nuts. Tighten them to the torques listed in this Chapter's Specifications.
17   The remainder of installation is the reverse of the removal steps,

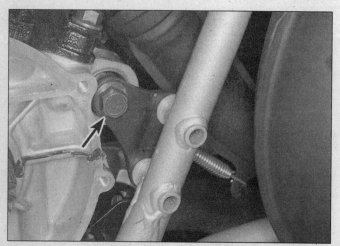

6.14a To detach the front end of the engine from the frame, remove the front mounting bolts (right bolt shown)

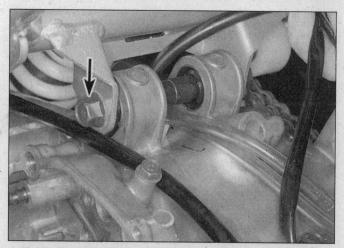

6.14b To detach the rear end of the engine from the frame, remove the nut for this bolt (arrow) and pull out the bolt

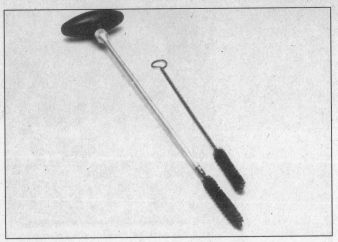

7.2 You'll need a selection of brushes for cleaning holes and passages in the engine components

7.3 An engine stand can be made from short lengths of lumber and lag bolts or nails

with the following additions:

a) *Use new O-rings when attaching the expansion chambers to the head (see Chapter 4)*

b) *If you need help routing hoses, cables and wires, refer to the routing diagrams at the end of this manual.*

c) *Adjust the throttle cable and clutch cable (see Chapter 1).*

d) *Fill the cooling system with a 50/50 mixture of antifreeze and water and fill the transmission with oil (see Chapter 1).*

e) *Run the engine and check for coolant, exhaust and oil leaks.*

7 Engine disassembly and reassembly - general information

Refer to illustrations 7.2 and 7.3

1   Before disassembling the engine, clean the exterior with a degreaser and rinse it with water. A clean engine will make the job easier and prevent the possibility of getting dirt into the internal areas of the engine.

2   In addition to the precision measuring tools mentioned earlier, you will need a torque wrench and oil gallery brushes **(see illustration)**. Some new, clean engine oil of the correct grade and type (two-stroke oil, four-stroke oil or both, depending on whether it's a top-end or bottom-end overhaul), some engine assembly lube (or moly-based grease) and a tube of RTV (silicone) sealant will also be required.

3   An engine support stand made from short lengths of 2 x 4's bolted together will facilitate the disassembly and reassembly proce-

dures **(see illustration)**. If you have an automotive-type engine stand, an adapter plate can be made from a piece of plate, some angle iron and some nuts and bolts.

4   When disassembling the engine, keep "mated" parts together (including gears, shift forks and shafts, etc.) that have been in contact with each other during engine operation. These "mated" parts must be reused or replaced as an assembly.

5   Engine/transmission disassembly should be done in the following general order with reference to the appropriate Sections.

Remove the cylinder head
Remove the reed valves
Remove the cylinders
Remove the pistons
Remove the clutch
Remove the primary drive gear
Remove the kickstarter mechanism
Remove the external shift mechanism
Remove the CDI magneto
Separate the crankcase halves
Remove the internal shift mechanism
Remove the transmission shafts and gears
Remove the crankshaft and connecting rods

6   Reassembly is the reverse of the disassembly sequence.

8 Cylinder head - removal, inspection and installation

Caution: *The engine must be completely cool before beginning this procedure, or the cylinder head may become warped.*

Note: *This procedure is described with the engine in the frame. If the engine has been removed, ignore the steps which don't apply.*

Removal

Refer to illustrations 8.4 and 8.6

1   Disconnect the spark plug wires from the spark plugs (see Chapter 1).

2   Remove the seat, the radiator cover, the fuel tank cover, the front fender, the front fender stays and the rear fender (see Chapter 8).

3   Remove the fuel tank (see Chapter 4).

4   The coolant hose adapter is bolted to the cylinder head by two Allen bolts at the rear of the head. The cylinder head is attached to the cylinders by 10 nuts **(see illustration)**. The nuts are numbered "1" through "10" (the numbers are cast into the head, right next to each head nut). Remove the two Allen bolts first (it's not necessary to disconnect the coolant hose from the adapter; the adapter stays with the hose when the head is removed). Then, beginning with nut No. 10, loosen the cylinder head nuts in two stages, in descending numerical order (10-9-8 . . . etc.). When all the nuts are loose, remove them.

8.4 Remove these two Allen bolts (arrows), then remove the 10 cylinder head nuts, starting with no. 10 and working down to no. 1

2A

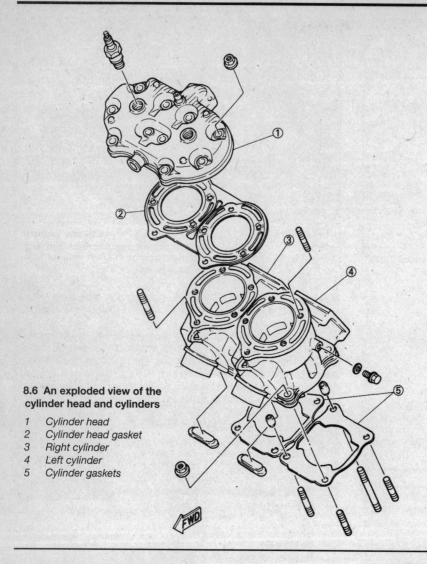

8.6 An exploded view of the cylinder head and cylinders

1 Cylinder head
2 Cylinder head gasket
3 Right cylinder
4 Left cylinder
5 Cylinder gaskets

9.2a Loosen the balance pipe clamps and slide them up the pipe

9.2b Disconnect the balance pipe from the rubber carburetor joints and remove it

5   Lift the cylinder head off the cylinders. If the head is stuck, use a wooden dowel inserted into a spark plug hole to lever the head off. Do NOT try to pry off the head with a screwdriver between the head and the cylinder; this will damage the sealing surfaces.

6   Rotate one piston to the top of its cylinder and stuff a clean rag into the other cylinder to prevent the entry of debris. Once this is done, remove the head gasket from the cylinder **(see illustration)**.

Inspection

7   Check the cylinder head gasket and the mating surfaces on the cylinder head and cylinder for leakage, which could indicate warpage.

8   Clean all traces of old gasket material from the cylinder head and cylinder. Be careful not to let any of the gasket material fall into the cylinder or coolant passages.

9   Inspect the head very carefully for cracks and other damage. If cracks are found, a new head will be required.

10   Using a precision straightedge and a feeler gauge, check the head gasket mating surface for warpage. Using the head bolt holes opposite one another, lay the straightedge across the front and rear surfaces of the head, across the ends and diagonally, and try to slip a feeler gauge under it, on either side of the combustion chamber. The feeler gauge thickness should be the same as the cylinder head warpage limit listed in this Chapter's Specifications. If the feeler gauge can be inserted between the head and the straightedge, the head is warped and must either be resurfaced or, if warpage is excessive, replaced with a new one.

11   To resurface the head, lay a piece of 400 to 600 grit emery paper on a perfectly flat surface, such as a piece of plate glass. Move the head in a figure-8 pattern over the sandpaper. Rotate the head 1/2 turn after each few figure-8 motions so you don't remove too much material from one side of the head. Don't remove any more material than necessary to correct the warpage.

Installation

12   Lay the new gasket in place on the cylinder. Never reuse the old gasket and don't use any type of gasket sealant.

13   Carefully lower the cylinder head over the studs.

14   Install the cylinder head nuts and tighten them evenly, in ascending numerical order, from 1 through 10, to the torque listed in this Chapter's Specifications. Install the head-to-coolant hose adapter bolts and tighten them to the torque listed in this Chapter's Specifications.

15   The remainder of installation is the reverse of the removal steps.

9   Reed valves - removal, inspection and installation

Removal

Note: *This procedure applies to either reed valve.*
Refer to illustrations 9.2a, 9.2b, 9.3a and 9.3b

1   Remove the carburetor (see Chapter 4).

2   Loosen and slide up the balance pipe clamps, then detach the balance pipe from the rubber intake joints **(see illustrations)**.

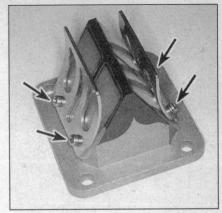

9.3a Remove the four carburetor joint Allen bolts (arrows) and remove the joint . . .

9.3b . . . then remove the reed valve (arrow) and gasket

9.6a To replace the reed valve stopper plates, remove these screws (arrows)

3   Remove the four Allen bolts from the rubber intake joint and remove the intake joint **(see illustrations)**. Remove the reed valve and gasket from the cylinder.

Inspection

Refer to illustrations 9.6a and 9.6b

4   Check the reed valve for obvious damage, such as cracked or broken reeds or stoppers. Also make sure there's no clearance between the reeds and the edges where they make contact with the seats.

5   If inspection doesn't show any obvious damage, connect a vacuum pump to the carburetor side of the reed valve assembly and apply vacuum. There should be little or no leakage.

6   The reed valve can be disassembled and the reeds replaced. Remove the screws and stoppers **(see illustration)**. The screws have locking agent on the threads, so you may need to use an impact driver. Remove the reeds and install new ones. Install the stoppers, aligning the cutout in the stopper with the cutout in the reed. Coat the screw threads with non-permanent thread locking agent, then tighten them to the torque listed in this Chapter's Specifications. After assembly, check the clearance between the reeds and reed stoppers **(see illustration)**. This clearance is referred to as the "valve stopper height" in the Specifications.

Installation

7   Installation is the reverse of the removal steps, with the following additions:

  a) *Use a new gasket between the reed valve assembly and cylinder.*
  b) *Tighten the intake joint bolts in a criss-cross pattern to the torque listed in this Chapter's Specifications.*

10 Cylinder - removal, inspection and installation

Removal

Refer to illustration 10.2
Note: *This procedure applies to either cylinder.*
1   Remove the cylinder head (see Section 8).
2   Remove the four nuts securing each cylinder to the crankcase **(see illustration)**.
3   Lift each cylinder straight up off the piston. If it's stuck, tap around its perimeter with a soft-faced hammer. Don't attempt to pry between the cylinder and the crankcase, as you'll ruin the sealing surfaces.
4   Locate the dowel pins (they may have come off with the cylinder or still be in the crankcase). Be careful not to let these drop into the engine. Stuff clean shop rags around the piston and remove the gasket and all traces of old gasket material from the surfaces of the cylinder and the crankcase.

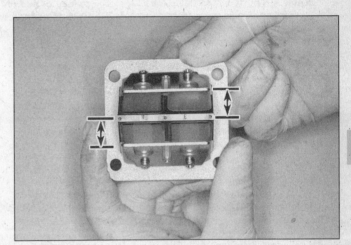

9.6b Measure the reed valve stopper height

Inspection

Refer to illustration 10.7

5   Check the top surface of the cylinder for warpage, using the same method as for the cylinder head (see Section 8). Measure along the studs and across the bore.

6   Check the cylinder walls carefully for scratches and score marks.

7   Using the appropriate precision measuring tools, check the cylinder's diameter at the top, center and bottom of the cylinder bore,

10.2 To detach a cylinder from the crankcase, remove all four nuts (two outer nuts of left cylinder shown; inner nuts not shown)

2A

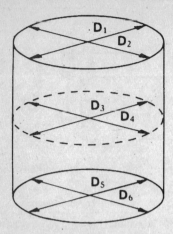

10.7 Measure the cylinder bore at the top, center and bottom, parallel to the crankshaft axis and across the crankshaft axis

11.3a The arrow mark on the piston points to the front of the engine; the 25 mark on this piston indicates that it's a first oversize

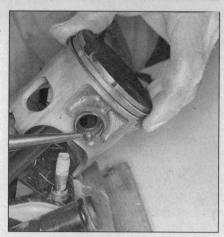

11.3b Wear eye protection and remove the circlip with a pointed tool or needle-nosed pliers

parallel to the crankshaft axis (see illustration). Next, measure the cylinder's diameter at the same three locations across the crankshaft axis. Compare the results to this Chapter's Specifications.

8   Differences between the top and bottom measurements indicate cylinder taper. Differences between the measurements parallel to and across the crankshaft axis indicate out-of-round. If the cylinder walls are tapered, out-of-round, worn beyond the specified limits, or badly scuffed or scored, you can have the cylinder rebored and honed by a dealer service department or a motorcycle repair shop. If a rebore is done, oversize pistons and rings will be required as well. **Note:** *Yamaha supplies pistons in two oversizes for these models.*

9   As an alternative, if the precision measuring tools are not available, a dealer service department or repair shop will make the measurements and offer advice concerning servicing of the cylinder.

10   If it's in reasonably good condition and not worn to the outside of the limits, and if the piston-to-cylinder clearance can be maintained properly, then the cylinder does not have to be rebored; honing is all that is necessary.

11   To perform the honing operation you will need the proper size flexible hone with fine stones as shown in *Maintenance techniques, tools and working facilities* at the front of this book, or a "bottle brush" type hone, plenty of light oil or honing oil, some shop towels and an electric drill motor. Hold the cylinder in a vise (cushioned with soft jaws or wood blocks) when performing the honing operation. Mount the hone in the drill motor, compress the stones and slip the hone into the cylinder. Lubricate the cylinder thoroughly, turn on the drill and move the hone up and down in the cylinder at a pace which will produce a fine crosshatch pattern on the cylinder wall with the crosshatch lines intersecting at approximately a 60-degree angle. Be sure to use plenty of lubricant and do not take off any more material than is absolutely necessary to produce the desired effect. Do not withdraw the hone from the cylinder while it is running. Instead, shut off the drill and continue moving the hone up and down in the cylinder until it comes to a complete stop, then compress the stones and withdraw the hone. Wipe the oil out of the cylinder. Remember, do not remove too much material from the cylinder wall. If you do not have the tools, or do not desire to perform the honing operation, a dealer service department or vehicle repair shop will generally do it for a reasonable fee.

12   Next, the cylinder must be thoroughly washed with warm soapy water to remove all traces of the abrasive grit produced during the honing operation. Be sure to run a brush through the bolt holes and flush them with running water. After rinsing, dry the cylinder thoroughly and apply a coat of light, rust-preventative oil to all machined surfaces.

Installation

13   Lubricate the piston with plenty of clean two-stroke engine oil.
14   Install the dowel pins, then lower a new cylinder base gasket

over them.
15   Make sure the piston ring gaps are aligned with the dowels in the ring lands. Install the cylinder over the studs and carefully lower it down until the piston crown fits into the cylinder liner. Push down on the cylinder, making sure the piston doesn't get cocked sideways, until the bottom of the cylinder liner slides down past the piston rings. Be sure not to rotate the cylinder, as this may snag the piston rings on the exhaust port. A wood or plastic hammer handle can be used to gently tap the cylinder down, but don't use too much force or the piston will be damaged.
16   The remainder of installation is the reverse of the removal steps.

11   Pistons and rings - removal, inspection and installation

Note: *This procedure applies to either piston.*
1   Each piston is attached to the connecting rod with a piston pin that's a "slip fit" in the piston and connecting rod needle bearing.
2   Before removing the piston from the rod, stuff a clean shop towel into the crankcase hole, around the connecting rod. This will prevent the circlips from falling into the crankcase if they are inadvertently dropped.

Removal

Refer to illustrations 11.3a, 11.3b, 11.4a and 11.4b
3   The piston should have an arrow mark on its crown that goes toward the exhaust (front) side of the engine (see illustration). If this mark is not visible due to carbon buildup, scribe an arrow into the piston crown before removal. Support the piston and pry the circlip out with a pointed tool or needle-nosed pliers (see illustration).
4   Push the piston pin out from the opposite end to free the piston from the rod (see illustration). You may have to deburr the area around the groove to enable the pin to slide out (use a triangular file for this procedure). If the pin won't come out, you can fabricate a piston pin removal tool from a long bolt, a nut, a piece of tubing and washers (see illustration).

Inspection

Refer to illustrations 11.6, 11.11, 11.13, 11.14a, 11.14b, 11.15, 11.16 and 11.17
5   Before the inspection process can be carried out, the piston must be cleaned and the old piston ring removed.
6   Carefully remove the rings from the piston (see illustration). Do not nick or gouge the piston in the process. A ring removal and installation tool will make this easier, but you can use your fingers if you

11.4a Push the piston pin partway out, then pull it the rest of the way

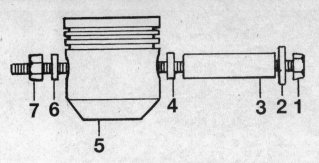

11.4b The piston pin should come out with hand pressure - if it doesn't, this removal tool can be fabricated from readily available parts

1	Bolt	5	Piston	A	Large enough for piston pin to fit inside
2	Washer	6	Washer (B)		
3	Pipe (A)	7	Nut (B)	B	Small enough to fit through piston pin bore
4	Padding (A)				

don't have one - just be sure not to cut yourself.

7   Scrape all traces of carbon from the top of the piston. A hand-held wire brush or a piece of fine emery cloth can be used once most of the deposits have been scraped away. Do not, under any circumstances, use a wire brush mounted in a drill motor to remove deposits from the piston; the piston material is soft and will be eroded away by the wire brush.

8   Use a piston ring groove cleaning tool to remove any carbon deposits from the ring groove. If a tool is not available, a piece broken off the old ring will do the job. Be very careful to remove only the carbon deposits. Do not remove any metal and do not nick or gouge the sides of the ring grooves.

9   Once the deposits have been removed, clean the piston with solvent and dry it thoroughly.

10   Normal piston wear appears as even, vertical wear on the thrust surfaces of the piston and slight looseness of the rings in their grooves.

11   Carefully inspect each piston for cracks around the skirt, at the pin bosses and at the ring lands. Make sure the ring locating dowels are secure in the ring lands **(see illustration)**.

12   Look for scoring and scuffing on the thrust faces of the skirt, holes in the piston crown and burned areas at the edge of the crown. If the skirt is scored or scuffed, the engine may have been suffering from oil starvation and/or abnormal combustion, which caused excessively high operating temperatures. A hole in the piston crown, an extreme to be sure, is an indication that abnormal combustion (pre-ignition) was occurring. Burned areas at the edge of the piston crown are usually evidence of spark knock (detonation). If any of the above problems exist, the causes must be corrected or the damage will occur again.

13   Measure the piston ring-to-groove clearance (side clearance) by laying a new piston ring in the ring groove and slipping a feeler gauge

11.6 Remove the piston rings with a ring removal and installation tool if you have one; you can use your fingers instead if you're careful

in beside it **(see illustration)**. Check the clearance at three or four locations around the groove. If the clearance is greater than specified, a new piston will have to be used when the engine is reassembled.

14   Measure the ring end gap. Push each piston ring into the cylinder from the top, down to the bottom of the ring travel area inside the cylinder. Square the ring in the bore by tapping it with the piston crown **(see illustration)**. Measure the gap between the ends of the ring with a

2A

11.11 There's a locating dowel in each ring land (arrow); center the ring gaps on these dowels

11.13 Measure side clearance between the rings and piston with a feeler gauge

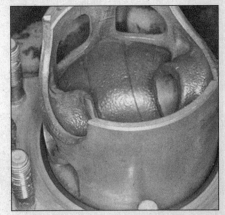

11.14a Use the piston to push the ring squarely into the bore . . .

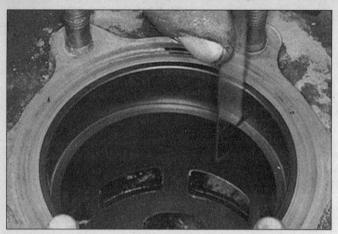

11.14b . . . then measure the ring end gap with a feeler gauge

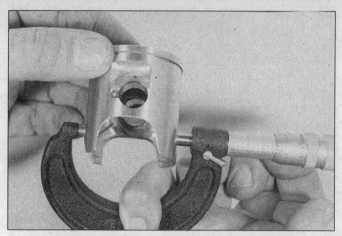

11.15 Measure the piston diameter with a micrometer

feeler gauge **(see illustration)**. Measure both rings; if either has a gap greater than the value listed in this Chapter's Specifications, replace both rings with new ones.

15   Check the piston-to-bore clearance by measuring the bore (see Section 11) and the piston diameter **(see illustration)**. Measure the piston across the skirt on the thrust faces at a 90-degree angle to the piston pin, at the specified distance up from the bottom of the skirt. Subtract the piston diameter from the bore diameter to obtain the clearance. If it is greater than specified, the cylinder will have to be rebored and a new oversized piston and rings installed. If the appropriate precision measuring tools are not available, the piston-to-cylinder clearance can be obtained, though not quite as accurately, using feeler gauge stock. Feeler gauge stock comes in 12-inch lengths and various thickness and is generally available at auto parts stores. To check the clearance, slip a piece of feeler gauge stock of the same thickness as the specified piston clearance into the cylinder along with appropriate piston. The cylinder should be upside down and the piston must be positioned exactly as it normally would be. Place the feeler gauge between the piston and cylinder on one of the thrust faces (90-degrees to the piston pin bore). The piston should slip through the cylinder (with the feeler gauge in place) with moderate pressure. If it falls through, or slides through easily, the clearance is excessive and a new piston will be required. If the piston binds at the lower end of the cylinder and is loose toward the top, the cylinder is tapered, and if tight spots are encountered as the piston/feeler gauge is rotated in the cylinder, the cylinder is out-of-round. Be sure to have the cylinder and piston checked by a dealer service department or a repair shop to confirm your findings before purchasing new parts.

16   Apply clean two-stroke oil to the pin, insert it into the piston and check for freeplay by rocking the pin back-and-forth **(see illustration)**. If the pin is loose, a new piston and possibly a new pin must be

installed. Check both for visible wear, replace whichever appears worn and repeat the freeplay check.

17   Repeat Step 15, this time inserting the piston pin into the connecting rod needle bearing **(see illustration)**. If it wobbles and the pin isn't worn, replace the needle bearing.

Installation

Refer to illustration 11.20

18   Install the piston with its arrow mark toward the exhaust side (front) of the engine. Lubricate the pin and the connecting rod needle bearing with two-stroke oil of the type listed in the Chapter 1 Specifications.

19   Install a new circlip in the groove in one side of the piston (don't reuse the old circlips). Push the pin into position from the opposite side and install another new circlip. Compress the circlips only enough for them to fit in the piston. Make sure the clips are properly seated in the grooves.

20   Locate the manufacturer's mark on the piston rings near one of the ends **(see illustration)**. Turn the rings so this mark is upward, then carefully spread them and install them in the ring grooves. Make sure the end gaps are centered on the dowel pin in each ring groove **(see illustration 11.11)**.

12   Clutch cable and lever - removal and installation

Refer to illustration 12.5

1   At the handlebar, peel back the rubber dust cover, back off the lockwheel and unscrew the clutch cable adjuster (see Section 21 in Chapter 1).

11.16 The piston and pin should be replaced if the pin wobbles inside the piston

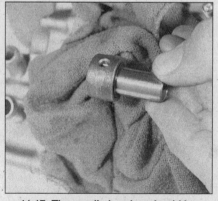

11.17 The needle bearing should be replaced if the pin wobbles inside it

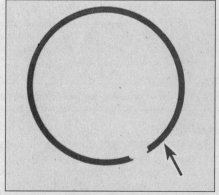

11.20 The manufacturer's mark (arrow) near the ring gap should be facing up when the ring is installed

12.5 To detach the clutch lever from the handlebar, remove these two bolts (arrows)

13.2 Unbolt the rear master cylinder and secure the brake pedal to the frame with a cable tie to provide clearance for removing the right crankcase cover

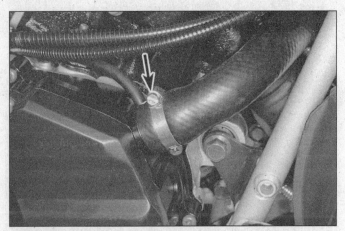

13.4 Before removing the right crankcase cover, loosen this hose clamp and detach the coolant inlet hose

13.5a Right crankcase cover screws

2   To disengage the upper end of the cable from the clutch lever, rotate the cable so the inner cable aligns with the slot in the lever, then slip the cable end plug out of the lever.
3   Trace the clutch cable down to the engine, unbolt the cable holder from the top of the crankcase and disengage the cable from the clutch push lever (see Section 21 in Chapter 1) .
4   Note the routing of the clutch cable, then remove the cable.
5   If you need to remove the clutch lever, simply remove the two clamp bolts (see illustration) and remove the lever assembly.
6   Slide the inner cable back and forth in the housing and make sure it moves freely. If it doesn't, try lubricating it as described in Chapter 1. If that doesn't help, replace the cable.
7   Installation is the reverse of removal. Make sure that the cable is correctly routed (refer to the hose and cable routing diagrams at the end of Chapter 12, if necessary). Adjust the clutch cable when you're done (see Section 21 in Chapter 1).

13 Clutch - removal, inspection and installation

Removal
Refer to illustrations 13.2, 13.4, 13.5a, 13.5b and 13.6a through 13.6l
1   Drain the transmission oil (see Chapter 1).
2   If the engine is installed in the frame, unbolt the rear brake master cylinder from the frame (see Chapter 7) and secure the rear brake pedal to the frame with a cable tie (see illustration) to provide enough clearance to remove the right crankcase cover.
3   Remove the kickstarter pedal (see Section 15).

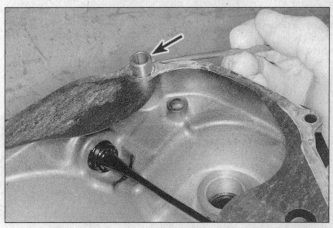

13.5b Locate the cover dowels (arrow) in the cover or in the crankcase, remove them and store them in plastic bags (rear dowel shown, front dowel not shown)

4   Disconnect the coolant inlet hose from the right crankcase cover (see illustration).
5   Remove the right crankcase cover screws (see illustration) and pull off the cover. If the cover is stuck, tap it gently with a rubber mallet to break the gasket seal. Don't pry against the mating surfaces of the cover and crankcase. Once the cover is off, locate the dowels (see illustration); they may have stayed in the crankcase or come off with the cover.

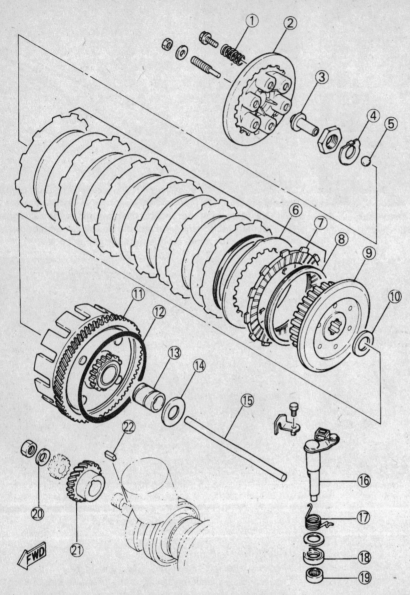

13.6a Clutch (Banshee) - exploded view

1 Clutch spring
2 Clutch pressure plate
3 Short pushrod
4 Lock washer
5 Ball
6 Clutch plate
7 Friction plate
8 Cushion ring
9 Clutch center
10 Thrust washer
11 Clutch housing
12 O-ring
13 Spacer bushing
14 Thrust washer
15 Long pushrod
16 Clutch push lever axle
17 Push lever axle spring
18 Oil seal
19 Bearing
20 Conical spring washer
21 Primary drive gear
22 Key

13.6b Remove the clutch spring bolts and springs (arrows) and pull off the pressure plate

13.6c Remove the friction plates, cushion rings and steel plates; if they stick together, carefully pry them loose

13.6d Remove the short pushrod (not shown), then using a magnet, remove the ball . . .

13.6e . . . and remove the long pushrod

13.6f Straighten the lockwasher tabs, then unscrew the clutch center nut and slide the lockwasher off the mainshaft . . .

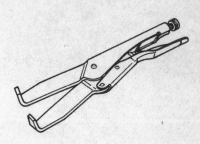

13.6g . . . to loosen the clutch center nut, you'll need a special tool to hold the clutch center; this is the factory tool, available at any Yamaha dealer . . .

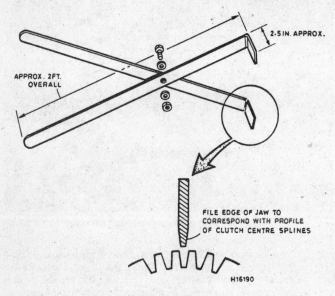

13.6h . . . you can make your own tool from steel scrap . . .

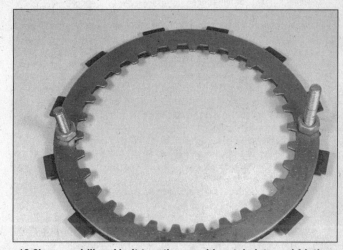

13.6i . . . or drill and bolt together an old metal plate and friction plate, slip them into their installed positions and wedge the primary gears . . .

Inspection

Refer to illustrations 13.8, 13.11, 13.12 and 13.13

7   Inspect the friction surface on the pressure plate for scoring or wear. Replace the pressure plate if any defects are found.

8   Inspect the edges of the slots in the clutch housing for indentations made by the friction plate tabs. If the indentations are deep, they

6   Refer to the accompanying illustrations to remove the clutch **(see illustrations)**. To prevent the clutch from turning while the bolts are loosened, wedge a copper washer or a rag between the primary drive and driven gears (see Section 14).

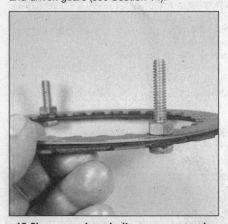

13.6j . . . use long bolts so you can grip them to pull the tool out when you're done

13.6k Remove the clutch center, its thrust washer and the clutch housing

13.6l Finally, remove the spacer bushing and thrust washer behind the clutch housing

13.8 Hold the clutch housing so it won't turn and try to rotate the primary driven gear; if there's any play, replace the clutch housing

13.11 Measure the clutch spring free length

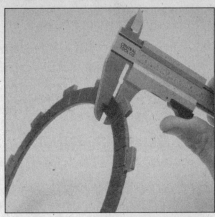

13.12 Measure the thickness of the friction plates

can prevent clutch release, so replace the housing. If the indentations can be easily removed with a file, the life of the housing can be prolonged for a little while longer. Also inspect the primary driven gear teeth **(see illustration)** for cracks, chips or excessive wear. If the primary driven gear is worn or damaged or the gear can be rotated separately from the clutch housing, the clutch housing must be replaced. Make sure that the lash number on the back of the primary driven gear matches the lash number on the back of the primary drive gear within the specified range (see Section 14).

9   Inspect the bushing surface in the center of the clutch housing for score marks, scratches and excessive wear. If it's worn, replace the clutch housing. If the bushing surface on the mainshaft is worn excessively, replace the mainshaft (see Section 19).

10   Inspect the clutch center's friction surface and slots for scoring, wear and indentations. Also check the splines in the middle of the clutch center. Replace the clutch center if problems are found.

11   Measure the free length of the clutch springs **(see illustration)** and compare the results to this Chapter's Specifications. If the springs have sagged, or if cracks are noted, replace them with new ones as a set.

12   If the lining material of the friction plates smells burnt or if it is glazed, new parts are required. If the metal clutch plates are scored or discolored, they must be replaced with new ones. Measure the thickness of the friction plates **(see illustration)** and replace with new parts any friction plates that are worn.

13   Lay the metal plates, one at a time, on a perfectly flat surface (such as a piece of plate glass) and check for warpage by trying to slip a feeler gauge between the flat surface and the plate **(see illustration)**. The feeler gauge should be the same thickness as the maximum warp listed in this Chapter's Specifications. Do this at several places around the plate's circumference. If the feeler gauge can be slipped under the plate, it is warped and should be replaced with a new one.

14   Inspect the tabs on the friction plates for excessive wear and mushroomed edges. They can be cleaned up with a file if the deformation is not severe. Check the friction plates for warpage as described in Step 13.

Installation

Refer to illustrations 13.15a and 13.15b

15   Installation is the reverse of the removal steps, with the following additions:

a) *Install a new lockwasher and position its tabs between the splines of the clutch center. Using the factory clutch holding tool or a suitable equivalent tool, tighten the clutch nut to the torque listed in this Chapter's Specifications, then bend the lockwasher tabs against two of the flats on the nut.*

b) *Coat the friction plates with clean engine oil before you install them.*

13.13 Check the metal plates for warpage

c) *Install a cushion ring, then a friction plate, then a metal plate; a cushion ring, a friction plate and a metal plate . . . etc. until they're all installed. Friction plates go on first and last, so the friction material contacts the metal surfaces of the clutch center and the pressure plate.*

d) *Note that the edges of the metal plates are cut away* **(see illustration)**. *This reduces clutch noise caused by the metal plates and the clutch center by allowing the plates to move outward under centrifugal force. As you install each metal plate, position these cutaways 60 degrees apart, in a clockwise direction, as shown.*

e) *Align the marks on the pressure plate and clutch center* **(see illustration)**.

f) *Apply grease to the ends of the clutch pushrods and the steel ball between the two pushrods.*

g) *Be sure to grease the O-ring on the water pump outlet tube with lightweight lithium soap base grease (see "Water pump - removal, inspection and installation" in Chapter 3).*

h) *Tighten the right crankcase cover screws evenly to the torque listed in this Chapter's Specifications.*

14   Water pump and primary drive gears - removal, inspection and installation

Removal

Refer to illustration 14.2

1   Remove the right crankcase cover (see Section 13).

2   Put a penny or a shop rag between the primary drive gear and the driven gear on the clutch housing, then loosen the water pump

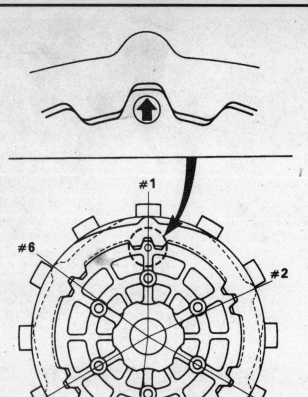

13.15a Install the metal plates with the cut-outs oriented
60 degrees apart, as shown

gear/primary drive gear retaining nut (see illustration).
3   Remove the clutch (see Section 13).
4   Remove the water pump gear/primary drive gear retaining nut and the washer.
5   Remove the water pump drive gear and the primary drive gear from the crankshaft. Locate the Woodruff key (see illustration 13.6a) - it might be in the crankshaft or it might have fallen out - and store it in a plastic bag.

14.2 Primary drive and driven gear selection

13.15b Align the arrow on the pressure plate
with the mark on the clutch center

Inspection

6   Check the gears for obvious damage such as chipped, pitted or broken teeth. Replace them if any of these problems are found. If it's necessary to replace the primary drive gear, make sure that the lash numbers on the back of the primary drive gear and the primary driven gear match within the following range, and that the sum of these two numbers is within the specified range of tolerance:

Installation

7   Installation is the reverse of removal, with the following additions:
a) Make sure the Woodruff key is in place on the crankshaft (see illustration 13.6a).
b) Wedge the gears using the same method used for removal, then tighten the nuts to the torques listed in this Chapter's Specifications.

2A

15   Kickstarter - removal, inspection and installation

Pedal

Removal

Refer to illustration 15.1

1   Look for a punch mark on the end of the kickstarter spindle. If you can't see one, make your own to align with the slit in the pedal shaft (see illustration).
2   Remove the pinch bolt and slide the pedal off the spindle.

15.1 Mark the alignment of the kickstarter pedal and shaft, then
remove the pinch bolt (arrow) and slide the pedal off

Inspection

3 Inspect the pedal for obvious wear and damage, such as bending or stripped splines. Replace worn or damaged parts. Inspect the pedal seal for signs of oil leakage. If it's been leaking, remove the right crankcase cover (see Section 13). Pry the seal out of the bore and tap in a new one with a socket the same diameter as the seal.

Installation

4 Slip the pedal onto the kickstarter spindle, aligning the marks. Install the nut and tighten it to the torque listed in this Chapter's Specifications.

Kickstarter mechanism

Removal

Refer to illustrations 15.7, 15.8, 15.10a, 15.10b and 15.10c

5 Remove the kickstarter pedal (see Steps 1 and 2 above).
6 Remove the right crankcase cover and the clutch (see Section 13).
7 Unhook the kickstarter spring from its pin on the crankcase (see illustration) and remove the kickstarter mechanism.
8 Disengage the return spring (see illustration) from the hole in the shaft and slide off the return spring, collar and thrust washer. Remove the clip and pinion gear.
10 Remove the idler gear snap-ring and washer, slip the idler gear off its shaft and remove the thrust washer (see illustrations).

Inspection

11 If the clip is damaged, install a new one.
12 Inspect all parts for wear or damage, paying special attention to the teeth on the pinion and idler gears. Replace worn or damaged parts.

Installation

13 Installation is the reverse of removal, with the following addition:

a) *Be sure the kickstarter stop rests against the protrusion on the crankcase. Place the protruding part of the kickstarter clip in the crankcase notch.*

---

16   External shift mechanism - removal, inspection and installation

---

Shift pedal

Removal

Refer to illustration 16.1

1 Look for alignment punch marks on the gearshift pedal and the end of the gearshift spindle. If there aren't any marks, make your own with a sharp punch, or draw a line across the end of the spindle in line with the split in the gearshift pedal (see illustration).

15.7 Unhook the return spring from the post on the crankcase and remove the kickstarter mechanism

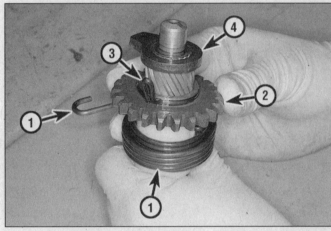

15.8 Kickstarter mechanism components:

1	Return spring	3	Clip
2	Kickstarter gear	4	Kickstarter shaft

2 Remove the gearshift pedal pinch bolt and slide the pedal off the gearshift spindle.

Inspection

Refer to illustration 16.4

3 Inspect the gearshift pedal for wear or damage, such as bending. Inspect the splines on the pedal and on the gearshift spindle for strip-

15.10a Remove the snap-ring . . .

15.10b . . . remove the washer and the idler gear . . .

15.10c . . . and remove the thrust washer

16.1 Mark the alignment of the gearshift pedal and spindle, remove the pinch bolt (arrow) and slide the gearshift pedal off the spindle

16.4 If the gearshift spindle seal (arrow) is leaking, remove the spindle, pry out the old seal and install a new one

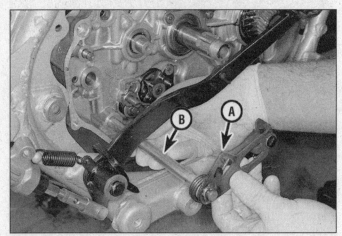

16.8 To remove the change lever (A), pull the gearshift spindle (B) out of the crankcase

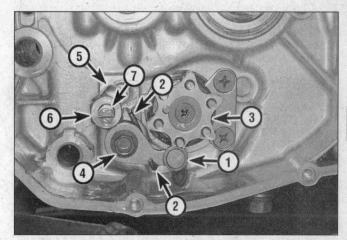

16.9 External shift linkage details

1	Stopper arm	5	Eccentric adjuster
2	Spring ends		lockwasher
3	Shift drum cam	6	Eccentric adjuster locknut
4	Stopper arm bolt	7	Eccentric adjuster

ping. If the splines are damaged, replace the pedal and/or spindle.

4 Inspect the gearshift spindle seal for signs of oil leakage (see illustration). If it's leaking, remove the left crankcase cover (see "CDI magneto - component replacement" in Chapter 9), remove the gearshift spindle as described below, then pry the seal out of the crankcase. Install a new seal by tapping it into place with a small deep socket that's the same diameter as the seal. Install the left crankcase cover.

Installation

5 Align the punch marks, install the gearshift pedal and tighten the pinch bolt securely.

External shift linkage

Removal

Refer to illustrations 16.8 and 16.9

6 Remove the gearshift pedal as described above.

7 Remove the clutch (see Section 13) and the kickstarter mechanism (see Section 15).

8 Note how the gearshift spindle return spring fits over the adjuster pin and note how the change lever's pawls engage the pins of the shift drum. To remove the change lever, pull the gearshift spindle out of the crankcase (see illustration).

9 Note how the stopper arm spring presses against the case and hooks around the stopper arm (see illustration). Remove the bolt and remove the stopper arm and spring.

Inspection

10 Inspect the gearshift spindle return spring and splines for damage. The return spring can be replaced separately, but if the splines are damaged, the spindle/change lever must be replaced.

11 Inspect the condition of the stopper arm and spring. Replace the stopper arm if it's worn where it contacts the shift drum. Replace the stopper arm spring if it's bent.

12 Inspect the shift cam pins for wear on their contact surfaces. If they're worn or damaged, replace the shift drum (you'll have to split the crankcase to replace the shift drum).

Installation

Refer to illustration 16.15

13 Install the stopper arm and spring on the crankcase. Make sure that the stopper arm spring is correctly positioned (see illustration 16.9). Apply non-permanent thread locking agent to the threads of the stopper arm bolt, then tighten the bolt to the torque listed in this Chapter's Specifications. Engage the roller end of the stopper arm with the neutral notch in the shift drum cam.

14 Carefully slide the gearshift spindle into the crankcase, taking care not to damage the seal on the other side. Make sure that the spindle return spring is correctly positioned, with its ends on either side of the

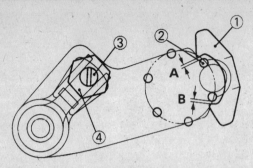

**16.15 Adjust the eccentric adjuster so that gaps
A and B are equal**

1 Change lever	3 Eccentric adjuster
2 Shift drum cam pins	4 Eccentric adjuster locknut

**17.9 Remove these bearing stopper plate screws (arrows) and
the stopper plate before separating the crankcase halves**

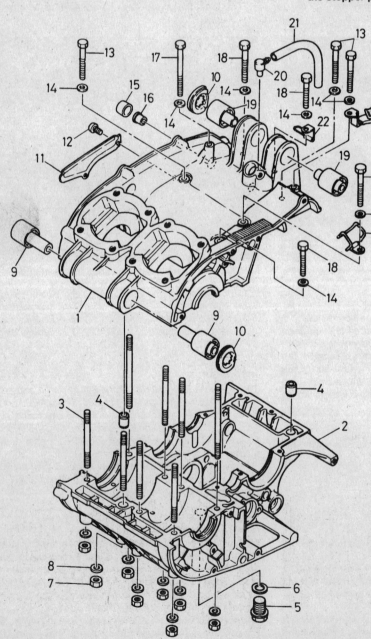

17.11 Crankcase (Banshee) – exploded view

1	Upper crankcase half
2	Lower crankcase half
3	Studs (8)
4	Dowels (2)
5	Drain plug
6	Sealing washer
7	Nuts (8)
8	Washers (8)
9	Front mounting bushings (2)
10	Front mounting bushing spacers (2)
11	Side cover
12	Side cover screws (2)
13	Bolts (4)
14	Washers (8)
15	Collar
16	Bushing
17	Bolt
18	Bolts (3)
19	Rear mounting bushing (2)
20	Pipe cap
21	Pipe
22	Clamp
23	Cable clip
24	Cable clip

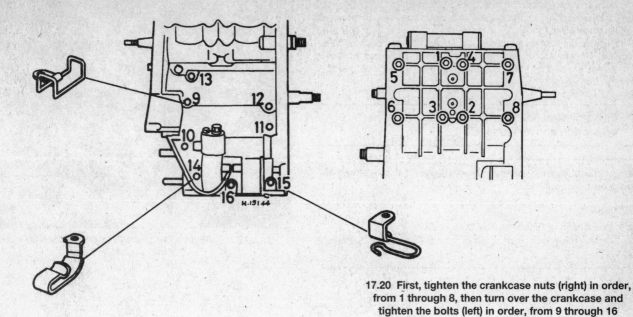

17.20 First, tighten the crankcase nuts (right) in order, from 1 through 8, then turn over the crankcase and tighten the bolts (left) in order, from 9 through 16

adjuster pin. Operate the gearshift spindle and verify that the external shift mechanism operates correctly. If it doesn't, adjust it as follows.

15   Straighten the lockwasher tab **(see illustration 16.9)**, loosen the locknut **(see illustration)** and turn the eccentric adjuster pin in or out until gap A and B are equal. Tighten the locknut and bend the lock-washer tab against the locknut.

16   The remainder of installation is the reverse of removal.

17   Refill the transmission oil (see Chapter 1).

17 Crankcase - disassembly and reassembly

1   To examine and repair or replace the crankshaft, connecting rods, bearings and transmission components, the crankcase must be split into two parts.

Disassembly

Refer to illustrations 17.9 and 17.11

2   Remove the engine from the vehicle (see Section 6).

3   Remove the cylinder head, cylinders and pistons (see Sections 8, 10 and 11).

4   Remove the CDI magneto (see Chapter 9).

5   Remove the clutch (see Section 13).

6   Remove the water pump and primary drive gears (see Section 14).

7   Remove the kickstarter (see Section 15). (It's not necessary to remove the idler gear.)

8   Remove the external shift mechanism (see Section 16).

9   Remove the bearing stopper plate for the transmission input shaft **(see illustration)**.

10   Check carefully to make sure there aren't any remaining components that attach the halves of the crankcase together.

11   There are eight upper crankcase bolts and eight lower crankcase nuts **(see illustration)**. Loosen the bolts evenly and gradually, in two or three stages, remove them, then turn the crankcase assembly upside down and remove the nuts the same way.

12   Separate the upper crankcase from the lower crankcase. If the case halves are stuck together, strike the front engine mount boss with a rubber mallet to knock the upper case half loose. Don't pry against the mating surfaces of the case halves or they'll leak.

13   Locate the crankcase dowels and store them in a plastic bag.

14   Refer to Sections 18 through 20 for information on the internal components of the crankcase.

Reassembly

Refer to illustration 17.20

15   Remove all traces of old gasket and sealant from the crankcase mating surfaces with a sharpening stone or similar tool. Be careful not to let any fall into the case as this is done and be careful not to damage the mating surfaces.

16   Check to make sure the dowel pins are in place in their holes in the mating surface of the lower crankcase half **(see illustration 17.11)**.

17   Pour some four-stroke engine oil over the transmission gears. Don't get any oil in the crankshaft cavity or on the crankcase mating surface.

18   Apply a coat of Yamabond No. 4 sealant, or a suitable equivalent, to the lower crankcase mating surface.

19   Carefully place the upper crankcase half onto the lower crankcase half.

20   Carefully turn the crankcase upside down and install the lower crankcase nuts. Tighten them gradually and evenly until they are snug, then tighten them in the indicated order **(see illustration)** to the torque listed in this Chapter's Specifications.

21   Turn the crankcase right side up and install the upper crankcase bolts. Tighten them gradually and evenly until they are snug, then tighten them in the indicated order **(see illustration 17.20)** to the torque listed in this Chapter's Specifications.

22   Turn the crankshaft and the transmission shafts. Make sure all three turn freely.

23   The remainder of assembly is the reverse of disassembly.

18 Crankcase components - inspection and servicing

1   Separate the crankcase and remove the following:
   a) *Shift drum and forks (see Section 19).*
   b) *Transmission shafts and gears (see Section 19).*
   d) *Crankshaft (see Section 20).*

2   Clean the crankcase halves thoroughly with new solvent and dry them with compressed air. All oil passages should be blown out with compressed air and all traces of old gasket should be removed from the mating surfaces. **Caution:** *Be very careful not to nick or gouge the crankcase mating surfaces or leaks will result. Check both crankcase halves very carefully for cracks and other damage.*

3   Carefully inspect the crankcase halves for cracks and any other damage. If either of them is damaged, replace the crankcase halves as a set.

4   Inspect the transmission and crankshaft bearings. If the bearings don't turn smoothly, replace them (transmission, see Section 19; crankshaft, see Section 20).

5   Replace the crankshaft oil seals whenever the crankcase is disassembled. The crankshaft seals are critical to the performance of two-stroke engines, so they should be replaced even if they look perfectly all right.

19 Transmission shafts and shift drum - removal, inspection and installation

Note: *When disassembling the transmission shafts, place the parts on a long rod or thread a wire through them to keep them in order and facing the proper direction.*

Removal

Refer to illustrations 19.2 and 19.3a through 19.3f

1   Remove the engine, then separate the case halves (see Sections 6 and 17).

19.2 Note how the gears fit together, then lift out the transmission shafts

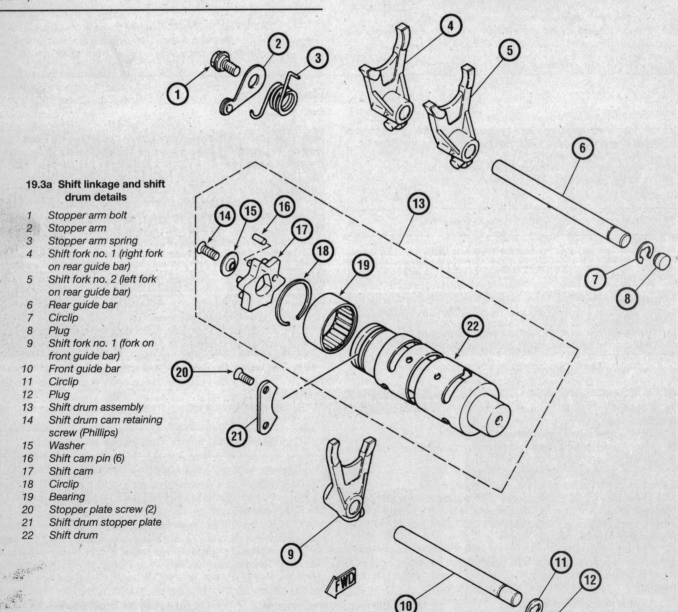

19.3a Shift linkage and shift drum details

1   Stopper arm bolt
2   Stopper arm
3   Stopper arm spring
4   Shift fork no. 1 (right fork on rear guide bar)
5   Shift fork no. 2 (left fork on rear guide bar)
6   Rear guide bar
7   Circlip
8   Plug
9   Shift fork no. 1 (fork on front guide bar)
10   Front guide bar
11   Circlip
12   Plug
13   Shift drum assembly
14   Shift drum cam retaining screw (Phillips)
15   Washer
16   Shift cam pin (6)
17   Shift cam
18   Circlip
19   Bearing
20   Stopper plate screw (2)
21   Shift drum stopper plate
22   Shift drum

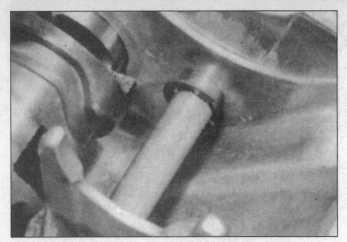

19.3b Remove the circlip from the front guide bar . . .

19.3c . . . pull out the front guide bar and remove the front shift fork

2   Remove the transmission shafts (see illustration).
3   Pull out the shift fork shafts and shift forks (see illustrations). Lift the shift drum out of the case half (see illustration).

Transmission shaft disassembly

Refer to illustrations 19.4a, 19.4b and 19.4c
4   Removal of the shaft components requires only a pair of snap-ring pliers to remove the snap-rings (see illustration). Slide the

components off the shafts and place them in order on a long rod or a piece of plastic pipe (see illustrations).

Inspection

Refer to illustrations 19.7a, 19.7b and 19.10
5   Wash all of the components in clean solvent and dry them off.
6   Inspect the shift fork grooves in the gears. If a groove is worn or scored, replace the affected part and inspect its corresponding shift fork.

19.3d Remove the circlip from the rear guide bar . . .

19.3e . . . pull out the guide bar and remove the rear shift forks

19.3f Remove the shift drum

19.4a Remove the snap-rings with snap-ring pliers

19.4b Rotate the thrust washers so tabs align with the shaft splines, then slide them off the shaft

2A

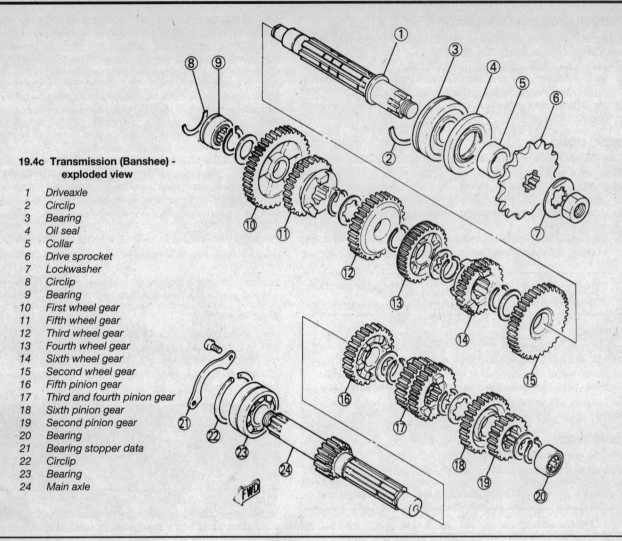

19.4c Transmission (Banshee) - exploded view

1   Driveaxle
2   Circlip
3   Bearing
4   Oil seal
5   Collar
6   Drive sprocket
7   Lockwasher
8   Circlip
9   Bearing
10 First wheel gear
11 Fifth wheel gear
12 Third wheel gear
13 Fourth wheel gear
14 Sixth wheel gear
15 Second wheel gear
16 Fifth pinion gear
17 Third and fourth pinion gear
18 Sixth pinion gear
19 Second pinion gear
20 Bearing
21 Bearing stopper data
22 Circlip
23 Bearing
24 Main axle

7   Check the shift forks for distortion and wear, especially at the fork ears **(see illustration)**. If they are discolored or severely worn they are probably bent. Inspect the guide pins and shift drum grooves for excessive wear and distortion and replace any defective parts with new ones **(see illustration)**.

8   Check the shift fork shafts evidence of wear, galling and other damage. Make sure the shift forks move smoothly on the shafts. If the bars are worn or bent, replace them with new ones.

9   Check the gear teeth for cracking and other obvious damage. Check the bushing surface in the inner diameter of the freewheeling gears for scoring or heat discoloration. Replace damaged parts.

10   Inspect the engagement dogs and dog holes on gears so equipped for excessive wear or rounding off **(see illustration)**. Replace the paired gears as a set if necessary.

11   Check the transmission shaft bearings in the crankcase for wear or heat discoloration and replace them if necessary (see Section 19).

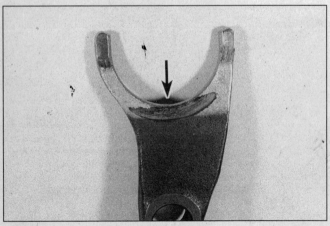

19.7a An arc-shaped burn mark like this means the fork was rubbing against a gear, probably due to bending or worn fork fingers

19.7b Unscrew the Phillips screw (arrow) to remove the shift drum cam and bearing

Transmission shaft assembly

12 Assembly of the transmission shafts is the reverse of the disassembly procedure, with the following additions:

a) *Make sure all components face in the correct direction* **(see illustration 19.4a)**. *Use new snap-rings, installed with their sharp sides facing away from the thrust washers.*

b) *Once assembled, make sure the gears mesh properly* **(see illustration 19.2).**

Installation

13 Installation is the basically the reverse of removal, but note the following points:

a) *Lubricate the transmission parts with four-stroke engine oil before assembling them.*

b) *After assembly, check the gears to make sure they're installed correctly. Move the shift drum through the gear positions and rotate the gears to make sure they mesh and shift correctly. If they don't, stop and find the problem before you reassemble the case halves.*

20 Crankshaft and connecting rods - removal, inspection and installation

Removal

Refer to illustration 20.2

1 Remove the engine and separate the crankcase halves (Sections 6 and 17). The transmission shafts need not be removed.

2 Remove the crankshaft and connecting rods from the lower case half. Remove the circlip **(see illustration)** that secures the right main bearing.

Inspection

Refer to illustrations 20.3, 20.4 and 20.6

Note: *Before tackling a crankshaft rebuild, check with your dealer. Yamaha sells complete, assembled crankshafts, or you can purchase replacement crank parts - flywheels, crankpins, thrust bearings, needle*

roller bearings, connecting rods, etc. Depending on the nature of the damage, it might be more cost effective to replace only the damaged part(s), or it might be more practical to replace the entire crankshaft. For example, the old bearings can be pressed off and new bearings pressed on without disassembling the crankshaft. But if a rod, big end bearing, crankpin or flywheel must be replaced, the crankshaft must be disassembled. If the crank is disassembled, it must be balanced after it has been reassembled. Balancing a two-stroke crankshaft is a difficult and very exacting procedure that is normally done only by a highly skilled motorcycle machinist. We don't recommend tackling a crank rebuild yourself (unless you're a machinist!).

3 Inspect the threads on the ends of the crankshaft. If they're damaged, try to clean them up with a thread die. Put the crankshaft on V-blocks and inspect the ball bearings on the ends of the crankshaft **(see illustration)**. The crankshaft should rotate freely and quietly. If either bearing is rough, noisy or otherwise damaged, have it replaced by your dealer or by a competent motorcycle machine shop (these two bearings can be replaced without disassembling the crankshaft.)

19.10 Check the slots (left arrow) and dogs (right arrow) for wear, especially at the edges; rounded corners cause the transmission to jump out of gear - new gears (bottom) have sharp corners

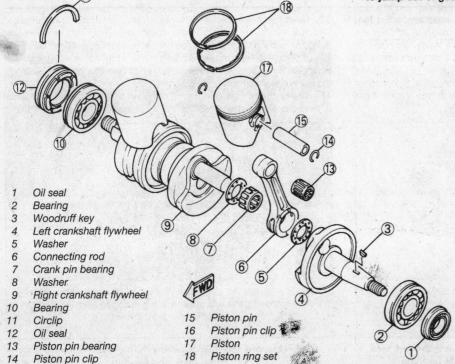

1	Oil seal
2	Bearing
3	Woodruff key
4	Left crankshaft flywheel
5	Washer
6	Connecting rod
7	Crank pin bearing
8	Washer
9	Right crankshaft flywheel
10	Bearing
11	Circlip
12	Oil seal
13	Piston pin bearing
14	Piston pin clip
15	Piston pin
16	Piston pin clip
17	Piston
18	Piston ring set

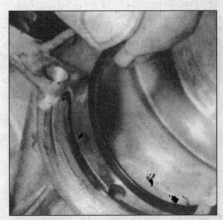

20.2 Be sure this circlip is in its groove in the right main bearing saddle when the crankshaft is reinstalled

20.3 Crankshaft (Banshee) – exploded view

2A

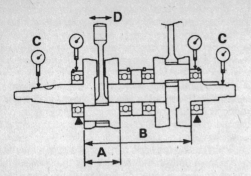

20.4 Crankshaft measurement points

A   *Width of left flywheels*
B   *Width of both flywheels and center bearings*
C   *Measure runout at these points*
D   *Connecting rod small-end side play*

4   With the crankshaft on the V-blocks, measure the width of the two left flywheels and the distance from the outside face of the left flywheel to the outside face of the right flywheel **(see illustration)**. Compare your measurements to the dimensions listed in this Chapter's Specifications. If either measurement exceeds the specified dimension, replace the crankshaft (or have it rebuilt).

5   With the crankshaft still on the V-blocks, measure the runout at the indicated points **(see illustration 20.4)** with a dial gauge and compare your measurements to the runout listed in this Chapter's Specifications. If the indicated runout is excessive at any point, have the crankshaft aligned by a dealer service department or by a competent machine shop (or replace it).

6   Measure the side clearance between the connecting rods and crankshaft with a feeler gauge **(see illustration)**. If it's more than the limit listed in this Chapter's Specifications, have the crankshaft rebuilt, or replace the crankshaft and connecting rods as an assembly.

7   With the crankshaft in V-blocks, use a dial indicator to measure the side play of the small end of each connecting rod. Move the rod side-to-side against the indicator pointer and compare the reading to the small-end side play value listed in this Chapter's Specifications. If it's beyond the limit, the crankshaft can be disassembled and the needle roller bearing replaced. However, this is a specialized job that

should be done by a Yamaha dealer or a competent motorcycle machine shop.

Installation

Refer to illustration 20.9

8   Install the circlip for the right outer main bearing in its groove in the right bearing saddle **(see illustration 20.2)**.

9   Make sure the small positioning pins for the center main bearings **(see illustration)** and the left outer main bearing are in place.

11   Place the crankshaft in the lower crankcase half with the right crank bearing up against the circlip.

12   Install *new* crankshaft seals on the ends of the crank. (Using the old seals will result in a loss of crankcase pressure, and performance will suffer.)

13   The remainder of installation is the reverse of removal.

21   Recommended start-up and break-in procedure

Note: *Any rebuilt engine needs time to break in, even if parts have been installed in their original locations. Yamaha specifies a 20-hour break-in period for these models when new; you can use this as a guide for breaking in a rebuilt engine.*

First 10 hours

1   Don't operate continuously at more than half throttle.

2   Let the engine cool for five to ten minutes after each hour of operation.

3   Vary engine speeds; don't operate continuously at one throttle setting.

10 to 20 hours

4   Don't operate continuously at more than three-quarters throttle.

5   Rev the engine freely, but don't use full throttle.

After 20 hours

6   Vary engine speeds occasionally. Don't operate at full throttle for prolonged periods.

7   Upon completion of the break-in rides, and after the engine has cooled down completely, recheck the transmission oil level (see Chapter 1).

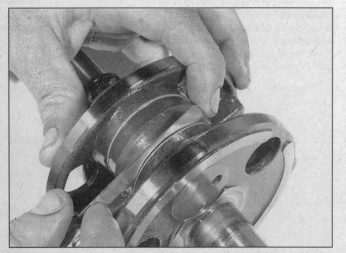

20.6 Check the connecting rod side clearance with a feeler gauge

20.9 The center bearings are located by these two positioning pins (arrows); the left outer main bearing is also located by another pin (not shown)

Chapter 2 Part B
Engine, clutch and transmission (Warrior models)

Contents

2B

Specifications

General

Bore	83 mm (3.268 inches)
Stroke	64.5 mm (2.539 inches)
Displacement	348 cc (21.2 cubic inches)

Rocker arms

Rocker arm inside diameter
  Standard .... 12.000 to 12.018 mm (0.4724 to 0.4731 inch)
  Limit .... 12.078 mm (0.4755 inch)
Rocker shaft outside diameter
  Standard .... 11.981 to 11.991 mm (0.4717 to 0.4721 inch)
  Limit .... 11.951 mm (0.4705 inch)
Shaft-to-arm clearance
  Standard .... 0.009 to 0.037 mm (0.0004 to 0.0015 inch)
  Limit .... 0.08 mm (0.0032 inch)

Camshaft

Lobe height (intake and exhaust)	40.62 to 40.72 mm (1.599 to 1.603 inches)
Camshaft runout limit	0.03 mm (0.001 inch)

Cylinder head, valves and valve springs

Cylinder head warpage limit	0.03 mm 0.0012 inch)
Valve stem runout limit	0.01 mm (0.0004 inch)
Valve stem diameter	
Intake	
Standard	6.975 to 6.990 mm (0.2746 to 0.2752 inch)
Limit	6.95 mm (0.274 inch)
Exhaust	
Standard	6.955 to 6.970 mm (0.2738 to 0.2744 inch)
Limit	6.915 mm (0.2722 inch)
Valve guide inside diameter	
Standard	7.000 to 7.012 mm (0.2756 to 0.2761 inch)
Limit	7.03 mm (0.277 inch)
Stem-to-guide clearance	
Standard	0.010 to 0.037 mm (0.0004 to 0.0015 inch)
Limit	0.08 mm (0.0031 inch)
Valve seat width	
Standard	1.0 to 1.2 mm (0.039 to 0.047 inch)
Limit	1.6 mm (0.063 inch)
Valve spring free length	
Inner spring	
Standard	39.9 mm (1.57 inch)
Limit	37.9 mm (1.49 inch)
Outer spring	
Standard	43.27 mm (1.70 inch)
Limit	41.27 mm (1.62 inch)
Valve spring bend limit	1.6 mm (0.063 inch)

Cylinder

Bore diameter	82.97 to 83.02 mm (3.267 to 3.269 inches)
Out-of-round limit	0.01 mm (0.0004 inch)
Taper limit	0.05 mm (0.002 inch)
Measuring point	40 mm (1.57 inches) from top of bore

Piston

Diameter	
1987 through 2001	82.020 to 82.070 mm (3.229 to 3.231 inches)
2002 and later	82.92 to 82.97 mm (3.265 to 3.267 inch)
Measuring point	5.5 mm (7/32 inch) from bottom of skirt
Piston-to-cylinder clearance	0.04 to 0.06 mm (0.0016 to 0.0024 inch)
Oversize pistons and rings	
First oversize	83.50 mm (3.287 inches)
Second oversize	84.00 mm (3.307 inches)
Piston pin bore	Not specified
Piston pin outer diameter	Not specified
Piston pin-to-piston clearance	Not specified
Ring side clearance	
Top	
Standard	
1999 through 2001	0.04 to 0.08 mm (0.0016 to 0.0032 inch)
2002 and later	0.03 to 0.09 mm (0.0012 to 0.0035 inch)
Limit	0.12 mm (0.0047 inch)
Second	
Standard	0.03 to 0.07 mm (0.0012 to 0.0028 inch)
Limit	0.12 mm (0.0047 inch)
Ring end gap	
Top	
Standard	0.2 to 0.4 mm (0.008 to 0.016 inch)
Limit	0.5 mm (0.02 inch)
Second	
Standard	0.2 to 0.4 mm (0.008 to 0.016 inch)
Limit	0.5 mm (0.02 inch)
Oil	
Standard	0.3 to 0.9 mm (0.012 to 0.035 inch)
Limit	not specified

Clutch

Spring free length
  Standard .... 47.8 mm (1.88 inches)
  Limit .... 46.5 mm (1.831 inches)
Metal plate thickness
  Nominal 2.0 mm plates .... 1.9 to 2.1 mm (0.0748 to 0.0827 inch)
  Nominal 1.6 mm plates .... 1.5 to 1.7 mm (0.059 to 0.066 inch)
Friction plate thickness
  Standard .... 2.94 to 3.06 mm (0.116 to 0.120 inch)
  Limit .... 2.8 mm (0.110 inch)
Friction and metal plate warpage limit .... 0.20 mm (0.008 inch)

Oil pump

Outer rotor-to-body clearance .... 0.04 to 0.09 mm (0.002 to 0.004 inch)
Inner-to-outer rotor clearance
  Standard .... 0.15 mm (0.006 inch) or less
  Limit .... 0.20 mm (0.008 inch)

Crankshaft and connecting rod

Runout limit .... 0.06 mm (0.0024 inch)
Assembly width .... 58.95 to 59.00 mm (2.321 to 2.323 inches)
Connecting rod big-end side clearance
  Standard .... 0.35 to 0.85 mm (0.014 to 0.033 inch)
  Limit .... 0.90 mm (0.035 inch)
Connecting rod small-end endplay
  Standard .... 0.8 to 1.0 mm (0.0315 to 0.0394 inch)
  Limit .... 2.0 mm (0.08 inch)

Torque specifications

Cylinder head Allen bolts .... 20 Nm (168 in-lbs) (1)
Cylinder head bolts .... 40 Nm (29 ft-lbs) (1)
Cylinder base Allen bolt .... 10 Nm (84 in-lbs)
Cam sprocket cover Allen bolts .... 10 Nm (84 in-lbs)
Oil check bolt .... 7 Nm (61 in-lbs)
Camshaft bearing retainer bolts .... 8 Nm (70 in-lbs)
Cam chain guide bolts .... 10 Nm (84 in-lbs) (2)
Camshaft sprocket bolt .... 60 Nm (43 ft-lbs)
Cam chain tensioner body bolts .... 10 Nm (84 in-lbs)
Cam chain tensioner cap bolt .... 23 Nm (184 in-lbs)
Crankcase bolts .... 10 Nm (84 in-lbs)
Crankcase cover bolts .... 10 Nm (84 in-lbs)
Main axle bearing retainer screws .... 10 Nm (84 in-lbs) (3)
Balancer shaft bearing retainer screws .... 7 Nm (61 in-lbs) (3)
Shift drum segment screw .... 12 Nm (108 in-lbs) (3)
Oil pump screws .... 7 Nm (61 in-lbs)
Clutch boss nut .... 80 Nm (58 ft-lbs) (1)
Clutch spring plate bolts .... 8 Nm (70 in-lbs)
Balancer shaft and driven gear nut .... 60 Nm (43 ft-lbs) (2)

1 Apply engine oil to the threads.
2 Use a new lockwasher.
3 Apply non-permanent thread locking agent to the screws.

2B

1   General information

The engine/transmission unit is of the air-cooled, single-cylinder four-stroke design. The two valves are operated by an overhead camshaft which is chain driven off the crankshaft. The engine/transmission assembly is constructed from aluminum alloy. The crankcase is divided vertically.

The crankcase incorporates a wet sump, pressure-fed lubrication system which uses a gear-driven rotor-type oil pump, an oil filter and separate strainer screen and an oil temperature warning switch.

Power from the crankshaft is routed to the transmission via a wet, multi-plate clutch. The clutch transmits power to the transmission; it's engaged and disengaged by a cable linkage. The transmission has six forward gears and one reverse gear.

2   Operations possible with the engine in the frame

The components and assemblies listed below can be removed without having to remove the engine from the frame. If, however, a number of areas require attention at the same time, removal of the engine is recommended.

Recoil starter (if equipped)
Starter motor
Starter reduction gears
Starter clutch
Alternator rotor and stator
Clutch
External shift mechanism
Cam chain tensioner
Camshaft
Rocker arms and shafts
Cylinder head
Cylinder and piston
Oil pump
Balancer gears

3   Operations requiring engine removal

It is necessary to remove the engine/transmission assembly from the frame and separate the crankcase halves to gain access to the following components:

Crankshaft and connecting rod
Transmission shafts
Shift drums and forks

4   Major engine repair - general note

1   It is not always easy to determine when or if an engine should be completely overhauled, as a number of factors must be considered.

2   High mileage is not necessarily an indication that an overhaul is needed, while low mileage, on the other hand, does not preclude the need for an overhaul. Frequency of servicing is probably the single most important consideration. An engine that has regular and frequent oil and filter changes, as well as other required maintenance, will most likely give many miles of reliable service. Conversely, a neglected engine, or one which has not been broken in properly, may require an overhaul very early in its life.

3   Exhaust smoke and excessive oil consumption are both indications that piston rings and/or valve guides are in need of attention. Make sure oil leaks are not responsible before deciding that the rings and guides are bad. Refer to Chapter 1 and perform a cylinder compression check to determine for certain the nature and extent of the work required.

4   If the engine is making obvious knocking or rumbling noises, the connecting rod and/or main bearings are probably at fault.

5   Loss of power, rough running, excessive valve train noise and high fuel consumption rates may also point to the need for an overhaul, especially if they are all present at the same time. If a complete tune-up does not remedy the situation, major mechanical work is the only solution.

6   An engine overhaul generally involves restoring the internal parts to the specifications of a new engine. During an overhaul the piston rings are replaced and the cylinder walls are bored and/or honed. If a rebore is done, then a new piston is also required. Generally the valves are serviced as well, since they are usually in less than perfect condition at this point. While the engine is being overhauled, other components such as the carburetor and the starter motor can be rebuilt also. The end result should be a like-new engine that will give as many trouble-free miles as the original.

7   Before beginning the engine overhaul, read through all of the related procedures to familiarize yourself with the scope and requirements of the job. Overhauling an engine is not all that difficult, but it is time consuming. Plan on the vehicle being tied up for a minimum of two (2) weeks. Check on the availability of parts and make sure that any necessary special tools, equipment and supplies are obtained in advance.

8   Most work can be done with typical shop hand tools, although a number of precision measuring tools are required for inspecting parts to determine if they must be replaced. Often a dealer service department or repair shop will handle the inspection of parts and offer advice concerning reconditioning and replacement. As a general rule, time is the primary cost of an overhaul so it doesn't pay to install worn or substandard parts.

9   As a final note, to ensure maximum life and minimum trouble from a rebuilt engine, everything must be assembled with care in a spotlessly clean environment.

5   Engine - removal and installation

Note: *Engine removal and installation should be done with the aid of an assistant to avoid damage or injury that could occur if the engine is dropped.*

Removal

1   Drain the engine oil (see Chapter 1).
2   Remove the main switch (see Chapter 9).
3   Remove the seat, the front panel and the front fender (see Chapter 8). Remove the front fender stay.
4   Remove the fuel tank, the carburetor and the exhaust system (see Chapter 4).
5   Disconnect the clutch cable (see Section 14). Be sure to detach the cable from any brackets and guides on the frame and the engine.
6   Disconnect and remove the select lever rod.
7   Detach the crankcase breather hose.
8   Remove the drive chain sprocket cover and the drive chain (see Chapter 7).
9   Remove the footpegs (see Chapter 8).
10   Disconnect the shift lever rod from the shift lever and from the reverse shift mechanism (see Section 16).
11   Disconnect the rear brake pedal assembly (see Chapter 7).
12   Label and disconnect the following electrical wires: spark plug wire (see Chapter 1), starter motor lead, engine ground lead, reverse switch lead, CDI magneto lead and neutral switch lead (see Chapter 9).
13   Remove the upper mounting bolts, the front mounting bolt, the rear upper mounting bolt and the rear lower mounting bolt.
14   Remove the engine. Have an assistant help you lift the engine. Remove the engine to the left side of the vehicle.
15   Slowly lower the engine to a suitable work surface.

Installation

Refer to illustrations 5.21 and 5.22

16   Check the rubber engine supports for wear or damage and

5.21 Make sure that the output axle turns in a counterclockwise direction when the transmission is in forward shift

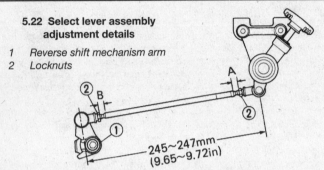

5.22 Select lever assembly adjustment details

1   *Reverse shift mechanism arm*
2   *Locknuts*

245~247mm
(9.65~9.72in)

replace them if necessary before installing the engine.

17   Make sure the rear of the vehicle is securely supported so it can't be knocked over during the remainder of this procedure.

18   With the help of an assistant, lift the engine up into the frame. Install the mounting bolts and nuts at the rear, front and top. The heads of all the mounting bolts face the right side of the vehicle. Finger-tighten the mounting bolts, but don't tighten them to the specified torque yet.

19   Tighten the engine mounting bolts and nuts securely.

20   Connect the select lever rod to the select lever, but do not connect it to the engine yet.

21   Push the select lever forward and verify that the transmission is in the forward mode as follows: Shift the transmission into sixth gear, return the decompression lever to its original position, pull the recoil starter lever and verify that the output axle turns in a counterclockwise direction **(see illustration)**. Return the transmission to Neutral.

22   Loosen both locknuts on the select lever rod **(see illustration)**, connect the select lever rod to the reverse shift mechanism, and adjust the rod length so that it is within the range shown in the accompanying illustration. Make sure that dimensions A and B are the same. Tighten the locknuts securely.

23   The remainder of installation is the reverse of removal, with the following additions:

a)   *Use new gaskets at all exhaust pipe connections.*
b)   *Adjust the clutch cable, throttle cable and rear brake pedal (see Chapter 1).*
c)   *Fill the engine with oil (see Chapter 1). Run the engine and check for leaks.*

24   Check the operation of the select lever. Make sure that the clutch lever must be operated before Reverse can be engaged and that there is an audible "click" sound (this indicates that engagement is positive). If not, go back and readjust the select lever rod.

6   Engine disassembly and reassembly - general information

Refer to illustrations 6.2 and 6.3

1   Before disassembling the engine, clean the exterior with a degreaser and rinse it with water. A clean engine will make the job easier and prevent the possibility of getting dirt into the internal areas of the engine.

2   In addition to the precision measuring tools mentioned earlier, you will need a torque wrench, a valve spring compressor, oil gallery brushes **(see illustration)**, a piston ring removal and installation tool, a piston ring compressor and a clutch holder tool (which is described in Section 8). Some new, clean engine oil of the correct grade and type, some engine assembly lube (or moly-based grease) and a tube of RTV (silicone) sealant will also be required.

3   An engine support stand made from short lengths of 2 x 4's bolted together will facilitate the disassembly and reassembly procedures **(see illustration)**. If you have an automotive-type engine stand, an adapter plate can be made from a piece of plate, some angle iron and some nuts and bolts.

4   When disassembling the engine, keep "mated" parts together (including gears, rocker arms and shafts, etc.) that have been in contact with each other during engine operation. These "mated" parts must be reused or replaced as an assembly.

5   Engine/transmission disassembly should be done in the following general order with reference to the appropriate Sections.

Remove the cam chain tensioner
Remove the cylinder head, rocker arms and camshaft
Remove the cylinder
Remove the piston
Remove the clutch
Remove the balancer gears
Remove the oil pump
Remove the external shift mechanism
Remove the alternator rotor

2B

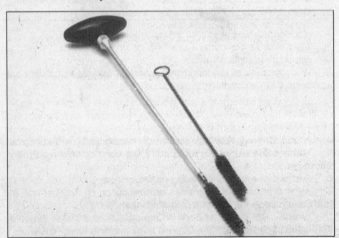

6.2 A selection of brushes is required for cleaning holes and passages in the engine compartment

6.3 An engine stand can be made from short lengths of lumber and lag bolts or nails

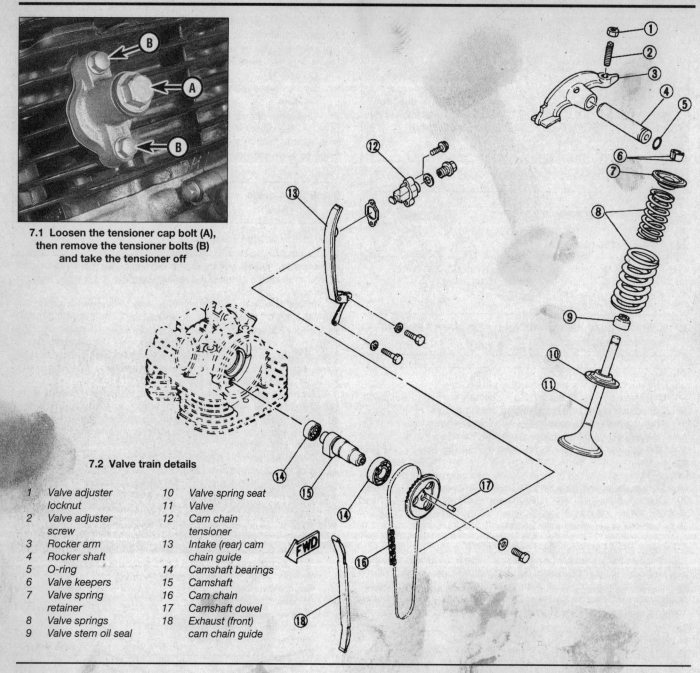

7.1 Loosen the tensioner cap bolt (A), then remove the tensioner bolts (B) and take the tensioner off

7.2 Valve train details

1	Valve adjuster locknut	10	Valve spring seat
2	Valve adjuster screw	11	Valve
3	Rocker arm	12	Cam chain tensioner
4	Rocker shaft	13	Intake (rear) cam chain guide
5	O-ring	14	Camshaft bearings
6	Valve keepers	15	Camshaft
7	Valve spring retainer	16	Cam chain
8	Valve springs	17	Camshaft dowel
9	Valve stem oil seal	18	Exhaust (front) cam chain guide

Separate the crankcase halves
Remove the shift drums and forks
Remove the transmission gears and shafts
Remove the balancer shaft
Remove the crankshaft and connecting rod

6   Reassembly is accomplished by reversing the general disassembly sequence.

7   Cam chain tensioner - removal and installation

Removal

Refer to illustrations 7.1 and 7.2

Caution: *Once you start to remove the tensioner bolts you must remove the tensioner all the way and reset it before tightening the bolts. The tensioner extends and locks in place, so if you loosen the bolts partway and then tighten them, the tensioner or cam chain will be damaged.*

1   Loosen the tensioner cap bolt **(see illustration)**.
2   Remove the tensioner mounting bolts and detach it from the cylinder block **(see illustration)**.
3   Remove the cap bolt and sealing washer from the tensioner body and wash them with solvent,

Installation

Refer to illustrations 7.7a and 7.7b

4   Clean all old gasket material from the tensioner body and engine.
5   Lubricate the friction surfaces of the components with moly-based grease.
6   Install a new tensioner gasket on the cylinder.
7   Lift the latch, compress the tensioner piston all the way into the body and release the latch **(see illustrations)**.
8   Position the tensioner body on the cylinder and install the bolts, tightening them to the torque listed in this Chapter's Specifications.
9   Install the cap bolt with a new sealing washer and tighten it to the torque listed in this Chapter's Specifications.

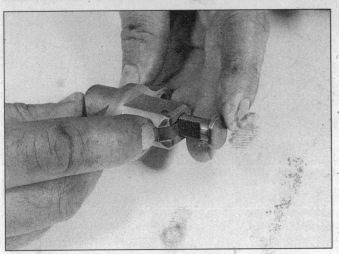

7.7a Lift the latch, press the piston into the tensioner
and release the latch

7.7b The piston should be retracted like this when
the tensioner is installed

8   Cylinder head, camshaft and rocker arms - removal, inspection and installation

Removal

Camshaft

Refer to illustrations 8.3, 8.4, 8.5, 8.7a, 8.7b and 8.8

1   Remove the engine from the frame (see Section 5).
2   Remove the valve adjusting hole covers (see Chapter 1).
3   Remove the Allen bolts and take off the cam sprocket cover **(see illustration)**.
4   Put the piston at top dead center on the compression stroke (see *Valve clearance - check and adjustment* in Chapter 1). The cam sprocket mark will align with the indicator cast into the cylinder head and the rocker arms will be loose when the cylinder is at TDC compression **(see illustration)**.

1987 and 1988 models (with recoil starter)

5   Prevent the crankshaft from turning. To do this, remove the recoil starter (see Section 19). Hold the recoil starter pulley with a clutch holder tool. If the factory tool or an equivalent isn't available, you can make your own from some steel strap, bent at the ends and bolted together in the middle **(see illustration)**.

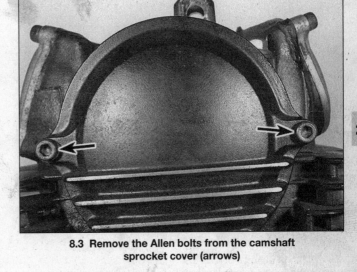

8.3 Remove the Allen bolts from the camshaft
sprocket cover (arrows)

8.4 With the engine at TDC compression, the sprocket line should
be even with the cast indicator in the cylinder head (arrows)

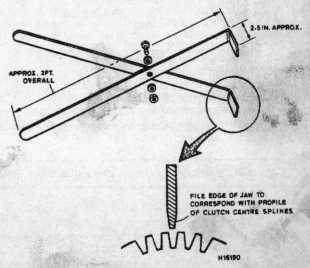

8.5 A clutch holding tool can be made from steel strap

2B

8.7a The camshaft dowel aligns with the sprocket line and the cast indicator

8.7b Bend back the lockwasher tabs, remove the two bolts and take off the lockwasher and retainer

8.8 Thread a 10 mm bolt into the camshaft and pull on it to remove the camshaft and outer bearing

1989 and later models (without recoil starter)

6   Remove the alternator outer cover (see Chapter 9) and place a wrench on the flats of the rotor (the rotor that fits into the outer cover, not the alternator rotor).

All models

7   Unbolt the cam sprocket and take it off the camshaft **(see illustration)**. Disengage the sprocket from the chain and support the chain with wire so it doesn't fall down off the crankshaft sprocket. Unbolt the camshaft retainer from the head **(see illustration)**.
8   Thread a 10 mm bolt into the end of the camshaft and use it as a handle to pull the camshaft out of the cylinder head **(see illustration)**. **Caution:** *The camshaft should come out easily. If it seems stuck, make sure it isn't caught on the rocker arms.*

Rocker arm

Refer to illustration 8.9

9   Thread a 6 mm bolt into the end of each rocker arm shaft **(see illustration)**. Support the rocker and use the bolt as a handle to pull out the shaft. **Note:** *If the shaft is stuck, it may be necessary to use a slide hammer. These can be rented from equipment rental yards (some auto parts stores also rent tools).*

Cylinder head

Refer to illustrations 8.10, 8.11 and 8.12

10   Remove the cylinder head Allen bolts **(see illustration)**.
11   Loosen the cylinder head bolts in several stages, in the reverse order of the tightening sequence **(see illustration)**.
12   Lift the cylinder head off the cylinder **(see illustration)**. If it's stuck, don't attempt to pry it off - tap around the sides of it with a plastic hammer to dislodge it. Be careful not to tap against the cooling fins;

8.9 Thread a bolt into each rocker shaft and pull it out

they're easily broken.
13   Locate the dowel pins **(see illustration 8.12)**. They may be in the cylinder or they may have come off with the head.

Cam chain and guide

Refer to illustrations 8.14a and 8.14b

14   Lift the front cam chain guide out of the cylinder **(see illustrations)**. If the rear guide or the cam chain need to be removed, remove the alternator rotor (see Chapter 9). The rear guide is bolted at the bottom.
15   Stuff clean rags into the cam chain openings so dirt, small parts or tools can't fall into them.

8.10 Remove the two Allen bolts

8.11 Cylinder head bolt TIGHTENING sequence

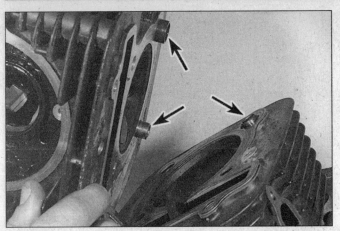

8.12 Lift the head off; the dowels and the O-ring that surrounds one of the dowels may come off with the head or stay in the cylinder (arrows)

8.14a Lift the front chain guide (arrow) . . .

Inspection

Camshaft, chain and guides

Refer to illustrations 8.17a and 8.17b

Note: *Before replacing camshafts or the cylinder head because of damage, check with local machine shops specializing in ATV or motorcycle engine work. In the case of the camshaft, it may be possible for cam lobes to be welded, reground and hardened, at a cost far lower than that of a new camshaft. If the bearing surfaces in the cylinder head are damaged, it may be possible for them to be bored out to accept bearing inserts. Due to the cost of a new cylinder head it is recommended that all options be explored before condemning it as trash!*

16   Rotate the cam bearings and check for roughness, looseness or noise. Check the sealed side of the outer bearing for signs of leakage. Replace the bearing(s) if problems are found.

17   Check the camshaft lobes for heat discoloration (blue appearance), score marks, chipped areas, flat spots and spalling **(see illustration)**. Measure the height of each lobe with a micrometer **(see illustration)** and compare the results to the minimum lobe height listed in this Chapter's Specifications. If damage is noted or wear is excessive, the camshaft must be replaced. Check the bearing surfaces for scoring or wear. Also, be sure to check the condition of the rocker arms, as described below.

18   Except in cases of oil starvation, the camshaft chain wears very little. If the chain has stretched excessively, which makes it difficult to maintain tension, replace it. To remove the chain from the crankshaft sprocket, remove the alternator rotor (see Chapter 9).

19   Check the sprocket for wear, cracks and other damage, replacing it if necessary. If the sprocket is worn, the chain is also worn, and pos-

8.14b . . . out of its cup (left arrow); to unbolt the rear chain guide (right arrows), remove these two bolts (arrows)

sibly the sprocket on the crankshaft. If wear this severe is apparent, the entire engine should be disassembled for inspection.

20   Check the chain guides for wear or damage. If they are worn or damaged, replace them.

Rocker arms, shafts and decompression lever

Refer to illustrations 8.21 and 8.22

21   Check the rocker arms for wear at the cam contact surfaces, inside the shaft bores and at the tips of the valve adjusting screws **(see illustration)**. Try to twist the rocker arms from side-to-side on the

8.17a Check the cam lobes for wear - here's a good example of damage which will require replacement (or repair) of the camshaft

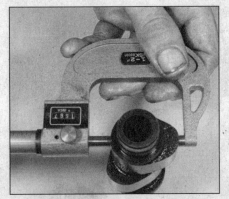

8.17b Measure the height of the cam lobes with a micrometer

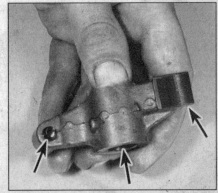

8.21 Check rocker arms for wear on the adjuster surface, inside the bore and on the cam contact surface (arrows)

2B

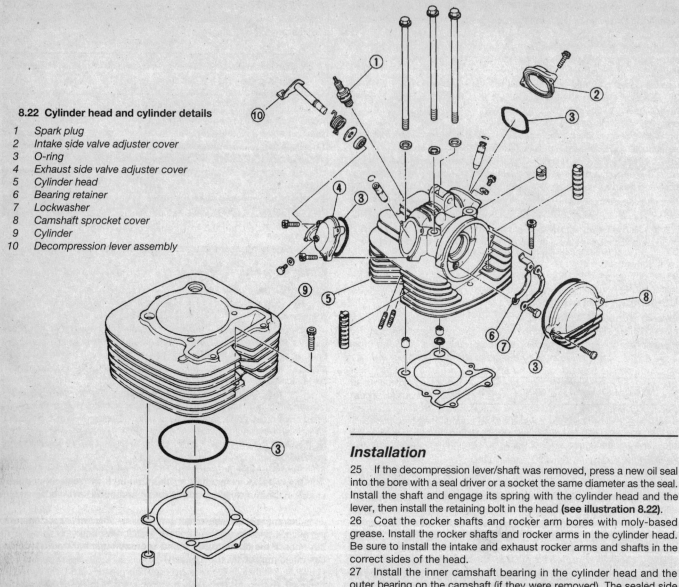

8.22 Cylinder head and cylinder details

1   Spark plug
2   Intake side valve adjuster cover
3   O-ring
4   Exhaust side valve adjuster cover
5   Cylinder head
6   Bearing retainer
7   Lockwasher
8   Camshaft sprocket cover
9   Cylinder
10   Decompression lever assembly

shafts. If they're loose on the shafts or if there's visible wear, measure the rocker arm shaft diameter and bore diameter with a micrometer and hole gauge. If the parts are worn beyond the limits listed in this Chapter's Specifications, replace them. Replace the rocker arm and shaft as a set.

22   Check the decompression lever (if equipped) and its shaft for wear, damage or a broken spring **(see illustration)**. If any problems are found, pull the lever/shaft out of the cover, together with the spring. Pry the shaft oil seal out of its bore.

Cylinder head

23   Check the cylinder head gasket and the mating surfaces on the cylinder head and cylinder for leakage, which could indicate warpage. Check the flatness of the cylinder head (see Section 10).

24   Clean all traces of old gasket material from the cylinder head and cylinder. Be careful not to let any of the gasket material fall into the crankcase, the cylinder bore or the bolt holes.

Installation

25   If the decompression lever/shaft was removed, press a new oil seal into the bore with a seal driver or a socket the same diameter as the seal. Install the shaft and engage its spring with the cylinder head and the lever, then install the retaining bolt in the head **(see illustration 8.22)**.

26   Coat the rocker shafts and rocker arm bores with moly-based grease. Install the rocker shafts and rocker arms in the cylinder head. Be sure to install the intake and exhaust rocker arms and shafts in the correct sides of the head.

27   Install the inner camshaft bearing in the cylinder head and the outer bearing on the camshaft (if they were removed). The sealed side of the outer bearing faces out (away from the cylinder head). Lubricate the camshaft bearings with engine oil.

28   Install the camshaft in the cylinder head with its lobes pointing down. The camshaft dowel should be up, so it aligns with the cast indicator in the cylinder head, when the camshaft is installed **(see illustration 8.4)**.

29   Install the bearing retainer and a new lockwasher **(see illustrations 8.7b and 8.22)**. Tighten the bearing retainer bolts to the torque listed in this Chapter's Specifications.

30   Install the three dowel pins and the O-ring that surrounds one of the dowels, then place the new head gasket on the cylinder **(see illustration 8.12)**. Never reuse the old gasket and don't use any type of gasket sealant.

31   Install the exhaust side cam chain damper, fitting the lower end into its notch **(see illustration 8.14b)**.

32   Carefully lower the cylinder head over the dowels and O-ring, guiding the cam chain through the slot in the cylinder head. It's helpful to have an assistant support the cam chain with a piece of wire so it doesn't fall and become kinked or detached from the crankshaft. When the head is resting on the cylinder, wire the cam chain to another component to keep tension on it.

33   Lubricate the threads of the cylinder head bolts with engine oil, then install them finger-tight. Tighten the four hex bolts in the correct sequence **(see illustration 8.11)**, in several stages, to the torque listed

in this Chapter's Specifications. After the hex bolts are tightened, tighten the two Allen bolts to the torque listed in this Chapter's Specifications.

34   Refer to the valve adjustment procedure in Chapter 1 and make sure the timing mark with the T next to it is aligned with the notch in the timing hole. If it's necessary to turn the crankshaft, hold the cam chain up so it doesn't fall off the crankshaft sprocket and become jammed.

35   Engage the camshaft sprocket with the timing chain so its dowel hole aligns with the dowel (see illustration 8.7a). Slip the sprocket onto the camshaft over the dowel, then install the sprocket bolt finger-tight. The line on the cam sprocket should be aligned with the cast indicator in the cylinder head (see illustration 8.4).

36   Twist the cam sprocket in both directions to remove the slack from the cam chain. Insert a screwdriver in the cam chain tensioner hole and push against the cam chain guide. With the guide pushed in, the cam sprocket line and cast indicator should line up (see illustration 8.4). If they don't, remove the cam sprocket from the chain, reposition it and try again. Don't continue with assembly until the marks are lined up correctly.

37   Tighten the cam sprocket bolt to the torque listed in this Chapter's Specifications.

38   Apply engine oil to a new O-ring for the cam sprocket cover. Install the O-ring and cover and tighten the Allen bolts to the torque listed in this Chapter's Specifications.

39   Install the cam chain tensioner (see Section 7).

40   Change the engine oil (see Chapter 1).

41   Adjust the valve clearance (see Chapter 1).

42   The remainder of installation is the reverse of removal.

9   Valves/valve seats/valve guides - servicing

1   Because of the complex nature of this job and the special tools and equipment required, servicing of the valves, the valve seats and the valve guides (commonly known as a valve job) is best left to a professional.

2   The home mechanic can, however, remove and disassemble the head, do the initial cleaning and inspection, then reassemble and deliver the head to a dealer service department or properly equipped vehicle repair shop for the actual valve servicing. Refer to Section 10 for those procedures.

3   The dealer service department will remove the valves and springs, recondition or replace the valves and valve seats, replace the valve guides, check and replace the valve springs, spring retainers and keepers (as necessary), replace the valve seals with new ones and reassemble the valve components.

4   After the valve job has been performed, the head will be in like-new condition. When the head is returned, be sure to clean it again very thoroughly before installation on the engine to remove any metal particles or abrasive grit that may still be present from the valve service operations. Use compressed air, if available, to blow out all the holes and passages.

10   Cylinder head and valves - disassembly, inspection and reassembly

1   As mentioned in the previous Section, valve servicing and valve guide replacement should be left to a dealer service department or other repair shop. However, disassembly, cleaning and inspection of the valves and related components can be done (if the necessary special tools are available) by the home mechanic. This way no expense is incurred if the inspection reveals that service work is not required at this time.

2   To properly disassemble the valve components without the risk of damaging them, a valve spring compressor is absolutely necessary. If the special tool is not available, have a dealer service department or vehicle repair shop handle the entire process of disassembly, inspection, service or repair (if required) and reassembly of the valves.

Disassembly

Refer to illustrations 10.7a and 10.7b

3   Remove the carburetor intake tube from the cylinder head (see Chapter 4).

4   Before the valves are removed, scrape away any traces of gasket material from the head gasket sealing surface. Work slowly and do not nick or gouge the soft aluminum of the head. Gasket removing solvents, which work very well, are available at most ATV shops and auto parts stores.

5   Carefully scrape all carbon deposits out of the combustion chamber area. A hand held wire brush or a piece of fine emery cloth can be used once most of the deposits have been scraped away. Do not use a wire brush mounted in a drill motor, or one with extremely stiff bristles, as the head material is soft and may be eroded away or scratched by the wire brush.

6   Before proceeding, arrange to label and store the valves along with their related components so they can be kept separate and reinstalled in the same valve guides they are removed from (again, plastic bags work well for this).

7   Compress the valve spring(s) on the first valve with a spring compressor, then remove the keepers and the retainer from the valve assembly (see illustration 7.2 and the accompanying illustration). Do not compress the spring(s) any more than is absolutely necessary. Carefully release the valve spring compressor and remove the spring(s), spring seat and valve from the head. If the valve binds in the guide (won't pull through), push it back into the head and deburr the area around the keeper groove with a very fine file or whetstone (see illustration).

10.7a Compress the valve springs with a valve spring compressor

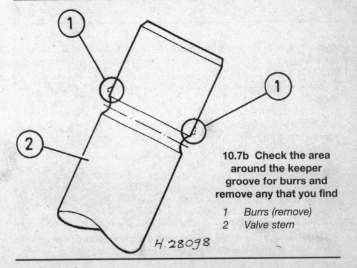

10.7b Check the area around the keeper groove for burrs and remove any that you find

1   *Burrs (remove)*
2   *Valve stem*

H.28098

8   Repeat the procedure for the remaining valve. Remember to keep the parts for each valve together so they can be reinstalled in the same location.

9   Once the valves have been removed and labeled, pull off the valve stem seals with pliers and discard them (the old seals should never be reused).

10   Next, clean the cylinder head with solvent and dry it thoroughly. Compressed air will speed the drying process and ensure that all holes and recessed areas are clean.

11   Clean all of the valve springs, keepers, retainers and spring seats with solvent and dry them thoroughly. Do the parts from one valve at a time so that no mixing of parts between valves occurs.

12   Scrape off any deposits that may have formed on the valve, then use a motorized wire brush to remove deposits from the valve heads and stems. Again, make sure the valves do not get mixed up.

Inspection

Refer to illustrations 10.14, 10.16, 10.17, 10.18a, 10.18b, 10.19a and 10.19b

13   Inspect the head very carefully for cracks and other damage. If cracks are found, a new head will be required. Check the cam bearing surfaces for wear and evidence of seizure. Check the camshaft for wear as well (see Section 8).

14   Using a precision straightedge and a feeler gauge, check the head gasket mating surface for warpage. Lay the straightedge lengthwise, across the head and diagonally (corner-to-corner), intersecting the head bolt holes, and try to slip a feeler gauge under it, on either side of each combustion chamber **(see illustration)**. The feeler gauge thickness should be the same as the cylinder head warpage limit listed in this Chapter's Specifications. If the feeler gauge can be inserted between the head and the straightedge, the head is warped and must either be machined or, if warpage is excessive, replaced with a new one.

15   Examine the valve seats in each of the combustion chambers. If they are pitted, cracked or burned, the head will require valve service that is beyond the scope of the home mechanic. Measure the valve seat width and compare it to this Chapter's Specifications. If it is not within the specified range, or if it varies around its circumference, valve service work is required.

16   Clean the valve guides to remove any carbon buildup, then measure the inside diameters of the guides (at both ends and the center of the guide) with a small hole gauge and a micrometer **(see illustration)**. Record the measurements for future reference. The guides are measured at the ends and at the center to determine if they are worn in a bell-mouth pattern (more wear at the ends). If they are, guide replacement is an absolute must.

17   Carefully inspect each valve face for cracks, pits and burned spots. Check the valve stem and the keeper groove area for cracks **(see illustration)**. Rotate the valve and check for any obvious indica-

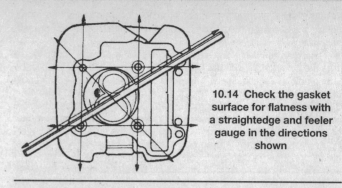

10.14 Check the gasket surface for flatness with a straightedge and feeler gauge in the directions shown

tion that it is bent. Check the end of the stem for pitting and excessive wear and make sure the bevel is the specified width. The presence of any of the above conditions indicates the need for valve servicing.

18   Measure the valve stem diameter **(see illustration)**. If the diameter is less than listed in this Chapter's Specifications, the valves will have to be replaced with new ones. Also check the valve stem for bending. Set the valve in a V-block with a dial indicator touching the middle of the stem **(see illustration)**. Rotate the valve and look for a reading on the gauge (which indicates a bent stem). If the stem is bent, replace the valve.

19   Check the end of each valve spring for wear and pitting. Measure the free length **(see illustration)** and compare it to this Chapter's Specifications. Any springs that are shorter than specified have sagged and should not be reused. Stand the spring on a flat surface and check it for squareness **(see illustration)**.

20   Check the spring retainers and keepers for obvious wear and cracks. Any questionable parts should not be reused, as extensive damage will occur in the event of failure during engine operation.

21   If the inspection indicates that no service work is required, the valve components can be reinstalled in the head.

Reassembly

Refer to illustrations 10.23, 10.24, 10.26 and 10.27

22   If the valve seats have been ground, the valves and seats should be lapped before installing the valves in the head to ensure a positive seal between the valves and seats. This procedure requires coarse and fine valve lapping compound (available at auto parts stores) and a valve lapping tool. If a lapping tool is not available, a piece of rubber or plastic hose can be slipped over the valve stem (after the valve has been installed in the guide) and used to turn the valve.

23   Apply a small amount of coarse lapping compound to the valve face **(see illustration)**, then slip the valve into the guide. **Note:** *Make sure the valve is installed in the correct guide and be careful not to get any lapping compound on the valve stem.*

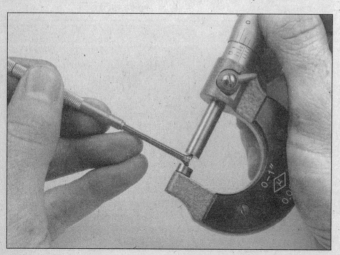

10.16 Measure the valve guide inside diameter with a hole gauge, then measure the gauge with a micrometer

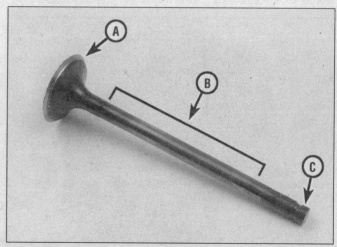

10.17 Check the valve face (A), stem (B) and keeper groove (C) for wear and damage

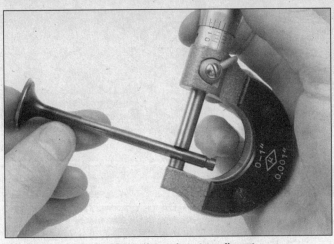

10.18a Measuring valve stem diameter

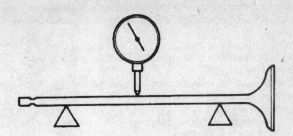

10.18b Check the valve stem for bends with a V-block (or V-blocks, as shown here) and a dial indicator

24   Attach the lapping tool (or hose) to the valve and rotate the tool between the palms of your hands. Use a back-and-forth motion rather than a circular motion. Lift the valve off the seat and turn it at regular intervals to distribute the lapping compound properly. Continue the lapping procedure until the valve face and seat contact area is of uniform width and unbroken around the entire circumference of the valve face and seat **(see illustration)**. Once this is accomplished, lap the valves again with fine lapping compound.

25   Carefully remove the valve from the guide and wipe off all traces of lapping compound. Use solvent to clean the valve and wipe the seat area thoroughly with a solvent soaked cloth. Repeat the procedure for the remaining valves.

26   Lay the spring seat in place in the cylinder head, then install new valve stem seals on both of the guides **(see illustration)**. Use an appropriate size deep socket to push the seals into place until they are properly seated. Don't twist or cock them, or they will not seal properly against the valve stems. Also, don't remove them again or they will be damaged.

27   Coat the valve stems with assembly lube or moly-based grease, then install one of them into its guide. Next, install the spring seat, springs and retainers, compress the springs and install the keepers. **Note:** *Install the springs with the tightly wound coils at the bottom (next to the spring seat).* When compressing the springs with the valve spring compressor, depress them only as far as is absolutely necessary to slip the keepers into place. Apply a small amount of grease to

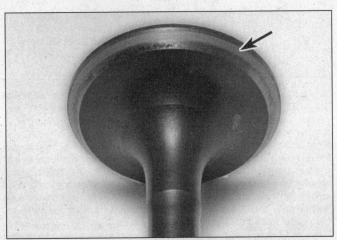

10.19a Measuring the free length of the valve springs

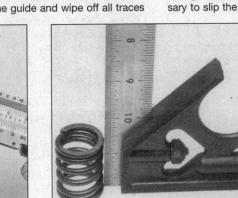

10.19b Checking the valve springs for squareness

10.23 Apply the lapping compound very sparingly, in small dabs, to the valve face only

10.24 After lapping, the valve face should exhibit a uniform, unbroken contact pattern (arrow)

10.26 Push the oil seal onto the valve guide (arrow)

2B

10.27 A small dab of grease will help hold the keepers in place on the valve while the spring compressor is released

11.3 Remove the Allen bolt that attaches the cylinder to the crankcase (arrow)

11.4 Lift the cylinder off and locate the dowels; the dowel inside the gasket loop has an O-ring (arrow) . . .

the keepers **(see illustration)** to help hold them in place as the pressure is released from the springs. Make certain that the keepers are securely locked in their retaining grooves.

28 Support the cylinder head on blocks so the valves can't contact the workbench top, then very gently tap each of the valve stems with a soft-faced hammer. This will help seat the keepers in their grooves.

29 Once all of the valves have been installed in the head, check for proper valve sealing by pouring a small amount of solvent into each of the valve ports. If the solvent leaks past the valve(s) into the combustion chamber area, disassemble the valve(s) and repeat the lapping procedure, then reinstall the valve(s) and repeat the check. Repeat the procedure until a satisfactory seal is obtained.

11 Cylinder - removal, inspection and installation

Removal

Refer to illustrations 11.3, 11.4 and 11.5

1 Following the procedure given in Section 8, remove the cylinder head. Make sure the crankshaft is positioned at Top Dead Center (TDC).

2 Lift out the cam chain front guide **(see illustration 8.14a)**.

3 Remove the Allen bolt that secures the base of the cylinder to the crankcase **(see illustration)**.

4 Lift the cylinder straight up to remove it **(see illustration)**. If it's stuck, tap around its perimeter with a soft-faced hammer (but don't tap on the cooling fins or they may break). Don't attempt to pry between the cylinder and the crankcase, as you'll ruin the sealing surfaces.

5 Locate the dowel pins (they may have come off with the cylinder or still be in the crankcase) **(see illustration 11.4 and the accompanying illustration)**. Be careful not to let these drop into the engine. Stuff rags around the piston and remove the gasket and all traces of old gasket material from the surfaces of the cylinder and the crankcase.

Inspection

Refer to illustration 11.8

6 Don't attempt to separate the liner from the cylinder.

7 Check the cylinder walls carefully for scratches and score marks.

8 Using the appropriate precision measuring tools, check the cylinder's diameter. Measure parallel to the crankshaft axis and across the crankshaft axis, at the depth from the top of the cylinder listed in this Chapter's Specifications **(see illustration)**. Average the two measurements and compare the results to this Chapter's Specifications. If the cylinder walls are tapered, out-of-round, worn beyond the specified limits, or badly scuffed or scored, have the cylinder rebored and honed by a dealer service department or an ATV repair shop. If a rebore is done, an oversize piston and rings will be required as well. **Note:** *Yamaha supplies pistons in two oversizes.*

9 As an alternative, if the precision measuring tools are not available, a dealer service department or repair shop will make the measurements and offer advice concerning servicing of the cylinder.

11.5 . . . there's also another dowel (left arrow); the cylinder base O-ring (right arrow) should be replaced whenever the cylinder is removed

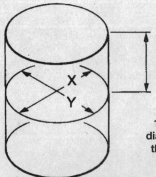

11.8 Measure the cylinder diameter in two directions, at the specified distance from the top of the cylinder

10 If it's in reasonably good condition and not worn to the outside of the limits, and if the piston-to-cylinder clearance can be maintained properly, then the cylinder does not have to be rebored; honing is all that is necessary.

11 To perform the honing operation you will need the proper size flexible hone with fine stones as shown in Maintenance techniques, tools and working facilities at the front of this book, or a "bottle brush" type hone, plenty of light oil or honing oil, some shop towels and an electric drill motor. Hold the cylinder block in a vise (cushioned with soft jaws or wood blocks) when performing the honing operation. Mount the hone in the drill motor, compress the stones and slip the hone into the cylinder: Lubricate the cylinder thoroughly, turn on the drill and move the hone up and down in the cylinder at a pace which will produce a fine crosshatch pattern on the cylinder wall with the

11.16 If you're experienced and very careful, the cylinder can be installed over the rings without a ring compressor, but a compressor is recommended

12.3a The arrow mark on top of the piston faces the exhaust (front) side of the engine

12.3b Wear eye protection and pry the snap-ring out of its groove with a pointed tool

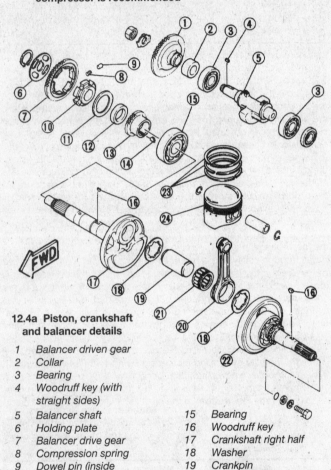

12.4a Piston, crankshaft and balancer details

1   Balancer driven gear
2   Collar
3   Bearing
4   Woodruff key (with straight sides)
5   Balancer shaft
6   Holding plate
7   Balancer drive gear
8   Compression spring
9   Dowel pin (inside compression spring)
10 Buffer boss
11 Plain washer
12 Collar
13 Oil pump drive gear
14 Woodruff key
15 Bearing
16 Woodruff key
17 Crankshaft right half
18 Washer
19 Crankpin
20 Connecting rod
21 Connecting rod needle roller bearing
22 Crankshaft left half
23 Piston rings
24 Piston

crosshatch lines intersecting at approximately a 60-degree angle. Be sure to use plenty of lubricant and do not take off any more material than is absolutely necessary to produce the desired effect. Do not withdraw the hone from the cylinder while it is running. Instead, shut off the drill and continue moving the hone up and down in the cylinder until it comes to a complete stop, then compress the stones and withdraw the hone. Wipe the oil out of the cylinder and repeat the proce-

dure on the remaining cylinder. Remember, do not remove too much material from the cylinder wall. If you do not have the tools, or do not desire to perform the honing operation, a dealer service department or vehicle repair shop will generally do it for a reasonable fee.

12   Next, the cylinder must be thoroughly washed with warm soapy water to remove all traces of the abrasive grit produced during the honing operation. Be sure to run a brush through the bolt holes and flush them with running water. After rinsing, dry the cylinder thoroughly and apply a coat of light, rust-preventative oil to all machined surfaces.

Installation

Refer to illustration 11.16

13   Lubricate the cylinder bore with plenty of clean engine oil. Apply a thin film of moly-based grease to the piston skirt.
14   Install the dowel pins, then lower a new cylinder base gasket over them **(see illustrations 11.4 and 11.5)**.
15   Attach a piston ring compressor to the piston and compress the piston rings. A large hose clamp can be used instead - just make sure it doesn't scratch the piston, and don't tighten it too much.
16   Install the cylinder and carefully lower it down until the piston crown fits into the cylinder liner **(see illustration)**. While doing this, pull the camshaft chain up, using a hooked tool or a piece of stiff wire. Push down on the cylinder, making sure the piston doesn't get cocked sideways, until the bottom of the cylinder liner slides down past the piston rings. A wood or plastic hammer handle can be used to gently tap the cylinder down, but don't use too much force or the piston will be damaged.
17   Remove the piston ring compressor or hose clamp, being careful not to scratch the piston.
18   The remainder of installation is the reverse of the removal steps.

12   Piston - removal, inspection and installation

1   The piston is attached to the connecting rod with a piston pin that's a slip fit in the piston and rod.
2   Before removing the piston from the rod, stuff a clean shop towel into the crankcase hole, around the connecting rod. This will prevent the snap-rings from falling into the crankcase if they are inadvertently dropped.

Removal

Refer to illustrations 12.3a, 12.3b, 12.4a and 12.4b

3   The piston should have an arrow mark on its crown that points toward the exhaust (front) side of the engine **(see illustration)**. If this mark is not visible due to carbon buildup, scribe an arrow into the piston crown before removal. Support the piston and pry the snap-ring out with a pointed tool **(see illustration)**.
4   Push the piston pin out from the opposite end to free the piston from the rod **(see illustration)**. You may have to deburr the area

2B

around the groove to enable the pin to slide out (use a triangular file for this procedure). If the pin won't come out, you can fabricate a piston pin removal tool from a long bolt, a nut, a piece of tubing and washers **(see illustration)**.

Inspection

Refer to illustrations 12.6, 12.11, 12.13, 12.14, 12.15 and 12.16

5   Before the inspection process can be carried out, the piston must be cleaned and the old piston rings removed.

6   Using a piston ring removal and installation tool, carefully remove the rings from the piston **(see illustration)**. Do not nick or gouge the piston in the process.

7   Scrape all traces of carbon from the top of the piston. A hand-held wire brush or a piece of fine emery cloth can be used once the majority of the deposits have been scraped away. Do not, under any circumstances, use a wire brush mounted in a drill motor to remove deposits from the piston; the piston material is soft and will be eroded away by the wire brush.

8   Use a piston ring groove cleaning tool to remove any carbon deposits from the ring grooves. If a tool is not available, a piece broken off the old ring will do the job. Be very careful to remove only the carbon deposits. Do not remove any metal and do not nick or gouge the sides of the ring grooves.

9   Once the deposits have been removed, clean the piston with solvent and dry them thoroughly. Make sure the oil return holes below the oil ring grooves are clear.

10   If the piston is not damaged or worn excessively and if the cylinder is not rebored, a new piston will not be necessary. Normal piston wear appears as even, vertical wear on the thrust surfaces of the piston and slight looseness of the top ring in its groove. New piston rings, on the other hand, should always be used when an engine is rebuilt.

11   Carefully inspect each piston for cracks around the skirt, at the pin bosses and at the ring lands **(see illustration)**.

12   Look for scoring and scuffing on the thrust faces of the skirt, holes in the piston crown and burned areas at the edge of the crown. If the skirt is scored or scuffed, the engine may have been suffering from overheating and/or abnormal combustion, which caused excessively high operating temperatures. The oil pump should be checked thoroughly. A hole in the piston crown, an extreme to be sure, is an indication that abnormal combustion (pre-ignition) was occurring. Burned areas at the edge of the piston crown are usually evidence of spark knock (detonation). If any of the above problems exist, the causes must be corrected or the damage will occur again.

13   Measure the piston ring-to-groove clearance (side clearance) by laying a new piston ring in the ring groove and slipping a feeler gauge in beside it **(see illustration)**. Check the clearance at three or four locations around the groove. Be sure to use the correct ring for each groove; they are different. If the clearance is greater then specified, a new piston will have to be used when the engine is reassembled.

14   Check the piston-to-bore clearance by measuring the bore (see Section 11) and the piston diameter **(see illustration)**. Measure the

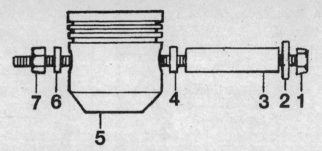

12.4b   The piston pin should come out with hand pressure - if it doesn't, this removal tool can be fabricated from readily available parts

1	Bolt	7	Nut (B)
2	Washer	A	Large enough for piston
3	Pipe (A)		pin to fit inside
4	Padding (A)	B	Small enough to fit
5	Piston		through piston pin bore
6	Washer (B)		

piston across the skirt on the thrust faces at a 90-degree angle to the piston pin, at the specified distance up from the bottom of the skirt. Subtract the piston diameter from the bore diameter to obtain the clearance. If it is greater than specified, the cylinder will have to be rebored and a new oversized piston and rings installed. If the appropriate precision measuring tools are not available, the piston-to-cylinder clearance can be obtained, though not quite as accurately, using feeler gauge stock. Feeler gauge stock comes in 12-inch lengths and various thicknesses and is generally available at auto parts stores. To check the clearance, slip a piece of feeler gauge stock of the same thickness as the specified piston clearance into the cylinder along with appropriate piston. The cylinder should be upside down and the piston must be positioned exactly as it normally would be. Place the feeler gauge between the piston and cylinder on one of the thrust faces (90-degrees to the piston pin bore). The piston should slip through the cylinder (with the feeler gauge in place) with moderate pressure. If it falls through, or slides through easily, the clearance is excessive and a new piston will be required. If the piston binds at the lower end of the cylinder and is loose toward the top, the cylinder is tapered, and if tight spots are encountered as the piston/feeler gauge is rotated in the cylinder, the cylinder is out-of-round. Be sure to have the cylinder and piston checked by a dealer service department or a repair shop to confirm your findings before purchasing new parts.

15   Apply clean engine oil to the pin, insert it into the piston and check for freeplay by rocking the pin back-and-forth **(see illustration)**. If the pin is loose, a new piston and possibly new pin must be installed.

16   Repeat Step 15, this time inserting the piston pin into the connecting rod **(see illustration)**. If the pin is loose, measure the pin diam-

12.6   Remove the piston rings with a ring removal and installation tool

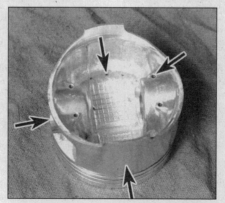

12.11   Check the piston pin bore and the piston skirt for wear, and make sure the internal holes are clear (arrows)

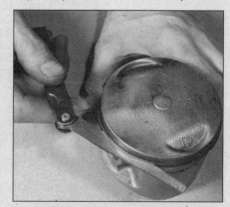

12.13   Measure the piston ring-to-groove clearance with a feeler gauge

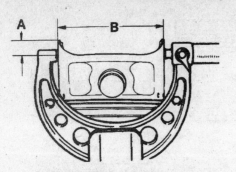

12.14 Measure the piston diameter with a micrometer

A Specified distance from bottom of piston
B Piston diameter

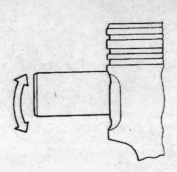

12.15 Slip the pin into the piston and try to wiggle it back-and-forth to check for looseness

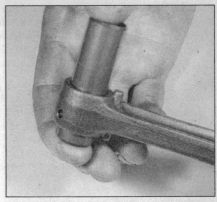

12.16 Slip the piston pin into the rod and try to rock it back-and-forth to check for looseness

12.18 Make sure both piston pin snap-rings are securely seated in the piston grooves

13.2 Check the piston ring end gap with a feeler gauge at the bottom of the cylinder

13.4 If the end gap is too small, clamp a file in a vise and file the ring ends (from the outside in only) to enlarge the gap slightly

eter and the pin bore in the rod (or have this done by a dealer or repair shop). A worn pin can be replaced separately; if the rod bore is worn, the rod and crankshaft must be replaced as an assembly.

17   Refer to Section 13 and install the rings on the piston.

Installation

Refer to illustration 12.18

18   Install the piston with its arrow mark toward the exhaust side (front) of the engine. Lubricate the pin and the rod bore with moly-based grease. Install a new snap-rings in the groove in one side of the piston (don't reuse the old snap-rings). Push the pin into position from

13.7a Installing the oil ring expander - make sure the ends don't overlap

the opposite side and install another new snap-ring. Compress the snap-rings only enough for them to fit in the piston. Make sure the clips are properly seated in the grooves **(see illustration)**.

13   Piston rings - installation

Refer to illustrations 13.2, 13.4, 13.7a, 13.7b, 13.9a, 13.9b, 13.10 and 13.12

1   Before installing the new piston rings, the ring end gaps must be checked.
2   Insert the top (No. 1) ring into the bottom of the first cylinder and square it up with the cylinder walls by pushing it in with the top of the piston. The ring should be about one-half inch above the bottom edge of the cylinder. To measure the end gap, slip a feeler gauge between the ends of the ring **(see illustration)** and compare the measurement to the Specifications.
3   If the gap is larger or smaller than specified, double check to make sure that you have the correct rings before proceeding.
4   If the gap is too small, it must be enlarged or the ring ends may come in contact with each other during engine operation, which can cause serious damage. The end gap can be increased by filing the ring ends very carefully with a fine file **(see illustration)**. When performing this operation, file only from the outside in.
5   Repeat the procedure for the second compression ring (ring gap is not specified for the oil ring rails or spacer).
6   Once the ring end gaps have been checked/corrected, the rings can be installed on the piston.
7   The oil control ring (lowest on the piston) is installed first. It is composed of three separate components. Slip the spacer into the groove, then install the upper side rail **(see illustrations)**. Do not use a

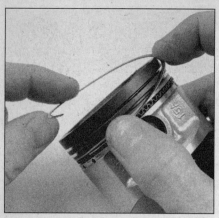

13.7b Installing an oil ring side rail - don't use a ring installation tool to do this

13.9a Install the middle ring with its identification mark up

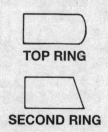

TOP RING

SECOND RING

13.9b The top and middle (second) rings can be identified by their profiles

piston ring installation tool on the oil ring side rails as they may be damaged. Instead, place one end of the side rail into the groove between the spacer expander and the ring land. Hold it firmly in place and slide a finger around the piston while pushing the rail into the groove (taking care not to cut your fingers on the sharp edges). Next, install the lower side rail in the same manner.

8   After the three oil ring components have been installed, check to make sure that both the upper and lower side rails can be turned smoothly in the ring groove.

9   Install the no. 2 (middle) ring next with its identification mark facing up **(see illustration)**. Do not mix the top and middle rings; they can be identified by their profiles **(see illustration)**.

10   To avoid breaking the ring, use a piston ring installation tool and make sure that the identification mark is facing up **(see illustration)**. Fit the ring into the middle groove on the piston. Do not expand the ring any more than is necessary to slide it into place.

11   Finally, install the no. 1 (top) ring in the same manner. Make sure the identifying mark is facing up. Be very careful not to confuse the top and second rings.

12   Once the rings have been properly installed, stagger the end gaps, including those of the oil ring side rails **(see illustration)**.

13.10 The top and middle rings have identification marks (arrows); these must be up when the rings are installed

14   Clutch cable and lever - removal and installation

1   Disconnect the clutch cable from the clutch lever at the handlebar (see "Clutch cable and lever - removal and installation" in Chapter 2A).

2   Loosen the two clutch cable locknuts at the cable bracket on the crankcase and disengage the cable from the bracket.

3   Disconnect the clutch cable from the push lever on top of the right crankcase cover.

4   If you want to remove the clutch lever assembly from the handlebar, simply remove the two clamp bolts and remove the lever assembly **(see illustration 12.5 in Chapter 2A)**.

5   Installation is the reverse of removal. When installing the clutch cable, refer to the cable routing diagrams at the end of Chapter 9 if you need help with cable routing.

15   Clutch - removal, inspection and installation

Removal

Refer to illustrations 15.4 and 15.7a through 15.7g

1   Drain the engine oil (see Chapter 1).

2   Disconnect the clutch cable from the push lever (see Section 14).

3   Remove the 13 right crankcase cover bolts and remove the right crankcase cover. Pull out the two dowel pins and save them in a plastic bag. Discard the old gasket.

13.12 Arrange the ring gaps like this
1   *Top compression ring*
2   *Oil ring lower rail*
3   *Oil ring upper rail*
4   *Second compression ring*

4   Remove the release mechanism components from the cover **(see illustration)**.

5   Inspect the push lever axle seal. If it's damaged or excessively worn, replace it. Dig out the old seal with a small screwdriver and tap a new seal into the cover with a small socket.

6   Inspect the teeth on the pinion gear and the short push rod for wear or damage. If the teeth are chewed up or excessively worn, replace them.

7   Remove the clutch components **(see illustration 15.4 and the accompanying illustrations)**. To prevent the clutch from turning while the nut is loosened, wedge a penny (or a shop rag) between the primary drive gear and the driven gear on the clutch housing, bend back the lockwasher and loosen the nut, then remove the penny.

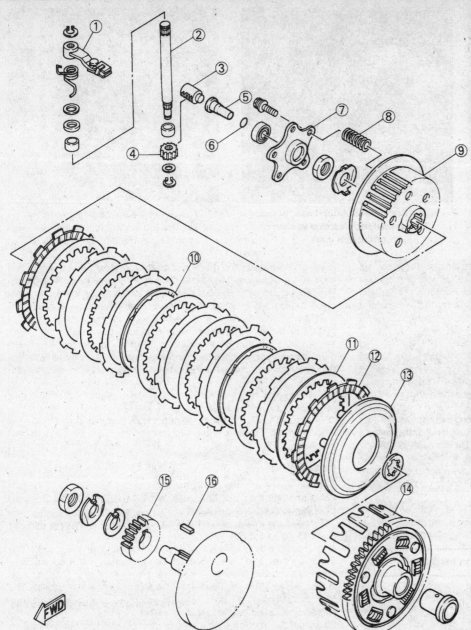

15.7a Remove the pushrod and O-ring . . .

15.7b . . . undo the spring plate bolts evenly, in a criss-cross pattern . . .

2B

15.4 An exploded view of the clutch assembly and release mechanism

1	Push lever	7	Pressure plate	13	Pressure plate
2	Push lever axle	8	Clutch spring	14	Clutch housing
3	Short pushrod	9	Clutch boss	15	Primary drive gear
4	Pinion gear	10	Cushion spring	16	Key
5	Long pushrod	11	Clutch plate		
6	O-ring	12	Friction plate		

15.7c . . . and remove the spring plate, bolts and springs

Inspection

Refer to illustrations 15.11, 15.12 and 15.13

8   Check the bolt posts and the friction surface on the pressure plate for damaged threads, scoring or wear. Replace the pressure plate if any defects are found.

9   Check the edges of the slots in the clutch housing for indentations made by the friction plate tabs. If the indentations are deep they can prevent clutch release, so the housing should be replaced with a new one. If the indentations can be removed easily with a file, the life of

the housing can be prolonged to an extent. Also, check the driven gear teeth for cracks, chips and excessive wear and the springs on the back side for breakage. If the gear is worn or damaged or the springs are broken, the clutch housing must be replaced with a new one. Check the bearing surface in the center of the clutch housing for score marks, scratches and excessive wear.

10   Check the splines of the clutch boss for indentations made by the tabs on the metal plates. Check the clutch boss friction surface for wear or scoring. Replace the clutch boss if problems are found.

15.7d Bend back the lockwasher and undo the nut as described in the text

15.7e Pull off the clutch boss, plates, cushion springs and pressure plate as a pack

15.7f Remove the thrust washer (arrow) . . .

15.7g . . . then pull off the clutch housing and remove the collar

11   Measure the free length of the clutch springs **(see illustration)** and compare the results to this Chapter's Specifications. If the springs have sagged, or if cracks are noted, replace them with new ones as a set.

12   If the lining material of the friction plates smells burnt or if it is glazed, new parts are required. If the metal clutch plates are scored or discolored, they must be replaced with new ones. Measure the thickness of the friction plates **(see illustration)** and replace with new parts any friction plates that are worn.

13   Lay the metal plates, one at a time, on a perfectly flat surface (such as a piece of plate glass) and check for warpage by trying to slip a feeler gauge between the flat surface and the plate **(see illustration)**. The feeler gauge should be the same thickness as the maximum warp listed in this Chapter's Specifications. Do this at several places around the plate's circumference. If the feeler gauge can be slipped under the plate, it is warped and should be replaced with a new one.

14   Check the tabs on the friction plates for excessive wear and mushroomed edges. They can be cleaned up with a file if the deformation is not severe. Check the friction plates for warpage as described in Step 13.

15   Check the clutch collar for score marks, heat discoloration and evidence of excessive wear.

16   Check the clutch spring plate for wear and damage. Rotate the inner race of the bearing and check for roughness, looseness or excessive noise.

Installation

Refer to illustrations 15.21 and 15.25

17   Lubricate the inner and outer surfaces of the clutch collar with moly-based grease and install it on the crankshaft.

18   Install the collar, clutch housing and thrust washer **(see illustrations 15.7g and 15.7f)**.

19   There are three different types of friction plate, one with a notch in one of its tabs and six without. Of the six without notches, two have cushion rings and are slightly narrower than the others. These two go in the third and fifth positions when the friction plates are installed. The friction plate marked with a notch in one of its tabs goes next to the clutch boss flange **(see illustration 15.7e)**.

20   Coat the friction plates with engine oil, then install the friction plates, metal plates and cushion springs on the clutch boss. Be sure to install them in the correct order **(see illustrations 15.4 and 15.7e)**.

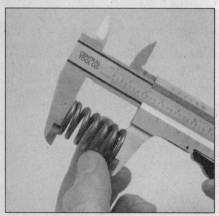

15.11 Measure the clutch spring free length

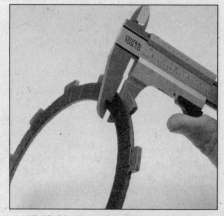

15.12 Measure the thickness of the friction plates

15.13 Check the metal plates for warpage

15.21 Align the arrows on clutch boss and pressure plate

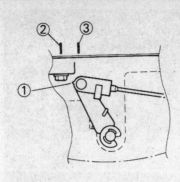

15.25 Position the push lever punch mark opposite the crankcase mark (1987 through 1989) or between the two crankcase marks (1990-on)

16.3a To remove the reverse lever arm, remove this bolt . . .

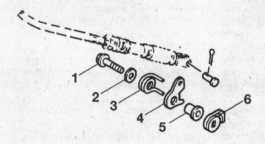

16.3b . . . and detach the lever components from the engine

1	Bolt	3	Spring	5	Collar
2	Washer	4	Outer lever	6	Inner lever

21   Install the pressure plate on the last friction plate, aligning the arrows on clutch boss and pressure plate **(see illustration)**.
22   Install a new lockwasher and the nut on the mainshaft. Hold the clutch as described in Step 7 and tighten the locknut to the torque listed in this Chapter's Specifications.
23   Bend one of the locknut tabs over to secure the nut.
24   Install the clutch springs and the spring plate **(see illustrations 15.7c and 15.7b)**. Tighten the bolts to the torque listed in this Chapter's Specifications in two or three stages, in a criss-cross pattern.
25   Install the short pushrod in the right crankcase cover, then install

the push lever axle in the right crankcase cover, install the pinion gear on the lower splined end of the axle and secure it with the washer and snap-ring. Make sure that the teeth of the pinion gear and the short pushrod mesh correctly. Before installing the spring and push lever on the upper splined end of the push lever axle, make sure that the push lever is correctly oriented. On 1987 through 1989 models, align the punch mark on the push lever with the mark on the crankcase; on 1990 and later models, align the punch mark on the push lever so that it's in the center of the two marks on the crankcase **(see illustration)**.
26   Make sure that all old gasket material is removed from the gasket mating surfaces of the crankcase and the right crankcase cover. Install a new gasket on the crankcase. Install the two dowel pins. Install the right crankcase cover and tighten the cover bolts to the torque listed in this Chapter's Specifications.

16 Reverse shift mechanism - removal, inspection and installation

Refer to illustrations 16.3a, 16.3b and 16.4

1   The reverse lock lever arm and shift drum detent ball are accessible from outside the engine. The crankcase must be disassembled for access to the reverse shift drum and forks.
2   Disconnect the select lever rod from the select lever.
3   Remove the bolt, washer, spring, outer lever, inner lever and collar **(see illustrations)**.

2B

16.4 Remove the bolt and sealing washer, then pull out the spring and remove the detent ball with a magnet

17.2 All three balancer gear marks must be in alignment to prevent severe ngine vibration

17.3 Bend back the lockwasher, wedge a rag between the gears to prevent rotation and unscrew the nut

17.4 Remove the balancer driven gear and the Woodruff key (arrow) . . .

17.5 . . . and slide off the collar

17.6a Remove the drive gear snap-ring . .

17.6b . . . and the holding plate

17.7a Pull off the drive gear . . .

17.7b . . . the six springs and the three dowels; a dowel goes inside every other spring

4   At the right rear corner of the engine, remove the bolt and sealing washer. Lift out the spring and detent ball with a magnet (see illustration).

5   Installation is the reverse of the removal steps, with the following additions:

a) Tighten the lever bolt securely, but don't overtighten it.
b) Use a new sealing washer on the detent ball bolt if the old one is worn or damaged. Tighten the detent ball bolt to the torque listed in this Chapter's Specifications.

17   Balancer gears - removal, inspection and installation

Removal

Refer to illustrations 17.2, 17.3, 17.4, 17.5, 17.6a, 16.6b, 17.7a, 17.7b, 17.8, 17.9a, 17.9b and 17.9c

1   Remove the clutch (see Section 15).
2   Turn the crankshaft so the match marks on the balancer drive and driven gears are aligned (see illustration).
3   Bend back the tab on the balancer gear lockwasher (see illustration 12.4a and the accompanying illustration). Wedge a rag between the teeth of the balancer drive and driven gears to prevent them from turning, undo the nut and remove the lockwasher.
4   Pull off the driven gear and remove the Woodruff key (see illustration).
5   Slide the collar off the end of the balancer (see illustration).
6   Remove the snap-ring and slide the holding plate off the end of the crankshaft (see illustrations).
7   Grasp the drive gear and pull it off the buffer boss (see illustra-

tion). The six springs and three pins will fall out as you do this, so be prepared to catch them (see illustration).
8   Place a puller on the buffer boss and pull it free of the crankshaft (see illustration). Note: *Yamaha recommends replacing the buffer boss and its Woodruff key with new ones whenever they are removed from the crankshaft.*
9   Once the buffer boss is loose, remove it, the plain washer, the collar, the oil pump drive gear and two Woodruff keys - one for the buffer boss and one for the oil pump drive gear (see illustrations).

17.8 Remove the buffer boss with a puller; replace the buffer boss and its Woodruff key with new ones whenever they're removed

17.9a Remove the plain washer and the oil pump drive gear . . .

17.9b . . . the buffer boss Woodruff key . .

17.9c . . . and the oil pump drive gear Woodruff key

Inspection

10 Check the gears for worn or damaged teeth and replace them as a set if problems are found.

11 Check the springs for distortion or fatigue and replace them as necessary.

12 Check the remaining components for wear and damage and replace any worn or damaged parts. Replace the lockwasher with a new one whenever it's removed.

13 Inspect the balancer and crankshaft ball bearings to the extent possible without disassembling the crankcase. If wear, looseness or roughness can be detected, the crankcase will have to be disassembled to replace the bearings.

Installation

Refer to illustration 17.14

14 Installation is the reverse of the removal steps, with the following additions:

a) *Use a new buffer boss and Woodruff key.*

b) *Apply engine oil to the crankshaft after installing the oil pump drive gear Woodruff key, and again after installing the buffer boss Woodruff key.*

c) *Install the buffer boss with the same tool used to install the crankshaft (see Section 24). The basic tool is crankshaft installer set YM-90050; you'll also need pot extension YM-33280, adapter YM-33279 and buffer boss installer set 98890-04088. If you don't have the correct special tool, take the engine to a Yamaha dealer and have the buffer boss installed.*

d) *Make sure the alignment marks on the buffer boss, drive gear and driven gear are lined up* **(see illustration 17.2)**.

e) *Use a new lockwasher and make sure its tab fits in the slot in the balancer shaft* **(see illustration)**. *Tighten the nut to the torque listed in this Chapter's Specifications.*

18 Oil pipe and pump - removal, inspection and installation

Note: *The oil pump can be removed with the engine in the frame.*

Oil pipe

Removal

Refer to illustration 18.2

1 Remove the clutch (Section 15).

2 Remove the union bolt and hex bolts that secure the oil pipe and remove the pipe **(see illustration)**.

Inspection

3 Check the oil pipe for bending and for cracks, especially where the banjo fittings are brazed to the pipe. Replace it if problems are found.

4 Clean the inside of the pipe with solvent to remove any clogging.

Installation

5 Installation is the reverse of the removal steps, with the following additions:

a) *Use new sealing washers on each side of the banjo fitting at both ends of the pipe.*

b) *Tighten the bolts to the torque listed in this Chapter's Specifications.*

17.14 Install the lockwasher so its tab fits into the shaft slot

18.2 Remove the union bolts at each end of the pipe; there are two sealing washers at each fitting

18.8a Loosen the pump cover screw (A) if you plan to take the pump apart; remove the mounting screws (B) . . .

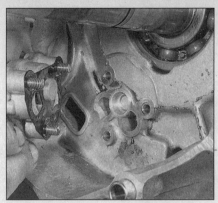

18.8b . . . and take the pump and gasket off the engine

18.9 Remove the oil pump assembly screw

Oil pump

Removal

Refer to illustrations 18.8a and 18.8b

6   Remove the clutch (see Section 15).

7   Remove the balancer drive gear and oil pump drive gear (see Section 17).

8   Rotate the oil pump driven gear for access to the mounting screws **(see illustration)**. If you're planning to disassemble the pump, loosen the assembly screw now while the pump is secured to the engine. Remove the mounting screws and take the pump and gasket off **(see illustration)**.

Inspection

Refer to illustrations 18.9, 18.10, 18.12a, 18.12b and 18.12c

9   Remove the oil pump assembly screw **(see illustration)**.

10   Remove the driven gear, shaft and pump cover from the pump body **(see illustration)**.

11   Wash all the components in solvent, then dry them off. Check the pump body, the rotors and the cover for scoring and wear. If any damage or uneven or excessive wear is evident, replace the pump. If you are rebuilding the engine, it's a good idea to install a new oil pump.

12   Place the rotors in the pump cover. Measure the clearance between the outer rotor and body, and between the inner and outer rotors, with a feeler gauge **(see illustrations)**. Place a straightedge across the pump body and rotors and measure the gap with a feeler gauge **(see illustration)**. If any of the clearances are beyond the limits listed in this Chapter's Specifications, replace the pump.

13   Check the pump driven gear for wear or damage. The gear and its

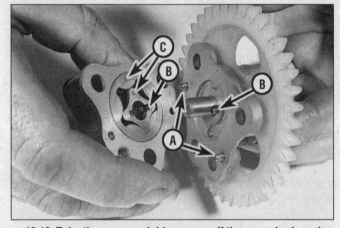

18.10 Take the cover and driven gear off the pump body and rotors; on reassembly, the dowels (A) must fit in the holes, the drive pin must fit in the slot (B) and the punch marks (C) must face the pump cover

drive pin are available separately, so if either needs to be replaced, push the drive pin out of the gear shaft and pull the gear out of the pump cover.

14   Reassemble the pump by reversing the disassembly steps, with the following additions:

a) *Before installing the cover, pack the cavities between the rotors with petroleum jelly - this will ensure the pump develops suction quickly and begins oil circulation as soon as the engine is started.*

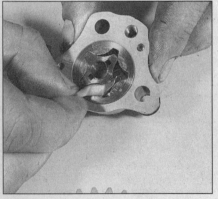

18.12a Measure the gap between the inner and outer rotors . . .

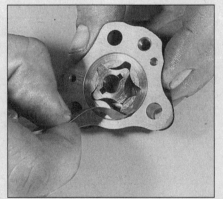

18.12b . . . between the outer rotor and body . . .

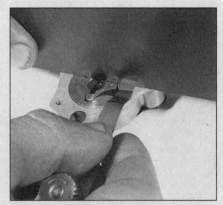

18.12c . . . and between the rotors and a straightedge; this gap isn't specified by Yamaha, but the pump should be replaced if it's significant

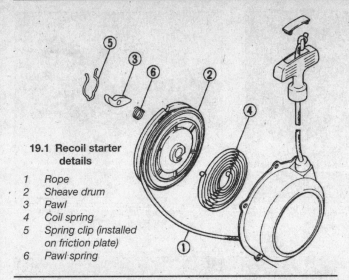

19.1 Recoil starter details

1   Rope
2   Sheave drum
3   Pawl
4   Coil spring
5   Spring clip (installed on friction plate)
6   Pawl spring

b)   Make sure the cover dowels and drive pin are in position (see illustration 18.10).
c)   Tighten the cover screw to the torque listed in this Chapter's Specifications.

Installation

15   Installation is the reverse of removal, with the following additions:

a)   Install a new gasket (see illustration 18.8b).
b)   Tighten the oil pump mounting screws to the torque listed in this Chapter's Specifications.

19   Recoil starter - removal, inspection and installation

Removal

Refer to illustration 19.1

1   Unbolt the recoil starter case from the left side of the engine (see illustration). Take the starter assembly off.
2   Pull the rope partway out and tie a knot in it so it won't be pulled into the case, then remove the cap and the starter handle.

Inspection

Warning: *Rewinding the coil spring is complicated and can be potentially dangerous. If you don't have experience with recoil starters, take the job to a Yamaha dealer or other qualified shop. If you do the job yourself, wear eye protection and heavy gloves in case the recoil spring flies out.*

3   Remove the nut, then the friction plate with its spring clip, the drive pawl, pawl spring, sheave drum and coil spring.
4   Check for obvious wear or damage, such as a broken rope. Replace worn or damaged parts.

Installation

5   Tie a knot in one end of the rope and pull it through the hole in the center of the sheave drum so the rope is in the sheave drum groove. Place the sheave drum on a work surface so the slit in its outer edge is up. Wind the rope 4-1/2 turns clockwise around the sheave drum, then lodge the rope in the slit in the edge of the sheave drum.
6   Install the pawl spring and pawl in the sheave drum.
7   Engage the hook on one end of the starter spring with the slit in the case (the slit closest to the outer edge of the case), then wind the spring clockwise, from the outside in, and engage the hook on its free end with the hook in the center of the case.
8   Install the spring clip and friction plate, engaging the ends of the spring clip with the starter pawl holes.
9   With the case down on a work surface, turn the sheave drum three turns clockwise to preload the starter spring. Pull the rope out through the starter case as you do this, then tie a temporary knot in the

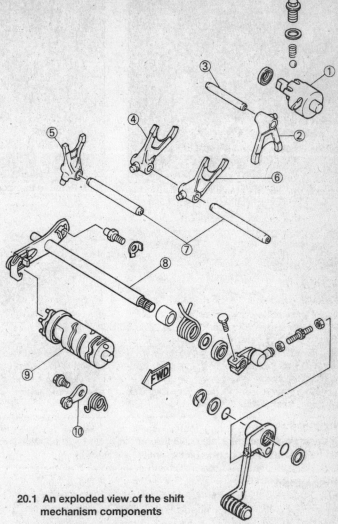

20.1 An exploded view of the shift mechanism components

1   Output axle shift drum
2   Output axle shift fork
3   Output axle guide bar
4   Right shift fork
5   Center shift fork
6   Left shift fork
7   Guide bar
8   Shift shaft
9   Shift drum
10 Stopper lever

rope so it won't be pulled back into the case.
10   Slip the starter handle into the rope and tie a permanent knot in its end, then install the cap.
11   Untie the temporary knot in the rope and let it back into the case.
12   Install the recoil starter on the engine, engaging it with the rotor. Install the case bolts and tighten them to the torque listed in this Chapter's Specifications.

20   External shift mechanism - removal, inspection and installation

Shift pedal

Removal

Refer to illustration 20.1

1   Look for alignment marks on the end of the shift pedal and shift shaft (see illustration). If they aren't visible, make your own marks with a sharp punch.
2   Remove the shift pedal pinch bolt and slide the pedal off the shaft.

2B

20.7 Pull the shift shaft out of the crankcase and remove the thrust washer (arrow)

20.8 Remove the stopper lever and spring

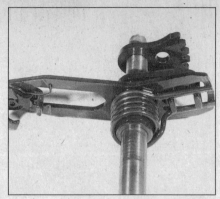

20.11 Check the shift shaft components for wear or damage

20.12 If the return spring post is loose, unscrew it, then reinstall it with thread locking agent and a new lockwasher

20.15a Pry apart the return spring and position it over the post

20.15b Make sure the ratchet pawls engage the shift drum pins

Inspection

3   Check the shift pedal for wear or damage such as bending. Check the splines on the shift pedal and shaft for stripping or step wear. Replace the pedal or shaft if these problems are found.

4   Check the shift shaft seal in the alternator cover for signs of leakage. If the seal has been leaking, remove the alternator cover (see Chapter 9). Pry the seal out of the cover, then tap in a new one with a seal driver or socket the same diameter as the seal.

Installation

5   Install the shift pedal. Line up its punch marks and tighten the pinch bolt to the torque listed in this Chapter's Specifications.

External shift linkage

Removal

Refer to illustrations 20.7 and 20.8

6   Remove the right crankcase cover (see Section 15).
7   Pull the shift shaft and its washer out of the crankcase **(see illustration)**.
8   Unbolt the stopper arm, then remove the arm and its spring **(see illustration)**.
9   Remove the Torx screw from the center of the shift drum segment.
10   Remove the shift drum segment and note the location of its dowel.

21.12a Using a soft face hammer, tap gently and evenly on the ends of the shafts as the case halves are separated

21.11 The bolts are different lengths; labeling them will speed reassembly

21.12b Pry only between the pry points . . .

21.12c . . . there's one at each end of the case

21.12d Lift the right case half off the left case half

Inspection

Refer to illustrations 20.11 and 20.12

11   Check the shift shaft for bends and damage to the splines **(see illustration)**. If the shaft is bent, you can attempt to straighten it, but if the splines are damaged it will have to be replaced. Check the condition of the return spring, shift arm and the pawl spring. Replace the shift shaft if they're worn, cracked or distorted.

12   Make sure the return spring post isn't loose **(see illustration)**. If it is, bend back its lockwasher and unscrew it. Apply a non-hardening locking compound to the threads, then reinstall the post with a new lockwasher and tighten it to the torque listed in this Chapter's Specifications.

Installation

Refer to illustrations 20.15a and 20.15b

13   Position the spring on the stopper arm, then install the stopper arm on the engine and tighten its bolt to the torque listed in this Chapter's Specifications.

14   Pull down the stopper arm and install the drum segment on the shift drum, making sure its dowel is located in the drum segment notch **(see illustration 20.8)**. Apply non-permanent thread locking agent to the threads of the shift drum segment Torx screw, then install it and tighten to the torque listed in this Chapter's Specifications. Make sure the stopper arm spring is correctly installed and that the roller end of the stopper arm engages a notch in the drum segment.

15   Place the washer on the shift shaft and slide it into the engine **(see illustration 20.7)**. Slide the shaft all the way in, making sure the return spring fits over the post and the pawls engage the drum segment pins **(see illustrations)**.

16   The remainder of installation is the reverse of the removal steps.

17   Check the engine oil level and add some, if necessary (see Chapter 1).

21.13 Make sure the case dowels (arrows) are in place

21 Crankcase - disassembly and reassembly

1   To examine and repair or replace the crankshaft, connecting rod, bearings and transmission components, the crankcase must be split into two parts.

Disassembly

Refer to illustrations 21.11, 21.12a, 21.12b, 21.12c, 21.12d and 21.13

2   Remove the engine from the vehicle (see Section 5).

3   Remove the carburetor (see Chapter 3).

4   Remove the alternator rotor and the starter motor (see Chapter 9).

5   Remove the clutch (see Section 15).

6   Remove the external shift mechanism (see Section 20).

7   Remove the reverse shift drum detent ball and spring (see Section 16).

8   Remove the cam chain tensioner, cylinder head, cam chain, cylinder and piston (see Sections 7, 8, 11 and 12).

9   Remove the oil pump (see Section 18).

10   Check carefully to make sure there aren't any remaining components that attach the upper and lower halves of the crankcase together.

11   There are 15 crankcase bolts; the bolt heads for all 15 bolts are on left side of the crankcase. Loosen the crankcase bolts in two or three stages, in a criss-cross pattern. Remove the bolts and label them; they are different lengths **(see illustration)**.

12   Tap gently on the ends of the transmission shafts, balancer shaft and crankshaft as the case halves are being separated **(see illustration)**. Carefully pry the crankcase apart at the pry points and lift the right half off the left half **(see illustrations)**. Don't pry against the mating surfaces or they'll develop leaks.

13   Locate the crankcase dowels **(see illustration)**. If they aren't secure in their holes, remove them and set them aside for safekeeping.

14   Refer to Sections 22 through 24 for information on the internal components of the crankcase.

Reassembly

Refer to illustrations 21.17 and 21.18

15   Remove all traces of old gasket and sealant from the crankcase mating surfaces with a sharpening stone or similar tool. Be careful not to let any fall into the case as this is done and be careful not to damage the mating surfaces.

16   Check to make sure the dowel pins are in place in their holes in the mating surface of the crankcase **(see illustration 21.13)**.

17   Coat both crankcase mating surfaces with Yamaha Quick Gasket (ACC-11001-05-01) or equivalent sealant **(see illustration)**.

18   Pour some engine oil over the transmission gears, balancer shaft and crankshaft bearing surfaces and the shift drums **(see illustration)**. Don't get any oil on the crankcase mating surfaces.

19   Carefully place the right crankcase half onto the left crankcase half. While doing this, make sure the transmission shafts, shift drums,

2B

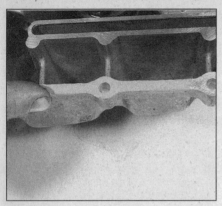

21.17 Coat both case halves with a thin film of sealant

21.18 Pour oil over the gears and shafts

22.3 Check the case bearings for roughness, looseness or noise

crankshaft and balancer fit into their ball bearings in the right crankcase half.

20   Install the crankcase bolts in the correct holes and tighten them so they are just snug. Then tighten them in two or three stages, in a criss-cross pattern, to the torque listed in this Chapter's Specifications (don't forget to install the copper washer).

21   Turn the transmission shafts to make sure they turn freely. Also make sure the crankshaft and balancer shaft turn freely.

22   The remainder of installation is the reverse of removal.

22   Crankcase components - inspection and servicing

Refer to illustration 22.3

1   Separate the crankcase and remove the following:

a) *Transmission shafts and gears*
b) *Middle drive gear*
c) *Crankshaft and main bearings*
d) *Shift drums and forks*

2   Clean the crankcase halves thoroughly with new solvent and dry them with compressed air. All oil passages should be blown out with compressed air and all traces of old gasket sealant should be removed from the mating surfaces. **Caution:** *Be very careful not to nick or gouge the crankcase mating surfaces or leaks will result. Check both crankcase sections very carefully for cracks and other damage.*

3   Check the bearings in the case halves **(see illustration)**. If they don't turn smoothly, replace them. For bearings that aren't accessible from the outside, a blind hole puller will be needed for removal. Drive the remaining bearings out with a bearing driver or a socket having an outside diameter slightly smaller than that of the bearing outer race. Before

installing the bearings, allow them to sit in the freezer overnight, and about fifteen-minutes before installation, place the case half in an oven, set to about 200-degrees F, and allow it to heat up. The bearings are an interference fit, and this will ease installation. **Warning:** *Before heating the case, wash it thoroughly with soap and water so no explosive fumes are present. Also, don't use a flame to heat the case. Install the bearings with a socket or bearing driver that bears against the bearing outer race.*

4   If any damage is found that can't be repaired, replace the crankcase halves as a set.

5   Assemble the case halves (see Section 21) and check to make sure the crankshaft and the transmission shafts turn freely.

23   Transmission shafts, balancer shaft and shift drum - removal, inspection and installation

Note: *When disassembling the transmission shafts, place the parts on a long rod or thread a wire through them to keep them in order and facing the proper direction.*

Removal

Refer to illustrations 23.3a, 23.3b, 23.3c, 23.4 and 23.5

1   Remove the engine and separate the case halves (see Sections 5 and 21, respectively).

2   The transmission components and shift drums remain in the left case half when the case is separated.

3   Pull out the guide bars and remove the shift forks and shift drum **(see illustration 20.1 and accompanying illustrations)**.

4   Lift the balancer shaft out of the crankcase **(see illustration)**.

5   Remove the drive axle and main axle **(see illustration)**.

23.3a Pull out each guide bar (arrows) . . .

23.3b . . . and remove the shift forks (the forks are marked L, C and R for left, center and right)

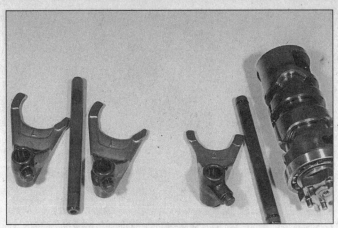

23.3c Keep the shift fork(s) with their original guide bars; don't mix them up!

23.4 Lift out the balancer shaft

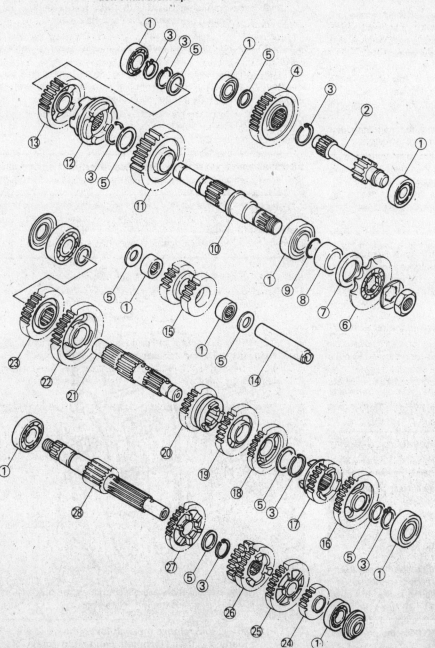

2B

23.5 Transmission gears and shafts (Warrior) – exploded view

1 Bearing
2 Reverse axle
3 Circlip
4 Reverse pinion gear (34 teeth)
5 Plain washer
6 Drive sprocket
7 Oil seal
8 Collar
9 O-ring
10 Output axle
11 Reverse wheel gear (33 teeth)
12 Dog clutch
13 Forward wheel gear (29 teeth)
14 Counter axle (10 teeth)
15 Counter wheel gear (20 teeth/14 teeth)
16 Second wheel gear (33 teeth)
17 Sixth wheel gear (23 teeth)
18 Fourth wheel gear (27 teeth)
19 Third wheel gear (29 teeth)
20 Fifth wheel gear (25 teeth)
21 Drive axle
22 First wheel gear (36 teeth)
23 Counter axle drive gear (27 teeth)
24 Second pinion gear (20 teeth)
25 Sixth pinion gear (29 teeth)
26 Third/fourth pinion gear (23 teeth/26 teeth)
27 Fifth pinion gear (28 teeth)
28 Main axle (first pinion gear: 16 teeth)

6   Before disassembling the shafts, note how they're assembled and how they fit together.

7   The only tool you will need to disassemble the shafts is an assortment of snap-ring pliers with the right size tips (or a single pair of multiple-tip snap-ring pliers with the right assortment of tip sizes).

8   The dog clutch, the gears and some of the washers must be reassembled in the same sequence and relationship to one another that they were in before the transmission was disassembled. One good way to achieve perfect order and correct orientation is to place the parts on a long rod or thread a wire through them as you disassemble the shafts.

Inspection

9   Wash all of the components in clean solvent and dry them off. Rotate the bearings, feeling for tightness, rough spots and excessive looseness, and listening for noises. If any of these parts are defective or excessively worn, replace them.

10   Inspect the shift fork grooves in the gears and the dog clutch. If a groove is worn or scored, replace the part and inspect its corresponding shift fork.

11   Check the shift forks for distortion and wear, especially at the fork ears **(see illustration 23.3c)**. If they are discolored or severely worn, they are probably bent. Inspect the guide pins for excessive wear and distortion and replace any defective parts with new ones.

12   Check the shift fork guide bars evidence of wear, galling and other damage. Make sure the shift forks move smoothly on the guide bars. If the shafts are worn or bent, replace them with new ones.

13   Check the edges of the grooves in the shift drums for signs of excessive wear.

14   Hold the inner race of the shift drum bearing with fingers and spin the outer race. Replace the bearing if it's rough, loose or noisy.

15   Check the gear teeth for cracking and other obvious damage. Check the bushing surface in the inner diameter of the freewheeling gears for scoring or heat discoloration. Replace damaged parts.

16   Inspect the engagement dogs and dog holes on gears so equipped for excessive wear or rounding off. Replace the paired gears as a set if necessary.

17   Inspect the transmission shaft bearings in the crankcase for wear or heat discoloration and replace them if necessary (see Section 22).

Installation

18   Installation is the basically the reverse of the removal procedure, but take note of the following points:

a) Use new snap-rings.
b) Align the flat on the end of the counter axle with the corresponding flat in the transmission case.
c) Lubricate the components with engine oil before assembling them.
d) After assembly, check the gears to make sure they're installed correctly. Move the shift drums through the gear positions and rotate the gears to make sure they mesh and shift correctly.

24   Crankshaft and connecting rod - removal, inspection and installation

Note: *The procedures in this section require special tools. If you don't have the necessary equipment or suitable substitutes, have the crankshaft removed and installed by a Yamaha dealer.*

Removal

Refer to illustrations 24.2 and 24.3

1   Remove the engine and separate the crankcase halves (Sections 5, 21 and 22). The transmission shafts need not be removed.

2   Generally, the crankshaft should stay in the left half of the case when the right half is lifted off **(see illustration 21.13)**. However, if the right bearing is tight enough, the crank might remain in the right crankcase half **(see illustration)**. If this happens, have the crankshaft

24.2 If the crankshaft stays in the right case half like this, have it removed by a Yamaha dealer

removed from the right case half by a Yamaha dealer or other repair shop.

3   The crankshaft may be loose enough in its bearing that you can lift it out of the left crankcase half. If not, push it out with tools YU-01135 and YM-1382 or equivalent **(see illustration)**.

Inspection

Refer to illustrations 24.4, 24.6 and 24.7

4   Measure the side clearance between connecting rod and crankshaft with a feeler gauge **(see illustration)**. If it's more than the limit listed in this Chapter's Specifications, replace the crankshaft and connecting rod as an assembly.

5   Set up the crankshaft in V-blocks with a dial indicator contacting the big end of the connecting rod. Move the connecting rod side-to-side against the indicator pointer and compare the reading to the value listed in this Chapter's Specifications. If it's beyond the limit, the

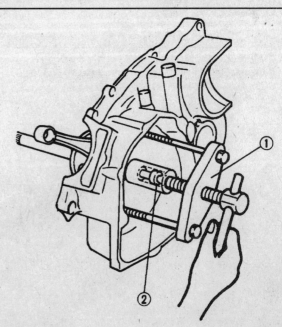

24.3 These special tools are used to push the crankshaft out of the left case half

1   Separating tool YU-01135
2   Puller attachment YU-01382

24.4 Measure the gap between the connecting rod and the crankshaft with a feeler gauge

24.6 Check the cam chain sprocket and the ball bearing on the end of the crankshaft

24.7 Measure runout on each side of the crankshaft (A); if the assembly width (B) is greater than specified, replace the crankshaft

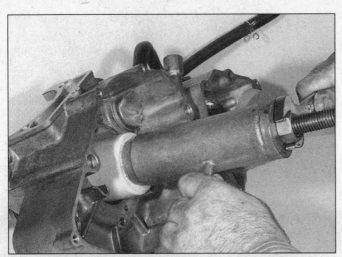

24.9 These tools are used to pull the crankshaft into the left case half

crankshaft can be disassembled and the needle roller bearing replaced. However, this is a specialized job that should be done by a Yamaha dealer or qualified machine shop.

6   Check the crankshaft splines, the cam chain sprocket, the ball bearing at the sprocket end of the crankshaft and the bearing journals for visible wear or damage (see illustration). Yamaha lists the ball bearing end of the crankshaft as a separately available part, but check with your dealer first; it may be more practical to replace the entire crankshaft if the ball bearing or cam sprocket is worn or damaged. Replace the crankshaft if any of the other conditions are found.

7   Set the crankshaft in a lathe or a pair of V-blocks, with a dial indicator contacting each end (see illustration). Rotate the crankshaft and note the runout. If the runout at either end is beyond the limit listed in this Chapter's Specifications, replace the crankshaft and connecting rod as an assembly.

8   Measure the assembly width of the crankshaft (see illustration 24.7). If it exceeds the limit listed in this Chapter's Specifications, replace the crankshaft.

Installation

Refer to illustration 24.9

9   Start the crankshaft into the left case half. If it doesn't go in easily, pull it in the rest of the way with Yamaha tools YU-90050, YM-1383 and YM-91044 (see illustration).

10   The remainder of installation is the reverse of the removal steps.

25   Initial start-up after overhaul

1   Make sure the engine oil level is correct, then remove the spark plug from the engine. Place the engine kill switch in the Off position and unplug the primary (low tension) wires from the coil.

2   Turn on the key switch and crank the engine over with the starter several times to build up oil pressure. Reinstall the spark plug, connect the wires and turn the switch to On.

3   Make sure there is fuel in the tank, then operate the choke.

4   Start the engine and allow it to run at a moderately fast idle until it reaches operating temperature. Loosen the oil gallery plug (see illustration 17.16 in Chapter 1). Oil should seep from the plug hole within one minute.

5   Check carefully for oil leaks and make sure the transmission and controls, especially the brakes, function properly before road testing the machine. Refer to Section 27 for the recommended break-in procedure.

6   Upon completion of the road test, and after the engine has cooled down completely, recheck the valve clearances (see Chapter 1).

2B

26 Recommended break-in procedure

1   Any rebuilt engine needs time to break in, even if parts have been installed in their original locations. For this reason, treat the machine gently for the first few miles to make sure oil has circulated throughout the engine and any new parts installed have started to seat.

2   Even greater care is necessary if the cylinder has been rebored or a new crankshaft has been installed. In the case of a rebore, the engine will have to be broken in as if the machine were new. This means greater use of the transmission and a restraining hand on the throttle for the first few operating days. There's no point in keeping to any set speed limit - the main idea is to vary the engine speed, keep from lugging the engine and to avoid full-throttle operation. These recommendations can be lessened to an extent when only a new crankshaft is installed. Experience is the best guide, since it's easy to tell when an engine is running freely. The following recommendations, which Yamaha provides for new machines, can be used as a guide:

Zero to ten hours: Operate at varying speeds and avoid using any one set speed. Don't operate the machine continuously at more than half throttle. After every hour of operation, let the engine cool for five to ten minutes.

Ten to 20 hours: Rev the engine freely, using all the gears, but don't operate at full throttle. Don't operate the machine continuously above three-quarters throttle.

After 20 hours: Consider the machine broken in. Operate occasionally at varying speeds, and avoid long periods at full throttle.

3   If a lubrication failure is suspected, stop the engine immediately and try to find the cause. If an engine is run without oil, even for a short period of time, irreparable damage will occur.

Chapter 3
Cooling system

Contents

Specifications

General

Coolant type	See Chapter 1
Mixture ratio	See Chapter 1
Radiator cap pressure rating	93 to 125 kPa (13.5 to 17.8 psi)

Torque specifications

Water pump access cover screws	7 Nm (61 in-lbs)
Water pump cover plate screws	8 Nm (70 in-lbs)

1 General information

The YFZ350 Banshee model is liquid-cooled. The liquid-cooling system uses a water/antifreeze mixture to carry away excess heat produced during the combustion process. The cylinders are surrounded by water jackets, through which the coolant is circulated by the water pump. The pump is mounted on the right side of the engine and is gear-driven off the right end of the crankshaft. Coolant is pumped through a radiator mounted below and in front of the handlebar.

The entire system is sealed and pressurized. The pressure is controlled by a valve which is part of the radiator cap. By pressurizing the coolant, the boiling point is raised, which prevents premature boiling of the coolant. An overflow hose, connected between the radiator filler neck and the reservoir tank, directs coolant to the tank when the radiator cap valve is opened by excessive pressure. The coolant is automatically siphoned back to the radiator through another hose as the engine cools.

Some cooling system inspection and service procedures are considered part of routine maintenance and are included in Chapter 1.

Warning 1: *Do not allow antifreeze to come in contact with your skin or painted surfaces of the vehicle. Rinse off spills immediately with plenty of water. Antifreeze is highly toxic if ingested. Never leave antifreeze lying around in an open container or in puddles on the floor; children and pets are attracted by its sweet smell and may drink it. Check with local authorities about disposing of used antifreeze. Many communities have collection centers which will see that antifreeze is disposed of safely.*

Warning 2: *Do not remove the radiator cap when the engine and radiator are hot. Scalding hot coolant and steam may be blown out under pressure, which could cause serious injury. To open the radiator cap, remove the rear screw from the right side panel on the inside of the fairing (if equipped). When the engine has cooled, lift up the panel and place a thick rag, like a towel, over the radiator cap; slowly rotate the cap counterclockwise to the first stop. This procedure allows any residual pressure to escape. When the steam has stopped escaping, press down on the cap while turning counterclockwise and remove it.*

2 Radiator cap - check

If problems such as overheating and loss of coolant occur, check the entire system as described in Chapter 1. The radiator cap opening pressure should be checked by a dealer service department or service station equipped with the special tester required to do the job. If the cap is defective, replace it.

3.3a **Loosen the hose clamp (arrow) that secures the lower radiator hose to the radiator, slide it back, pull off the hose and drain the coolant**

3 Radiator - removal and installation

Refer to illustrations 3.3a, 3.3b, 3.4, 3.5a and 3.5b
Warning: *The engine must be completely cool before beginning this procedure.*
1   Remove the seat, the radiator cover, the fuel tank cover, the front fender and the front fender stays (see Chapter 8).
2   Remove the fuel tank (see Chapter 4).
3   Place a large drain pan under the lower radiator hose, loosen the lower radiator hose clamp **(see illustration)**, detach the lower hose from the radiator and drain the coolant. Loosen the hose clamp and detach the upper hose from the radiator **(see illustration)**.

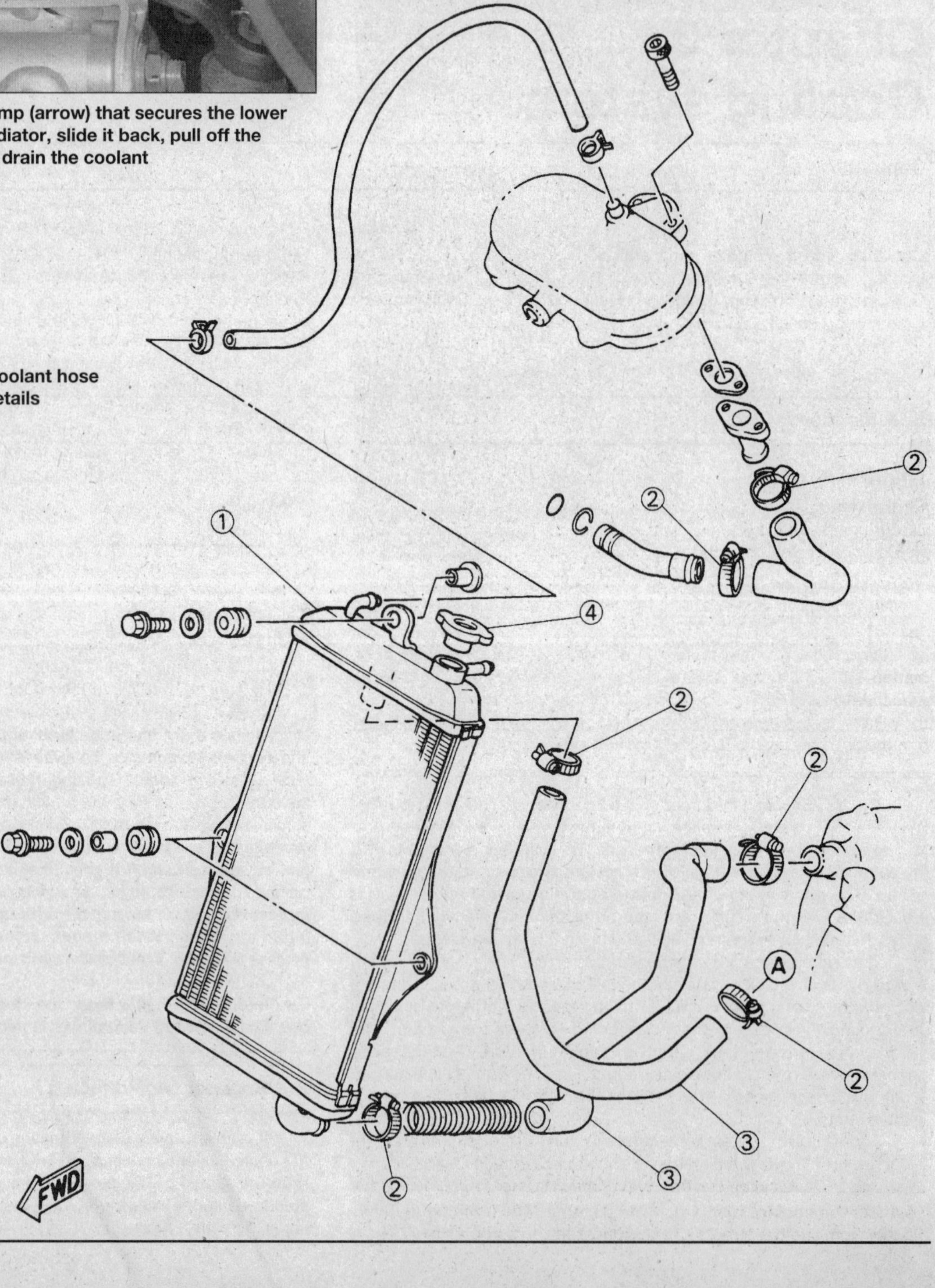

3.3b **Radiator and coolant hose installation details**

1 *Radiator*
2 *Hose clamps*
3 *Radiator hoses*
4 *Radiator filler cap*
5 *Bypass hose*

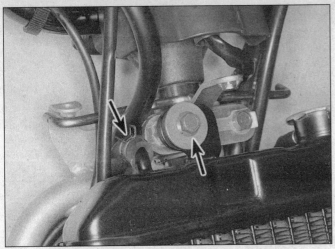

3.4 Coolant bypass hose (left arrow) and radiator upper bolt (right arrow)

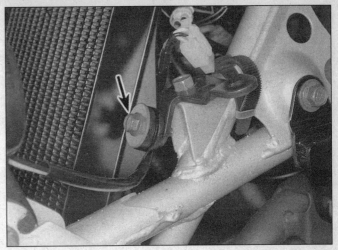

3.5a Here's the lower left radiator mounting bolt (arrow) . . .

3.5b . . . and the lower right mounting bolt (arrow); replace the rubber grommets if they're damaged or worn

4   Detach the overflow hose from the radiator filler neck (see illustration 19.7 in Chapter 1). Detach the bypass hose from the radiator (see illustration).
5   Remove the upper radiator mounting bolt (see illustration 3.4) and the two lower mounting bolts (see illustrations).

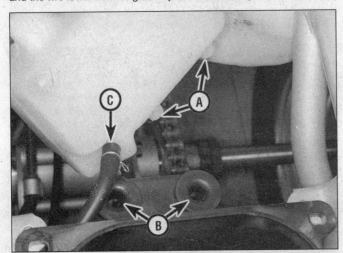

4.4 Lift the coolant reservoir and disengage the positioning pins (A) from the grommets (B), then detach the siphon hose (C)

6   Remove the radiator.
7   Carefully inspect the radiator for signs of leaks and any other damage. If repairs are necessary, take the radiator to a reputable radiator repair shop. If the radiator is clogged, or if large amounts of rust or scale have formed, the repair shop will also do a thorough cleaning job.
8   Make sure the spaces between the cooling tubes and fins are clear. If necessary, use compressed air or running water to remove anything that may be clogging them. If the fins are bent or flattened, straighten them very carefully with a small screwdriver.
9   Inspect the radiator hoses for cracks, tears and other damage. Be sure to replace the hoses if they are damaged or deteriorated.
10   Installation is the reverse of the removal procedure.
11   Refill the cooling system with the recommended coolant (see Chapter 1).

3

4   Coolant reservoir - removal and installation

Refer to illustration 4.4
1   Drain the cooling system (see Chapter 1).
2   Remove the seat (see Chapter 8).
3   Detach the overflow (upper) hose from the coolant reservoir.
4   Place a container under the reservoir to catch spilled coolant. Lift up the coolant reservoir and disengage the two positioning pins on the underside of the reservoir from the two rubber grommets (see illustration). Detach the siphon (lower) hose from the reservoir. Remove the reservoir.
5   Wash out the reservoir with clean water. If there are any deposits inside the reservoir, try to knock them loose with a high-pressure garden hose nozzle or blow them out with compressed air. Inspect the reservoir for cracks. If it's damaged, replace it. Using a cracked reservoir could allow the engine to overheat.
6   Installation is the reverse of removal.
7   Be sure to fill the cooling system when you're done (see Chapter 1).

5   Water pump - inspection and replacement

Inspection

Refer to illustrations 5.3a and 5.3b
1   Inspect the area around the water pump for coolant leaks. Try to determine whether the leak is simply the result of a loose hose clamp or deteriorated hose, a damaged pump cover gasket or a bad seal.
2   If the leak appears to be caused by a loose hose clamp, tighten the clamp, clean up the area around the leak, run the engine and verify

5.3a To get to the water pump cover plate, remove these three screws (arrows) and the access cover . . .

5.3b . . . then remove the cover plate screws and the plate

that the leak has been fixed. If the leak appears to be caused by a damaged hose, drain the coolant (see Chapter 1) and replace the hose.

3   To determine whether the pump is leaking because of a bad cover gasket, remove the access cover **(see illustration)** and inspect the area around the cover plate. If the pump is leaking because of a bad gasket, drain the coolant (see Chapter 1), remove the cover plate **(see illustration)** and replace the gasket. Carefully remove all of the old gasket material from the gasket mating surfaces of the pump housing and the cover plate. Install a new gasket, install the plate and tighten the cover plate screws to the torque listed in this Chapter's Specifications.

4   If there is coolant in the transmission oil, or transmission oil in the coolant, the seal for the impeller shaft is leaking. You'll have to remove the right crankcase cover to replace the seal (see below).

Replacement

Refer to illustrations 5.9, 5.11a, 5.11b, 5.11c, 5.11d, 5.12, 5.15, 5.16 and 5.18

5   Drain the coolant and the transmission oil (see Chapter 1).

6   Unbolt the rear brake master cylinder (see Chapter 7) and secure the rear brake lever to the frame with a cable tie to provide clearance for removing the right crankcase cover.

7   Remove the water pump access cover **(see illustration 5.3a)**.

8   Remove the right crankcase cover (see "Clutch - removal, inspection and installation" in Chapter 2A).

9   Before disassembling the pump, inspect the condition of the pump-to-cylinder head hose **(see illustration 3.3b)** and the O-ring **(see illustration)** that seals the plastic pump outlet tube between the

5.9 Replace the pump outlet tube O-ring (arrow) if it's deteriorated

pump and the pump-to-cylinder head hose. If either is damaged or worn, be sure to replace it.

10   Remove the water pump cover plate **(see illustration 5.3b)**.

11   Remove the circlip, washer, impeller shaft driven gear and drive pin **(see illustrations)**.

12   Remove the impeller shaft **(see illustration)**.

13   Inspect the impeller shaft for corrosion. If the shaft is heavily corroded, replace the impeller and shaft as a single assembly. And be

5.11a To release the water pump impeller shaft, remove the driven gear circlip . . .

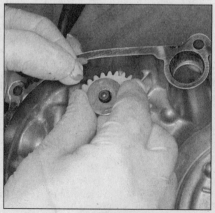

5.11b . . . remove the washer . . .

5.11c . . . remove the driven gear . . .

5.11d . . . and remove the drive pin

5.12 Remove the water pump impeller and shaft

5.15 Inspect the water pump seal; the WATER SIDE marking on the seal must face the impeller

15   Inspect the impeller shaft seal (see illustration). If it's damaged, replace it. Flip the crankcase cover over and inspect the bearing (see illustration 5.11d) on the other side. If the seal has been leaking, the bearing may be damaged too. To check the bearing, put your index finger in the center of the bearing, push in and rotate the bearing, and note whether the bearing turns smoothly. If it's rough, replace it.
16   To replace the seal or bearing, tap them out from the inner (engine) side of the right crankcase cover with a deep socket or bearing driver (see illustration). Bearings are easier to remove if you slowly heat the crankcase cover in an oven (do NOT use a hot plate or torch) to a temperature of 200 to 250 degrees F.
17   Tap in the new bearing and seal from the outer side, again, with a deep socket. Make sure that the manufacturer's serial number on the bearing faces outward and the "WATER SIDE" mark on the seal faces toward the impeller (see illustration 5.15).
18   Lightly grease the impeller shaft and insert it through the seal and bearing. Install the drive pin, impeller shaft driven gear, washer and circlip. Make sure that the driven gear is correctly engaged with the drive pin (see illustration) before installing the circlip.
19   Grease the pump outlet tube O-ring with lightweight lithium soap base grease.
20   Install a new pump cover gasket, install the pump cover and tighten the pump cover screws to the torque listed in this Chapter's Specifications.
21   The remainder of installation is the reverse of removal.
22   Fill the cooling system with the recommended coolant (see Chapter 1), run the engine and check for leaks.

3

sure to flush the system thoroughly (see "Cooling system - draining, flushing and refilling" in Chapter 1). Also, inspect the internal condition of the radiator.
14   Inspect the impeller blades. If they're cracked, replace the impeller/shaft assembly.

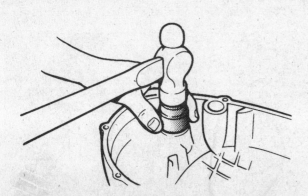
5.16 Slowly heat the crankcase cover and drive out the impeller shaft bearing and seal with a socket or driver

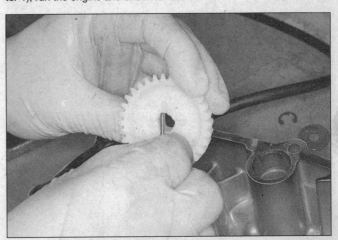
5.18 The impeller drive pin must align with two of the grooves in the gear

Notes

Chapter 4 Part A
Fuel and exhaust systems (Banshee models)

Contents

Specifications

General
Fuel type .... Premium unleaded gasoline mixed with 2-stroke oil

Carburetor
Main jet
  Through 2001 210
  2002 and later 200
Main air jet 1.6
Needle jet O-8
Jet needle 5N7-3
Pilot jet 25
Pilot air screw setting .... See Chapter 1
Float height
  Through 2001 .... 20.0 to 22 mm (51/64 to 55/64 inch)
  2002 and later .... 20.5 to 21.5 mm (13/16 to 27/32 inch)
Fuel level .... 0.5 to 1.5 mm (0.02 to 0.06 inch)

Torque specifications
Exhaust pipe stay .... 25 Nm (18 ft-lbs)
Muffler .... 35 Nm (25 ft-lbs)

* Standard specifications are for temperatures consistently above 32-degrees F (0-degrees C). Cold weather specifications are for temperatures between 5-degrees and 41-degrees F (minus 15-degrees and plus 5-degrees C). Extremely cold weather specifications are for temperatures between minus 22-degrees and plus 14-degrees F (minus 30-degrees and minus 10-degrees C).

4A

1 General information

The fuel system consists of the fuel tank, fuel tap, filter screen, carburetors, hoses and throttle cables.

The Mikuni carburetors on these models are controlled by a thumb lever on the right handlebar. For cold starting, an enrichment circuit is actuated by a choke knob mounted on the carburetor.

The exhaust system consists of an expansion chamber, pipe and muffler.

Many of the fuel system service procedures are considered routine maintenance items and for that reason are included in Chapter 1.

2 Fuel tank - removal and installation

Warning: *Gasoline is extremely flammable, so take extra precautions when you work on any part of the fuel system. Don't smoke or allow open flames or bare light bulbs near the work area, and don't work in a garage where a natural gas-type appliance (such as a water heater or clothes dryer) is present. Since gasoline is carcinogenic, wear latex gloves when there's a possibility of being exposed to fuel, and, if you get fuel on your skin, rinse it off immediately with soap and water. Mop up any spills immediately and do not store fuel-soaked rags where they could ignite. When you perform any kind of work on the fuel system,* *wear safety glasses and have an extinguisher suitable for a class B type fire (flammable liquids) on hand.*

Refer to illustrations 2.2a, 2.2b, 2.3 and 2.6

1   Remove the seat, the radiator cover, the fuel tank cover, the front fender and the front fender stays, and the rear fender (see Chapter 8).

2   Remove the fuel tank front mounting bolts **(see illustrations)**. Make sure the fuel tap is turned off.

3   Disconnect the fuel line from the fuel tap **(see illustration)**.

4   Lift the fuel tank off the vehicle.

5   Before installing the tank, inspect the condition of the rubber mounting grommets. If they're hard, cracked, or otherwise deteriorated, replace them.

6   Installation is the reverse of removal. Don't pinch any control cables or wires when placing the tank in position on the frame. Make sure the metal collars **(see illustration)** are installed in the mounting grommets before installing the fuel tank mounting bolts.

3   Fuel tank - cleaning and repair

1   The fuel tank is plastic and can't be repaired by traditional welding or brazing techniques. All repairs to the fuel tank should be carried out by a professional who has experience in this critical and potentially dangerous work. Even after cleaning and flushing of the fuel system, explosive fumes can remain and ignite during repair of the tank.

2   If the fuel tank is removed from the vehicle, it should not be placed in an area where sparks or open flames could ignite the fumes coming out of the tank. Be especially careful inside garages where a natural gas-type appliance is located, because the pilot light could cause an explosion.

4   Idle fuel/air mixture adjustment

Idle fuel/air mixture on these vehicles is adjusted as part of the idle speed adjustment procedure (see Chapter 1).

5   Carburetor overhaul - general information

1   Poor engine performance, hesitation, hard starting, stalling, flooding and backfiring are all signs that major carburetor maintenance may be required.

2   Keep in mind that many so-called carburetor problems are really not carburetor problems at all, but mechanical problems within the engine or ignition system malfunctions. Try to establish for certain that the carburetor is in need of maintenance before beginning a major overhaul.

3   Check the fuel tap and its strainer screen, the fuel line, the intake tube clamps, the reed valve, the air filter element, the crankcase compression and vacuum, the spark plug and the ignition timing before

2.2a Remove one mounting bolt from each rear corner of the fuel tank . . .

assuming that a carburetor overhaul is required. If the vehicle has been unused for more than a month, refer to Chapter 1, drain the float chamber and refill the tank with fresh fuel.

4   Most carburetor problems are caused by dirt particles, varnish and other deposits which build up in and block the fuel and air passages. Also, in time, gaskets and O-rings shrink or deteriorate and cause fuel and air leaks which lead to poor performance.

5   When the carburetor is overhauled, it is generally disassembled completely and the parts are cleaned thoroughly with a carburetor cleaning solvent and dried with filtered, unlubricated compressed air. The fuel and air passages are also blown through with compressed air to force out any dirt that may have been loosened but not removed by the solvent. Once the cleaning process is complete, the carburetor is reassembled using new gaskets, O-rings and, generally, a new inlet needle valve and seat.

6   Before disassembling the carburetor, make sure you have all necessary O-rings and other parts, some carburetor cleaner, a supply of rags, some means of blowing out the carburetor passages and a clean place to work.

6   Carburetors - removal and installation

Warning: *Gasoline is extremely flammable, so take extra precautions when you work on any part of the fuel system. Don't smoke or allow open flames or bare light bulbs near the work area, and don't work in a garage where a natural gas-type appliance (such as a water heater or clothes dryer) is present. If you spill any fuel on your skin, rinse it off immediately with soap and water. When you perform any kind of work on the fuel system, wear safety glasses and have a fire extinguisher suitable for a class B type fire (flammable liquids) on hand.*

2.2b . . . and one from each front corner

2.3 Disconnect the fuel line (arrow) from the fuel tap

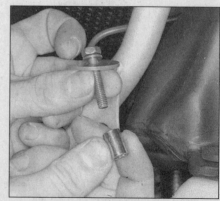

2.6 Don't forget the collars in the grommets

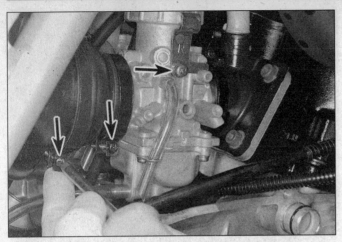

6.3 Loosen the clamping band screws (left arrows); remove the stopper plate screw (right arrow) if you'll need to unscrew the carburetor top

6.4a Unscrew the carburetor top . . .

Removal

Refer to illustrations 6.3, 6.4a, 6.4b, 6.4c, 6.4d, 6.5a, 6.5b, 6.5c and 6.6

1　Remove the fuel tank (see Section 2).
2　Drain the fuel from the carburetor float chamber (see Chapter 1).
3　Loosen the screws on the clamps that attach the intake ducts to the air cleaner housing and the carburetors **(see illustration)**.
4　If you just want to remove the carburetor bodies, remove the stopper plate from each carburetor **(see illustration 6.3)**, unscrew the carburetor cap from the carburetor body and pull up the throttle piston **(see illustrations)**. If you also want to remove the throttle pistons, pull up the spring and detach the retainer and cable from each piston **(see illustrations)**.
5　Disconnect the fuel lines from the carburetors and disconnect the overflow hoses from the carburetor float bowls **(see illustrations)**.
6　Loosen the screws on the clamps that attach the carburetors to the reed valve bodies **(see illustration)**.

6.4b . . . and pull out the throttle piston; the piston slot must align with the protrusion in the carburetor body when the piston is reinstalled

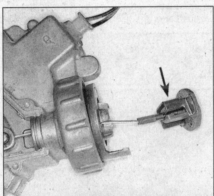

6.4c . . . slide the cable retainer (arrow) off the jet needle holder (spring and throttle piston removed for clarity) . . .

6.4d . . . and slip the cable sideways out of the jet needle holder

4A

6.5a Follow the fuel lines from the T-fitting to each carburetor and disconnect them

6.5b Disconnect the fuel transfer hose (arrow) from both carburetors

6.5c Disconnect the overflow hose from each carburetor float bowl

7   Work the carburetors free of the intake ducts and the reed valve bodies, then stuff clean rags into the intake ports in the cylinders to prevent the entry of dirt or other objects.

Installation

Refer to illustrations 6.8a and 6.8b

8   Installation is the reverse of the removal steps, with the following additions:

a) *Inspect the intake ducts and the reed valve bodies for cracks, deterioration or other damage. If they're damaged, replace them (to replace the reed valve bodies, see "Reed valve - removal, inspection and installation" in Chapter 2A).*

b) *Make sure the O-ring in the carburetor top is in good condition and replace it if necessary* **(see illustration)**.

c) *Slide the throttle piston into the carburetor, making sure its groove is aligned with the protrusion in the carburetor body* **(see illustration 6.4b)**.

d) *After screwing the carburetor top onto the carburetor, align one of the ridges on the edge of the carburetor top with one of the notches in the stopper plate* **(see illustration)** *before tightening the stopper plate screw.*

e) *Adjust throttle lever freeplay and idle speed (see Chapter 1).*

7   Carburetors - disassembly, cleaning and inspection

Warning: *Gasoline is extremely flammable, so take extra precautions when you work on any part of the fuel system. Don't smoke or allow open flames or bare light bulbs near the work area, and don't work in a garage where a natural gas-type appliance (such as a water heater or clothes dryer) is present. Since gasoline is carcinogenic, wear latex gloves when there's a possibility of being exposed to fuel, and, if you*

6.6 Loosen the screws on the clamps that attach the carburetors to the reed valve bodies

get fuel on your skin, rinse it off immediately with soap and water. Mop up any spills immediately and do not store fuel-soaked rags where they could ignite. When you perform any kind of work on the fuel system, wear safety glasses and have an extinguisher suitable for a class B type fire (flammable liquids) on hand.

Disassembly

Refer to illustrations 7.2a through 7.2k

1   Remove the carburetors (see Section 6). Set the carburetors on a clean working surface.

2   Refer to the accompanying illustrations to disassemble each carburetor **(see illustrations)**.

6.8a Replace the O-ring (arrow) if it's damaged or deteriorated

6.8b Align one of the two notches in the stopper with one of the ridges on the carburetor top (arrow)

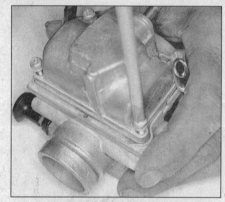

7.2a Remove the screws and lift off the float chamber and gasket

7.2b Lift off the baffle (arrow)

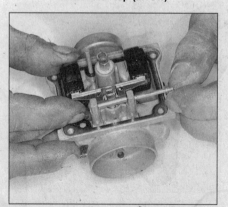

7.2c Push the float pivot pin partway out and pull it the rest of the way

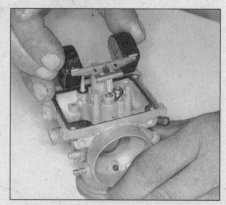

7.2d Lift the needle valve out of the seat

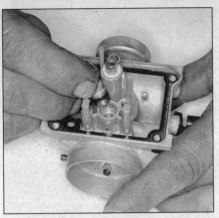

7.2e Pull out the needle valve seat and O-ring and unscrew the main jet (arrow)

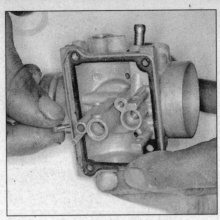

7.2f Unscrew the pilot jet

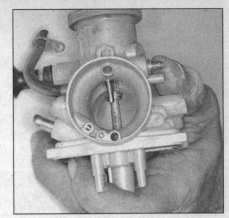

7.2g Push the needle jet partway out, then pull it from above the rest of the way

Cleaning

Caution: *Use only a carburetor cleaning solution that is safe for use with plastic parts (be sure to read the label on the container).*

3   Submerge the metal components in the carburetor cleaner for approximately thirty minutes (or longer, if the directions recommend it).

4   After the carburetor has soaked long enough for the cleaner to loosen and dissolve most of the varnish and other deposits, use a brush to remove the stubborn deposits. Rinse it again, then dry it with compressed air. Blow out all of the fuel and air passages in the main and upper body. **Caution:** *Never clean the jets or passages with a piece of wire or a drill bit, as they will be enlarged, causing the fuel and air metering rates to be upset.*

Inspection

5   Check the operation of the choke plunger. If it doesn't move smoothly, replace it, along with the return spring. If the plunger O-rings are deteriorated or damaged, replace them.

6   Check the tapered portion of the pilot screw for wear or damage. Replace the pilot screw if necessary.

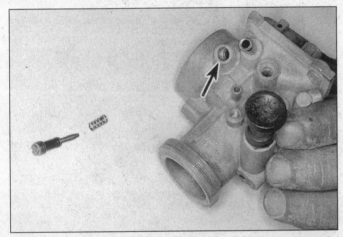

7.2h Remove the pilot screw and spring from their bore (arrow)

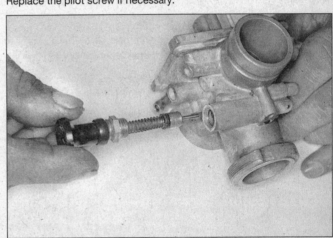

7.2i Unscrew the choke plunger

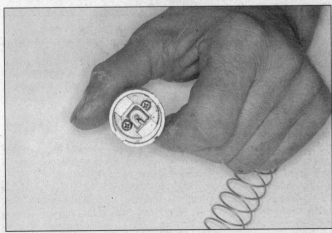

7.2j Remove these two screws to detach the jet needle holder from the piston . . .

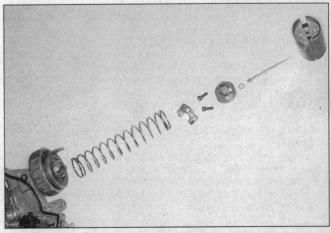

7.2k . . . then remove the jet needle, washer and clip from the throttle piston

4A

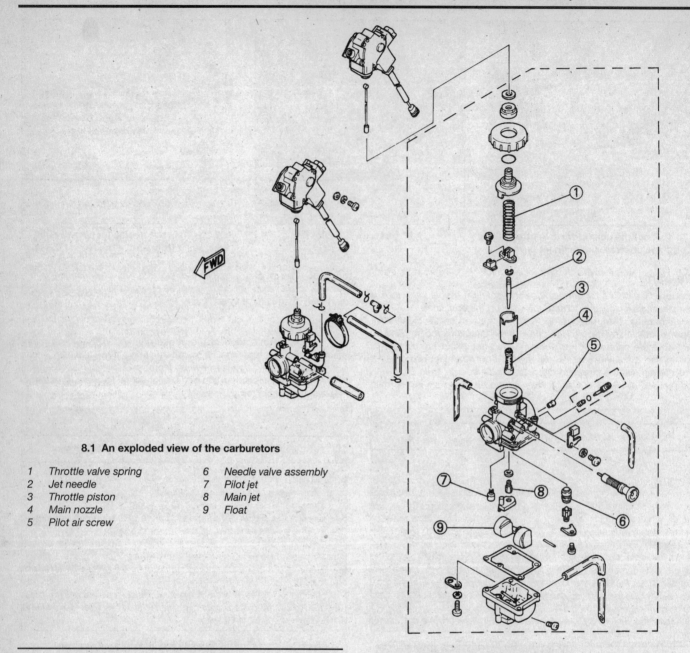

8.1 An exploded view of the carburetors

1	Throttle valve spring	6	Needle valve assembly
2	Jet needle	7	Pilot jet
3	Throttle piston	8	Main jet
4	Main nozzle	9	Float
5	Pilot air screw		

7   Check the carburetor body, float chamber and top cover for cracks, distorted sealing surfaces and other damage. If any defects are found, replace the faulty component, although replacement of the entire carburetor will probably be necessary (check with your parts supplier for the availability of separate components).

8   Check the jet needle for straightness by rolling it on a flat surface (such as a piece of glass). Replace it if it's bent or if the tip is worn.

9   Check the tip of the fuel inlet valve needle. If it has grooves or scratches in it, it must be replaced. Push in on the rod in the other end of the needle, then release it - if it doesn't spring back, replace the valve needle.

10   Check the float chamber gasket and the drain plug (in the float chamber). Replace them if they're damaged.

11   Slide the throttle piston up and down in its bore to make sure it moves smoothly. If it doesn't, or if the throttle piston shows wear or damage, replace the carburetor.

12   Check the floats for damage. This will usually be apparent by the presence of fuel inside one of the floats. If the floats are damaged, they must be replaced.

8   Carburetors - reassembly and float height check

Refer to illustrations 8.1 and 8.5

1   Reassembly is the reverse of disassembly **(see illustration)**, with the following additions. **Caution:** *When installing the jets, be careful not to overtighten them - they're made of soft material and can strip or shear easily.*

2   Install the clip on the jet needle if it was removed. Place it in the needle groove listed in this Chapter's Specifications.

3   Install the pilot screw along with its spring, washer and O-ring, turning it in until it seats lightly. Now, turn the screw out the number of turns listed in the Chapter 1 Specifications.

4   Reverse the disassembly steps to install the jets.

5   Invert the carburetor. Attach the fuel inlet valve needle to the float. Set the float into position in the carburetor, making sure the valve needle seats correctly. Install the float pivot pin. To check the float height, hold the carburetor upside down. Measure the distance from the float chamber gasket surface to the top of the float and compare your mea-

8.5 Hold the carburetor upside down and measure float height from the gasket surface

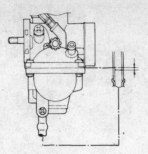

9.2 A ruler and a clear plastic tube can be used to measure fuel level if you don't have the special tool

surement to the float height listed in this Chapter's Specifications **(see illustration)**. If it isn't as specified, bend the tang on the float to change it. **Note:** *Setting the float level is a preliminary adjustment. After the carburetor has been reinstalled, the fuel level must be checked and, if necessary, adjusted (see Section 9).*

6   Install the float chamber gasket. Place the float chamber on the carburetor and install the screws, tightening them securely.

9   Fuel level - check and adjustment

Refer to illustration 9.2

Warning: *Gasoline is extremely flammable, so take extra precautions when you work on any part of the fuel system. Don't smoke or allow open flames or bare light bulbs near the work area, and don't work in a garage where a natural gas-type appliance (such as a water heater or clothes dryer) is present. Since gasoline is carcinogenic, wear latex gloves when there's a possibility of being exposed to fuel, and, if you get fuel on your skin, rinse it off immediately with soap and water. Mop up any spills immediately and do not store fuel-soaked rags where they could ignite. When you perform any kind of work on the fuel system, wear safety glasses and have an extinguisher suitable for a class B type fire (flammable liquids) on hand.*

1   Park the vehicle on a level surface and make sure the carburetor

is level. If necessary, adjust its position slightly by raising the front or rear end.

2   Attach the Yamaha service tool to the drain fitting on the bottom of the carburetor float bowl. This is a clear plastic tube graduated in millimeters. You can also use a length of clear plastic tubing and an accurate ruler **(see illustration)**. Hold the free end of the tube vertically against the float chamber cover.

3   Unscrew the drain screw at the bottom of the float chamber a couple of turns, then start the engine and let it idle - fuel will flow into the tube. Wait for the fuel level to stabilize, then note how far the fuel level is below the line on the float chamber cover.

4   Measure the distance between the indicator line and the top of the fuel in the tube or gauge. This distance is the fuel level.

5   Compare your reading to the value listed in this Chapter's Specifications. If the fuel level is not correct, remove the float chamber cover and bend the float tang up or down as necessary, then recheck the fuel level.

10   Air cleaner housing - removal and installation

Refer to illustrations 10.4 and 10.5

1   Remove the seat (see Chapter 8).

2   Remove the air filter element (see Chapter 1).

3   Loosen the screws for the hose clamps that secure the air intake ducts to the air cleaner housing **(see illustration 6.3)**.

4   Detach the wiring harnesses and hoses from the hooks on the side of the air cleaner housing **(see illustration)**.

5   Remove the air cleaner housing mounting bolts **(see illustration)** and remove the air cleaner housing.

6   Installation is the reverse of removal. Be sure to inspect the drain tube before installing the air cleaner housing (see "Air filter element and drain tube - cleaning" in Chapter 1).

4A

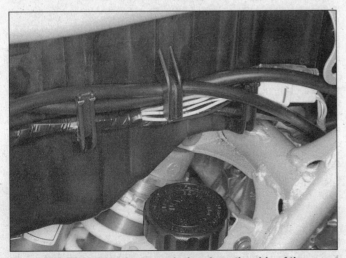

10.4 Detach the hoses and wires from the side of the air cleaner housing . . .

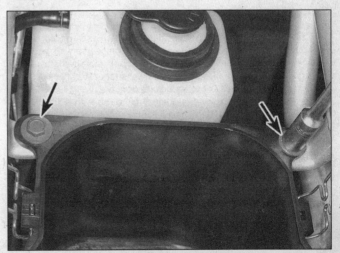

10.5 . . . and remove these bolts (arrows)

11.3a Remove the cover screws (arrows) . . .

11.3b . . . and lift off the cover for access to the lever and cable

11 Throttle cables, throttle switch and carburetor switch - removal, installation and adjustment

Throttle cables

Removal

Refer to illustrations 11.3a, 11.3b, 11.3c, 11.5a, 11.5b, 11.5c, 11.6a and 11.6b

1   The "throttle cable" is actually five cables. The main cable connects the throttle lever on the handlebar to two cables - one per carburetor - inside a junction housing. Each of these two cables is connected at its lower end to a lever inside the carburetor switch housing. A short cable connects each lever to the piston.

2   Loosen the cable adjuster at the handlebar all the way (see Chapter 1).

3   Remove the cover from the throttle housing on the handlebar and disconnect the cable from the lever inside (see illustrations). If necessary, remove the throttle housing clamp screws and detach the throttle housing from the handlebar (see illustration).

4   Detach the carburetor top and the carburetor switch housing from the carburetor (see Section 6). Disconnect the lower end of the short cable from the carburetor throttle piston (see illustrations 6.4c and 6.4d).

5   Remove the cover from the right side of the carburetor switch housing (see illustration). Detach the cable from the lever inside the switch housing (see illustrations). Remove the cable from the vehicle, noting how it's routed.

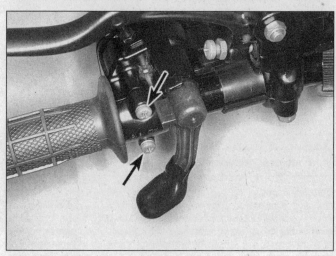

11.3c The throttle housing clamp screws (arrows) are underneath

6   Remove the cover from the left side of the switch housing and remove the short cable that connects the switch to the throttle piston (see illustrations).

Inspection

7   Inspect the components inside the switch housing for wear and damage. Replace the housing if problems are found.

11.5a Remove the screws and rubber cover (arrows) . . .

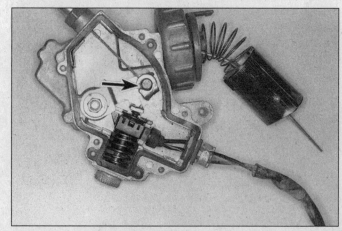

11.5b . . . lift off the cover and detach the long cable from the lever (arrow)

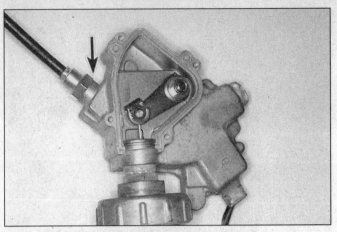

11.5c Unscrew the cable nut (arrow)

11.6a Remove the cover screws . . .

Installation

Refer to illustration 11.8

8   If the throttle housing was removed, install it on the handlebar and tighten its clamp screws loosely. Position the throttle housing so that its protrusion is aligned with the notch in the handlebar spacer collar that fits between the brake master cylinder and the throttle housing **(see illustration)**. Install the clamp and screws and tighten them securely.

9   Reverse the disconnection steps to connect the cables to the switch housing.

10   Route the cable into place. Make sure it doesn't interfere with any other components and isn't kinked or bent sharply. Reverse the disconnection steps to reconnect the cable to the throttle lever at the handlebar.

11   Reconnect the carburetor top to the switch housing, then install them on the carburetor and reinstall it in the vehicle.

12   Operate the lever and make sure it returns to the idle position by itself under spring pressure. **Warning:** *If the lever doesn't return by itself, find and solve the problem before continuing with installation. A stuck lever can lead to loss of control of the vehicle.*

Adjustment

13   Adjust the throttle cable (see "Throttle cable and speed limiter - check and adjustment" in Chapter 1).

14   Turn the handlebar back and forth to make sure the cables don't cause the steering to bind.

15   Once you're sure the cables operate properly, install the cover on the throttle lever housing.

16   With the engine idling, turn the handlebar through its full travel (full left lock to full right lock) and note whether idle speed increases. If it does, the cable is routed incorrectly. Correct this dangerous condition before riding the vehicle.

Throttle switch

Refer to illustration 11.18

17   Remove the throttle housing cover **(see illustration 11.3a)**.

18   Remove the switch mounting screw **(see illustration)**. Pull up the gasket where it passes over the switch grommet and pull the grommet out of the notch in the throttle housing.

19   Installation is the reverse of the removal steps.

11.6b . . . lift off the cover and detach the short cable from the lever

4A

11.8 Align the protrusion (arrow) with the spacer collar notch

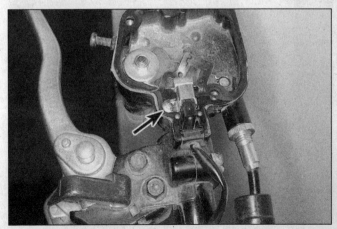

11.18 Pull back the gasket and remove the screw (arrow)

11.20 Try cleaning the switch contacts

11.21 Unscrew the hex (arrow) to separate the carburetor top from the switch housing

12.1 To detach the heat shield from the middle exhaust pipe, remove these two screws (arrows)

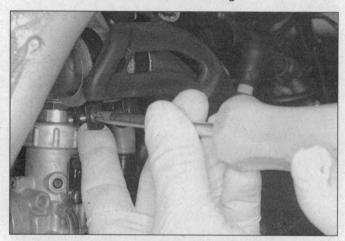

12.2a To detach the rear exhaust pipe and muffler, loosen the clamp screw below the rear end of the heat shield . . .

Carburetor switch

Refer to illustrations 11.20 and 11.21

20   The switch is located inside the switch housing **(see illustration)**. Before replacing the switch, check its contacts and try cleaning them.

21   The switch and housing are replaced as a unit. Undo the nut at the bottom of the switch to separate the housing from the carburetor top **(see illustration)**.

12 Exhaust system - removal and installation

Refer to illustrations 12.1, 12.2a, 12.2b, 12.2c, 12.2d, 12.3, 12.4, 12.5a, 12.5b, 12.5c, 12.5d and 12.6

Note: *The following procedure applies to both exhaust pipes.*

1   If you just want to replace the heat shield, it can be detached from

12.2b . . . remove the bolt that attaches the rear pipe to the frame bracket . . .

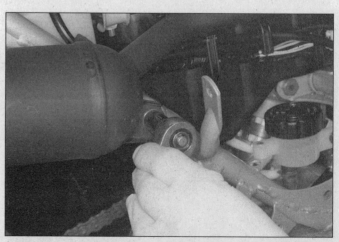

12.2c . . . remove the bolt that attaches the muffler front bracket to the frame . . .

12.2d . . . unbolt the muffler upper bracket from the frame and separate the rear pipe and muffler from the middle pipe

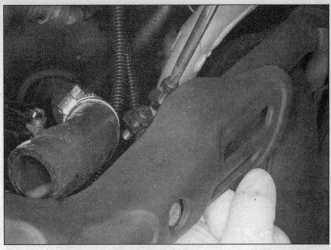

12.3 To separate the middle exhaust pipe from the front exhaust pipe, loosen this clamp screw and pull the middle pipe to the rear

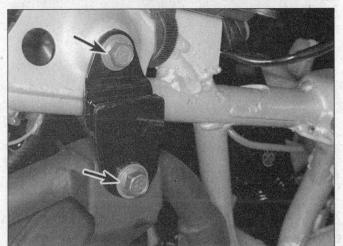

12.4 To detach the front exhaust pipe from the frame, remove these two bolts (arrows) and the front pipe bracket

12.5a To detach the expansion chamber, remove this spring . . .

4A

the middle exhaust pipe simply by removing two screws (see illustration). (Conversely, it's not necessary to remove the heat shield in order to remove the middle exhaust pipe.)

2   Remove the rear exhaust pipe and muffler (see illustrations).

3   Loosen the clamp screws from each end of the middle exhaust pipe (see illustration) and remove the middle exhaust pipe.

4   Remove the front exhaust pipe bracket (see illustration).

5   Remove the expansion chamber springs (see illustrations) and remove the expansion chamber.

12.5b . . . this one (springs for both pipes visible) . . .

12.5c . . . and this one

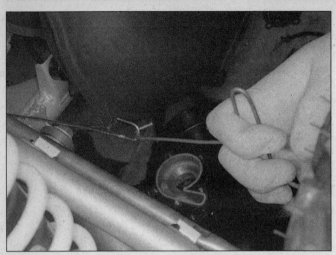

12.5d A hooked tool like this is handy - and safer - for removing exhaust springs

6   Installation is the reverse of removal, with the following additions:

a) *Be sure to install a new O-ring at the cylinder head* **(see illustration).**

b) *Inspect the joints between the front exhaust pipe and middle exhaust pipe, and between the middle pipe and rear pipe. If they're cracked, deteriorated or leaking, replace them.*

c) *Tighten the muffler mounting bolt, clamp screws, heat shield screws and front exhaust pipe bracket bolts securely, but don't overtighten them and strip the threads.*

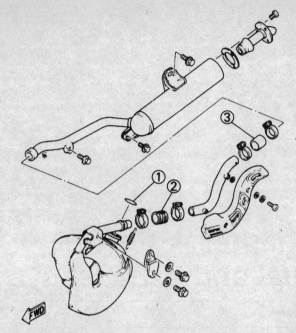

12.6 An exploded view of the exhaust system for one cylinder (left exhaust shown, right exhaust identical)

1   O-ring
2   Front exhaust pipe-to-middle exhaust pipe joint
3   Middle exhaust pipe-to-rear exhaust pipe joint

Chapter 4 Part B
Fuel and exhaust systems (Warrior models)

Contents

Specifications

General

Fuel type Unleaded gasoline subject to local regulations; minimum octane 91 RON (86 pump octane)

Carburetor

Main jet	145
Main air jet	0.6
Jet needle	
1987 through 2001	5J18-3
2002 and later	
Non-Califorrnia	5J18-3
California	5J18-1
Pilot jet	42.5
Pilot air jet	
Pilot air jet 1	1.0
Pilot air jet 2	0.7
Pilot screw setting	1-1/4 turns out
Float valve seat	2.5
Float height	
1987 through 2001	11.9 to 12.9 mm (15/32 to 1/2 inch)
2002 and later	11.4 to 13.4 mm (29/64 to 17/32 inch)
Fuel level	
1987 through 2001	2.5 to 4.5 mm (0.098 to 0.178 inch)
2002 and later	2 to 3 mm (0.080 to 0.120 inch)

Tightening torques

Exhaust pipe-to-cylinder head flange nuts	12 Nm (104 in-lbs)
Heat shield screws	8 Nm (70 in-lbs)
Muffler-to-frame bolt	27 Nm (19 ft-lbs)
Muffler clamp bolt	20 Nm (168 in-lbs)

1   General information

The fuel system consists of the fuel tank, fuel tap, filter screen, carburetor and connecting lines, hose and control cables.

The Mikuni carburetor installed on these vehicles is controlled by two cables, one that lifts the jet needle and another that operates a butterfly-type throttle valve. The two cables are controlled by a single throttle cable, which in turn is operated by a thumb lever on the right handlebar. For cold starting, an enrichment circuit is actuated by a choke knob mounted on the carburetor.

The exhaust system consists of a pipe and a muffler/silencer.

Many of the fuel system service procedures are considered routine maintenance items and for that reason are included in Chapter 1.

2   Fuel tank - removal and installation

Warning: *Gasoline is extremely flammable, so take extra precautions when you work on any part of the fuel system. Don't smoke or allow open flames or bare light bulbs near the work area, and don't work in a garage where a natural gas-type appliance (such as a water heater or clothes dryer) with a pilot light is present. Since gasoline is carcinogenic, wear latex gloves when there's a possibility of being exposed to fuel, and, if you spill any fuel on your skin, rinse it off immediately with soap and water. Mop up any spills immediately and do not store fuel-soaked rags where they could ignite. When you perform any kind of work on the fuel system, wear safety glasses and have a fire extinguisher suitable for a class B type fire (flammable liquids) on hand.*

1   Remove the main switch (see Chapter 9).

2   Remove the front panel, front fender, seat and fuel tank cover (see Chapter 8).

3   Remove the two forward and two rear fuel tank mounting bolts.

4   Lift up the rear of the tank and disconnect the fuel line from the fuel tap.

5   Remove the fuel tank.

6   Before installing the tank, check the condition of the rubber mounting dampers - if they're hardened, cracked, or show any other signs of deterioration, replace them.

7   Installation is the reverse of removal. Don't pinch any control cables or wires.

3   Fuel tank - cleaning and repair

1   The fuel tank is plastic and can't be repaired by traditional welding or brazing techniques. All repairs to the fuel tank should be carried out by a professional who has experience in this critical and potentially dangerous work. Even after cleaning and flushing of the fuel system, explosive fumes can remain and ignite during repair of the tank.

2   If the fuel tank is removed from the vehicle, it should not be placed in an area where sparks or open flames could ignite the fumes coming out of the tank. Be especially careful inside garages where a natural gas-type appliance is located, because the pilot light could cause an explosion.

4   Idle fuel/air mixture adjustment

Refer to illustration 4.3

1   Idle fuel/air mixture on these vehicles is preset at the factory and should not need adjustment unless the carburetor is overhauled or the pilot screw, which controls the mixture adjustment, is replaced.

2   The engine must be properly tuned up before making the adjustment (valve clearances set to specifications, spark plug in good condition and properly gapped).

3   To make an initial adjustment, turn the pilot screw clockwise until

4.3 The pilot screw (arrow) adjusts idle fuel/air mixture

it seats lightly, then back it out the number of turns listed in this Chapter's Specifications **(see illustration)**. **Caution:** *Turn the screw just far enough to seat it lightly. If it's bottomed hard, the screw or its seat may be damaged, which will make accurate mixture adjustments impossible.*

4   Warm up the engine to normal operating temperature. Shut it off and connect a tune-up tachometer, following the tachometer manufacturer's instructions.

5   Restart the engine and compare idle speed to the value listed in the Chapter 1 Specifications. Adjust it if necessary.

5   Carburetor overhaul - general information

1   Poor engine performance, hesitation, hard starting, stalling, flooding and backfiring are all signs that major carburetor maintenance may be required.

2   Keep in mind that many so-called carburetor problems are really not carburetor problems at all, but mechanical problems within the engine or ignition system malfunctions. Try to establish for certain that the carburetor is in need of maintenance before beginning a major overhaul.

3   Check the fuel tap and its strainer screen, the fuel line, the intake manifold clamps and Allen bolts, the O-ring between the intake manifold and cylinder head, the air filter element, the cylinder compression, the spark plug and the ignition timing before assuming that a carburetor overhaul is required. If the vehicle has been unused for more than a month, refer to Chapter 1, drain the float chamber and refill the tank with fresh fuel.

4   Most carburetor problems are caused by dirt particles, varnish and other deposits which build up in and block the fuel and air passages. Also, in time, gaskets and O-rings shrink or deteriorate and cause fuel and air leaks which lead to poor performance.

5   When the carburetor is overhauled, it is generally disassembled completely and the parts are cleaned thoroughly with a carburetor cleaning solvent and dried with filtered, unlubricated compressed air. The fuel and air passages are also blown through with compressed air to force out any dirt that may have been loosened but not removed by the solvent. Once the cleaning process is complete, the carburetor is reassembled using new gaskets, O-rings and, generally, a new inlet needle valve and seat.

6   Before disassembling the carburetors, make sure you have a carburetor rebuild kit (which will include all necessary O-rings and other parts), some carburetor cleaner, a supply of rags, some means of blowing out the carburetor passages and a clean place to work.

6.4 Carburetor nuts (left arrows) and manifold Allen bolts (right arrows)

6 Carburetor - removal and installation

Warning: *Gasoline is extremely flammable, so take extra precautions when you work on any part of the fuel system. Don't smoke or allow open flames or bare light bulbs near the work area, and don't work in a garage where a natural gas-type appliance (such as a water heater or clothes dryer) with a pilot light is present. Since gasoline is carcinogenic, wear latex gloves when there's a possibility of being exposed to fuel, and, if you spill any fuel on your skin, rinse it off immediately with soap and water. Mop up any spills immediately and do not store fuel-soaked rags where they could ignite. When you perform any kind of work on the fuel system, wear safety glasses and have a fire extinguisher suitable for a class B type fire (flammable liquids) on hand.*

Removal

Refer to illustration 6.4

1 Remove the fuel tank (see Section 2).
2 Remove the throttle cable housing (see Section 11).
3 Loosen the clamping bands on the air cleaner duct between the air cleaner housing and the carburetor and remove the duct.
4 Remove the carburetor mounting nuts **(see illustration)** and detach the carburetor from the intake manifold.
5 If you plan to replace the manifold gasket, remove the nuts and separate the intake manifold from the carburetor **(see illustration 6.4)**.
6 Inspect the intake manifold and air cleaner duct for cracks, deterioration or other damage. Inspect the condition of the O-ring between the carburetor and the manifold. If it looks damaged or worn, replace it. Very small defects in the O-ring can affect carburetor performance, so it's a good idea to replace the O-ring whenever it's removed.
7 After the carburetor has been removed, stuff clean rags into the intake port in the cylinder head to prevent the entry of dirt or other objects.

Installation

8 Installation is the reverse of removal.
9 Adjust throttle lever freeplay (see Chapter 1).

7 Carburetors - disassembly, cleaning and inspection

Warning: *Gasoline (petrol) is extremely flammable, so take extra precautions when you work on any part of the fuel system. Don't smoke or allow open flames or bare light bulbs near the work area, and don't work in a garage where a natural gas-type appliance (such as a water heater or clothes dryer) with a pilot light is present. Since gasoline is carcinogenic, wear latex gloves when there's a possibility of being exposed to fuel, and, if you spill any fuel on your skin, rinse it off imme-*

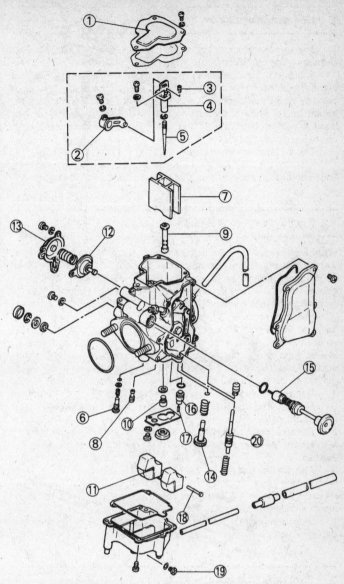

7.2a Warrior carburetor (1987 models) – exploded view

1	Carburetor cap	12	Coasting enricher
2	Throttle lever		diaphragm
3	Spring	13	Coasting enricher cover
4	Needle holder	14	Throttle stop screw
5	Jet needle	15	Starter plunger assembly
6	Pilot screw		(choke)
7	Piston valve	16	Valve seat
8	Pilot jet	17	Valve
9	Main nozzle	18	Float pivot pin
10	Main jet	19	Float chamber drain screw
11	Float	20	Accelerator plunger

diately with soap and water. Mop up any spills immediately and do not store fuel-soaked rags where they could ignite. When you perform any kind of work on the fuel system, wear safety glasses and have a fire extinguisher suitable for a class B type fire (flammable liquids) on hand.

Disassembly

Refer to illustrations 7.2a through 7.2u

1 Remove the carburetor from the machine as described in Section 6. Set it on a clean working surface.
2 Refer to the accompanying illustrations to disassemble the carburetor **(see illustrations)**.

4B

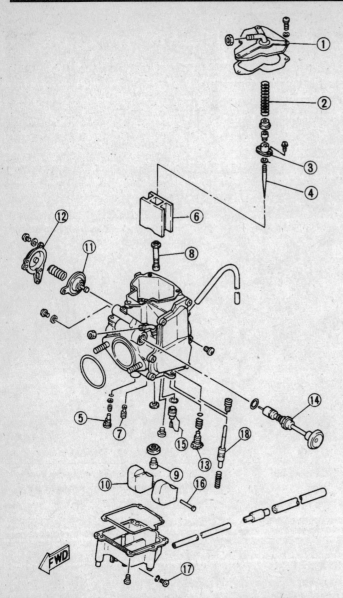

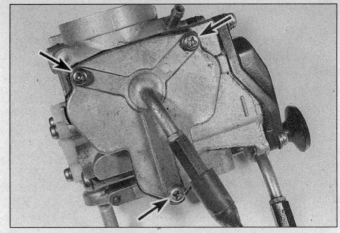

7.2c Remove the screws from the cap (arrows) . . .

7.2d . . . and lift the cap, together with the spring, cable and jet needle components

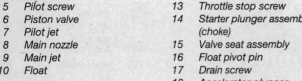

7.2b Warrior carburetor (1988 and later models) – exploded view

1	Carburetor cap	11	Coasting enricher diaphragm
2	Spring	12	Coasting enricher diaphragm cover
3	Needle holder		
4	Jet needle	13	Throttle stop screw
5	Pilot screw	14	Starter plunger assembly (choke)
6	Piston valve		
7	Pilot jet	15	Valve seat assembly
8	Main nozzle	16	Float pivot pin
9	Main jet	17	Drain screw
10	Float	18	Accelerator plunger

Cleaning

Caution: *Use only a carburetor cleaning solution that is safe for use with plastic parts (be sure to read the label on the container).*

3   Submerge the metal components in the carburetor cleaner for approximately thirty minutes (or longer, if the directions recommend it).

4   After the carburetor has soaked long enough for the cleaner to loosen and dissolve most of the varnish and other deposits, use a brush to remove the stubborn deposits. Rinse it again, then dry it with compressed air. Blow out all of the fuel and air passages in the main and upper body. **Caution:** *Never clean the jets or passages with a*

7.2e Remove the cover . . .

piece of wire or a drill bit, as they will be enlarged, causing the fuel and air metering rates to be upset.

Inspection

5   Check the operation of the choke plunger. If it doesn't move smoothly, replace it, along with the return spring. If the plunger O-ring is deteriorated or damaged, replace it.

6   Check the tapered portion of the pilot screw for wear or damage. Replace the pilot screw if necessary.

7   Check the carburetor body, float chamber and top cover for

7.2f . . . rotate the throttle pulley . . .

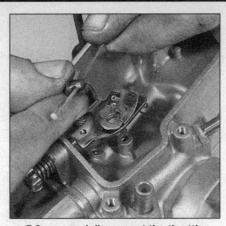

7.2g . . . and disconnect the throttle valve cable

7.2h Remove the screws and take off the float chamber . . .

7.2i . . . remove the main jet ring . . .

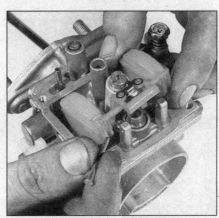

7.2j . . . pull out the float pivot pin . . .

7.2k . . . and unhook the needle valve; bend the tang (arrow) if necessary to change float level

7.2l Remove the retainer screw, lift out the needle valve seat and discard its O-ring

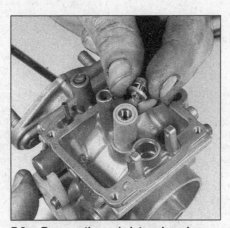

7.2m Remove the main jet and washer . . .

7.2n . . . the pilot jet . . .

cracks, distorted sealing surfaces and other damage. If any defects are found, replace the faulty component, although replacement of the entire carburetor will probably be necessary (check with your parts supplier for the availability of separate components).

8   Check the jet needle for straightness by rolling it on a flat surface (such as a piece of glass). Replace it if it's bent or if the tip is worn.

9   Check the tip of the fuel inlet valve needle. If it has grooves or scratches in it, it must be replaced. Push in on the rod in the other end of the needle, then release it - if it doesn't spring back, replace the valve needle.

10   Check the float chamber O-ring and the drain plug (in the float

chamber). Replace them if they're damaged.

11   Operate the throttle shaft to make sure the throttle butterfly valve opens and closes smoothly. If it doesn't, replace the carburetor.

12   Check the floats for damage. This will usually be apparent by the presence of fuel inside one of the floats. If the floats are damaged, they must be replaced.

13   Check the coasting enricher diaphragm for splits, holes and general deterioration. Holding it up to a light will help to reveal problems of this nature.

14   Check the piston valve in the carburetor body for wear or damage. If it's worn or damaged, replace the carburetor.

4B

7.2o . . . and the pilot screw, together with its spring, washer and O-ring

7.2p Remove the main nozzle . . .

7.2q . . . on installation, the shouldered end is up

7.2r Unscrew the choke knob

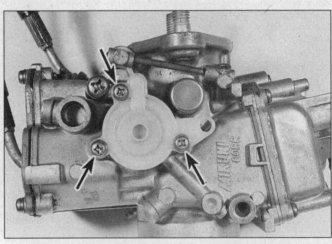

7.2s Remove the coasting enricher cover screws (arrows) . . .

8   Carburetors - reassembly and float height check

Refer to illustration 8.6

1   Reassembly is the reverse of disassembly, with the following additions. **Caution:** *When installing the jets, be careful not to over-tighten them - they're made of soft material and can strip or shear easily.* **Note:** *When reassembling the carburetor, be sure to use the new O-rings, gaskets and other parts supplied in the rebuild kit.*
2   Install the clip on the jet needle if it was removed. Place it in the needle groove listed in this Chapter's Specifications.

3   Install the pilot screw (if removed) along with its spring, washer and O-ring, turning it in until it seats lightly. Now, turn the screw out the number of turns listed in this Chapter's Specifications.
4   Install the coasting enricher valve into the carburetor body. Seat the bead of the diaphragm into the groove in the carburetor body, making sure the diaphragm isn't distorted or kinked **(see illustration 7.2t)**.
5   Reverse the disassembly steps to install the jets.
6   Invert the carburetor. Attach the fuel inlet valve needle to the float. Set the float into position in the carburetor, making sure the valve needle seats correctly. Install the float pivot pin. To check the float height, hold the carburetor so the float hangs down, then tilt it back until the

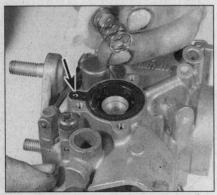

7.2t . . . and lift out the spring and diaphragm; the locating tab (arrow) fits into the notch on installation

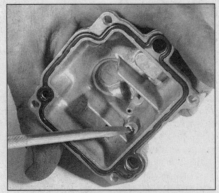

7.2u Unscrew the choke (starter) jet from the bottom of the float chamber

8.6 Hold the carburetor upside down and measure float height from the O-ring surface

valve needle is just seated. Measure the distance from the float chamber gasket surface to the top of the float and compare your measurement to the float height listed in this Chapter's Specifications **(see illustration)**. If it isn't as specified, bend the tang on the float to change it **(see illustration 7.2j)**.

7 Install the O-ring into the groove in the float chamber. Place the float chamber on the carburetor and install the screws, tightening them securely.

9 Fuel level - check and adjustment

Refer to illustration 9.2

Warning: *Gasoline (petrol) is extremely flammable, so take extra precautions when you work on any part of the fuel system. Don't smoke or allow open flames or bare light bulbs near the work area, and don't work in a garage where a natural gas-type appliance (such as a water heater or clothes dryer) with a pilot light is present. Since gasoline is carcinogenic, wear latex gloves when there's a possibility of being exposed to fuel, and, if you spill any fuel on your skin, rinse it off immediately with soap and water. Mop up any spills immediately and do not store fuel-soaked rags where they could ignite. When you perform any kind of work on the fuel system, wear safety glasses and have a fire extinguisher suitable for a class B type fire (flammable liquids) on hand.*

1 Park the vehicle on a level surface and make sure the carburetor is level. If necessary, adjust its position slightly by placing a floor jack under the engine and raising it.

2 Attach Yamaha service tool YM-01312 to the drain fitting on the bottom of the carburetor float bowl. This is a clear plastic tube graduated in millimeters. An alternative is to use a length of clear plastic tubing and an accurate ruler **(see illustration)**. Hold the graduated tube (or the free end of the clear plastic tube) vertically against the float chamber cover.

3 Unscrew the drain screw at the bottom of the float chamber a couple of turns, then start the engine and let it idle - fuel will flow into the tube. Wait for the fuel level to stabilize, then note how far the fuel level is below the line on the float chamber cover.

4 Measure the distance between the line and the top of the fuel in the tube or gauge. This distance is the fuel level.

5 Compare your reading to the value listed in this Chapter's Specifications. If the fuel level is not correct, remove the float chamber cover and bend the float tang up or down as necessary, then recheck the fuel level.

10 Air cleaner housing - removal and installation

Removal

1 Remove the fuel tank (see Section 2).

2 Loosen the clamps and detach the intake duct between the air cleaner housing and the carburetor.

9.2 A ruler and a clear plastic tube like this one can be used to measure fuel level if you don't have the special tool

3 Remove the air cleaner housing bolts. Lift the air cleaner housing out of the frame.

4 Installation is the reverse of removal.

11 Throttle cables - removal, installation and adjustment

1 These vehicles have three throttle cables. One runs from the throttle lever housing on the handlebar to the cable housing. Two run from the cable housing to the carburetor, one to the piston valve and one to the throttle valve.

Removal

Refer to illustrations 11.3, 11.4, 11.5, 11.8a and 11.8b

2 Remove the front fender (see Chapter 8).

3 Remove the fuel tank (see Section 2). Unhook the rubber retainer for the throttle cable housing and move it out of the way **(see illustration)**.

4 Remove the cover screws and lift the cover from the cable housing **(see illustration)**.

5 Loosen the throttle cable at the handlebar adjuster as much as possible. Lift the upper slider (the one that contains the handlebar cable) and detach the cable from it **(see illustration)**. Lift the other slider (with the two carburetor cables) and detach the cables.

6 Remove the sliders and spring.

7 Refer to Section 8 to disconnect the cables from the carburetor.

8 Remove the cover from the throttle housing on the handlebar, remove the lever components and disconnect the cable **(see**

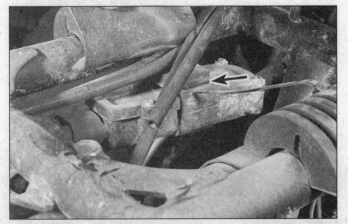

11.3 Detach the retaining band (arrow) from the throttle cable housing and move it aside

11.4 Remove the cover screws and lift off the cover

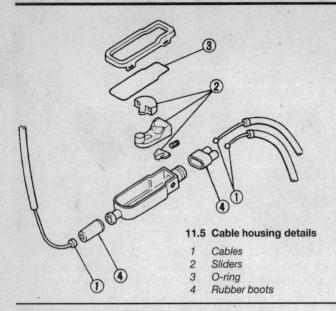

11.5 Cable housing details

1   *Cables*
2   *Sliders*
3   *O-ring*
4   *Rubber boots*

illustrations). Remove the cable, noting how it's routed.
9   If necessary, remove the throttle housing clamp screws and detach the throttle housing from the handlebar **(see illustration 11.3c in Chapter 4A)**.

Installation

10   If the throttle housing was removed, install it on the handlebar and tighten its clamp screws loosely. Position the housing so its protrusion is aligned with the notch in the handlebar spacer **(see illustration 11.8 in Chapter 4A)**. Install the clamp and screws and tighten them securely.
11   Route the cable into place. Make sure it doesn't interfere with any other components and isn't kinked or bent sharply.
12   Lubricate the end of the cable with multi-purpose grease and connect it to the slider in the throttle housing. Do the same with the two carburetor cables.
13   Reverse the disconnection steps to connect the throttle cable to the handlebar lever. Operate the lever and make sure it returns to the idle position by itself under spring pressure. **Warning:** *If the lever does-n't return by itself, find and solve the problem before continuing with installation. A stuck lever can lead to loss of control of the vehicle.*

Adjustment

14   Follow the procedure outlined in Chapter 1, *Throttle operation/grip freeplay - check and adjustment*, to adjust the cable.
15   Turn the handlebar back and forth to make sure the cables don't cause the steering to bind.

11.8b . . . and lift off the cover for access to the lever and cable

11.8a Remove the cover screws (arrows) . . .

16   Once you're sure the cables operate properly, install the covers on the throttle lever housing and cable housing.
17   With the engine idling, turn the handlebar through its full travel (full left lock to full right lock) and note whether idle speed increases. If it does, a cable is routed incorrectly. Correct this dangerous condition before riding the vehicle.
18   Install the fuel tank and front fender.

12   Exhaust system - removal and installation

Refer to illustration 12.1

1   Remove the exhaust pipe holder nuts and slide the holder off the mounting studs **(see illustration)**.
2   If necessary, unbolt the heat shield and remove it from the exhaust pipe.
3   Remove the muffler/silencer mounting bolts.
4   Pull the exhaust system forward, separate the pipe from the cylinder head and remove the system from the machine.
5   Installation is the reverse of removal, with the following additions:

a) *Be sure to install a new gasket at the cylinder head.*
b) *Tighten the muffler mounting bolts, clamp bolts, heat shield bolts and exhaust pipe-to-cylinder head flange nuts to the torques listed in this Chapter's Specifications.*

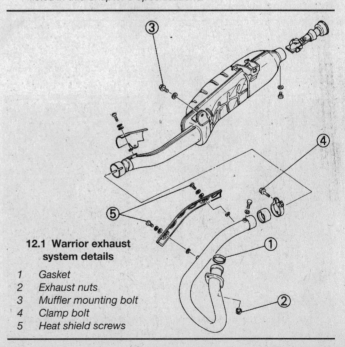

**12.1 Warrior exhaust
system details**

1   *Gasket*
2   *Exhaust nuts*
3   *Muffler mounting bolt*
4   *Clamp bolt*
5   *Heat shield screws*

55555555

Chapter 5
Ignition system

Contents

Specifications

Spark plug cap resistance
  Banshee .... 5 K-ohms
  Warrior .... 10 K-ohms
Ignition coil resistance (at 20-degrees C/68-degrees F)
  Banshee
    Primary resistance .... 0.28 to 0.38 ohms
    Secondary resistance .... 4.7 to 7.1 K-ohms
  Warrior
    1987 through 2001
      Primary resistance .... 0.73 to 0.98 ohms
      Secondary resistance .... 5.06 to 6.85 K-ohms
    2002 and later
      Primary resistance .... 0.018 to 0.28 ohms
      Secondary resistance .... 6.32 to 9.48 K-ohms
CDI magneto resistance (at 20-degrees C/68-degrees F)
  Pick-up coil resistance
    Banshee .... 94 to 140 ohms
    Warrior
      1987 through 1989 .... 180 to 220 ohms
      1990 through 2001 .... 171 to 209 ohms
      2002 and later .... 459 to 561 ohms
  Source coil resistance
    Banshee .... 13.7 to 20.5 ohms
    Warrior .... 270 to 330 ohms

2.5 Unscrew the spark plug cap from the plug wire and measure its resistance with an ohmmeter

2.16 A simple spark gap testing fixture can be made from a block of wood, two nails, a large alligator clip, a screw and a piece of wire

1   General information

These vehicles are equipped with a fully transistorized, breakerless ignition system. The system consists of the following components:

CDI magneto
CDI unit
Battery and fuse (Warrior models only)
Ignition coil
Spark plug(s)
Engine kill (stop) and main (key) switches
Primary and secondary (HT) circuit wiring

The transistorized ignition system functions on the same principle as a DC ignition system with the CDI magneto and CDI unit performing the tasks previously associated with the breaker points and mechanical advance system. As a result, adjustment and maintenance of ignition components is eliminated (with the exception of spark plug replacement). As a safety measure on Banshee models, switches at the carburetor and in the throttle housing are designed to cut off the ignition if a throttle problem occurs and the operator releases the throttle lever.

Because of their nature, the individual ignition system components can be checked but not repaired. If ignition system troubles occur, and the faulty component can be isolated, the only cure for the problem is to replace the part with a new one. Keep in mind that most electrical parts, once purchased, can't be returned. To avoid unnecessary expense, make very sure the faulty component has been positively identified before buying a replacement part.

2   Ignition system - check

Warning: *Because of the very high voltage generated by the ignition system, extreme care should be taken when these checks are performed.*

1   If the ignition system is the suspected cause of poor engine performance or failure to start, a number of checks can be made to isolate the problem.
2   Make sure the ignition kill (stop) switch is in the Run or On position.

Engine will not start

Refer to illustration 2.5

3   Disconnect the spark plug wire(s) from the spark plug(s) (see Chapter 1). Connect the wire to a spare spark plug and lay the plug on the engine with the threads contacting the engine. If necessary, hold the spark plug with an insulated tool. Crank the engine over and make

sure a well-defined, blue spark occurs between the spark plug electrodes. **Warning:** *Don't remove the spark plug from the engine to perform this check - atomized fuel being pumped out of the open spark plug hole could ignite, causing severe injury!*
4   If no spark occurs, the following checks should be made:
5   Unscrew the spark plug cap from the plug wire and check the cap resistance with an ohmmeter **(see illustration)**. If the resistance is infinite, replace it with a new one.
6   Make sure all electrical connectors are clean and tight. Check all wires for shorts, opens and correct installation. The connectors are designed to be weather-tight, but since these vehicles are operated off road, mud and water can be thrown onto the connectors. It's a good idea to clean mud, sand, salt, weeds, etc. from the outside of the connectors, then disconnect each one, clean its terminals and reconnect it.
7   On Warrior models, check the battery voltage with a voltmeter. If the voltage is less than 12-volts, recharge the battery.
8   On Warrior models, check the main fuse and fuse connections (see Chapter 9). If the fuse is blown, replace it; if the connections are loose or corroded, clean or repair them.
9   Check the ignition coil primary and secondary resistance (see Section 3).
10   Check the CDI magneto pick-up coil and source coil resistance (see Section 4).
11   Check the ignition switch operation (see Chapter 9).
12   Check the kill switch operation (see Chapter 9).
13   On Banshee models, check the ignition cutoff system operation (see Chapter 9).
14   If the preceding checks produce positive results but there is still no spark at the plug, refer to Section 5 for information on the CDI unit.

Engine starts but misfires

Refer to illustration 2.16

15   If the engine starts but misfires, make the following checks before deciding that the ignition system is at fault.
16   The ignition system must be able to produce a spark across a six millimeter (1/4-inch) gap (minimum). A simple test fixture **(see illustration)** can be constructed to make sure the minimum spark gap can be jumped. Make sure the fixture electrodes are positioned six millimeters apart.
17   Connect one of the spark plug wires to the protruding test fixture electrode, then attach the fixture's alligator clip to a good engine ground.
18   Crank the engine over with the key in the On position and see if well-defined, blue sparks occur between the test fixture electrodes. If so, the ignition coil is functioning properly. If the spark will not jump the gap, or if it is weak (orange colored), refer to Steps 5 through 11 of this Section and perform the component checks described.

**3.1a Ignition system component
locations (Banshee models)**

1   Ignition coil
2   Main switch
3   Spark plug
4   CDI magneto
5   CDI unit
6   CDI magneto pick-up coil
7   Throttle control unit
8   Throttle lever switch
9   Left carburetor switch
10 Right carburetor switch
11 Kill switch

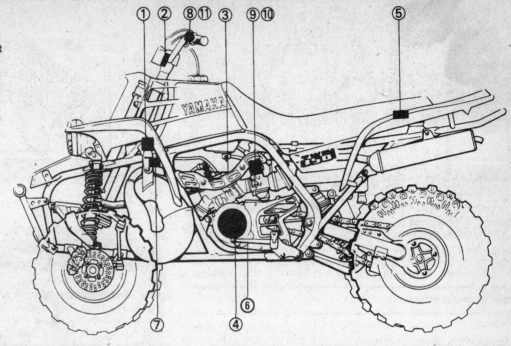

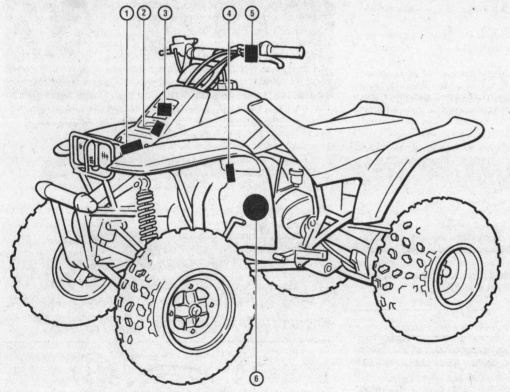

**3.1b Ignition system component
locations (Warrior models)**

1   CDI unit
2   Ignition coil
3   Main switch
4   Spark plug
5   Kill switch
6   CDI magneto

5

3   Ignition coil - check and replacement

Check

Refer to illustrations 3.1a, 3.1b, 3.4a and 3.4b

1   To access the coil on Banshee models, remove the fuel tank (see Chapter 4) and the front fender (see Chapter 8); the coil **(see illustration)** is located right behind the steering shaft. To get to the coil on Warrior models, remove the front panel (see Chapter 8); the coil **(see illustration)** is located behind this panel.

2   Inspect the coil for cracks and other obvious damage. If the coil is obviously damaged, replace it.
3   Unplug the primary circuit electrical connectors from the coil and remove the spark plug wire(s) from the spark plug(s). Mark the locations of all wires before disconnecting them.
4   Check the coil primary resistance with an ohmmeter. On Banshee models, attach the ohmmeter leads to the coil primary terminals **(see illustration)**. On Warrior models, attach one ohmmeter lead to the primary terminals and the other ohmmeter lead to the coil base **(see illustration)**.

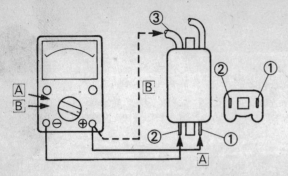

3.4a Checking the ignition coil resistance (Banshee models)

1   *Primary terminal and primary connector terminal (orange wire)*
2   *Primary terminal and primary connector terminal (black wire)*
3   *Spark plug wire*
A   *Measure primary resistance between these terminals*
B   *Measure secondary resistance between these terminals*

5   Place the ohmmeter selector switch in the Rx1 position and compare the measured resistance to the value listed in this Chapter's Specifications.
6   If the coil primary resistance is as specified, check the coil secondary resistance by disconnecting the meter leads and attaching them between the spark plug wire terminal and the primary terminal (see illustration 3.4a or 3.4b). (On Banshee models, check secondary resistance at both caps; you can attach the other lead to either primary terminal.)
7   Place the ohmmeter selector switch in the Rx1000 position and compare the measured resistance to the values listed in this Chapter's Specifications.
8   If the primary and secondary resistances are not as specified, unscrew the spark plug cap from the plug wire and check the resistance between the primary terminal and the end of the spark plug wire. If it is now within specifications, the spark plug cap is bad. If it's still not as specified, replace the coil.

Replacement

9   Disconnect the spark plug wire(s) from the plug(s) and unplug the coil primary circuit electrical connector(s), if you haven't already done so.
10   Support the coil with one hand and remove the coil mounting bolts, then lift the coil out. On Warrior models, note that one mounting bolt secures a coil primary wire.
11   Installation is the reverse of removal.

---

4   CDI magneto - check

Check

Refer to illustration 4.1

1   Trace the CDI wiring harness, which exits the engine cover on the left side of the vehicle, to the CDI electrical connector(s) on the left side of the frame (see illustration). Disconnect the connector(s).
2   On Banshee models, the CDI magneto wires are red, green, white/green and white/red and there's one connector; on Warrior models, the wires are red, gray, blue, yellow, green and brown, and there are two connectors (one for the pick-up coils, one for the source coil). Note: For the following tests, connect the ohmmeter to the CDI side of the connector (the terminals for the wires leading back to the engine), not the wiring harness side of the connector.

Banshee models

Refer to illustration 4.3

3   Connect the ohmmeter between the connector terminals for the white/green and white/red wires (see illustration). These are the pick-up coil wires. Compare your measurement with the value listed in this Chapter's Specifications.

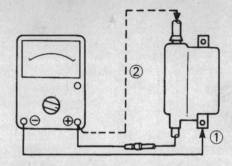

3.4b Checking the ignition coil resistance (Warrior models)

1   *Primary resistance*
2   *Secondary resistance*

4.1 Follow the wiring harness from the left crankcase cover to the CDI unit connector (arrow) and check its wire colors (Banshee shown)

4   Connect the ohmmeter between the connector terminals for the red and green wires. These are the source coil wires. Compare your measurement with the value listed in this Chapter's Specifications.

Warrior models

Refer to illustration 4.5

5   Connect the ohmmeter between the connector terminals for the yellow wire and the green wire, and between the connector terminals for the gray wire and the blue wire (see illustration). These are the pick-up coil wires. Compare your readings with the value listed in this Chapter's Specifications.
6   Connect the ohmmeter between the connector terminals for the brown wire and the red wire. These are the source coil wires. Compare the readings with the value listed in this Chapter's Specifications.

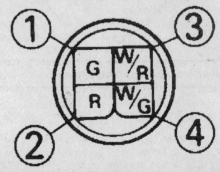

4.3 Terminal guide for CDI magneto connector (Banshee models)

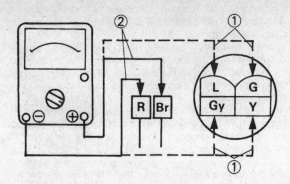

4.5 Terminal guide for CDI magneto connector (Warrior models)

1   *Pick-up coil connector*
2   *Source coil connector*

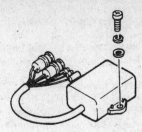

5.2 The Warrior CDI unit is under the front panel

All models

7   If the indicated resistance is incorrect for the pick-up coil or for the source coil on either model, replace the defective component (Banshee models, see "CDI Magneto - component replacement" in Chapter 9; Warrior models, see "Alternator charging coils and rotor - check and replacement" in Chapter 9).

5   CDI unit - check and replacement

Check

1   The CDI unit can only be diagnosed by a process of elimination, i.e. if all other possible causes have been checked and verified to be operating correctly, the CDI unit is defective. The CDI unit is expensive, and cannot be returned once you have purchased it, so have a Yamaha dealer test the CDI unit before you buy a new one.

Replacement

Refer to illustrations 5.2 and 5.3

2   On Banshee models, remove the seat; on Warrior models, remove the front panel (see Chapter 8) **(see illustration)**.
3   Unplug the electrical connectors to the CDI unit and remove the retaining bolts **(see illustration)**. Remove the CDI unit.
4   Installation is the reverse of removal.

6   Ignition timing - general information and check

General information

1   Ignition timing need not be checked unless you're troubleshooting a problem such as loss of power. The ignition timing cannot be adjusted and none of the ignition system parts is subject to mechanical wear, so there's no need for regular checks.
2   The ignition timing is checked with the engine running at the idle speed listed in the Chapter 1 Specifications. Inexpensive neon timing lights should be adequate in theory, but in practice may produce such dim pulses that the timing marks are hard to see. If possible, one of the more precise xenon timing lights should be used, powered by an external source of the appropriate voltage. Note: Don't use the vehicle battery on Warrior models; stray pulses within the electrical system can produce an incorrect reading.

Check

Banshee models

Refer to illustration 6.6

3   Remove the left crankcase cover (see "CDI magneto - removal and installation" in Chapter 9).

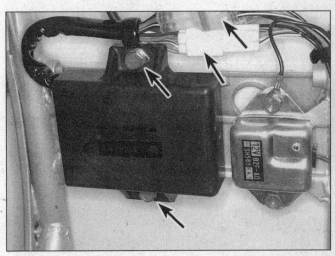

5.3 Disconnect the CDI unit electrical connectors (arrows) and remove the mounting bolts (arrows) (Banshee shown)

4   Hook up a timing light in accordance with the manufacturer's instructions.
5   Warm up the engine until it's running at the idle speed listed in the Chapter 1 Specifications.
6   With the timing light on and the engine running at the specified idle speed, verify that the stationary pointer on the crankcase is within the firing range indicated on the flywheel **(see illustration)**.
7   If the stationary point is not within the firing range indicated on the flywheel, inspect the flywheel and pick-up assembly (see "CDI magneto - removal and installation" in Chapter 9). Make sure they're both tight and undamaged.
8   Install the left crankcase cover (see "CDI magneto - removal and installation" in Chapter 9).

5

6.6 The index mark on the crankcase (upper arrow) should align with the firing mark on the CDI magneto rotor (lower arrow)

Warrior models

9   Warm the engine to normal operating temperature, make sure the transmission is in Neutral, then shut the engine off.

10   Remove the timing hole plug **(see illustration 27.7 in Chapter 1)**.

11   Connect the timing light and a tune-up tachometer to the engine, following manufacturer's instructions.

12   Start the engine. Make sure it idles at the speed listed in the Chapter 1 Specifications. Adjust if necessary.

13   Point the timing light into the timing window. At idle, notch at the top of the timing window should be between the two lines on either side of the F mark on the alternator rotor **(see illustration 27.8 in Chapter 1)**.

14   If the timing is incorrect and all other ignition components have tested as good, the CDI unit may be defective. Have it tested by a Yamaha dealer.

15   When the check is complete, grease the timing hole plug O-ring, then install the O-ring and plug and disconnect the test equipment.

7   RPM limiter – description and check

1   1997 and later models include an engine speed (RPM) limiter that causes the engine to misfire if it's revved above 2300 rpm with the parking brake engaged. The system consists of control circuitry inside the CDI unit and a parking brake switch. This reminds the rider that the parking brake is engaged.

2   To check the system, set the parking brake, place the transmission in Neutral and rev the engine. If it starts to misfire at 2300 rpm, the system is working. If you aren't sure about the engine speed, connect a tachometer to the spark plug wire, following the tachometer manufacturer's instructions.

3   If the revs above 2300 rpm with the parking brake on, follow the wiring harness from the parking brake switch on the right handlebar to the connector and disconnect it (the wires are black and green/yellow). Connect an ohmmeter to the switch side of the connector and set it to Rx1 or ohms x 1.

4   With the parking brake engaged, the ohmmeter should indicate continuity (little or no resistance). With the parking brake released, the ohmmeter should indicate no continuity (infinite resistance). If the switch doesn't perform as described, replace it.

5   If the switch does work properly and the engine revs over 2300 rpm with the parking brake on, check the wiring from the parking brake switch to the CDI unit for breaks or bad connections.

6   If the switch and wiring are good, the problem may be in the CDI unit's internal circuitry. Since the CDI unit can't be returned once purchased, have the system checked by a Yamaha dealer or other qualified ATV shop before replacing it.

Chapter 6
Steering, suspension and final drive

Contents

Specifications

Tie-rod balljoint spacing (distance between balljoint centerlines)
Banshee .... 361 mm (14.2 inches)
Warrior .... 325 mm (12.8 inches)
Rear spring preload (installed length)
Banshee
Standard .... 218.5 mm (8.6 inches)
Minimum (hardest setting) .... 210.5 mm (8.3 inches)
Maximum (softest setting)... 225.5 mm (8.8 inches)
Warrior
Standard .... 227.5 mm (8.96 inches)
Minimum (hardest setting) .... 220.5 mm (8.68 inches)
Maximum (softest setting)... 235.5 mm (9.27 inches)
Rear axle runout limit .... 1.5 mm (0.06 inch)
Wheel rim runout limit (vertical and lateral)..................... 2.0 mm (0.008 inch)

Torque specifications

Steering
Handlebar bracket bolts .... 20 Nm (14 ft-lbs)
Steering shaft nut .... 30 Nm (22 ft-lbs)
Steering shaft (upper) bearing bolts .... 23 Nm (17 ft-lbs)
Steering knuckle arm to knuckle bolts .... 38 Nm (27 ft-lbs)
Tie-rod nuts .... 25 Nm (18 ft-lbs)
Tie-rod locknuts... 30 Nm (22 ft-lbs)

Front suspension
Front shock absorber bolts and nuts .... 45 Nm (32 ft-lbs)
Balljoint castle nuts... 25 Nm (18 ft-lbs)
Balljoints (Warrior)... 85 Nm (61 ft-lbs)
Front suspension arm pivot bolts (Warrior) .... 45 Nm (32 ft-lbs)
Front suspension arm pivot bolt nuts (Banshee) .... 30 Nm (22 ft-lbs)

6

Torque specifications (continued)

Rear suspension

Rear shock absorber
    Upper shock-to-frame bracket bolt
        Banshee .... 30 Nm (22 ft-lbs
        Warrior .... 30 Nm (23 ft-lbs)
    Lower shock-to-relay arm bolt
        Banshee .... 30 Nm (22 ft-lbs)
        Warrior .... 32 Nm (23 ft-lbs)
Rear axle ring nuts*
    Inner nut initial torque
        Banshee .... 130 Nm (94 ft-lbs)
        Warrior .... 55 Nm (40 ft-lbs)
    Outer nut torque .... 190 Nm (140 ft-lbs)
    Inner nut final torque .... 240 Nm (170 ft-lbs)
Relay arm and connecting rod
    Banshee
        Relay arm-to-frame .... 30 Nm (22 ft-lbs)
        Relay arm-to-connecting rod .... 30 Nm (22 ft-lbs)
        Connecting rod-to-swingarm bolt .... 30 Nm (22 ft-lbs)
    Warrior
        Relay arm-to-frame .... 48 Nm (35 ft-lbs)
        Relay arm-to-connecting rod .... 33 Nm (23 ft-lbs)
        Connecting rod-to-swingarm bolt .... 48 Nm (35 ft-lbs)
Swingarm pivot bolt and nut .... 85 Nm (61 ft-lbs)

Final drive

Front sprocket nut
    Banshee .... 80 Nm (58 ft-lbs)
    Warrior... 75 Nm (54 ft-lbs)
Rear sprocket nuts .... 60 Nm (43 t-lbs)

Apply non-permanent thread locking agent to the threads.

1 General information

The front suspension consists of upper and lower control arms on each side of the vehicle, supported by a shock absorber with a concentric coil spring.

The steering system consists of knuckles mounted at the outer ends of the front suspension and connected to a steering shaft by tie-rods. The steering shaft is turned by a one-piece handlebar.

The rear suspension on all models consists of a single shock absorber with concentric coil spring, progressive linkage and a steel swingarm. Final drive is by a chain and sprockets.

2 Handlebar - removal and installation

Removing the handlebar to service other components

Refer to illustration 2.5

1   If you're removing the handlebar simply to gain access to the steering shaft, it's not necessary to remove the clutch lever bracket, the left switch housing, the throttle cable housing or the front brake master cylinder.

2   Pull the fuel tank breather hose out of the hole in the handlebar trim cover (the plastic cover in the center that houses the main switch on Banshee models and the indicator lights on Warrior models), if applicable.

3   To remove the handlebar cover on Banshee models, remove the two mounting screws and pull off the cover (see "Ignition main (key) switch - check and replacement" in Chapter 9). To remove the cover

on Warrior models, simply pull it straight up (see "Indicator light system - check and replacement" in Chapter 9). To remove the cover, you'll have to disconnect any electrical connectors, some of which might be located under the radiator cover (Banshee models) or behind the front body panel (Warrior models), in which case you'll need to remove the cover or panel (see Chapter 8).

4   Look for a punch mark on the front of each handlebar bracket. If you can't find the factory punch marks, make your own marks to ensure that the brackets are correctly oriented when they're reinstalled.

5   Remove the handlebar bracket bolts **(see illustration)**, remove the upper bracket halves, then lift the handlebar off the lower bracket halves. **Caution:** *Support the handlebar assembly with a piece of wire or rope; allowing it to hang free will damage the cables, hoses and wiring.*

6   Installation is the reverse of removal. Make sure that the factory punch marks (or the ones you made prior to disassembly) face to the front. Tighten the handlebar bracket bolts to the torque listed in this Chapter's Specifications.

Replacing the handlebar

7   If you're replacing the handlebar, remove all cable ties, then remove the clutch lever bracket (see "Clutch cable and lever - removal and installation" in Chapter 2A), the left switch housing (see "Handlebar switch housing - removal and installation" in Chapter 9), the throttle cable housing **(see illustration 11.3c in Chapter 4A)** and the front brake master cylinder (see "Front brake master cylinder - removal, overhaul and installation" in Chapter 8).

8   Follow Steps 2 through 5 above.

9   Installation is the reverse of removal. Tighten the handlebar bracket bolts to the torque listed in this Chapter's Specifications.

2.5 Mark the front side of each bracket, then remove the bracket bolts and lift off the bracket and handlebar

3 Steering shaft - removal, inspection and installation

Removal

Refer to illustrations 3.5, 3.7 and 3.9

1   Remove the handlebar and brackets (see Section 2).
2   On Banshee models, remove the radiator cover, the fuel tank cover and the front fender (see Chapter 8).
3   On Banshee models, remove the radiator (see Chapter 3).
4   On Warrior models, remove the front panel (see Chapter 8).
5   Straighten the lockwasher tabs and remove the two nuts, the lockwasher, the washer and the steering shaft bearing halves **(see illustration)**.

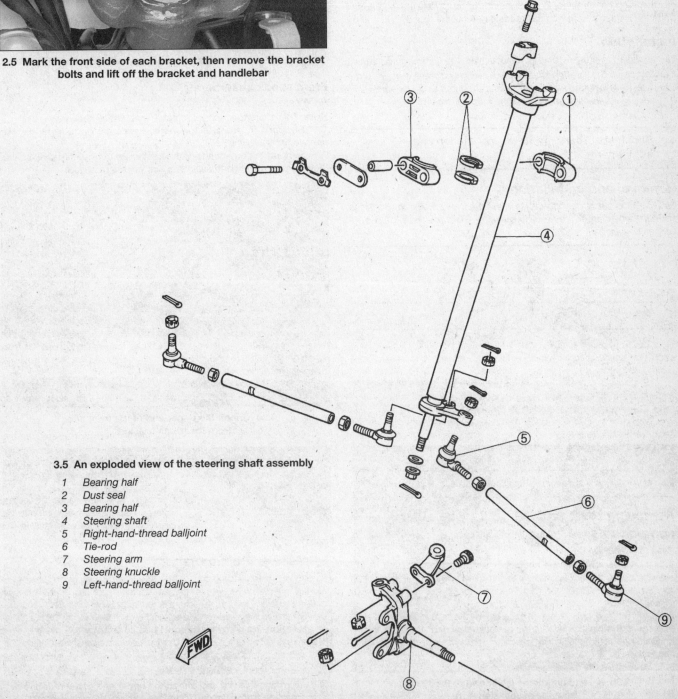

3.5 An exploded view of the steering shaft assembly

1   *Bearing half*
2   *Dust seal*
3   *Bearing half*
4   *Steering shaft*
5   *Right-hand-thread balljoint*
6   *Tie-rod*
7   *Steering arm*
8   *Steering knuckle*
9   *Left-hand-thread balljoint*

6   Disconnect the inner ends of the tie-rods from the steering shaft (see Section 5).

7   Remove the cotter pin and nut from the bottom of the steering shaft **(see illustration)**.

8   Remove the steering shaft from the vehicle.

9   Pry out the seals, unscrew the retainer with a hex bit and remove the lower bearing from the frame **(see illustration)**.

Inspection

10   Clean all the parts with solvent and dry them thoroughly, using compressed air, if available.

11   Inspect the steering shaft bearings and seals for wear, deterioration or damage. Replace them if there's any doubt about their condition.

12   Inspect the steering shaft and its integral steering arm for bending or other signs of damage. Do not attempt to repair any steering components. Replace them with new parts if defects are found.

Installation

13   Installation is the reverse of removal, with the following additions:

  a) *Lubricate the steering shaft upper bearing and seals with grease.*

  b) *Use new locknuts and cotter pins and tighten all fasteners to the torque values listed in this Chapter's Specifications.*

---

4   Shock absorbers - removal, installation and adjustment

Removal and installation

Warning: *Do not attempt to disassemble these shock absorbers. They are nitrogen-charged under high pressure. Replace the shocks and springs as a unit.*

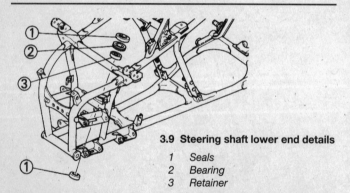

3.9 Steering shaft lower end details

  1   *Seals*
  2   *Bearing*
  3   *Retainer*

4.3b . . . and unbolt the lower end of the shock from the suspension arm

3.7 To detach the lower end of the steering shaft from the frame, remove this cotter pin and nut (arrow)

Front shock absorbers

Refer to illustrations 4.3a and 4.3b

Note: *This procedure applies to either front shock absorber.*

1   Support the front of the vehicle securely on jackstands and remove the front wheels.

2   Support the outer ends of the front lower arms with jackstands so they won't drop when the shock absorbers are removed.

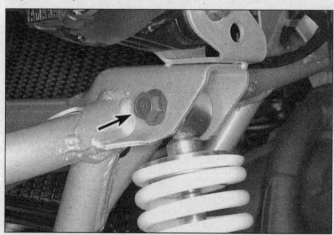

4.3a Unbolt the upper end of the front shock from the frame bracket . . .

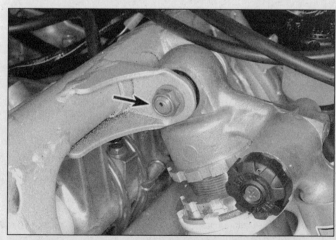

4.8a Remove this nut and unbolt the upper end of the rear shock from the frame (arrow) (Banshee shown, Warrior similar)

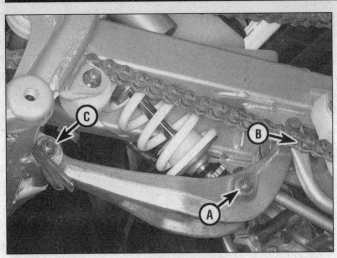

4.8b Remove the nut and bolt and separate the lower end of the shock from the relay arm

- A   Shock absorber nut and bolt
- B   Relay arm to tie-rod nut and bolt (behind chain)
- C   Relay rod to frame nut and bolt

3   Remove the nuts and bolts that attach the upper end of the shock to the frame bracket and the lower end to the bracket on the lower control arm bracket **(see illustrations)**. Separate the shock from the frame bracket and from the control arm bracket and lift it out.

4   Inspect the shock absorber for signs of wear or damage such as oil leaks, bending, a weak spring and worn bushings. Replace both shock absorbers as a pair if any problems are found.

5   Installation is the reverse of the removal steps. Tighten the nuts and bolts to the torque listed in this Chapter's Specifications.

Rear shock absorber

Refer to illustrations 4.8a, 4.8b, 4.8c and 4.8d

6   Jack up the rear end of the vehicle and support it securely on jackstands.

7   On Warrior models, loosen the clamp screws and remove the remote reservoir from the clamps. Do NOT disconnect the hose that connects the remote reservoir to the rear shock.

8   Remove the mounting bolt and nut at the top of the shock **(see illustration)**, then remove the nut, washer, lower shock mounting bolt and assorted spacers, bushings, etc. at the lower end of the shock **(see illustrations)**. To ensure that the various washers, spacers, bushings, etc. are installed in the correct sequence and relationship to one another, it's a good idea to immediately install all parts on the lower shock mounting bolt in the order in which they were removed. Separate the shock from the upper mounting bracket and from the relay arm and lift it out of the vehicle.

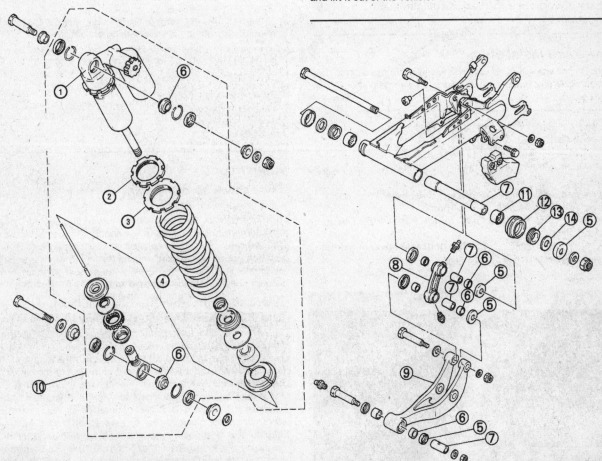

4.8c Rear suspension (Banshee) – exploded view

1	Compression damping adjuster knob	6	Bushing	11	Bearing
2	Spring preload adjuster locknut	7	Collar	12	Chain guide
3	Spring preload adjuster nut	8	Connecting rod	13	Oil seal
4	Rebound damping adjuster nut	9	Relay arm	14	Washer
5	Thrust cover	10	Rear shock absorber assembly		

6

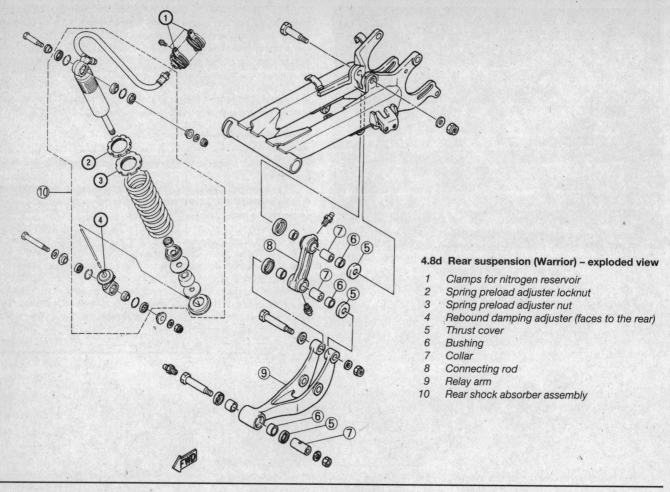

4.8d Rear suspension (Warrior) – exploded view

1   *Clamps for nitrogen reservoir*
2   *Spring preload adjuster locknut*
3   *Spring preload adjuster nut*
4   *Rebound damping adjuster (faces to the rear)*
5   *Thrust cover*
6   *Bushing*
7   *Collar*
8   *Connecting rod*
9   *Relay arm*
10 *Rear shock absorber assembly*

9   Installation is the reverse of the removal steps, with the following additions:

  a) *Make sure that you install all parts, in order, when reattaching the lower end of the shock to the relay arm.*
  b) *Tighten the nut and bolt to the torque listed in this Chapter's Specifications.*
  c) *Install a thrust washer on each side of the pivot pin.*
  d) *Use a new cotter pin in the pivot pin.*

4.10 Here's a front spring preload adjuster ring (left arrow) and lug (right arrow); A is the softest position and E is the hardest

Adjustment

Front shock absorbers

Refer to illustration 4.10

10   Front shock absorber spring preload is adjusted by turning the adjuster ring at the bottom of the shock with a spanner wrench **(see illustration)**. (The spanner should be in your machine's toolkit; if not, you can obtain one at any Yamaha dealer.) The adjuster ring has five positions: A, B, C, D and E. A is the softest position and E is the stiffest; position B is the standard setting.

Rear shock absorber (Banshee models)

Refer to illustrations 4.12a, 4.12b, 4.12c and 4.13

11   The rear shock absorber is fully adjustable for spring preload, compression damping and rebound damping.

12   Spring preload is adjusted by changing the length of the spring. Loosen the preload adjuster locknut at the top of the shock, then turn the adjuster nut with a spanner wrench **(see illustrations)**. (The spanner should be in your machine's toolkit; if not, you can obtain one at any Yamaha dealer.) Turn the adjuster clockwise to reduce spring length or counterclockwise to increase spring length. Each turn of the adjuster nut changes spring length by 1.5 mm (0.06 inch). Alter the spring length in increments of 3 mm (0.12 inch), then measure the spring length **(see illustration)** and compare your measurement to the typical spring lengths listed in this Chapter's Specifications. **Caution:** *Do NOT attempt to turn the spring preload adjuster beyond the maximum or minimum setting.* Tighten the locknut when you're done.

13   Rebound damping force is adjusted by turning the adjuster at the bottom of the shock **(see illustration)**. Turning the adjuster clockwise increases the rebound damping force (slower rebound); turning the adjuster counterclockwise decreases the rebound damping force (faster rebound). The rebound damping adjuster has a range of 20 clicks. To set

4.12a Here's a rear spring preload adjuster locknut (1) and adjusting nut (2); the compression damping adjuster (3) is on Banshee models only

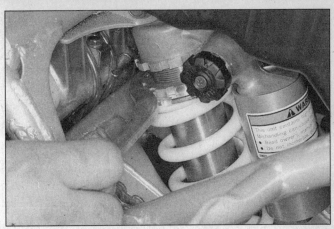

4.12b You need a special spanner wrench to turn the preload adjuster nut (it should be in your toolkit)

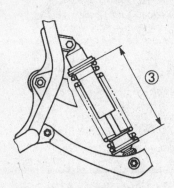

4.12c Measure the length of the spring and compare your measurement to the spring lengths listed in this Chapter's Specifications

4.13 The Banshee rebound damping adjuster ring is at the lower end of the shock

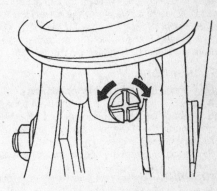

4.17 The Warrior rebound damping adjuster knob is at the lower end of the shock

the rebound damping adjuster to its standard position, turn it all the way in, then back it out 12 clicks. **Caution:** *Do NOT attempt to turn the rebound adjuster beyond the maximum or minimum setting.*

14 Compression damping force is adjusted by turning the knob **(see illustration 4.12a)** on the nitrogen reservoir. Turning the knob clockwise increases the compression damping force; turning the knob counterclockwise decreases it. The compression damping adjuster

knob has a range of 20 clicks. To set the compression damping adjuster knob to its standard position, back it out all the way, then turn it in 11 clicks. **Caution:** *Do NOT attempt to turn the compression damping adjuster knob beyond the maximum or minimum setting.*

Rear shock absorber (Warrior models)
Refer to illustration 4.17

15 The rear shock absorber is adjustable for spring preload and rebound damping.
16 To adjust spring preload, refer to Step 12 above.
17 Rebound damping force is adjusted by turning the adjuster at the bottom of the shock **(see illustration)**. Turning the adjuster clockwise increases the rebound damping force (slower rebound damping); turning the adjuster counterclockwise decreases the rebound damping force (faster rebound damping). The rebound damping adjuster has a range of 20 clicks. To set the rebound damping adjuster to its standard position, turn it all the way in, then back it out 12 clicks. **Caution:** *Do NOT attempt to turn the rebound adjuster beyond the maximum or minimum setting.*

5 Tie-rods - removal, inspection and installation

Removal
Refer to illustrations 5.2 and 5.3

1 If both of the tie-rods are to be removed, mark them "Left" and "Right" so they're not accidentally switched during reassembly.
2 Remove the cotter pin from the nut at the outer end of the tie-rod and undo the nut **(see illustration)**.

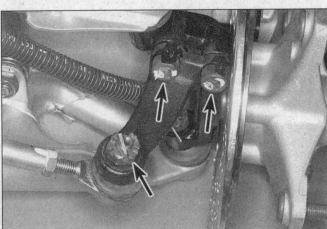

5.2 The steering arm is attached to the tie-rod by a nut and cotter pin (lower arrow) and to the steering knuckle by bolts (upper arrows)

6

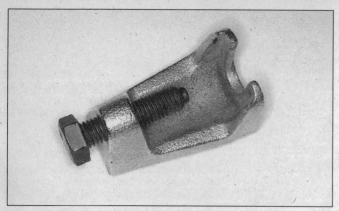

**5.3 This automotive tie-rod puller will work on
tie-rod ends and balljoints**

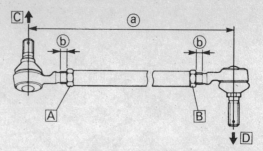

5.7 Tie-rod details

A   Tie-rod locknut   D   Outer stud
B   Tie-rod locknut   a   Tie-rod length
C   Inner stud   b   Exposed threads (must
                                 be the same length)

3   Separate the tie-rod stud from the knuckle with a tie rod puller or "pickle fork" balljoint separator **(see illustration). Caution:** *It's very easy to damage the rubber boot on the tie-rod with a pickle fork separator. If you're going to use the tie-rod again, it's best to use another type of tool.*
4   Repeat Steps 1 and 2 to disconnect the inner end of the tie rod from the steering shaft **(see illustration 3.5)**.

Inspection

5   Check the tie-rod shaft for bending or other damage and replace it if any problems are found. Don't try to straighten the shaft.
6   Check the tie-rod balljoint boots for cracks or deterioration. Twist and rotate the threaded studs. They should move easily, without roughness or looseness. If a boot or stud show any problems, unscrew the tie-rod end from the tie-rod and install a new one.

Installation

Refer to illustration 5.7
7   Thread the tie-rod ends onto the tie-rods until the length between stud centerlines is as listed in this Chapter's Specifications **(see illustration)**. The length of exposed threads on each end of the tie-rod must be even. The flat on the tie-rod that's used to adjust toe-in goes at the outer end of the tie-rod.
8   The remainder of installation is the reverse of the removal steps, with the following additions:

a) Use new cotter pins and bend them to hold the nuts securely.
b) Check front wheel toe-in and adjust as necessary (see Chapter 1).

6   Steering knuckles - removal, inspection, and installation

Removal

Refer to illustration 6.5
1   Jack up the front end of the vehicle and support it securely on jackstands. Remove the front wheels.
2   Disconnect the outer end of the tie-rod from the steering knuckle, or unbolt the steering arm from the knuckle **(see illustration 5.2)**.
3   Remove the outer disc cover, the front brake caliper, the wheel hub and the inner disc cover (see Chapter 7).
4   Remove the front shock absorber (see Section 4).
5   Remove the cotter pin and nut from the upper and lower balljoint studs **(see illustration)**.
6   Separating the balljoints from the steering knuckle requires a separator tool. Automotive tie-rod separator tools are suitable (try it for fit before you buy it, if possible) and can be rented from tool yards or purchased inexpensively **(see illustration 5.3)**.
7   If balljoint separation proves difficult, the knuckle and suspension arms can be removed as a single assembly, then taken to a Yamaha dealer for balljoint removal.

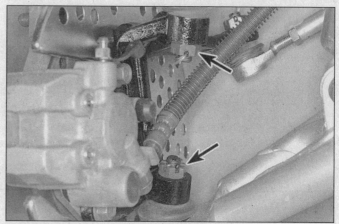

**6.5 The upper and lower balljoints are secured by castle
nuts and cotter pins (arrows)**

Inspection

8   Inspect the knuckle carefully for cracks, bending or other damage. Replace it if any problems are found. If the vehicle has been in a collision or has been bottomed hard, it's a good idea to have the knuckle magnafluxed by a machine shop to check for hidden cracks.

Installation

9   Installation is the reverse of removal, with the following addition: Use new cotter pins and tighten the nuts to the torque listed in this Chapter's Specifications.

7   Suspension arms and balljoints - removal, inspection and installation

Suspension arms

Removal

Refer to illustrations 7.4a through 7.4e
1   Securely block both rear wheels so the vehicle won't roll. Loosen the front wheel nuts with the tires still on the ground, then jack up the front end, support it securely on jackstands and remove the front wheels.
2   On Banshee models, remove the front bumper (see Chapter 8). Remove the front fender (see Chapter 8) and expansion chamber (see Chapter 4) from the side you're working on.
3   Remove the steering knuckle (see Section 6). If you're removing an upper arm, disengage the brake hose from the arm **(see illustration 14.2a in Chapter 7)**.
4   Remove the pivot bolts and nuts and remove the suspension arm **(see illustrations)**.

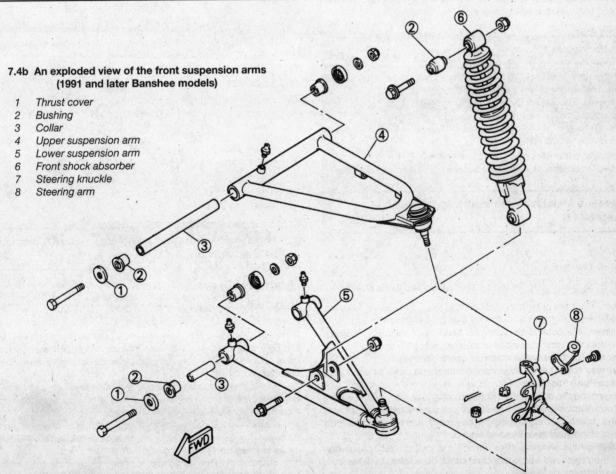

7.4a Front suspension (1987 through 1990 Banshee) – exploded view

1   Thrust cover
2   Bushing
3   Collar
4   Upper suspension arm
5   Lower suspension arm
6   Front shock absorber
7   Steering knuckle
8   Steering arm

7.4b An exploded view of the front suspension arms (1991 and later Banshee models)

1   Thrust cover
2   Bushing
3   Collar
4   Upper suspension arm
5   Lower suspension arm
6   Front shock absorber
7   Steering knuckle
8   Steering arm

FWD

6

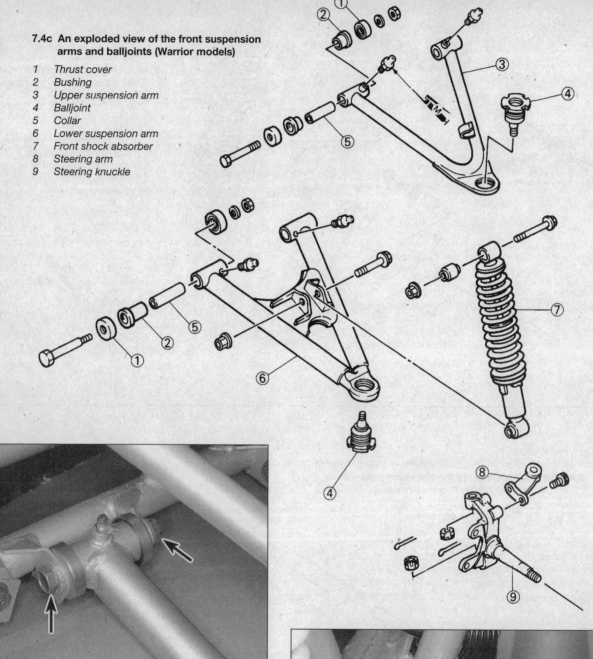

7.4c An exploded view of the front suspension arms and balljoints (Warrior models)

1   Thrust cover
2   Bushing
3   Upper suspension arm
4   Balljoint
5   Collar
6   Lower suspension arm
7   Front shock absorber
8   Steering arm
9   Steering knuckle

7.4d Each lower suspension arm pivots on two bolts like this

Inspection

5   Inspect the suspension arm(s) for bending, cracks or corrosion. Replace damaged parts. Don't attempt to straighten them.
6   Inspect all rubber bushings for cracks or deterioration. Check the inner collars on the lower suspension arms for damage or corrosion. Inspect the pivot bolts for wear as well. Replace the bushings and pivot bolts if they're worn or deteriorated.
7   Check the balljoint boot for cracks or deterioration. Twist and rotate the threaded stud. It should move easily, without roughness or looseness. On Banshees, the balljoints can't be replaced separately from the suspension arms. If the boot or stud show any problems, replace the suspension arm together with the balljoint. On Warriors, see Step 10 below.

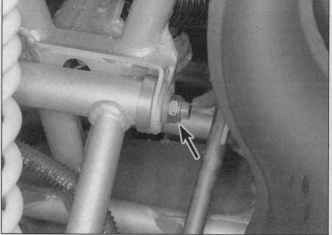

7.4e The upper suspension arms pivot

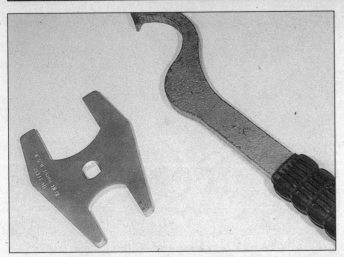

8.3a The special tool on the left is used with hex axle nuts; the one on the right is used with cogged axle nuts

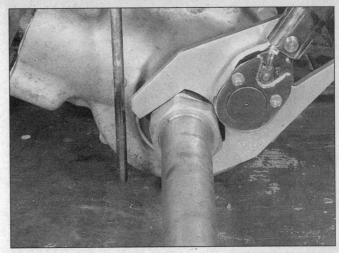

8.3b Tighten the axle nuts in sequence (see text); when tightening with the tool shown, place the torque wrench at a right angle to the tool

Installation

8   Installation is the reverse of removal, but don't torque the suspension fasteners while the vehicle is off the ground. Tighten the nuts and bolts *slightly* while the vehicle is jacked up, then tighten them to the torque listed in this Chapter's Specifications after the vehicle is resting on its wheels.

Balljoints

9   On Banshee models, the balljoints are an integral part of the suspension arms; they cannot be separated. If the balljoint or the suspension arm is damaged or worn, they must be replaced as a single assembly.

10   On Warrior models, the balljoints can be unscrewed from the suspension arms **(see illustration 7.4c)** and replaced separately. If you install a new balljoint, be sure to tighten it to the torque listed in this Chapter's Specifications. Because of its castellated design, the balljoint must be installed with a special Yamaha wrench (YM-01405). If you don't have one of these tools, have a dealer torque the new balljoint(s) for you.

8.3c Large pipe wrenches with lengths of pipe over them will also work, but may mar the nuts

8   Rear axle - removal, inspection and installation

Warning: *The axle nuts are secured with thread locking agent and tightened to a very high torque. When tightening or loosening them with the vehicle jacked up, be sure the vehicle is securely positioned on jackstands so it can't fall.*

Removal

Refer to illustrations 8.3a, 8.3b, 8.3c, 8.7a, 8.7b, 8.9a and 8.9b

1   Block the front wheels so the vehicle won't roll.

2   Jack up the rear end of the vehicle and support it securely, positioning the jackstands so they won't obstruct removal of the axle. The supports must be secure enough so the vehicle won't be knocked off of them while the axle is removed. Remove the rear wheels.

3   Turn the inner axle nut 1/8 turn clockwise (viewed from the left side of the vehicle) to unlock the outer nut. Unscrew the outer nut counterclockwise off its threads, then unscrew the inner nut. Let them hang on the axle for now. **Note:** *You'll need a wrench that will fit on the axle nuts, which measure 49.5 mm across the flats. There's a special Yamaha tool, manufactured by Kent Moore Tool Co., which you may be able to order* **(see illustrations)**. *If not, a tool can be made from a piece of 1/4-inch or thicker steel plate. In an emergency, a pair of pipe wrenches can be used, but they may mar the nuts* **(see illustration)**.

4   Remove the rear hubs (see Chapter 7).

5   Remove the skid plate under the swingarm (see Chapter 8).

8.7a Slide the sprocket hub off the axle splines

6   Remove the drive chain (see Section 12).

7   Slip the nuts off the rear axle and remove the rear sprocket (see Section 13). Slide off the sprocket hub and check the seal for signs of leakage **(see illustrations)**.

6

8.7b Check the axle seal for signs of leakage

8.9a Tape a large socket over the hub threads, then
tap on the socket to free the axle

8.9b Pull the axle out from the right side of the hub

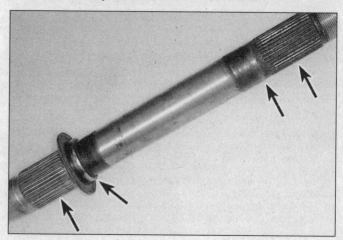

8.10 Inspect the splines and seal contact areas (arrows)

8   Remove the rear brake caliper (see Chapter 7).
9   Clean any foreign material from the left side of the axle so it won't
be pulled into the rear hub during removal. Temporarily install the left
rear hub, then place a large socket over the exposed end of the axle to
protect it **(see illustration)**. Tap on the left end of the axle with a soft
faced hammer to free it, then pull it out of the axle housing **(see illustration)**.

Inspection

Refer to illustrations 8.10 and 8.12

10   Check the axle for obvious damage, such as step wear of the
splines or bending, and replace it as necessary **(see illustration)**.
11   Inspect the brake disc and replace it if necessary (see Chapter 7).
12   Place the axle in V-blocks and set up a dial indicator to contact
each of the outer ends in turn **(see illustration)**. Rotate the axle and
compare runout to the value listed in this Chapter's Specifications. If
runout is excessive, replace the axle.
13   Inspect the hub seals and bearings (see Chapter 7).
14   Inspect the sprockets and drive chain (Sections 12 and 13).

Installation

Refer to illustration 8.22

15   Install the rear hub and brake disc if they were removed.
16   Lubricate the axle splines and the lips of the hub oil seals with
multi-purpose grease. Install the axle from the right side of the vehicle.
Place the right wheel hub on the axle and place a large socket over the
exposed end of the axle. Tap the axle into position, aligning the splines
of the axle with those of the hub.
17   Install the brake caliper (see Chapter 7).

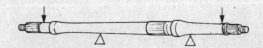

8.12 Place the axle in a pair of V-blocks and measure
runout with a dial indicator at the ends (arrows)

18   Install the rear sprocket (Section 13).
19   Slip the axle nuts over the axle, but don't thread them on yet. Apply
a drop of non-permanent thread locking agent to the axle threads.
20   Install the swingarm skid plate.
21   Install the wheel hubs, washers and nuts. Secure the hub nuts
with new cotter pins and bend them correctly (see Chapter 7).
22   Tighten the inner axle nut against the hub to the initial torque listed
in this Chapter's Specifications **(see illustration 8.3b)**. **Note:** *The
Yamaha tool is designed to work with a torque wrench. If you make your
own tool or use pipe wrenches, you'll need to find a way to torque the
nuts accurately. You can do this by hanging a weight on the end of the
tool at a measured distance from the center of the axle* **(see illustration)**.
23   Hold the inner nut so it won't turn and tighten the outer nut
against it to the torque listed in this Chapter's Specifications.
24   Now hold the outer nut so it won't turn and tighten the inner nut
against the outer nut to the final torque listed in this Chapter's Specifications.
25   The remainder of installation is the reverse of the removal steps.
26   Check drive chain freeplay and adjust as necessary (see Chapter 1).

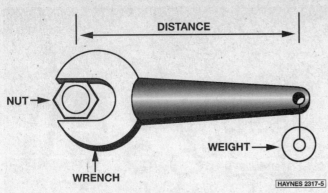

8.22 Length in feet times weight in pounds equals foot-pounds of torque

9 Swingarm bearings - check

1   Remove the rear wheels (see Chapter 7), then remove the rear shock absorber (see Section 4).

2   Grasp the rear of the swingarm with one hand and place your other hand at the junction of the swingarm and the frame. Try to move the rear of the swingarm from side-to-side. If the bearings are worn, they will allow some freeplay, which produces movement between the swingarm and the frame at the front (the swingarm will move forward and backward at the front, not from side-to-side). If any play is noted, the bearings should be replaced with new ones (see Sections 10 and 11).

3   Next, move the swingarm up and down through its full travel. It should move freely, without any binding or rough spots. If it does not move freely, remove the swingarm (see Section 10) and inspect the bearings (see Section 11).

10 Shock linkage and swingarm - removal and installation

1   If the swingarm is being removed just for bearing replacement, the brake assembly, rear hub and rear axle need not be removed from the swingarm.

Removal

Refer to illustrations 10.7a, 10.7b, 10.8a and 10.8b

2   Raise the rear end of the vehicle and support it securely on jackstands.

3   Remove the rear wheels, the rear wheel hubs, the brake caliper and the brake disc (see Chapter 7).

4   Unbolt the swingarm protector from the swingarm. Remove the master link and take the drive chain off the sprockets (see Section 12).

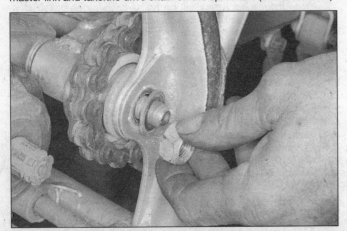

10.8a Remove the swingarm locknut and washer . . .

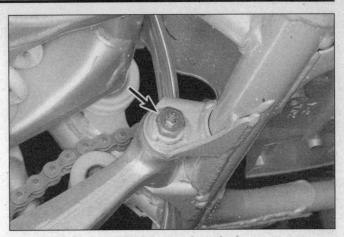

10.7a To detach the relay arm from the frame, remove this nut and bolt (arrow)

10.7b To detach the upper end of the connecting rod from the swingarm, remove this nut and bolt (arrows)

5   If you're replacing the swingarm, remove the rear axle (see Section 8).

6   Support the swingarm so it won't drop, then detach the lower end of the shock absorber from the relay arm (see Section 4).

7   Remove the relay arm and the connecting rod **(see illustration 4.8b, 4.8c or 4.8d and the accompanying illustrations)**.

8   Unscrew the locknut, then pull the pivot bolt out of the swingarm **(see illustration 4.8c or 4.8d and the accompanying illustrations)**.

9   Pull the swingarm back and away from the vehicle.

10   Inspect the pivot bearings in the swingarm for dryness or deterioration (see Section 11).

6

10.8b . . . then pull out the swingarm pivot bolt

11.4 Inspect the swingarm bearings for damage or wear

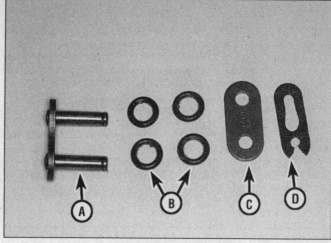

12.2 Master link details

A Link   B O-rings   C Plate   D Clip

Installation

11 Lift the swingarm into position in the frame. Install the pivot bolt and locknut to hold the swingarm in the frame, but don't tighten them yet.

12 Raise and lower the swingarm several times, moving it through its full travel to seat the bearings and pivot bolt.

13 Tighten the pivot bolt and locknut to the torque listed in this Chapter's Specifications.

14 The remainder of installation is the reverse of the removal steps.

11 Swingarm bearings - replacement

Refer to illustration 11.4

1 The swingarm pivot bolt rides on two needle roller bearings.

2 Remove the swingarm (see Section 10).

3 Remove the collar and pry the seal from each side of the swingarm.

4 Inspect the swingarm pivot bearing in each end of the swingarm **(see illustration)**. If either bearing is rough or loose, or has excessive play, replace the bearings as a set.

5 Remove the bearings with a blind hole puller and slide hammer. If you don't have the proper tools, have the bearings replaced by a Yamaha dealer or machine shop.

6 While the bearings are removed, remove the collar, clean it thoroughly, inspect it for burrs, scoring and other damage. If the collar is damaged or worn, replace it. Lubricate the collar with grease and insert it back into the swingarm (make sure that the pivot bore is clean).

7 Tap new bearings into position with a bearing driver or socket just slightly smaller than the diameter of the outer race.

8 Pack the bearings with waterproof lithium-based wheel bearing grease.

9 Tap new seals into position with a seal driver or a socket just slightly smaller than the outside diameter of the seal.

12 Drive chain - removal, cleaning, inspection and installation

Removal

Refer to illustration 12.2

1 Turn the rear wheels to place the drive chain master link where it's easily accessible **(see illustration 8.3 in Chapter 1)**.

2 Remove the clip and plate and pull the master link out of the chain **(see illustration)**.

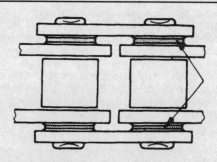

12.6 There are tiny O-rings between the chain plates; do not wash them in anything besides kerosene

3 Remove the left crankcase cover (Banshee models, see "CDI magneto - component replacement" in Chapter 9; Warrior models, see "Alternator charging coils and rotor - check and replacement" in Chapter 9).

4 Lift the chain off the sprockets and remove it from the vehicle.

5 Check the chain guide and rollers on the swingarm and frame for wear or damage and replace them as necessary (see Chapter 1).

Cleaning and inspection

Refer to illustration 12.6

6 The drive chain has small rubber O-rings between the chain plates **(see illustration)**. Soak the chain in kerosene and use a brush to work the solvent into the spaces between the links and plates. **Caution:** *Do NOT use steam, high-pressure washes or solvents, all of which can damage the O-rings, to clean the chain. Use only kerosene.*

7 Wipe the chain dry, then inspect it carefully for worn or damaged links. Replace the chain if wear or damage is found at any point.

8 If the chain is worn or damaged, inspect the sprockets. If they're worn or damaged, replace them also. **Caution:** *Do NOT install a new chain on worn sprockets; it will wear out quickly.*

9 Lubricate the chain (Yamaha recommends 30 to 50-weight engine oil only, not chain lube).

Installation

10 Installation is the reverse of removal. Be sure to install the master link clip so its opening faces the back of the vehicle when the master link is in the upper chain run **(see illustration 8.3 in Chapter 1)**.

11 Adjust the chain when you're done (see Chapter 1).

13 Sprockets - check and replacement

Refer to illustrations 13.2, 13.4 and 13.6

1   Whenever the sprockets are inspected, the chain should be inspected and replaced if it's worn. Installing a worn chain on new sprockets will cause them to wear quickly.

2   Check the teeth on the engine sprocket and rear sprocket for wear **(see illustration)**. The engine sprocket is visible through the cover slots.

3   If the sprockets are worn, remove the chain (see Section 12) and the left rear wheel and hub (see Chapter 7).

4   To remove the engine sprocket, bend back the lockwasher **(see illustration)** and remove the nut. Pull the sprocket off the transmission shaft.

5   Inspect the seal behind the engine sprocket. If it has been leaking, pry it out (take care not to scratch the seal bore) and tap in a new seal with a socket the same diameter as the seal.

6   To remove the rear sprocket, bend back the lockwashers **(see illustration)**. Undo the nuts and slip the sprocket over the end of the axle.

7   Installation is the reverse of the removal steps. Be sure to use new lockwashers on the rear sprocket bolts. Tighten the sprocket bolts

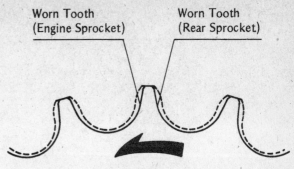

13.2 Inspect the sprockets in the areas indicated to see if they're worn excessively

to the torque listed in this Chapter's Specifications.

8   Install the chain (see Section 12).

9   Adjust the chain when you're done (see Chapter 1).

13.4 Bend back the lockwasher tab (arrow), remove the nut and pull the sprocket off the transmission shaft

13.6 There are three pairs of sprocket nuts (arrows), each secured by a double-ended lockplate

6

Notes

Chapter 7
Brakes, wheels and tires

Contents

Specifications

Brakes

Brake pedal height	See Chapter 1
Brake pad thickness (limit)	
Front	0.8 mm (0.03 inch)
Rear	1.0 mm (0.04 inch)
Brake disc	
Maximum runout	0.5 mm (0.02 inch)
Minimum allowable thickness	3.0 mm (0.12 inch)
Parking brake cable length	46 to 50 mm (1.8 to 1.9 inches)

Wheels and tires

Tire pressures	See Chapter 1
Tire tread depth	See Chapter 1

Torque specifications

Wheel lug nuts	45 Nm (32 ft-lbs)
Front hub nuts	85 Nm (61 ft-lbs)
Front brake caliper bolts	
Banshee	
1987 through 1989	23 Nm (17 ft-lbs)
1990 on	28 Nm (20 ft-lbs)
Warrior	
1987 and 1988	23 Nm (17 ft-lbs)
1989 on	28 Nm (20 ft-lbs)
Brake hose-to-caliper banjo bolts	27 Nm (19 ft-lbs)
Front brake disc retaining bolts	28 Nm (20 ft-lbs)
Rear brake caliper	
Caliper-to-bracket bolts	23 Nm (17 ft-lbs)
Pad retaining bolts	18 Nm (156 in-lbs)
Front master cylinder	
Brake hose banjo bolt	25 Nm (18 ft-lbs)
Handlebar clamp bolts	10 Nm (86 in-lbs)
Rear hub nuts and through-bolts	100 Nm (72 ft-lbs)
Rear axle ring nuts	See Chapter 6

*Refer to marks cast into the drum (they supersede information printed here)

7

1   General information

The vehicles covered by this manual are equipped with three hydraulically-operated disc brakes: a disc at each front wheel and a single disc on the rear axle. The front brakes are operated by a lever-actuated master cylinder on the right end of the handlebar; the rear brake is operated by a pedal-actuated master cylinder on the right side of the vehicle, right behind the right footrest. The rear brake caliper is equipped with a parking brake system, which is actuated by a lever on the left end of the handlebar.

All models are equipped with wheels which require very little maintenance and allow tubeless tires to be used. **Caution:** *Brake components rarely require disassembly. Do not disassemble components unless absolutely necessary.*

2   Wheels - inspection, removal and installation

Inspection

1   Clean the wheels thoroughly to remove mud and dirt that may interfere with the inspection procedure or mask defects. Make a general check of the wheels and tires as described in Chapter 1.

2   The wheels should be visually inspected for cracks, flat spots on the rim and other damage. Since tubeless tires are involved, look very closely for dents in the area where the tire bead contacts the rim. Dents in this area may prevent complete sealing of the tire against the rim, which leads to deflation of the tire over a period of time.

3   If damage is evident, the wheel will have to be replaced with a new one. Never attempt to repair a damaged wheel.

Removal

4   Securely block the wheels at the opposite end of the vehicle from the wheel being removed, so it can't roll.

5   Loosen the lug nuts on the wheel being removed. Jack up one end of the vehicle and support it securely on jackstands.

6   Remove the lug nuts and pull the wheel off.

Installation

7   Position the wheel on the studs. Make sure the directional arrow on the tire points in the forward rotating direction of the wheel.

8   Install the wheel nuts with their tapered sides toward the wheel. This is necessary to locate the wheel accurately on the hub.

9   Snug the wheel nuts evenly in a criss-cross pattern.

10   Remove the jackstands, lower the vehicle and tighten the wheel nuts, again in a criss-cross pattern, to the torque listed in this Chapter's Specifications.

3   Tires - general information

1   Tubeless tires are used as standard equipment on this vehicle. Unlike motorcycle tires, they run at very low air pressures and are completely unsuited for use on pavement. Inflating ATV tires to excessive pressures will rupture them, making replacement of the tire necessary.

2   The force required to break the seal between the rim and the bead of the tire is substantial, much more than required for motorcycle tires, and is beyond the capabilities of an individual working with normal tire irons or even a normal bead breaker. A special bead breaker is required for ATV tires; it produces a great deal of force and concentrates it in a relatively small area.

3   Also, repair of the punctured tire and replacement on the wheel rim requires special tools, skills and experience that the average do-it-yourselfer lacks.

4   For these reasons, if a puncture or flat occurs with an ATV tire, the wheel should be removed from the vehicle and taken to a dealer service department or a repair shop for repair or replacement of the tire. The accompanying illustrations can be used as a guide to tire replacement in an emergency, provided the necessary bead breaker is available.

4   Front wheel hub and bearing - removal and installation

Removal

Refer to illustrations 4.2, 4.3, 4.4 and 4.6

Note: *This procedure applies to either front hub.*

1   Remove the front wheel (see Section 2).

2   Remove the disc outer cover **(see illustration)**, if equipped. (All models except the earliest Warrior have disc covers.)

3   Bend back the cotter pin and pull it out of the hub nut **(see illustration).**

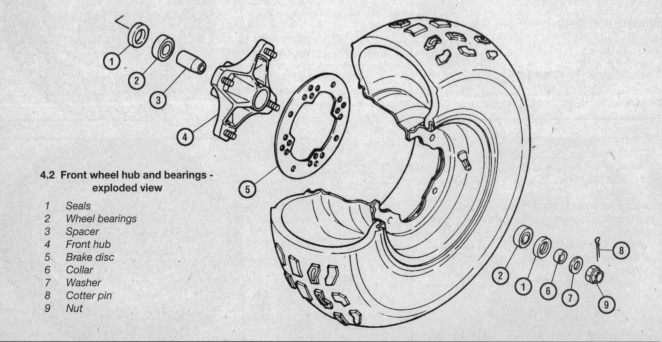

4.2 Front wheel hub and bearings - exploded view

1   *Seals*
2   *Wheel bearings*
3   *Spacer*
4   *Front hub*
5   *Brake disc*
6   *Collar*
7   *Washer*
8   *Cotter pin*
9   *Nut*

TIRE CHANGING SEQUENCE - TUBED TIRES

 A Deflate tire. After pushing tire beads away from rim flanges push tire bead into well of rim at point opposite valve. Insert tire lever next to valve and work bead over edge of rim.

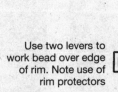 Use two levers to work bead over edge of rim. Note use of rim protectors **B**

 C Remove inner tube from tire

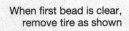 When first bead is clear, remove tire as shown **D**

 E To install, partially inflate inner tube and insert in tire

Work first bead over rim and feed valve through hole in rim. Partially screw on retaining nut to hold valve in place. **F**

 G Check that inner tube is positioned correctly and work second bead over rim using tire levers. Start at a point opposite valve.

Work final area of bead over rim while pushing valve inwards to ensure that inner tube is not trapped. **H**

4.3 Bend back the cotter pin and pull it out

4.4 Have someone firmly apply the front brakes while
you crack the hub nut loose

4   Have an assistant apply the front brake while you loosen the hub nut **(see illustration)**. Remove the hub nut and the washer.

5   Remove the front brake caliper and inner disc cover (see Section 6). (The inner cover itself doesn't interfere with hub removal, but the caliper can't be removed without detaching the inner cover from the steering knuckle.) It's not necessary to disconnect the brake hose from the caliper; set the caliper aside and hang it from the suspension with a coat hanger.

6   Pull the hub off the spindle. If the hub is stuck, remove it with a puller **(see illustration)**.

Bearing inspection and replacement

Refer to illustration 4.10

7   Wipe off the spindle and hub. **Caution:** *Do NOT immerse the hub in any kind of cleaning solvent. The sealed hub bearings, which cannot be disassembled and repacked, could be damaged if any solvent enters them.*

8   Insert your fingers into each hub bearing and turn the bearing. If the bearing feels rough or dry, replace it.

9   Pry out the old seals **(see illustration 4.2)** and discard them.

10   To drive each bearing from the hub, lay the hub on a workbench, with the outer side of the hub facing down, then insert a soft metal (brass) drift into the hub from the inner side of the hub, push the floating spacer to the side and tap gently against the inner face of the outer bearing **(see illustration)**. Then flip over the hub, inner side facing down, insert the drift from the outer side of the hub, and drive out the inner bearing the same way.

11   To install the new bearings, drive them into place with an old socket. The socket must have an outside diameter that's the same, or slightly smaller than, the outer diameter of the bearings. **Caution:** *Do NOT strike the center race or the ball bearings.*

12   Tap new inner and outer seals into place with a block of wood. Do NOT use the old seals.

4.6 You may need a slide hammer and adapter to pull
the hub off the spindle

Installation

13   Installation is the reverse of removal. Lubricate the spindle with wheel bearing grease. Tighten the hub nut to the torque listed in this Chapter's Specifications. If necessary, tighten it an additional amount to align the cotter pin slots. Don't loosen the nut to align the slots. Install a new cotter pin and bend it to secure the nut.

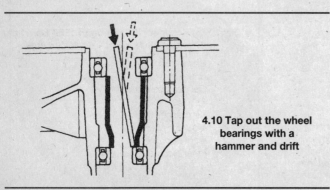

4.10 Tap out the wheel
bearings with a
hammer and drift

5.2 Loosen - but don't remove - the brake pad retaining bolts
while the caliper is still bolted to the steering knuckle

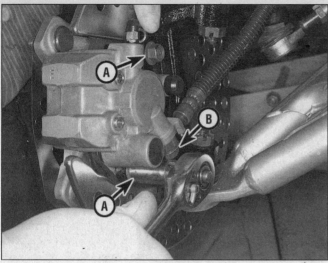

5.3 Caliper mounting bolts (A) and brake hose banjo bolt (B); be sure the neck of the brake hose fits in the stop groove as shown

5   Front brake pads - replacement

Refer to illustrations 5.2, 5.3, 5.5a, 5.5b, 5.5c, 5.7, 5.8a and 5.8b
Note: *Always replace both pairs of brake pads at the same time.*
1   Remove the front wheel (see Section 2). Remove the outer disc cover.
2   On 1990 and later Banshees and on 1989 and later Warriors, loosen the brake pad retaining bolts **(see illustration)**. (The pad retaining bolts are easier to loosen while the caliper is still bolted to the steering knuckle.)
3   If you're removing the caliper to overhaul it on a 1990 or later Banshee, or on a 1989 or later Warrior, remove the brake hose-to-caliper banjo bolt **(see illustration)** and disconnect the brake hose from the caliper now. On earlier models, each brake hose is screwed directly into the caliper; on these models, loosen the brake hose now, then unscrew it after the caliper is removed by turning the caliper. If you're only removing the caliper to replace the brake pads, or to remove the steering knuckle, do NOT disconnect the brake hose from the caliper.
4   Unbolt the caliper from the steering knuckle **(see illustration 5.3)**.
5   Remove the inner disc cover **(see illustrations)**, or detach the hub (see Section 4) and pull it off just far enough to clear the caliper **(see illustration)**. The inner disc cover bolts are difficult to remove and install on some models; you might find that sliding the hub out is actually a little less trouble than detaching the inner disc cover. However, if you're removing components in order to remove the steering knuckle, you will need to remove the inner disc cover anyway.

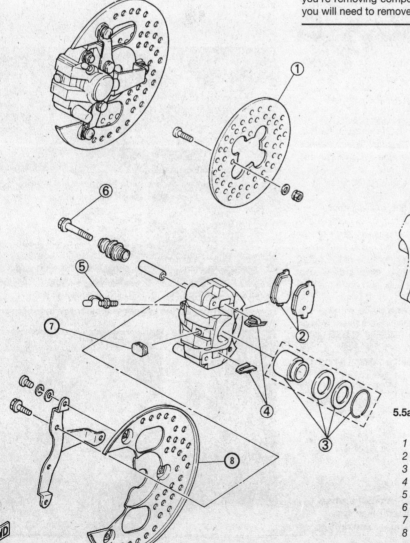

5.5a Front caliper (1987 through 1989 Banshee, 1987 and 1988 Warrior) – exploded view

1   *Brake disc*
2   *Brake pads*
3   *Caliper piston assembly*
4   *Pad springs*
5   *Air bleeder valve*
6   *Mounting bolt*
7   *Inspection plug*
8   *Inner disc cover*

7

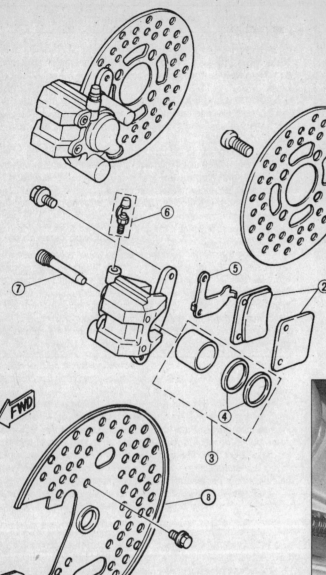

5.5b Front caliper (1990-on Banshee, 1989-on Warrior) – exploded view

1   Brake disc
2   Brake pads
3   Caliper piston assembly
4   Piston assembly
5   Shim
6   Bleeder valve
7   Mounting bolt
8   Inner disc cover

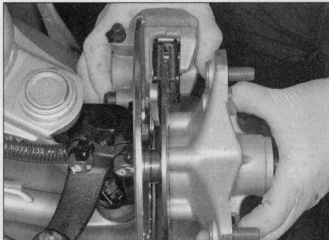

5.5c You may need to remove the hub nut and slide the hub off partway so the caliper will clear the inner cover

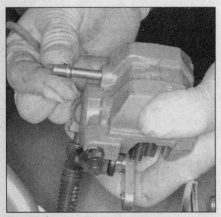

5.7 Remove the caliper, then remove the pad retaining bolts

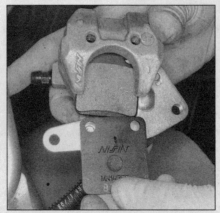

5.8a Remove the outer brake pad . . .

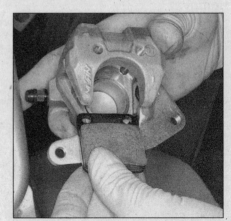

5.8b . . . and the inner pad

6.4 Carefully blow compressed air into the fluid outlet to push the piston out of the caliper; keep your fingers out of the way to prevent injury

6.6 Remove the piston from the bore

6.7 Remove the old piston seal from its groove in the bore with a toothpick (if you use a metal tool, don't scratch the bore)

6   Remove the caliper. If you're only removing the caliper to replace the brake pads, hang the caliper from the suspension with a coat hanger. **Caution:** *Do NOT allow the caliper to hang from its brake hose.*

7   On 1990 and later Banshee models and on 1989 and later Warrior models, remove the brake pad retaining bolts **(see illustration)**.

8   Remove the brake pads **(see illustrations)**.

9   On older models, remove the pad springs from the caliper **(see illustration 5.5a)** and inspect them. If they're damaged or distorted, replace them.

10   On newer models, remove the shim from the inner brake pad and install it on the new inner pad.

11   Installation is the reverse of removal. Using a C-clamp, depress the piston back into the caliper bore to provide enough room for the new pads to clear the disc. Be sure to tighten the caliper bolts to the torque listed in this Chapter's Specifications. On 1990 and later Banshee models and on 1989 and later Warrior models, tighten the brake pad bolts securely.

12   Replace the brake pads on the other front caliper.

6   Front brake caliper - removal, overhaul and installation

Warning: *The dust created by the brake system may contain asbestos, which is harmful to your health. Never blow it out with compressed air and don't inhale any of it. An approved filtering mask should be worn when working on the brakes. Do not, under any circumstances, use petroleum-based solvents to clean brake parts. Use brake cleaner only!* **Note:** *This procedure applies to both front calipers.*

Removal

1   Disconnect the brake hose from the caliper, remove the caliper from the steering knuckle and remove the brake pads, shims and pad springs (see Section 5).

Overhaul

Refer to illustrations 6.4, 6.6 and 6.7

2   Clean the exterior of the caliper with denatured alcohol or brake system cleaner.

3   On 1987 through 1989 Banshee models and on 1987 and 1988 Warrior models, remove the pad springs and the wire retainer for the dust seal **(see illustration 5.5a)**.

4   Place a few rags between the piston and the caliper frame to act as a cushion, lay the caliper on the work bench so that the piston is facing down, toward the work bench surface, then use compressed air, directed into the fluid inlet **(see illustration)**, to remove the piston. Use only small quick blasts of air to ease the piston out of the bore. If a piston is blown out with too much force, it might be damaged. **Warning:** *Never place your fingers in front of the piston in an attempt to*

catch or protect it when applying compressed air. Doing so could result in serious injury.

5   If compressed air isn't available, reconnect the caliper to the brake hose and pump the brake lever until the piston is free. (You'll have to put brake fluid in the master cylinder reservoir and get most of the air out of the hose to use this method.)

6   Once the piston is protruding from the caliper, remove it **(see illustration)** and the old dust seal **(see illustration 5.5a or 5.5b)**.

7   Using a wood or plastic tool, remove the piston seal **(see illustration)**.

8   Clean the piston and piston bore with denatured alcohol, fresh brake fluid or brake system cleaner and dry them off with filtered, unlubricated compressed air. Inspect the surfaces of the piston and the piston bores for rust, corrosion, nicks, burrs and loss of plating. If you find defects on the surface of either piston or piston bore, replace the piston and caliper assembly (the piston is matched to the caliper). If the caliper is in bad shape, inspect the master cylinder too.

9   Lubricate the new piston seal with clean brake fluid and install it in its groove in the caliper bore. Make sure it's not twisted and is fully and correctly seated.

10   Lubricate the piston with clean brake fluid and install it into its bore in the caliper. Using your thumbs, push the piston all the way in; make sure it doesn't become cocked in the bore.

11   Install the new dust seal. Make sure that the inner lip of the seal is seated in its groove in the piston and the outer circumference of the seal is seated in its groove in the caliper bore.

12   On 1987 through 1989 Banshee models and on 1987 and 1988 Warrior models, install the wire dust seal retainer and install the pad springs **(see illustration 5.5a)**.

13   Install the brake pads (see Section 5).

Installation

14   On 1987 through 1989 Banshee models, and on 1987 and 1988 Warrior models, screw the brake hose into the caliper now by turning the caliper onto the threaded end of the hose. Tighten the hose securely.

15   Install the caliper and brake pads (see Sections 5 and 6).

16   On 1990 and later Banshee models, and on 1989 and later Warrior models, connect the brake hose-to-caliper banjo bolt **(see illustration 5.3)**. Be sure to use new sealing washers. Tighten the banjo bolt to the torque listed in this Chapter's Specifications.

17   Remove and overhaul the other front brake caliper.

18   Bleed the front brake system (see Section 15).

7   Front brake disc - inspection, removal and installation

Note: *This procedure applies to both front discs.*

1   Remove the front wheels (see Section 2).

7

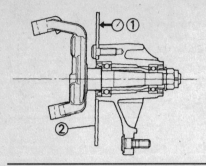

7.3 To measure front disc runout, position a dial indicator (1) so that its probe is about half an inch from the outer edge of the disc (2)

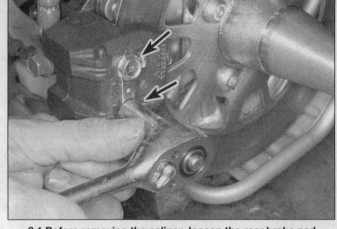

8.1 Before removing the caliper, loosen the rear brake pad retaining bolts (arrows)

Inspection

Refer to illustration 7.3

2   Visually inspect the surface of the disc for score marks and other damage. Light scratches are normal after use and won't affect brake operation, but deep grooves and heavy score marks will reduce braking efficiency and accelerate pad wear. If the disc is badly grooved it must be machined or replaced.

3   To check disc runout, mount a dial indicator with the plunger on the indicator touching the surface of the disc about 1/2-inch from the outer edge **(see illustration)**. Slowly turn the wheel hub and watch the indicator needle, comparing your reading with the disc runout limit listed in this Chapter's Specifications. If the runout is greater than allowed, replace the disc.

4   The disc must not be machined or allowed to wear to a thickness less than the minimum listed in this Chapter's Specifications. The thickness of the disc can be checked with a micrometer. If the thickness of the disc is less than the minimum, it must be replaced.

Removal and installation

5   Remove the front wheel hub (see Section 4).

6   To detach the brake disc from the hub, remove the four disc retaining bolts.

7   Installation is the reverse of removal. Tighten the disc retaining bolts to the torque listed in this Chapter's Specifications.

8   Rear brake pads - replacement

Refer to illustrations 8.1, 8.2, 8.3, 8.4a, 8.4b and 8.5

Warning: *The dust created by the brake system may contain asbestos, which is harmful to your health. Never blow it out with compressed air and don't inhale any of it. An approved filtering mask should be worn when working on the brakes. Do not, under any circumstances, use petroleum-based solvents to clean brake parts. Use brake cleaner only!*

1   Loosen the brake pad retaining bolts **(see illustration)**. (The brake pad retaining bolts are easier to loosen while the caliper is still bolted onto the caliper bracket.)

2   If you're planning to overhaul the caliper, remove the brake hose-

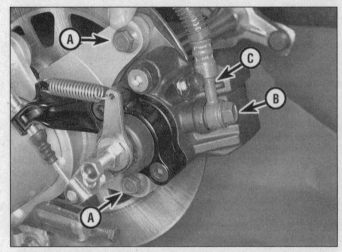

8.2   Rear caliper mounting bolts (A) and brake hose banjo bolt (B); be sure to place the neck of the brake hose in its notch (C)

to-caliper banjo bolt **(see illustration)**, disconnect the brake hose from the caliper and discard the old sealing washers. If you're simply replacing the brake pads, or if you're only removing the caliper to remove other components, such as the axle, do NOT disconnect the brake hose.

3   Remove the brake caliper bolts **(see illustration 8.2)** and remove the caliper **(see illustration)**. While the caliper is off the disc, tie it up out of the way.

4   Remove the brake pad retaining bolts and lockplate, then remove

8.3 To remove the caliper, pull it straight back

8.4a Remove the outer brake pad . . .

8.4b . . . and the inner pad

the brake pads **(see illustrations).**

5   Remove the shim from the inner pad (the pad closest to the piston) and install it on the new inner pad. Be sure to install the shim so that its arrow mark points in the same direction that the disc rotates when the vehicle is moving forward **(see illustration).**

6   Installation is otherwise the reverse of removal. Be sure to tighten the caliper retaining bolts and the pad retaining bolts to the torque listed in this Chapter's Specifications.

9   Rear brake caliper - removal, overhaul and installation

Warning: *The dust created by the brake system may contain asbestos, which is harmful to your health. Never blow it out with compressed air and don't inhale any of it. An approved filtering mask should be worn when working on the brakes. Do not, under any circumstances, use petroleum-based solvents to clean brake parts. Use brake cleaner only!*

Removal

1   Disconnect the parking brake cable (see Section 16).

2   Disconnect the brake hose from the caliper, remove the caliper and remove the brake pads (see Section 8).

Overhaul

Refer to illustration 9.10

3   Clean the exterior of the caliper with denatured alcohol or brake system cleaner.

4   Loosen the parking brake lever adjuster bolt locknut (see Section 16), remove the parking brake lever adjuster bolt and remove the parking brake lever and return spring.

5   Remove the parking brake case Allen bolts and detach the case assembly and remove the old gasket.

6   Remove the cover, spring, adjuster nut and bearing from the parking brake case.

7   Remove the caliper bracket bolt, dust boots, C-washer, caliper pin dust boot and bracket from the caliper.

8   Place a few rags between the piston and the caliper frame to act as a cushion, lay the caliper on the work bench so that the piston is facing down, toward the work bench surface, then use compressed air, directed into the fluid inlet **(see illustration 6.4),** to remove the piston. Use only small quick blasts of air to ease the piston out of the bore. If a piston is blown out with too much force, it might be damaged. **Warning:** *Never place your fingers in front of the piston in an attempt to catch or protect it when applying compressed air. Doing so could result in serious injury.*

9   If compressed air isn't available, reconnect the caliper to the brake hose and pump the brake lever until the piston is free. (You'll have to put brake fluid in the master cylinder reservoir and get most of the air out of the hose to use this method.)

10   Once the piston is protruding from the caliper, remove it **(see illustration 6.6)** and remove the old dust seal **(see illustration).**

11   Using a wood or plastic tool, remove the piston seal **(see illustration 6.7).**

12   Clean the piston and piston bore with denatured alcohol, fresh brake fluid or brake system cleaner and dry them off with filtered, unlubricated compressed air. Inspect the surfaces of the piston and the piston bores for rust, corrosion, nicks, burrs and loss of plating. If you find defects on the surface of either piston or piston bore, replace the piston and caliper assembly (the piston is matched to the caliper). If the caliper is in bad shape, inspect the master cylinder too.

13   Lubricate the new piston seal with clean brake fluid and install it in its groove in the caliper bore. Make sure it's not twisted and is fully and correctly seated.

14   Lubricate the piston with clean brake fluid and install it into its bore in the caliper. Using your thumbs, push the piston all the way in; make sure it doesn't become cocked in the bore.

15   Install the new dust seal. Make sure that the inner lip of the seal is seated in its groove in the piston and the outer circumference of the seal is seated in its groove in the caliper bore.

16   Reassembly of the parking brake case is essentially the reverse of

8.5 Make sure the arrow mark on the pad shim points in the same direction as forward disc rotation

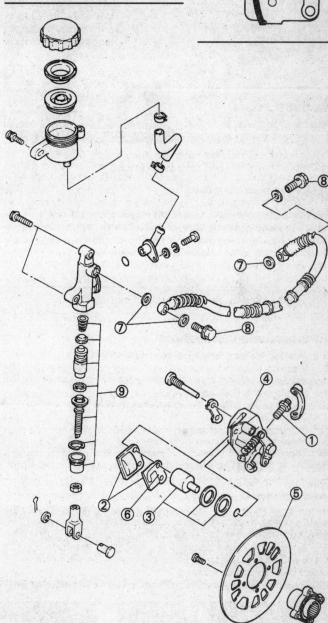

9.10 Rear brake caliper and master cylinder - exploded view

1	Bleeder valve	5	Brake disc
2	Brake pads	6	Shim
3	Caliper piston assembly (piston, piston seal, dust seal)	7	Copper sealing washer
		8	Banjo bolt
4	Brake caliper	9	Master cylinder piston assembly

disassembly. Make sure that the tab on the bearing race is aligned with the slit in the parking brake case, and be sure to grease the bearing and races. Tighten the parking brake case bolts to the torque listed in this Chapter's Specifications. When installing the parking brake lever, make sure the punch mark on the adjuster bolt locknut is aligned with the punch mark on the lever.

10.2 Remove the cotter pin, then unscrew the nut and remove the washer

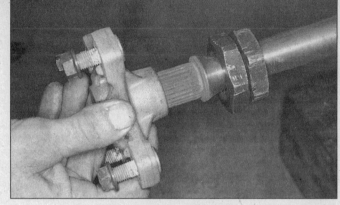

10.4 Pull the hub off and clean the splines

Installation

17   Install the caliper and brake pads (see Sections 8 and 9).
18   Connect the brake hose-to-caliper banjo bolt **(see illustration 8.2)**. Be sure to use new sealing washers. Tighten the banjo bolt to the torque listed in this Chapter's Specifications.
19   Bleed the front brake system (see Section 15).

10   Rear wheel hubs - removal and installation

Refer to illustrations 10.2 and 10.4
1   Remove the rear wheels (see Section 2).
2   Bend back the cotter pin and pull it out of the hub nut **(see illustration)**.
3   Apply the parking brake to lock the rear axle. Unscrew the hub nut and remove the washer.
4   Pull the hub off the axleshaft **(see illustration)**. Clean the hub and the axle splines.
5   Installation is the reverse of removal.

11   Rear brake disc - inspection, removal and installation

Inspection

1   Visually inspect the surface of the disc for score marks and other damage. Light scratches are normal after use and won't affect brake operation, but deep grooves and heavy score marks will reduce braking efficiency and accelerate pad wear. If the disc is badly grooved it must be machined or replaced.

2   To check disc runout, mount a dial indicator with the plunger on the indicator touching the surface of the disc about 1/2-inch from the outer edge **(see illustration 7.3)**. Slowly turn the wheel hub and watch the indicator needle, comparing your reading with the disc runout limit listed in this Chapter's Specifications. If the runout is greater than allowed, replace the disc.
3   The disc must not be machined or allowed to wear to a thickness less than the minimum listed in this Chapter's Specifications. The thickness of the disc can be checked with a micrometer. If the thickness of the disc is less than the minimum, it must be replaced.

Removal and installation

Refer to illustration 11.6
4   Remove the right rear wheel hub (see Section 10).
5   Remove the rear caliper (see Section 9).
6   Remove the disc retaining bolts **(see illustration)** and remove the disc.
7   Installation is the reverse of removal. Be sure to tighten the disc retaining bolts to the torque listed in this Chapter's Specifications.

12   Front brake master cylinder - removal, overhaul and installation

1   If the front brake master cylinder is leaking fluid, or if the lever does not produce a firm feel when the brake lever is applied, and bleeding the brakes does not help, master cylinder overhaul is recommended. Before disassembling the master cylinder, read through the entire procedure and make sure that you have the correct rebuild kit. Also, you will need some new, clean brake fluid of the recommended

11.6 To detach the rear disc from the axle, remove these four Allen bolts

12.4 Pull back the rubber boot and remove the banjo bolt; use new sealing washers on assembly

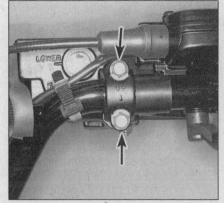

12.5 Remove the master cylinder clamp bolts (arrows); the arrow on the clamp must point up when installed

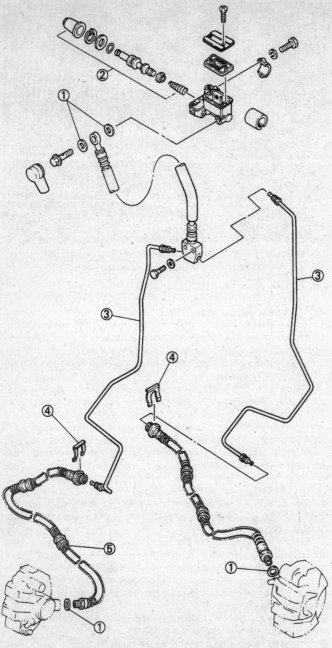

12.7 Front master cylinder and brake hose details

1	*Sealing washers*	*3*	*Metal brake lines*
2	*Master cylinder*	*4*	*Brake line clips*
	piston assembly	*5*	*Brake flexible hoses*

type, some clean rags and internal snap-ring pliers. **Note:** *To prevent damage to the paint from spilled brake fluid, always cover the top cover or upper fuel tank when working on the master cylinder.*

2   **Caution:** *Disassembly, overhaul and reassembly of the brake master cylinder must be done in a spotlessly clean work area to avoid contamination and possible failure of the brake hydraulic system components.*

Removal

Refer to illustrations 12.4 and 12.5

3   Remove the reservoir cover retaining screw. Remove the reservoir and the rubber diaphragm. Siphon as much brake fluid from the reservoir as you can to avoid spilling it on the bike.

4   Pull back the rubber dust boot and loosen the brake hose banjo

12.14 Place the master cylinder protrusion in the spacer notch, then tighten the clamp bolts

bolt **(see illustration)** and separate the brake hose from the master cylinder. Wrap the end of the hose in a clean rag and suspend the hose in an upright position or bend it down carefully and place the open end in a clean container. The objective is to prevent excessive loss of brake fluid, fluid spills and system contamination.

5   Remove the master cylinder mounting bolts **(see illustration)** and separate the master cylinder from the handlebar. **Caution:** *Do not tip the master cylinder upside down or any brake fluid still in the reservoir will run out.*

Overhaul

Refer to illustration 12.7

6   Remove the brake lever pivot bolt nut, remove the pivot bolt and remove the lever.

7   Carefully remove the rubber dust boot from the end of the piston **(see illustration)**. Using snap-ring pliers, remove the snap-ring and slide out the piston assembly and the spring.

8   Lay the parts out in the order in which they're removed to prevent confusion during reassembly.

9   Clean all of the parts with brake system cleaner (available at motorcycle dealerships and auto parts stores), isopropyl alcohol or clean brake fluid. **Caution:** *Do not, under any circumstances, use a petroleum-based solvent to clean brake parts. If compressed air is available, use it to dry the parts thoroughly (make sure it's filtered and unlubricated). Check the master cylinder bore for corrosion, scratches, nicks and score marks. If damage is evident, the master cylinder must be replaced with a new one. If the master cylinder is in poor condition, then the calipers should be checked as well.*

10   The dust seal, piston assembly and spring are included in the rebuild kit. Use all of the new parts, regardless of the apparent condition of the old ones.

11   Before reassembling the master cylinder, soak the piston and the rubber cup seals in clean brake fluid for ten or fifteen minutes. Lubricate the master cylinder bore with clean brake fluid, then carefully insert the piston and related parts in the reverse order of disassembly. Make sure the lips on the cup seals do not turn inside out when they are slipped into the bore.

12   Depress the piston, then install the snap-ring (make sure the snap-ring is properly seated in the groove). Install the rubber dust boot (make sure the lip is seated properly in the piston groove).

13   Lubricate the brake lever pivot bolt and the friction surface on the lever that pushes against the piston assembly.

Installation

Refer to illustration 12.14

14   Attach the master cylinder to the handlebar. Make sure that the arrow on the clamp is pointing up **(see illustration 12.5)** and that the protrusion on the master cylinder fits into the notch in the handlebar spacer **(see illustration)**. Tighten the bolts to the torque listed in this

7

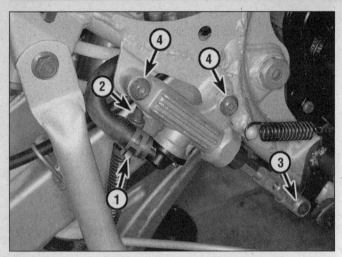

13.4 Rear master cylinder installation details

1	*Reservoir hose clamp*	3	*Pushrod clevis*
2	*Hose to caliper*	4	*Mounting bolts*

14.2a Replace cracked or deteriorated rubber hoses; this one is mounted on an upper suspension arm

Chapter's Specifications.

15   Connect the brake hose to the master cylinder, using new sealing washers. Tighten the banjo bolt to the torque listed in this Chapter's Specifications.

16   Fill the master cylinder with the recommended brake fluid (see Chapter 1), then bleed the front brake system (see Section 15).

13   Rear brake master cylinder - removal, overhaul and installation

1   If the rear brake master cylinder is leaking fluid, or if the lever does not produce a firm feel when the brake pedal is applied, and bleeding the brakes does not help, master cylinder overhaul is recommended. Before disassembling the master cylinder, read through the entire procedure and make sure that you have the correct rebuild kit. Also, you will need some new, clean brake fluid of the recommended type, some clean rags and internal snap-ring pliers. **Note:** *To prevent damage to the paint from spilled brake fluid, always cover the top cover or upper fuel tank when working on the master cylinder.*

2   **Caution:** *Disassembly, overhaul and reassembly of the brake master cylinder must be done in a spotlessly clean work area to avoid contamination and possible failure of the brake hydraulic system components.*

Removal

Refer to illustration 13.4

3   Unscrew the reservoir cover and siphon as much brake fluid from the reservoir as you can to avoid spilling it on the bike.

4   Pull back the brake hose clamp **(see illustration)** and detach the brake hose coming from the master cylinder reservoir. Plug or pinch off the end of the hose and suspend the hose in an upright position or bend it down carefully and place the open end in a clean container. Try to prevent excessive loss of brake fluid, fluid spills and system contamination.

5   Disconnect the pushrod clevis from the rear brake pedal **(see illustration 9.10)**.

6   Remove the master cylinder mounting bolts **(see illustration 13.4)** and detach the master cylinder from the frame. Remove the banjo bolt to disconnect the brake hose (to the rear caliper) from the master cylinder. Discard the old sealing washers.

Overhaul

7   Back off the pushrod clevis locknut, mark the position of the clevis by marking the threads with a large felt pen or some other suitable

marking agent, then unscrew the clevis from the pushrod. Unscrew and remove the locknut from the pushrod. Carefully remove the rubber dust boot from the pushrod. Using snap-ring pliers, remove the snap-ring and slide out the piston assembly and the spring.

8   Lay the parts out in the order in which they're removed to prevent confusion during reassembly.

9   Clean all of the parts with brake system cleaner (available at motorcycle dealerships and auto parts stores), isopropyl alcohol or clean brake fluid. **Caution:** *Do not, under any circumstances, use a petroleum-based solvent to clean brake parts. If compressed air is available, use it to dry the parts thoroughly (make sure it's filtered and unlubricated). Check the master cylinder bore for corrosion, scratches, nicks and score marks. If damage is evident, the master cylinder must be replaced with a new one. If the master cylinder is in poor condition, then the calipers should be checked as well.*

10   The dust seal, piston assembly and spring are included in the rebuild kit. Use all of the new parts, regardless of the apparent condition of the old ones.

11   Before reassembling the master cylinder, soak the piston and the rubber cup seals in clean brake fluid for ten or fifteen minutes. Lubricate the master cylinder bore with clean brake fluid, then carefully insert the piston and related parts in the reverse order of disassembly. Make sure the lips on the cup seals do not turn inside out when they are slipped into the bore.

12   Depress the piston, then install the snap-ring (make sure the snap-ring is properly seated in the groove).

13   Install the rubber dust boot onto the pushrod, push it all the way on and make sure the lip is seated correctly over the ridge on the end of the master cylinder. Install the locknut on the pushrod. Screw it on beyond the mark you made for the clevis prior to disassembly. Screw the clevis onto the pushrod. Make sure that it's aligned with the mark you made before disassembly. Tighten the locknut securely.

Installation

14   Connect the rear caliper brake hose to the master cylinder, using new sealing washers. Tighten the banjo bolt to the torque listed in this Chapter's Specifications.

15   Install the master cylinder on the frame and install - but don't tighten - the master cylinder retaining bolts.

16   Reattach the pushrod clevis to the rear brake pedal.

17   Tighten the rear brake master cylinder retaining bolts to the torque listed in this Chapter's Specifications.

18   Reattach the reservoir hose to the master cylinder. Use a new hose clamp.

19   Fill the master cylinder with the recommended brake fluid (see Chapter 1), then bleed the front brake system (see Section 15).

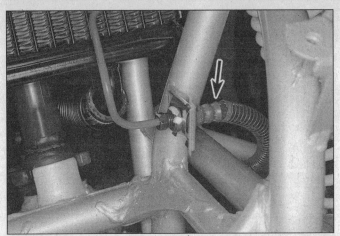

14.2b Check the junctions between brake hoses and their metal fittings (arrow); pull off the clip and unscrew the flare nut to disconnect the hose

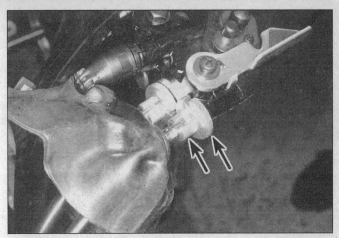

16.2 The parking brake adjuster (left arrow) and locknut (right arrow) are under this cover

14 Brake hoses - inspection and replacement

Inspection

Refer to illustration 14.2a and 14.2b

1   Once a week or, if the motorcycle is used less frequently, before every ride, check the condition of the brake hoses.
2   Twist and flex the rubber hoses while looking for cracks, bulges and seeping fluid **(see illustration)**. Check extra carefully around the areas where the hoses connect with the metal fittings, **(see illustration)**, as these are common areas for hose failure.
3   Inspect the metal banjo fittings connected to the brake hoses. If the fittings are rusted, scratched or cracked, replace them.

Replacement

4   Cover the surrounding area with plenty of rags, then disconnect the ends of the hose. If you're replacing a front brake hose, you'll need to remove the front brake caliper and unscrew the caliper from the hose on 1987 through 1989 Banshee models and 1987 and 1988 Warrior models. On later models, simply remove the banjo bolt from the caliper and disconnect the hose. Discard the old sealing washers.
5   To disconnect a front brake hose from a metal line, pull off the metal clip **(see illustration 14.2b)** with a pair of pliers, then unscrew the fitting.
6   All rear brake hoses are attached to the rear master cylinder and to the rear caliper by banjo bolts.
7   Position the new hose, making sure it isn't twisted or otherwise strained, between the two components. Where a hose is attached by a banjo bolt, use new sealing washers on both sides of the fitting, and tighten banjo bolts to the torque listed in this Chapter's Specifications. On non-banjo fittings, tighten the fitting securely.
8   Flush the old brake fluid from the system, refill the system with the recommended fluid (see Chapter 1) and bleed the air from the system (see Section 15). Check the operation of the brakes carefully before riding the motorcycle.

15 Brake system - bleeding

1   Bleeding the brake system removes all the air bubbles from the brake fluid reservoirs, the lines and the brake calipers. Bleeding is necessary whenever a brake system hydraulic connection is loosened, when a component or hose is replaced, or when the master cylinder or caliper is overhauled. Leaks in the system may also allow air to enter, but leaking brake fluid will reveal their presence and warn you of the need for repair.

2   To bleed the brakes, you will need some new, clean brake fluid of the recommended type (see Chapter 1), a length of clear vinyl or plastic tubing, a small container partially filled with clean brake fluid, some rags and a wrench to fit the brake caliper bleeder valves.
3   Cover the fuel tank and any other painted surfaces near the reservoir to prevent damage in the event that brake fluid is spilled.
4   Remove the front reservoir cover screws and remove the cover and diaphragm (or, on rear brakes, simply unscrew the reservoir cover). Slowly pump the brake lever (or brake pedal) a few times, until no air bubbles can be seen floating up from the holes at the bottom of the reservoir. Doing this bleeds the air from the master cylinder end of the line. Top up the reservoir with new fluid, then install the reservoir diaphragm and cover, but don't tighten the screws (or cover); you may have to remove the cover and diaphragm several times during the procedure.
5   Remove the rubber dust cover from the bleeder valve on the caliper and slip a box wrench over the bleeder. Attach one end of the clear vinyl or plastic tubing to the bleed valve and submerge the other end in the brake fluid in the container.
6   Carefully pump the brake lever or brake pedal three or four times and hold it while opening the caliper bleeder valve. When the valve is opened, brake fluid will flow out of the caliper into the clear tubing and the lever will move toward the handlebar (or the pedal will move down). Retighten the bleeder valve, then release the brake lever or pedal.
7   Repeat this procedure until no air bubbles are visible in the brake fluid leaving the caliper and the lever or pedal is firm when applied.
Note: *Remember to add fluid to the reservoir as the level drops. Use only new, clean brake fluid of the recommended type. Never re-use the fluid lost during bleeding.*
8   Keep an eye on the fluid level in the reservoir, especially if there's a lot of air in the system. Every time you crack open the bleeder valve, the fluid level in the reservoir drops a little. Do not allow the fluid level to drop below the lower mark during the bleeding process. If the level looks low, remove the reservoir cover and add some fluid.
9   When you're done, inspect the fluid level in the reservoir one more time, add some fluid if necessary, then install the diaphragm and reservoir cover and tighten the screws securely. Wipe up any spilled brake fluid and check the entire system for leaks. **Note:** *If bleeding is difficult, it may be necessary to let the brake fluid in the system stabilize for a few hours (it may be aerated). Repeat the bleeding procedure when the tiny bubbles in the system have settled out.*

16 Parking brake system - adjustment

Refer to illustrations 16.2 and 16.3

1   Apply the rear brake pedal two or three times.
2   Peel back the rubber dust cover, then loosen the locknut at the

7

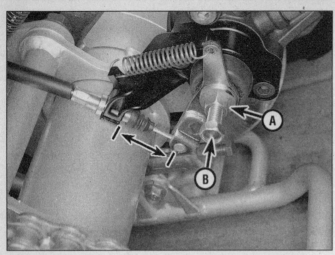

16.3 Loosen the locknut (A), use the adjuster (B) to make the
initial adjustment, then set the final dimension
with the handlebar adjuster

17.4 Hub bolts and nuts (arrows); the lower bolt secures
the chain adjusters

lever on the handlebar **(see illustration)** and back off the cable adjuster all the way.

3   Loosen the locknut and adjuster bolt at the parking brake lever on the rear brake caliper **(see illustration)**.

4   Slowly screw in the adjuster bolt until it feels tight, then back it out 1/4-turn. Tighten the locknut.

5   Turn the cable adjuster in or out to bring the length of the cable from the centerline of the parking brake lever clevis to the cable bracket **(see illustration 16.3)** within the dimensions listed in this Chapter's Specifications.

6   After adjusting the parking brake cable, raise the rear of the machine so that the wheels are off the ground, spin the rear wheels and verify that there is no drag. If there is, repeat this procedure.

17   Rear axle hub and bearings - removal, inspection and installation

Refer to illustration 17.4

1   Jack up the rear end of the vehicle and support it securely on jackstands.

2   Remove the rear wheels (see Section 2).

3   Remove the drive chain and rear axle (see Chapter 6).

4   If you need to remove the hub to replace it or the swing-arm, unbolt it from the swingarm and take it off the vehicle **(see**

illustration)**. The seals and hub bearings can be inspected and replaced with the hub installed on the vehicle.

Inspection and bearing replacement

Refer to illustrations 17.5, 17.6 and 17.7

5   Pry out the seal from each side of the hub **(see illustration)**.

6   Spin the bearing inside each end of the hub and check for roughness, looseness or noise **(see illustration)**.

7   Insert a metal drift or punch into the hub and tilt it so it pushes the spacer aside and catches the edge of the bearing on the far side **(see illustration)**. Tap gently against the bearing, on opposite sides of the bearing, to drive it from the hub. Insert the drift from the other side and drive the other bearing out in the same way. Remove the spacers.

8   The new bearings should be sealed on both sides. Place one of the new bearings in the hub. Tap the bearing into position with a bearing driver or socket the same diameter as the bearing outer race.

9   Install the spacers, with the shorter one on the left side of the hub.

10   Install the remaining bearing in the same manner.

11   Install a new seal in each side of the hub with its lip facing into the hub. Coat the seal lips with multi-purpose grease.

Installation

12   Installation is the reverse of removal. Be sure to tighten the hub nuts and bolts to the torque listed in this Chapter's Specifications.

13   Adjust the drive chain when you're done (see Chapter 1).

17.5 Pry the seal out of each side

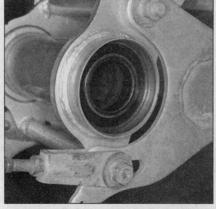

17.6 Spin the bearing in each side of the hub and check for wear

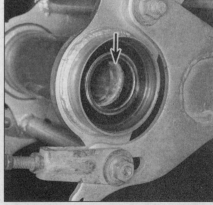

17.7 Insert a drift from the far side and catch the edge of the bearing (arrow), then tap on the drift to force the bearing out

Chapter 8
Bodywork and frame

Contents

1 General information

This Chapter covers the procedures necessary to remove and install the body panels and other body parts. Since many service and repair operations on these vehicles require removal of the panels and/or other body parts, the procedures are grouped here and referred to from other Chapters.

In the case of damage to the panels or other body parts, it is usually necessary to remove the broken component and replace it with a new (or used) one. The material that the plastic body parts is composed of doesn't lend itself to conventional repair techniques. There are, however, some shops that specialize in "plastic welding", so it would be advantageous to check around first before throwing the damaged part away.

Note: *When attempting to remove any body panel, first study the panel closely, noting any fasteners and associated fittings, to be sure of returning everything to its correct place on installation. In some cases, the aid of an assistant will be required when removing panels, to help avoid damaging the surface. Once the visible fasteners have been removed, try to lift off the panel as described but DO NOT FORCE the panel - if it will not release, check that all fasteners have been removed and try again. Where a panel engages another by means of tabs and slots, be careful not to break the tabs or to damage the bodywork. Remember that a few moments of patience at this stage will save you a lot of money in replacing broken panels!*

2.1 **To release the seat, pull up this latch**

2 Seat - removal and installation

Refer to illustrations 2.1, 2.3a and 2.3b

1   Lift the latch at the rear of the seat **(see illustration)** and lift the back end of the seat.

2   Disengage the lobes at the front end of the seat from their corresponding receptacles in the frame and lift the seat off the vehicle.

3   Installation is the reverse of removal. Insert the lobe(s) at the front of the seat into the corresponding receptacle(s) in the frame **(see illustrations)**.

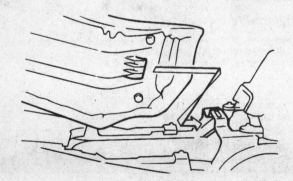

2.3a **There's a single hook at the front of the seat on Banshees – make sure it engages its catch**

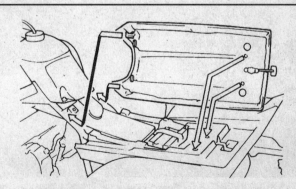

2.3b **On Warriors, be sure the hooks at the front of the seat engage their catches and the pins fit into their holes**

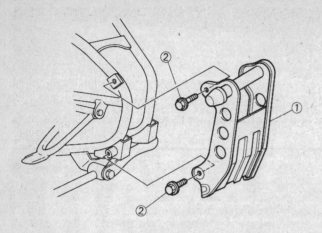

3.1 Front bumper details (Warrior shown, Banshee similar)

1   Bumper   *2   Mounting bolts*

4.1a To detach the Banshee radiator cover, remove the upper screw and one on each side . . .

4.1b . . . and pull off the cover

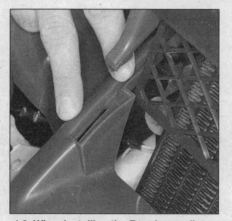

4.2 When installing the Banshee radiator cover, insert the tabs at the lower edge of the cover into their slots

5.3a To detach the fuel tank cover, remove the front screw from each side (right screw shown) . . .

3   Front bumper - removal and installation

Refer to illustration 3.1

1   Remove the bumper mounting bolts **(see illustration)** and separate the bumper from the vehicle.
2   Installation is the reverse of removal. Tighten the bumper bolts securely.

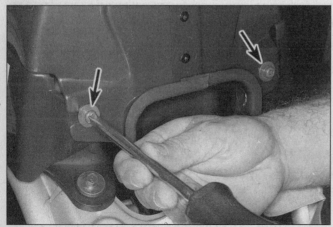

5.3b . . . the two screws at the rear . . .

4   Radiator cover/front panel - removal and installation

Radiator cover (Banshee)

Refer to illustrations 4.1a, 4.1b and 4.2

1   Remove the cover retaining screws and remove the cover **(see illustrations)**.
2   Installation is the reverse of removal. Make sure that the tabs at the lower leading edge of the cover fit into their respective slots in the fender **(see illustration)**.

Front panel (Warrior)

3   Remove the panel mounting screws, two at the forward edge, one on each side and two at the trailing edge.
4   Work the panel free of the vehicle and lift it off.
5   Installation is the reverse of removal.

5   Fuel tank cover - removal and installation

Refer to illustrations 5.3a, 5.3b, 5.3c and 5.4

1   On Banshee models, remove the radiator cover; on Warrior models, remove the front panel (see Section 4).
2   Remove the fuel tank filler cap.
3   Remove the fuel tank cover retaining screws at the front and rear

5.3c ... then lift off the cover (late Banshee shown; others similar)

5.4 When installing the fuel tank cover, hook the tabs on the lower edges into their slots

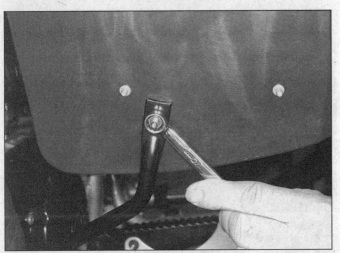

6.1 Remove the nuts to detach the front fenders from the stays

6.2a To detach the front fender panel, remove the nut from the underside of each fender ...

of the cover, then lift off the cover **(see illustrations).**

4   Installation is the reverse of removal. Make sure that the tabs on the lower edges of the cover (if equipped) are inserted into their corresponding slots in the front fender **(see illustration).**

6   Front fender - removal and installation

Refer to illustrations 6.1, 6.2a, 6.2b and 6.2c

1   Detach the fenders from the left and right fender stays **(see illustration).**

2   Remove the fender retaining nuts and screws and remove the front fender **(see illustrations).**

3   Installation is the reverse of removal.

6.2b ... remove these two screws (arrows) from the upper front portion of the panel ...

6.2c ... and lift the fender panel off the machine

8

7.1a To detach the mudguards from the rear fenders, remove these screws (arrows) (left side shown) . . .

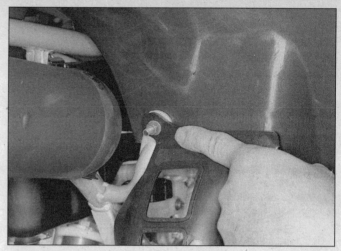

7.1b . . . the mudguards and the rear fenders are attached to the frame by nuts and the inner mudguard screws (right side shown)

7   Rear fender mudguards - removal and installation

Refer to illustrations 7.1a and 7.1b

1   Remove the mudguard retaining nuts and screws **(see illustrations)**.
2   Installation is the reverse of removal.

8   Rear fender - removal and installation

Refer to illustrations 8.3, 8.4a and 8.4b

1   Remove the seat (see Section 2).
2   Remove the rear fender mudguards (see Section 7).
3   Detach the fenders from the fender stays **(see illustration)**.
4   Remove the rear fender retaining screws **(see illustrations)** and remove the fender assembly.
5   Installation is the reverse of removal.

9   Rear bumper - removal and installation

Refer to illustration 9.1

1   To remove the rear bumper, remove the four mounting bolts **(see illustration)**.
2   Installation is the reverse of removal.

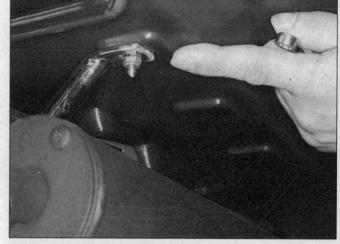

8.3 To detach the rear fenders from the stays, remove these nuts (right stay shown)

8.4a To remove the rear fender panel, remove four center screws (arrows) . . .

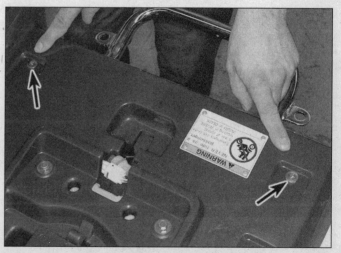

8.4b . . . and two rear screws (arrows)

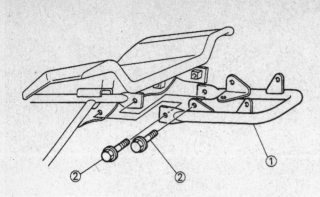

9.1 Rear bumper installation details

1   *Bumper*   2   *Mounting bolts*

10.1 The footrest is secured by Allen bolts and its plate by hex bolts

10   Footrests - removal and installation

Refer to illustration 10.1
1   To detach a footrest, remove the two Allen bolts that attach it to the foot plate and remove the two bolts that attach it to the frame **(see illustration)**.
2   To detach the plate, remove the footrest (see Step 1), then remove the nut that attaches the plate to the frame **(see illustration 10.1)**.
3   Installation is the reverse of removal.

11   Swingarm protector - removal and installation

Refer to illustrations 11.1a and 11.1b
1   Remove the protector bolts and nuts and remove the protector **(see illustrations)**.
2   Installation is the reverse of removal.

12   Frame - general information, inspection and repair

1   All models use a double-cradle frame made of cylindrical steel tubing.
2   The frame shouldn't require attention unless accident damage has occurred. In most cases, frame replacement is the only satisfactory remedy for such damage. A few frame specialists have the jigs and other equipment necessary for straightening the frame to the required standard of accuracy, but even then there is no simple way of assessing to what extent the frame may have been over-stressed.
3   After the machine has accumulated a lot of miles, the frame should be examined closely for signs of cracking or splitting at the welded joints. Corrosion can also cause weakness at these joints. Loose engine mount bolts can cause elongation of the bolt holes and can fracture the engine mounting points. Minor damage can often be repaired by welding, depending on the nature and extent of the damage.
Remember that a frame that is out of alignment will cause handling problems. If misalignment is suspected as the result of an accident, it will be necessary to strip the machine completely so the frame can be thoroughly checked.

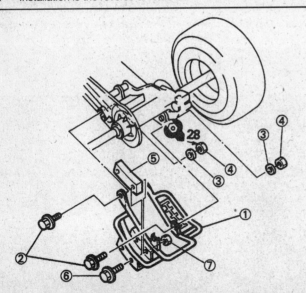

11.1a Swingarm protector installation details (Banshee)

1	*Swingarm protector*	5	*Bracket*
2	*Mounting bolts*	6	*Mounting bolt*
3	*Washer*	7	*Nut*
4	*Nut*		

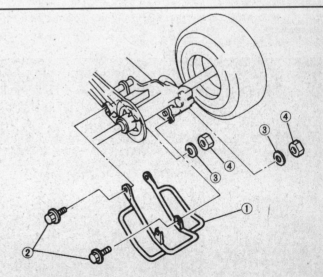

11.1b Swingarm protector installation details (Warrior)

1	*Swingarm protector*	3	*Washers*
2	*Mounting bolts*	4	*Nuts*

8

Notes

Chapter 9
Electrical system

Contents

Specifications

Battery type/capacity (Warrior)	GM12CZ-4A/12V 12 Ah
Main fuse rating	30 amps

Bulbs

Warrior
Headlight(s)	
1987 and 1988	25/25 watts
1989 through 1994	Two 25/25 watts
1995 on	Two 30/30 watts
Tail light	3.8 watts
Neutral and Reverse indicator lights	3.4 watts

Banshee
Headlight(s)	
1987 through 1989	30/30 watts
1990 on	Two 30/30 watts
Tail light	3.8 watts

Lighting system (Banshee)

Lighting voltage	
2500 rpm	11.5 volts
8000 rpm	16.3 volts
Lighting coil resistance	0.28 to 0.3 ohms at 20-degrees C (68 degrees F)

Indicator light system (Warrior)

Reverse switch relay coil resistance	72 to 88 ohms
Neutral switch relay coil resistance	72 to 88 ohms

Charging system (Warrior)

Magneto

Charging current output	
At 3000 rpm	12 amps or more
At 8000 rpm	17 amps or more
Charging coil (stator coil) resistance	0.70 to 0.86 ohms at 20-degrees C (68-degrees F)

Voltage regulator

No-load regulated voltage	14.0 to 15.0 volts at 5000 rpm

Starting system (Warrior)

Brush length	
Standard	12.0 mm (0.47 inch)
Minimum	3.5 mm (0.14 inch)
Commutator diameter	
Standard	28 mm (1.10 inch)
Minimum	27 mm (1.06 inch)
Mica depth	0.4 to 0.8 mm (0.03 to 0.04 inch)
Starting circuit cut-off relay resistance	72 to 88 ohms

Torque specifications

Alternator cover bolts (inner and outer)	10 Nm (84 in-lbs)
Alternator rotor bolt	50 Nm (36 ft-lbs)
Charging coil/CDI magneto screws	7 Nm (61 inch-lbs)*
Starter motor mounting bolts	10 Nm (84 in-lbs)
Starter clutch Torx bolts	30 Nm (22 ft-lbs)*

*Apply non-permanent thread locking agent to the threads.

1   General information

Banshee

The electrical system on Banshee models consists of a capacitive discharge ignition (CDI) system (see Chapter 5) and a lighting circuit. All models have a headlight, or headlights, and a tail light. Some vehicles originally sold in Maine and New Hampshire also have a brake light.

There is no electric starter or battery. The engine is started by a kickstarter and turned off by a kill switch on the left handlebar or by a key-operated ignition switch.

Warrior

Warrior are equipped with a 12-volt electrical system. The components include a three-phase permanent magnet alternator and a regulator/rectifier unit. The regulator/rectifier unit maintains the charging system output within the specified range to prevent overcharging and converts the alternating current (AC) output of the alternator to direct current (DC) to power the lights and other components and to charge the battery.

The lighting system consists of a headlight, or headlights, a tail light and a couple of indicator lights, for Neutral and Reverse. Some vehicles originally sold in Maine and New Hampshire also have a brake light.

An electric starter mounted to the engine case behind the cylinder is standard equipment. Some models are also equipped with a recoil (pull-rope) type starter as well. The starting system includes the motor, the battery, the starter relay and starting circuit cut-off relay and the various wires and switches. If the engine kill switch and the main key switch are both in the On position, the cut-off relay allows the starter motor to operate only if the transmission is in Neutral. **Note:** *Keep in mind that electrical parts, once purchased, can't be returned. To avoid unnecessary expense, make very sure the faulty component has been positively identified before buying a replacement part.*

2   Electrical troubleshooting

A typical electrical circuit consists of an electrical component, the switches, relays, etc. related to that component and the wiring and connectors that hook the component to both the battery and the frame. To aid in locating a problem in any electrical circuit, wiring diagrams are included at the end of this Chapter.

Before tackling any troublesome electrical circuit, first study the appropriate diagrams thoroughly to get a complete picture of what makes up that individual circuit. Trouble spots, for instance, can often be narrowed down by noting if other components related to that circuit are operating properly or not. If several components or circuits fail at one time, chances are the fault lies in the fuse or ground connection, as several circuits often are routed through the same fuse and ground connections.

Electrical problems often stem from simple causes, such as loose or corroded connections or a blown fuse. Prior to any electrical troubleshooting, always visually check the condition of the fuse, wires and connections in the problem circuit.

If testing instruments are going to be utilized, use the diagrams to plan where you will make the necessary connections in order to accurately pinpoint the trouble spot.

The basic tools needed for electrical troubleshooting include a test light or voltmeter, a continuity tester (which includes a bulb, battery and set of test leads) and a jumper wire, preferably with a circuit breaker incorporated, which can be used to bypass electrical components. Specific checks described later in this Chapter may also require an ammeter or ohmmeter.

Voltage checks should be performed if a circuit is not functioning properly. Connect one lead of a test light or voltmeter to either the negative battery terminal or a known good ground. Connect the other lead to a connector in the circuit being tested, preferably nearest to the battery or fuse. If the bulb lights, voltage is reaching that point, which means the part of the circuit between that connector and the battery is problem-free. Continue checking the remainder of the circuit in the same manner. When you reach a point where no voltage is present, the problem lies between there and the last good test point. Most of the time the problem is due to a loose connection. Since these vehicles are designed for off-road use, the problem may also be water or corrosion in a connector. Keep in mind that some circuits only receive voltage when the ignition key is in the On position.

One method of finding short circuits is to remove the fuse and connect a test light or voltmeter in its place to the fuse terminals. There should be no load in the circuit. Move the wiring harness from side-to-side while watching the test light. If the bulb lights, there is a short to ground somewhere in that area, probably where insulation has rubbed off a wire. The same test can be performed on other components in the circuit, including the switch.

A ground check should be done to see if a component is grounded properly. Disconnect the battery and connect one lead of a self-powered test light (such as a continuity tester) to a known good ground. Connect the other lead to the wire or ground connection being tested. If the bulb lights, the ground is good. If the bulb does not light, the ground is not good.

A continuity check is performed to see if a circuit, section of circuit or individual component is capable of passing electricity through it. Disconnect the battery and connect one lead of a self-powered test light (such as a continuity tester) to one end of the circuit being tested and the other lead to the other end of the circuit. If the bulb lights, there is continuity, which means the circuit is passing electricity through it properly. Switches can be checked in the same way.

Remember that all electrical circuits are designed to conduct electricity from the battery, through the wires, switches, relays, etc. to the electrical component (light bulb, motor, etc.). From there it is directed to the frame (ground) where it is passed back to the battery. Electrical problems are basically an interruption in the flow of electricity from the battery or back to it.

3 Battery (Warrior) - inspection and maintenance

1   Most battery damage is caused by heat, vibration, and/or low electrolyte levels, so keep the battery securely mounted, check the electrolyte level frequently and make sure the charging system is functioning properly. The battery used on these vehicles is a maintenance free (sealed) type and therefore doesn't require the addition of water. However, the following checks should still be regularly performed. **Warning:** *Always disconnect the negative cable first and connect it last to prevent sparks which could the battery to explode.*
2   Refer to Chapter 1 for electrolyte level and specific gravity checking procedures.
3   Inspect the base inside of the battery for sediment, which is the result of sulfation caused by low electrolyte levels. These deposits will cause internal short circuits, which can quickly discharge the battery. Look for cracks in the case and replace the battery if either of these conditions is found.
4   Inspect the battery terminals and cable ends for tightness and corrosion. If corrosion is evident, disconnect the cables from the battery, disconnecting the negative (-) terminal first, and clean the terminals and cable ends with a wire brush or knife and emery paper. Reconnect the cables, connecting the negative cable last, and apply a

thin coat of petroleum jelly to the cables to slow further corrosion.
5   The battery case should be kept clean to prevent current leakage, which can discharge the battery over a period of time (especially when it sits unused). Wash the outside of the case with a solution of baking soda and water. Do not get any baking soda solution in the battery cells. Rinse the battery thoroughly, then dry it.
6   If acid has been spilled on the frame or battery box, neutralize it with a baking soda and water solution, then touch up any damaged paint. Make sure the battery vent tube (if equipped) is directed away from the frame and is not kinked or pinched **(see illustrations 26.12a and 26.12b in Chapter 1).**
7   If the vehicle sits unused for long periods of time, disconnect the cables from the battery terminals. Charge the battery approximately once every month (see Section 4).

4 Battery (Warrior) - charging

1   If the machine sits idle for extended periods or if the charging system malfunctions, the battery can be charged from an external source.
2   To properly charge the battery, you will need a charger of the correct rating, a hydrometer, a clean rag and a syringe for adding distilled water to the battery cells.
3   The maximum charging rate for any battery is 1/10th of the rated amp-hour capacity. As an example, the maximum charge rate for a 14 amp/hour battery would be 1.4 amps. If the battery is charged at a higher rate, it could overheat, causing the plates inside the battery to buckle.
4   Do not allow the battery to be subjected to a so-called quick charge (high charge rate over a short period of time) unless you are prepared to buy a new battery.
5   When charging the battery, always remove it from the machine and be sure to check the electrolyte level before hooking up the charger. Add distilled water to any cells that are low.
6   Loosen the cell caps, hook up the battery charger leads (positive lead to battery positive terminal, negative lead to battery negative terminal), cover the top of the battery with a clean rag, then, and only then, plug in the battery charger. **Warning:** *The hydrogen gas escaping from a charging battery is explosive, so keep open flames and sparks well away from the area. Also, the electrolyte is extremely corrosive and will damage anything it comes in contact with,*
7   Allow the battery to charge until the specific gravity is as specified (refer to Chapter 1 for the specific gravity checking procedure). The charger must be unplugged and disconnected from the battery when making specific gravity checks. If the battery overheats or gases excessively, the charging rate is too high. Either disconnect the charger or lower the charging rate to prevent damage to the battery.
8   If one or more of the cells do not show an increase in specific gravity after a long slow charge, or if the battery as a whole does not seem to want to take a charge, it's time for a new battery.
9   When the battery is fully charged, unplug the charger first, then disconnect the leads from the battery. Install the cell caps and wipe any electrolyte off the outside of the battery case.
10   If the recharged battery discharges rapidly when left disconnected, it's likely that an internal short caused by physical damage or sulfation has occurred. A new battery will be required. A sound battery will tend to lose its charge at about 1-percent per day.

5 Main fuse (Warrior) - check and replacement

1   The main (30-amp) fuse is mounted in a plastic and rubber holder located below the left fender. A spare 30-amp fuse is also stored here. If you can't find the fuse, trace the red wire from the battery to the rectifier/regulator (not the thicker red wire to the starter); the main fuse is installed in this wire.
2   To remove the main fuse, simply pull the two halves of the rubber cover apart and pull out the fuse. A break in the element (wire) inside the fuse indicates a blown fuse.

9

3   If the fuse has blown, be sure to inspect the wiring harness very carefully for evidence of a short circuit. Look for bare wires and chafed, melted or burned insulation. If the fuse is replaced before the cause is located, the new fuse will blow immediately.

4   Never, under any circumstances, use a higher rated fuse or bridge the fuse terminals, as damage to the electrical system - or even a fire - could result.

5   Occasionally a fuse will blow or cause an open circuit for no obvious reason. Corrosion of the fuse ends and fuse holder terminals may occur and cause poor fuse contact. If this happens, remove the corrosion with a wire brush or emery paper, then spray the fuse end and terminals with electrical contact cleaner.

6   Lighting system - check

Banshee

Note: *The following tests apply to single and dual-headlight models.*

1   The lighting system on these models is powered by a lighting coil located on the left side of the engine, under the CDI rotor. There is no battery or charging system.

2   Remove the front and rear fenders (see Chapter 8).

Headlight not working

3   If only one headlight is out on a dual-headlight model, try installing the bulb from the working headlight.

4   If this solves the problem, replace the defective bulb.

5   If this doesn't solve the problem, test the system as follows.

Headlight bulb and socket

6   If the headlight doesn't come on in HI beam, or LO beam, or both, remove the headlight bulb (see Section 7) and inspect the filaments. If either filament is obviously broken, replace the bulb. (The upper filament is usually the LO beam filament; the lower filament is usually for HI beam.)

7   If the filaments look okay, check the continuity between each bulb terminal and ground (the metal base of the bulb). There are two circuits inside the bulb: HI beam terminal to ground, and LO beam terminal to ground. If there's no continuity in either or both circuits, replace the bulb.

8   Install the bulb in the headlight socket and check the socket terminals for continuity with an ohmmeter: Backprobe the socket terminals for HI beam (yellow wire) and ground (black wire), and for LO beam (green wire) and ground (black wire). If there's no continuity between either or both terminals and ground, replace the headlight bulb socket.

Voltage regulator

Note: *You will need a voltmeter capable of measuring alternating current (AC) voltage for this test. The lighting coil output is not rectified from AC to direct current (DC), so a DC voltmeter won't work.*

9   Connect the positive lead of an AC voltmeter to the yellow lead (HI beam) and the negative lead to the black (ground) wire. Start the engine and turn the headlight switch to the HI beam position. Note the indicated voltage at 2500 rpm, and at 8000 rpm, respectively, then compare your readings to the lighting voltage listed in this Chapter's Specifications. **Caution:** *Do NOT rev the engine at 8000 rpm in Neutral for more than one or two seconds.*

10   Connect the positive lead of the voltmeter to the green lead (LO beam) and the negative lead to the black (ground) wire and repeat the above test for the LO beam circuit.

11   If the lighting voltage is okay, check the headlight dimmer switch (see Section 14).

12   If the lighting voltage at 2500 rpm is lower than specified, check the lighting coil (see Step 14).

13   If the lighting voltage at 8000 rpm is higher than specified, replace the voltage regulator (see Section 26).

Lighting coil

14   Follow the wiring harness from the grommet in the left crankcase

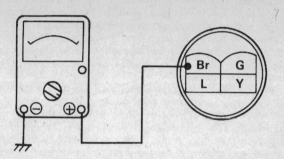

6.26 Headlight dimmer switch connector terminals (Warrior)

cover to the connector on the left side of the air cleaner housing. Disconnect the connector.

15   Connect the leads of an ohmmeter to the terminals for the yellow and black wires from the CDI magneto (these are the lighting coil leads), measure the lighting coil resistance and compare your measurement to the lighting coil resistance listed in this Chapter's Specifications.

16   If the resistance is out of specification, replace the lighting coil (see Section 25).

17   If the resistance is okay, inspect the lighting system wire harness for breaks or bad connections (see the wiring diagrams at the end of this Chapter). Pay special attention to the connectors. Inspect all connectors in the harness, including the ones inside the headlight housing. Clean off all accumulated mud and grime, then disconnect each connector and clean the terminals.

Taillight not working

Taillight bulb and socket

18   If the taillight doesn't come on, remove the taillight bulb (see Section 9) and inspect the filament. If the filament is obviously broken, replace the bulb.

19   If the filament looks okay, check the continuity between the bulb terminal and ground (the metal base of the bulb). If there's no continuity between the terminal and ground, replace the bulb.

20   Install the bulb in the headlight socket and check the socket terminal for continuity with an ohmmeter: backprobe the socket terminal and ground. If there's no continuity between the socket terminal and ground, replace the tail light bulb socket.

21   If there is continuity between the bulb socket and ground, troubleshoot the remainder of the lighting circuit as described above, beginning with Step 6.

Warrior

Note: *The following tests apply to single and dual-headlight models.*

22   The battery provides power for operation of the headlights, tail light, brake light (if equipped) and instrument cluster lights. If none of the lights operate, always check battery voltage before proceeding. Low battery voltage indicates either a faulty battery, low battery electrolyte level or a defective charging system. Refer to Chapter 1 and Section 3 of this Chapter for battery checks and Sections 21 through 24 for charging system tests.

23   Remove the front panel (see Chapter 8).

Headlight(s) not working

Refer to illustration 6.26

24   If only one headlight is out on a dual-headlight model, try installing the bulb from the working headlight. If this solves the problem, replace the defective bulb. If not, test the system as follows.

25   Disconnect the electrical connector from the wires to the headlight dimmer switch.

26   Connect the positive lead of a voltmeter to the terminal for the brown wire and the negative lead to ground **(see illustration)**. Turn the main switch to ON and measure battery voltage between the terminal for the brown lead and ground.

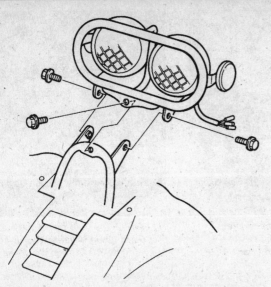

7.1a On Warriors, remove these three bolts, then remove the
headlights and guard as a single assembly

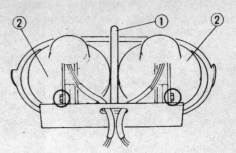

7.1b To detach either headlight (2) from the guard (1),
remove the indicated bolt

27 If battery voltage is less than 12 volts, check the battery (see Section 3), the main fuse (see Section 5) and the main switch (see Section 12).
28 If battery voltage is 12 volts or more, check the dimmer switch (see Section 14).

Tail light not working

29 If the tail light fails to work, check the bulb and the bulb terminals first.
30 If the bulb and terminals are good, disconnect the tail light electrical connector. Connect a voltmeter negative lead to the black wire in the wiring harness and the positive lead to the blue wire. With the main key switch and lighting switch On, the voltmeter should indicate 12 volts or more.

  a) If there's voltage at the terminals, the bulb is burned out or the bulb socket is corroded.
  b) If there's no voltage, the problem lies in the wiring or one of the switches in the circuit (see Sections 13 and 14).

31 If no voltage is indicated, check the ground wire and the wiring between the tail light and the lighting switch, then check the switch.

Neutral indicator light

32 If the neutral light fails to operate when the transmission is in Neutral, check the fuse and the bulb (see Section 11). If the bulb and fuse

are in good condition, check for battery voltage at the wire attached to the neutral switch on the left side of the engine. If battery voltage is present, check the neutral switch (see Section 16).
33 If no voltage is indicated, check the wiring to the bulb, to the switch and between the switch and the bulb for open circuits and poor connections.

Brake light switch (some Maine and New Hampshire models)

34 If the brake light doesn't work and the bulb is good, check the switch adjustment (see Section 4 in Chapter 1). If the switch is adjusted correctly, disconnect the switch wiring connector and connect an ohmmeter between the terminals in the switch side of the harness. The ohmmeter should indicate continuity when the switch plunger extends and no continuity when it retracts. If not, unscrew the switch nut, remove the switch body from the bracket and install a new switch.

7   Headlight bulb - replacement

Refer to illustrations 7.1a, 7.1b, 7.2a, 7.2b, 7.3a, 7.3b and 7.4
Warning: *If the headlight has just burned out, give it time to cool before changing the bulb to avoid burning your fingers.*
Note: *The following procedure applies to all single and dual-headlight models. The accompanying photos depict a late-model Banshee, but the headlights on all Banshee and Warrior models, whether square or round, are basically the same design.*
1   On Warrior models, remove the headlight(s) and guard as a single assembly **(see illustration)**, then detach the headlight(s) from the guard **(see illustration)**.
2   Remove the headlight cover screws and separate the headlight and cover from the headlight housing **(see illustrations)**.

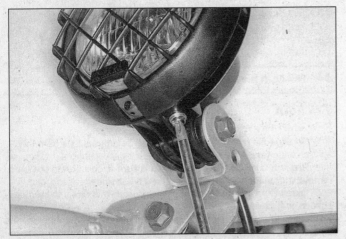

7.2a Remove the headlight cover screws
(other screw not visible) . . .

7.2b . . . and remove the headlight and cover from the housing
(Banshee shown; Warrior similar)

9

7.3a Pull off the rubber cover . . .

7.3b . . . turn the bulb socket
counterclockwise and remove
it from the headlight case

7.4 Pull the bulb out of the socket; if
you're going to reuse the same bulb,
do NOT touch the glass

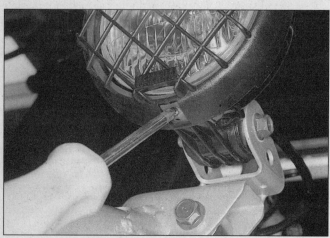

8.3a The headlight adjusting screw is mounted below each
headlight on Banshee models

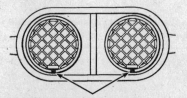

8.3b Warrior headlight
adjusting screws (arrows)

9.1a Remove the lens screws . . .

3   Pull the rubber cover off the bulb. Twist the bulb socket counter-clockwise and remove it from the headlight case **(see illustrations)**.
4   Pull the bulb out **(see illustration)**. If you're going to reuse the same bulb, don't touch the glass.
5   Installation is the reverse of the removal procedure, with the following additions:

a) *Be sure not to touch the bulb with your fingers - oil from your skin will cause the bulb to overheat and fail prematurely. If you do touch the bulb, wipe it off with a clean rag dampened with rubbing alcohol.*
b) *Align the tab on the metal bulb flange with the slot in the headlight case.*
c) *Make sure the TOP mark (if applicable) on the headlight cover is facing up.*
d) *On Warrior models, reattach the headlight(s) to the guard and install the headlight/guard assembly* **(see illustration 7.2)**.

8   Headlight aim - check and adjustment

Refer to illustrations 8.3a and 8.3b

1   An improperly adjusted headlight may cause problems for oncoming traffic or provide poor, unsafe illumination of the terrain ahead. Before adjusting the headlight, be sure to consult with local traffic laws and regulations. Yamaha doesn't provide specifications for headlight adjustment.
2   The headlight beam can be adjusted vertically. Before performing the adjustment, make sure the fuel tank is at least half full, and have an

assistant sit on the seat.
3   Insert a Phillips screwdriver into the vertical adjuster screw **(see illustrations)**, then turn the adjuster as necessary to raise or lower the beam.

9   Tail light and brake light bulbs - replacement

Tail light

Refer to illustrations 9.1a, 9.1b and 9.2

1   Remove the tail light lens screws and detach the lens from the tail light housing **(see illustrations)**.
2   Press the bulb into its socket and turn it counterclockwise to remove it from the tail light housing **(see illustration)**.
3   Inspect the socket terminals for corrosion and clean them if necessary.
4   Press the bulb into its socket, then turn it clockwise to engage the pins, locking the bulb into place.
5   Install the lens and tighten the screws securely (but not so tight that it cracks the plastic).

9.1b . . . and separate the lens from the tail light housing

9.2 Press the tail light bulb into the socket, turn it counterclockwise and pull it out of the tail light housing

Brake light (some Maine and New Hampshire models)

6 The brake light bulb on vehicles so equipped is replaced in the same way as the tail light bulb.

10 Brake light switch (Maine and New Hampshire models) - check and replacement

1 Some Maine and New Hampshire models are equipped with a brake light. On these models, the brake light is operated by a brake light switch at the rear brake pedal (see illustration 4.8 in Chapter 1).

Check

2 Using a test light connected to a good ground, check for voltage to the brake light switch. If there's no voltage present, check the wire between the switch and the main harness.
3 If voltage is available, touch the probe of the test light to the other terminal of the switch, then depress the brake pedal - if the test light doesn't light up, replace the switch.
4 If the test light does light, check the wiring between the switch and the brake lights.

Replacement

5 Unplug the switch electrical connector.
6 Disconnect the spring from the switch.
7 Hold the switch body from turning and rotate the adjuster nut all the way up until it clears the switch threads, then lift it out.
8 Installation is the reverse of removal. Be sure to adjust the switch when you're done (see "Brake system - general check" in Chapter 1).

11 Indicator light system (Warrior) - check and replacement

Check

Refer to illustrations 11.3, 11.4a and 11.4b

1 These models are equipped with indicator lights for Neutral and Reverse. If an indicator light isn't working, remove the bulb (see below) and inspect the bulb filament. If it's broken, replace the bulb. If the filament is okay, inspect the bulb terminal for corrosion. If the terminal is corroded, try cleaning it with a wire brush, then install the bulb and determine whether it works. If it still doesn't work, check the indicator light system as follows.
2 Disconnect the connector to the Neutral (or the Reverse) switch

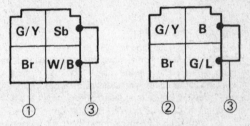

11.3 To bypass the Neutral switch (1) or Reverse switch (2), bridge the indicated connector terminals with a jumper wire (3)

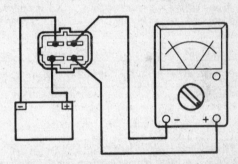

11.4a Hook up the battery and ohmmeter as shown; with battery voltage applied, there should be infinite resistance, but when the battery is disconnected, there should be no resistance

relay. The Neutral and Reverse switch relays are located right behind the battery, next to the rectifier/regulator. The Neutral relay connector is located to the left of the rectifier/regulator, and has white/black and sky blue wires. The Reverse relay connector is on the right side of the rectifier/regulator and has green/blue and black wires.
3 Hook up a jumper wire to the indicated terminals of the Neutral (or Reverse) switch relay connector (see illustration), then turn the main switch to ON, shift into Neutral (or Reverse), and verify whether the Neutral or Reverse light now comes on. If the Neutral (or Reverse) light now does come on, replace the Neutral (or Reverse) switch (see Section 16). If it doesn't, check the relay.
4 To check either relay, unplug the electrical connector, remove the relay and, using a 12-volt battery and an ohmmeter, test it as follows: First, check the relay contacts. Connect the battery and ohmmeter as shown (see illustration). With the battery connected to the indicated terminals of the relay, there should be infinite resistance at the other two terminals; with the battery disconnected, there should be no resistance at these terminals. Now, check the relay coil resistance: Set the

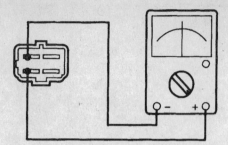

11.4b Touch the leads of the ohmmeter to the two terminals you just powered with the battery and measure relay coil resistance

battery and jumper wires aside and touch the leads of the ohmmeter to the two terminals you just powered up with the battery **(see illustration)**. Measure the resistance of the relay coil and compare your measurement to the relay coil resistance listed in this Chapter's Specifications. If the relay fails either of these tests, replace it.

Replacement

Bulb

Refer to illustrations 11.5 and 11.6

5   Pull the handlebar cover clips free of the handlebar, disconnect the indicator light electrical leads and remove the cover **(see illustration)**.

6   To replace either bulb, pull the rubber socket cover, socket and bulb out of the handlebar cover **(see illustration 11.5)**, pull the bulb and socket out of the rubber cover **(see illustration)**, press the bulb into its socket, turn it counterclockwise and pull the bulb out of the socket.

7   If the socket contact is dirty or corroded, clean it with a wire brush and spray it with electrical contact cleaner before installing the new bulb.

8   Push the new bulb into its socket, turn it clockwise and release it. Install the bulb and socket in the rubber cover, install the rubber cover in the handlebar cover, reconnect the electrical leads and install the handlebar cover on the handlebar.

12   Ignition main (key) switch - check and replacement

Check

1   Follow the wiring harness from the ignition main switch to the connector and disconnect it. To get to the switch connector on Banshee models, remove the fuel tank (see Chapter 4). To get to the switch connector on Warrior models, remove the front panel (see Chapter 8).

2   Using an ohmmeter, check the continuity at the indicated terminals of the switch connector (see the wiring diagrams at the end of this

11.5 Free the rubber housing and bulb socket from the handlebar cover . . .

Chapter). There should be continuity between the indicated terminals when the switch is in the indicated position.

3   If the switch fails either test, replace it.

Replacement

Refer to illustrations 12.4a and 12.4b

4   If you're working on a Banshee, remove the handlebar cover screws and lift off the cover **(see illustrations)**.

5   If you're working on a Warrior, remove the front panel (see Chapter 8) and disconnect the switch connector.

6   Unscrew the switch locknut **(see illustration 12.4a)** and remove the switch.

7   Installation is the reverse of removal.

13   Ignition cutoff system (Banshee) - check and control unit replacement

1   The ignition cutoff system, known as the Throttle Override System (T.O.R.S.), consists of the CDI magneto, the CDI unit, the ignition coil, the spark plugs, the engine kill switch, a throttle switch inside the throttle housing, the two carburetor switches and a system control unit. If the throttle cable or one of the throttle pistons sticks in an open-throttle position, the system shorts the ignition current to ground, shutting off the ignition circuit.

Check

2   Remove the seat, the front fender and the rear fender (see Chapter 8).

11.6 . . . then pull the bulb and socket out of the rubber housing; push the bulb into the socket and turn counterclockwise to remove

12.4a Remove the screws (arrows) . . .

12.4b . . . and lift off the handlebar cover (Banshee shown); unscrew the plastic nut to remove the ignition main switch

15.1a Remove the clamp screws (arrows) . . .

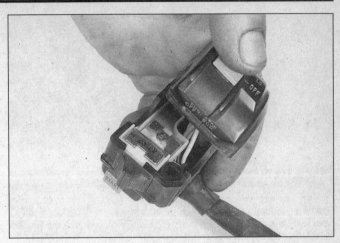

15.1b . . . and separate the switch housing (the handlebar switches are inside)

System

3   If the ignition system tests in Section 2 in Chapter 5 show that there's no spark at the plug, or if the throttle has stuck and the engine failed to shut off, test the ignition cutoff system. It will quickly tell you whether the ignition cutoff system has failed; further checks will be needed to identify the faulty component.

4   Locate the control unit near the left front fender (**see illustration 3.1a** in Chapter 5). Disconnect the control unit electrical connector (black, yellow/black and black/white wires), then try to start the engine.

5   If the engine won't start, the control unit is good; the problem is elsewhere. Check the spark plugs and the ignition coil (see Chapter 5), the CDI magneto source coil and pickup coil (see Section 4 in Chapter 5), and the engine kill switch (see Section 14).

6   If the engine does start, the throttle switch, carburetor switch or control unit may be defective.

Throttle switch

7   Check and, if necessary, adjust the throttle lever freeplay (see Chapter 1). (The following test won't be accurate if the freeplay is incorrect.)

8   Remove the fuel tank (see Chapter 4).

9   Follow the wiring harness from the throttle switch (located inside the throttle housing on the right handlebar) along the right end of the handlebar and down the steering shaft to the connector (black/yellow wire and black wire).

10   Connect the positive lead of an ohmmeter to the switch connector terminal (on the *switch* side of the connector, not the harness side) for the black/yellow wire and connect the ohmmeter negative lead to switch connector terminal for the black wire.

11   Operate the throttle lever and note the indicated resistance reading. There should be no continuity when the throttle is closed (lever released) and continuity when the throttle is open (lever applied). If the throttle switch doesn't operate as described, replace the throttle assembly (see Section 11 in Chapter 4).

Carburetor switch

12   Trace the black/yellow wire to the connector for the left carburetor switch (the switches are mounted inside the throttle cable housing on each carburetor). The right carburetor switch has a yellow/black wire.

13   Connect the positive lead of the ohmmeter to the switch connector terminal (on the switch side of the connector, not the harness side) for the black/yellow wire and the negative lead to the terminal for the black wire.

14   Operate the throttle lever and check the ohmmeter reading. There should be continuity when the throttle is closed (lever released) and no continuity when the throttle is open (lever applied). If the switch fails to operate as described, replace it (see Section 11 in Chapter 4).

15   Test the right carburetor switch the same way (the hot lead for the right carburetor switch is yellow/black, instead of black/yellow).

Control unit replacement

16   If the throttle switch, carburetor switch and system wiring are good, and the test in Steps 4 through 6 indicates a problem in the ignition cutoff system, the control unit may be defective.

17   Before replacing the control unit, check the throttle and carburetor switches as described above and make sure they're good.

18   Check all wiring and connections in the ignition circuit carefully. If you can, borrow a control unit from a friend and substitute it for the one in your vehicle.

19   To replace the control unit, disconnect its electrical connector and remove the mounting screw. Installation is the reverse of removal.

20   Install the rear fender, front fender and seat (see Chapter 8).

14   Handlebar switches - check

1   Switch problems are caused by dirty or corroded contacts, by wear or by broken parts. If something inside a switch breaks, the entire switch housing must be replaced as a single assembly. Individual parts are not available.

2   On Banshee models, remove the fuel tank (see Chapter 4) and/or the radiator cover (see Chapter 8), as necessary; on Warrior models, remove the front panel (see Chapter 8) and/or the fuel tank (see Chapter 4), as necessary.

3   Trace the wiring harness from the malfunctioning switch down to its electrical connector and unplug it. **Note:** *On Warrior models, to prevent the possibility of a short circuit, disconnect the battery negative cable before making the following checks.*

4   Using an ohmmeter or test light, check for continuity between the terminals of the switch harness with the switch in the various positions (see the continuity charts in the wiring diagrams at the end of this Chapter). Continuity should exist between the terminals connected by a solid line when the switch is in the indicated position.

5   If the continuity check indicates a problem exists, disassemble the switch housing (see Section 15) and spray the switch contacts with electrical contact cleaner. If they are accessible, the contacts can be scraped clean with a knife or polished with crocus cloth. If switch components are damaged or broken, replace the switch housing assembly.

15   Handlebar switch housing - removal and installation

Refer to illustrations 15.1a and 15.1b

1   The handlebar switch housing is composed of two halves that clamp around the bars. If you need to clean or inspect a switch, or remove the handlebar, simply remove the clamp screws and pull the switch halves away from the handlebars (**see illustrations**).

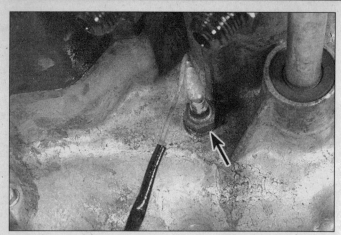

16.1a The Neutral switch (arrow) is located on the left side of the engine, right in front of the shift shaft

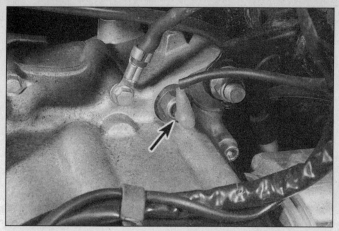

16.1b The Reverse switch (arrow) is located on the left side of the engine, above the crankcase, right behind the ground lead

2   To replace the switch housing, trace the switch harness down to the electrical connector(s), unplug it, and separate the harness from any tie wraps and retainers.

3   When installing the switch housing, make sure the wiring harness is properly routed to avoid pinching or stretching the wires.

16 Neutral and reverse switches (Warrior) - check and replacement

Check

Refer to illustrations 16.1a and 16.1b

Note: *The neutral and reverse switches are part of the indicator light system. For a step-by-step description of how to test the entire system, see Section 11.*

1   Disconnect the electrical connector from the switch being tested. The neutral switch **(see illustration)** is located on the left side of the engine, near the shift shaft. The reverse switch **(see illustration)** is located on the left side of the engine, behind the ground lead.

2   Connect one lead of an ohmmeter to a good ground and the other lead to the terminal post on the switch.

3   If you're testing the Neutral switch, there should be no resistance between the switch and ground when the transmission is in Neutral. In any other gear, there should be infinite resistance.

4   If you're testing the Reverse switch, there should be infinite resistance when the shift select lever is in Reverse. In any other gear, there should be no resistance.

5   If the switch doesn't check out as described, replace it.

Replacement

6   Unplug the electrical connector and unscrew the switch.

7   Before installing the new switch, wrap the threads of the new switch with Teflon tape or apply a thin coat of RTV sealant to them.

8   Install the switch in the case with a new sealing washer and tighten it to the torque listed in this Chapter's Specifications.

9   Reconnect the switch wires.

17 Starter circuit (Warrior) – check and component replacement

Description

1   The starter circuit consists of the starter motor, the starter relay, the starting circuit cut-off relay, the neutral relay, the clutch switch, the neutral switch and the reverse switch.

2   When the main (key) switch is ON and the engine kill switch is at RUN, the starter motor can be operated when (1) the transmission is in Neutral and the select lever is in the FORWARD position; or, (2) the

clutch lever is pulled in (the starter motor will operate with the engine kill switch at OFF, but the engine won't start).

3   The starting circuit cut-off relay prevents the starter motor from operating when the transmission is in gear (or the select lever is in Reverse) and the clutch is engaged. See the wiring diagrams at the end of this Chapter for details.

Check

4   Turn on the headlights. If they don't work, check the main fuse (see Section 5) and the battery (see Section 3).

5   If the headlights work, try cranking the starter. If it doesn't crank, the problem may be in the starter itself (see Sections 18 and 19), in the electrical cables between the battery and the starter relay, or in the starter relay.

1987 models

Starter relay

Refer to illustration 17.7

6   Check the starter relay as follows.

7   Locate the starter relay behind the battery, beneath the left rear fender **(see illustration)**.

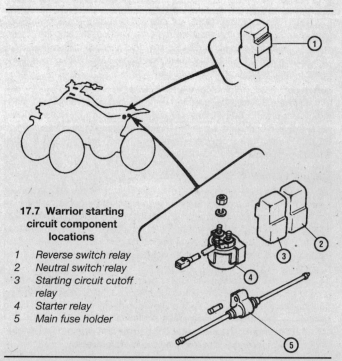

17.7 Warrior starting circuit component locations

1   Reverse switch relay
2   Neutral switch relay
3   Starting circuit cutoff relay
4   Starter relay
5   Main fuse holder

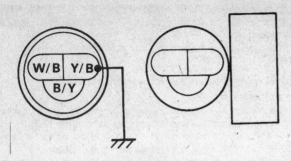

17.17 Ground the terminal for the yellow/black wire, turn the main switch to ON and push the starter button; the starter motor should crank the engine

8   Pull back the rubber covers from the terminal nuts, remove the nuts and disconnect the starter relay cables. Disconnect the remaining electrical connector from the starter relay.

9   Pull the relay's rubber mount off the metal bracket and pull the relay out of the mount.

10   Connect an ohmmeter or a battery-powered test lamp between the cable terminals on the starter relay **(see illustration 17.7)**. The ohmmeter should indicate infinite resistance or the test lamp should stay out.

11   Connect a jumper wire from one of the small relay terminals to the battery positive terminal. Connect another jumper wire from the relay's remaining small terminal to the battery negative terminal. The ohmmeter should not indicate little or no resistance or the test lamp should light.

12   If the starter relay doesn't perform as described, replace it.

13   Installation is the reverse of removal.

14   Reconnect the negative battery cable after all the other electrical connections are made.

Starting circuit cut-off relay

Refer to illustration 17.17

15   Remove the front panel (see Chapter 8).

16   Locate the electrical connector for the CDI unit (white/black, yellow/black and black/yellow wires) and disconnect it.

17   **Warning:** *Make sure the transmission is in Neutral for this step.* Using a jumper wire, ground the terminal for the yellow/black wire **(see illustration)**. Turn the main switch to ON and push the starter button. The starter motor should crank the engine.

18   If the starter motor does not crank the engine, check the main fuse (see Section 5), the main switch (see Section 12) and the starter switch (see Section 14) and replace any defective component(s).

19   If the main fuse, the main switch and the starter switch are okay, replace the starting circuit cut-off relay.

17.26 Disconnect the electrical connector and press the retainer prong (arrow) to free the clutch switch

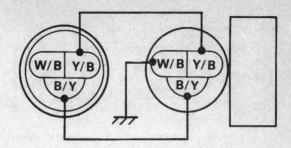

17.23 Clutch switch and CDI unit test connections (1987 Warrior)

Neutral switch relay

20   If the starter motor does crank the engine in Step 17, turn the main switch to ON, shift into Neutral, move the drive select lever to Forward and verify that the Neutral indicator light comes on.

21   If the Neutral indicator light does not come on, check the bulb (see Section 11), the Neutral switch (see Section 16) and the Reverse switch (see Section 16). Replace any defective components.

22   If the Neutral indicator bulb, the Neutral switch and the Reverse switch are okay, replace the Neutral switch relay.

Clutch switch and CDI unit

Refer to illustrations 17.23 and 17.26

23   If the Neutral indicator light does come on in Step 20, connect the indicated terminals of the CDI unit connector together and to ground as shown **(see illustration)**.

24   Turn the main switch to ON, put the engine kill switch in the RUN position and push the starter switch. The starter should crank the engine.

25   Disconnect the ground lead from the CDI connector (the CDI side), turn the main switch to ON, put the engine kill switch in the RUN position, pull in the clutch lever and push the starter switch. The starter should crank the engine.

26   If the starter doesn't crank the engine in Steps 24 and 25, check the engine kill switch (see Section 14) and the clutch switch **(see illustration)**. To check the clutch switch, use an ohmmeter to verify that it has no continuity when the clutch lever is released, and that it does have continuity when the clutch lever is applied. Replace either component if it's defective. To replace the engine kill switch, you'll have to replace the entire left switch housing (see Section 14). To replace the clutch switch, unplug the electrical connector, squeeze the prong that secures the switch to the clutch lever bracket and remove the switch. When installing a new clutch switch, make sure it's correctly seated; the prong should snap into place when the new switch is fully seated in the clutch lever bracket.

27   If the engine kill switch and the clutch switch are okay, replace the CDI unit.

28   If the starter cranks the engine in Step 25, turn the main switch to ON, turn the engine kill switch to OFF, pull in the clutch lever and push the starter switch. The starter should crank the engine.

29   If the starter still doesn't crank the engine, inspect the connectors and wires in the starter circuit. Look for an open or short in the circuit (see wiring diagrams at the end of this chapter) and repair as necessary.

30   If everything else checks out, and there is neither an open or short in the starting circuit, the CDI unit is probably defective. To make sure, take the CDI unit to a Yamaha dealer and have it professionally checked before replacing it.

1988 and later models

31   If the battery and the main fuse are both okay, check the main switch (see Section 12). Repair or replace the main switch as necessary.

32   If the main switch is okay, check the starter switch (see Section 14). Repair the starter switch or replace the left switch housing as necessary.

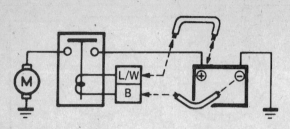

17.36 Starter relay test connections (1988 and later Warrior)

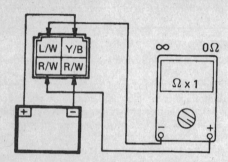

17.40 Starting circuit cutoff relay test connections 1988 and later Warrior)

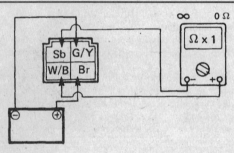

17.44 Neutral relay test connections (1988 and later Warrior)

33   If the starter switch is okay, check the engine kill switch (see Section 14). Repair the stop switch or replace the left switch housing as necessary.

34   If the engine kill switch is okay, check the clutch switch (see Step 26). Repair or replace the clutch switch as necessary.

35   If the clutch switch is okay, check the starter relay as described below.

Starter relay

Refer to illustration 17.36

36   Disconnect the electrical connector for the starter relay (blue/white and black wires) and connect the starter relay connector terminals to the battery as shown **(see illustration)**. The starter motor should operate.

37   If the starter motor doesn't operate, replace the starter relay (see Steps 11 through 14).

38   If the starter motor does operate in Step 37, check the starting circuit cut-off relay.

Starting circuit cut-off relay

Refer to illustration 17.40

39   Disconnect the electrical connector for the starting circuit cut-off relay (red/white, red/white, blue/white and yellow/black wires) **(see illustration 17.7)**.

40   Connect an ohmmeter (set to ohm X 1) to the indicated terminals of the starting circuit cut-off relay connector **(see illustration)**. Using a pair of jumper wires, connect the battery to the indicated terminals of the connector and verify that there is continuity between the first two terminals. Disconnect the battery jumpers and verify that the there is

no continuity between the indicated terminals.

41   If the resistance at the connector is not as specified, replace the starting circuit cut-off relay.

42   If the resistance at the connector is as specified, check the neutral relay.

Neutral relay/neutral switch/reverse switch

Refer to illustration 17.44

43   Disconnect the electrical connector for the neutral relay (sky blue, green/yellow, white/black and brown) **(see illustration 17.7)**.

44   Connect an ohmmeter (set to ohm X 1) to the indicated terminals of the neutral relay connector **(see illustration)**. Using a pair of jumper wires, connect the battery to the indicated terminals of the connector and verify that there is continuity between them. Disconnect the battery jumpers and verify that the there is no continuity between the indicated terminals.

45   If the resistance at the connector is not as specified, replace the neutral relay.

46   If the resistance at the connector is as specified, check the neutral switch (see Section 16). If the neutral switch is okay, check the reverse switch (see Section 16).

47   If everything else checks out, and there is neither an open, ground or short in the starting circuit, the CDI unit is probably defective. To make sure, take the CDI unit to a Yamaha dealer and have it professionally checked before replacing it.

18   Starter motor (Warrior) - removal and installation

Removal

1   Disconnect the cable from the negative terminal of the battery.

2   Pull back the rubber boot and remove the nut retaining the starter cable to the starter. Remove the starter mounting bolts.

3   Lift the outer end of the starter up a little bit and slide the starter out of the engine case. **Caution:** *Don't drop or strike the starter - its magnets may be demagnetized, which will ruin it.*

4   Check the condition of the O-ring on the end of the starter that fits into the engine and replace it if necessary.

Installation

5   Remove any corrosion or dirt from the mounting lugs on the starter and the mounting points on the crankcase.

6   Apply a little engine oil to the O-ring and install the starter by reversing the removal procedure.

19   Starter motor (Warrior) - disassembly, inspection and reassembly

1   Remove the starter motor (see Section 18).

Disassembly

Refer to illustrations 19.2a, 19.2b, 19.3, 19.4 and 19.5

2   One of the through-bolts should be centered between alignment marks **(see illustrations)**. Make your own marks if they aren't visible.

3   Unscrew the two through-bolts, then remove the cover with its O-ring from the motor **(see illustration)**.

4   Remove the bracket with its O-ring and the brush set from the motor **(see illustration)**.

5   Slide off the insulating washer and shim(s) from the armature, noting their locations, and withdraw the armature from the housing **(see illustration)**.

Inspection

Refer to illustrations 19.6, 19.8, 19.9a, 19.9b, 19.10 and 19.15

Note: *Check carefully which components are available as replacements before starting overhaul procedures.*

6   Lift the brush springs and slide the brushes out of their holders **(see illustration)**.

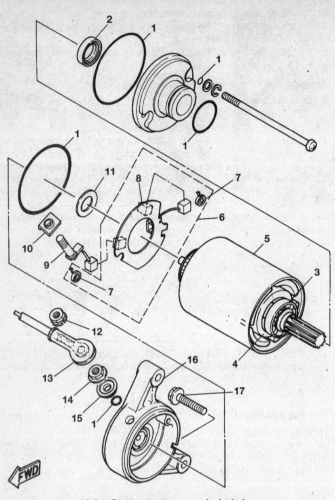

19.2a Starter motor – exploded view

1	O-rings	10	Insulator
2	Seal	11	Shim(s)
3	Bearing	12	Cable nut
4	Armature	13	Rubber cover and cable
5	Starter housing	14	Terminal nut
6	Brush set	15	Insulator
7	Brush springs	16	Bracket
8	Brush plate	17	Mounting bolt
9	Terminal bolt		

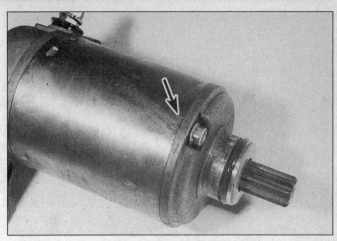

19.2b Position of the through-bolts is indicated by alignment marks (arrow)

19.3 Remove the through-bolts and pull the cover off

7   The parts of the starter motor that most likely will require attention are the brushes. If one brush must be replaced, replace both of them. The brushes are replaced together with the terminal bolt and the brush plate. Brushes must be replaced if they are worn excessively, cracked, chipped, or otherwise damaged. Measure the length of the brushes and compare the results to the brush length listed in this Chapter's Specifications. If either of the brushes is worn beyond the specified limits, replace them both.

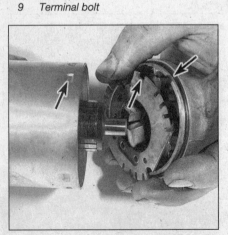

19.4 Pull the bracket and brush plate off the housing; the housing tab, brush plate slot and bracket slot (arrows) must be aligned on assembly

19.5 Pull the armature out of the housing and note the location of the shims on each end

19.6 Detach the positive brush from the brush plate and lift the plate out

9

19.8 Check the commutator for cracks
and discoloring, then measure
the diameter

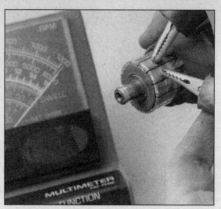

19.9a Continuity should exist between the
commutator bars

19.9b There should be no continuity
between each commutator bar
and the armature shaft

8   Inspect the commutator for scoring, scratches and discoloration. The commutator can be cleaned and polished with 600-grit emery paper, but do not remove copper from the commutator. After cleaning, clean out the grooves and wipe away any residue with a cloth soaked in an electrical system cleaner or denatured alcohol. Measure the commutator diameter and compare it to the diameter listed in this Chapter's Specifications **(see illustration)**. If it's less than the service limit, the motor must be replaced with a new one.

9   Using an ohmmeter or a continuity test light, check for continuity between the commutator bars **(see illustration)**. Continuity should exist between each bar and all of the others. Also, check for continuity between the commutator bars and the armature shaft **(see illustration)**. There should be no continuity between the commutator and the shaft. If the checks indicate otherwise, the armature is defective.

10   Check the undercut of the mica between the commutator bars **(see illustration)**. If it isn't deep enough, carefully scrape away mica with a broken-off piece of hacksaw blade until the undercut is as listed in this Chapter's Specifications.

11   Check the seal in the cover for wear or damage. Check the bearing on the armature for roughness, looseness or loss of lubricant. Check with a motorcycle shop or Yamaha dealer to see if the seal and bearing can be replaced separately; if this isn't possible, replace the starter motor.

12   Inspect the bushing in the bracket. Replace the starter motor if the bushing is worn or damaged.

13   Check the starter pinion for worn, chipped or broken teeth. If the gear is damaged or worn, replace the starter motor.

14   Inspect the insulating washers and shims for signs of damage and replace if necessary.

19.10 Measure the depth of
the mica and undercut it if
necessary

15   Check the magnets inside the starter housing for damage or loss of magnetism **(see illustration)**. Replace the starter motor if the magnets are damaged.

Reassembly

Refer to illustration 19.18

16   Lift the brush springs and slide the brushes back into position in their holders.

17   Make sure the shim(s) are in place on the bracket end of the armature.

18   Install the brush plate in the bracket, making sure its notch is correctly aligned with the housing notch **(see illustration)**. Insert the terminal bolt through the bracket, then install the O-ring, insulator and nut on the terminal bolt.

19   Insert the armature in the housing, locating the brushes to the commutator bars **(see illustration 19.18)**. Check that each brush is securely pressed against the commutator by its spring and is free to move easily in its holder.

20   Install the large O-ring and housing on the bracket; make sure the tab on the housing aligns with the notches in the brush plate and bracket **(see illustration 19.4)**.

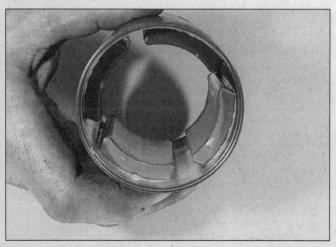

19.15 Replace the starter if the magnets inside the
housing are damaged or weak

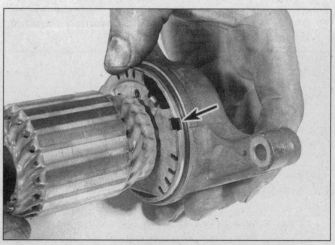

19.18 Align the brush plate and bracket notches (arrow)

20.2a Pull off the starter wheel gear (arrow) . . .

20.2b . . . then remove the needle roller bearing and washer

20.3 The idle gear shaft should pull out of the crankcase easily; if
not, remove the snap-ring and washer, then slide the gear and
two needle roller bearings off the shaft

21   Apply a smear of grease to the cover seal lip.
22   Slide the shim(s) onto the front end of the armature shaft. Fit the
large O-ring to the housing and carefully slide the front cover into position, aligning the marks on each side of the through-bolt hole (see
illustration 19.2b).
23   Fit the through-bolts and tighten them securely.

20 Starter clutch and reduction gears (Warrior) - removal, inspection and installation

Removal

Refer to illustrations 20.2a, 20.2b and 20.3

1   Refer to Section 23 and remove the alternator cover and rotor.
2   Pull the starter wheel gear off the end of the crankshaft, then
remove the bearing and plain washer (see illustrations).
3   Support the starter idle gear and pull its shaft out of the
crankcase, together with the snap-ring, washer and two needle roller
bearings (see illustration).

Inspection

Refer to illustrations 20.6 and 20.8

4   Check the gears for worn or broken teeth. Check the shafts and
the friction surface on the gears for wear or damage and replace any
parts that show defects.
5   Since needle roller bearing wear is difficult to see, the bearings

20.6 Check the starter clutch for visible wear and damage

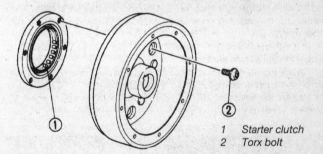

1   Starter clutch
2   Torx bolt

20.8 Remove the six Torx bolts, then remove the starter clutch

should be replaced if there's any doubt about their condition.
6   Check the starter clutch in the back of the alternator rotor for visible wear and damage and replace it as described below if problems
are found (see illustration).
7   Place the alternator rotor in the starter clutch. Hold the alternator
rotor with one hand so its open side is toward you and the starter
wheel gear is away from you. Try to rotate the starter wheel gear with
the other hand. The gear should rotate counterclockwise (anti-clockwise) smoothly, but not rotate clockwise at all.
8   If the gear rotates both ways or neither way, or if its movement is
rough, remove the Torx bolts and separate the starter clutch from the
alternator rotor (see illustration).
9   Install the starter clutch in the alternator rotor with its arrow mark
facing away from the rotor. Before you tighten the Torx bolts, place the
starter wheel gear in the rotor and try to turn it both ways. It should turn

9

counterclockwise (anti-clockwise) but not clockwise, as described in Step 7. If the gear turns the wrong way, the starter clutch is installed backwards.

10 Apply non-permanent thread locking agent to the threads of the Torx bolts and tighten them to the torque listed in this Chapter's Specifications.

Installation

11 Installation is the reverse of the removal steps, with the following addition: Lubricate the gears, bearings and shafts with clean engine oil.

21 Charging system testing (Warrior) - general information and precautions

1 If the performance of the charging system is suspect, the system as a whole should be checked first, followed by testing of the individual components (the alternator and the regulator/rectifier). **Note:** *Before beginning the checks, make sure the battery is fully charged and that all system connections are clean and tight.*

2 Checking the output of the charging system and the performance of the various components within the charging system requires the use of an ohmmeter; voltmeter or ammeter (depending on model); or the equivalent multimeter.

3 When making the checks, follow the procedures carefully to prevent incorrect connections or short circuits, as irreparable damage to electrical system components may result if short circuits occur.

4 If the necessary test equipment is not available, it is recommended that charging system tests be left to a dealer service department or a reputable ATV repair shop.

22 Charging system (Warrior) - output test

1 If a charging system problem is suspected, perform the following checks. Start by checking the fuse (see Section 5) and battery (see Section 3 and Chapter 1). If necessary, charge the battery (see Section 4).

2 With the engine idling, attach the positive lead of a 0 to 20 volt voltmeter to the positive (+) battery terminal and the negative lead to the battery negative (-) terminal.

3 Start the engine and let it warm up to normal operating temperature.

4 Slowly increase the engine speed to 5000 rpm and compare the voltmeter reading to the value listed in this Chapter's Specifications.

5 If the voltage output is as specified, the alternator is functioning properly.

6 If the voltage output is higher than specified, verify that the rectifier/regulator is connected to the system. If the rectifier/regulator is connected, and voltage output is higher than specified, replace the rectifier/regulator.

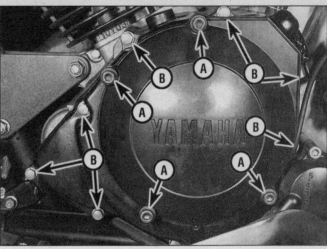

23.6a The alternator outer cover is secured by Allen bolts (A); the main cover is secured by hex bolts (B) (two rear bolts hidden) . . .

7 If the voltage output is lower than specified, check and, if necessary, replace the main fuse (see Section 5).

8 If the main fuse is okay, check and, if necessary, replace the charging coil (see Section 23).

23 Alternator charging coils and rotor (Warrior) - check and replacement

Charging coil check

1 Locate and disconnect the coil connector on the left side of the vehicle frame. The connector can be identified by its three white wires.

2 Connect an ohmmeter between each of the terminals in the side of the connector that runs back to the engine (connect the positive lead to one of the terminal and the negative lead to each of the two remaining terminals in turn). If the readings are outside the range listed in this Chapter's Specifications, replace the charging coils as described below.

3 Connect the ohmmeter between a good ground on the vehicle and each of the connector terminals in turn. The meter should indicate infinite resistance (no continuity). If not, replace the charging coils.

Charging coil and CDI magneto replacement

Refer to illustrations 23.6a, 23.6b, 23.7, 23.8, 23.10 and 23.11

4 Drain the engine oil (see Chapter 1).

5 If the vehicle has a recoil starter, remove it (see Chapter 2B).

23.6b . . . the lower rear bolt has a sealing washer

23.7 Hold the rotor with a wrench (or use a clutch holding tool if the vehicle has a recoil starter) and undo the bolt with a socket . . .

23.8 . . . then pull the rotor out

23.10 The charging coils and CDI magneto are secured by Phillips screws (arrows)

6   If you're working on a machine without a recoil starter, remove the outer cover from the left crankcase cover **(see illustrations)**.

7   Remove the bolt that secures the rotor to the alternator rotor. If the vehicle has a recoil starter, hold the rotor from turning with a clutch holding tool of the type described in Chapter 2 or a chain wrench. If it doesn't have a recoil starter, hold the rotor with a large open end or adjustable wrench **(see illustration)**.

8   Pull the rotor out of the cover **(see illustration)**.

9   Remove the cover bolts **(see illustrations 23.6a and 23.6b)**. Pull the cover off the engine. You may need to pull firmly to overcome the resistance of the rotor magnets, but don't use excessive force. If the cover seems to be stuck, check to make sure all fasteners have been removed.

10   Remove the charging coil screws and the CDI magneto screws **(see illustration)**, then remove the charging coils and CDI magneto together (they're replaced as a unit).

11   Check the seal in the cover for wear or damage. Spin the bearing inner race with a finger and check for roughness, looseness or noise. If the bearing or seal needs to be replaced, remove the Torx screws, take off the retainer, pry out the seal and remove the bearing **(see illustration 23.8 and the accompanying illustration)**.

23.11 Left side crankcase details

1   Intake cam chain guide
2   Plain washer
3   Bearing
4   Starter wheel gear
5   Woodruff key for alternator rotor
6   Starter idle gear shaft
7   Needle roller bearings
8   Starter idle gear
9   Plain washer
10   Snap-ring
11   Alternator cover dowels
12   Cover gasket
13   Alternator rotor
14   Charging coils
15   Timing plug
16   O-ring
17   Alternator cover
18   Bearing
19   Oil seal
20   Rotor (recoil starter type shown)
21   O-ring
22   Outer cover

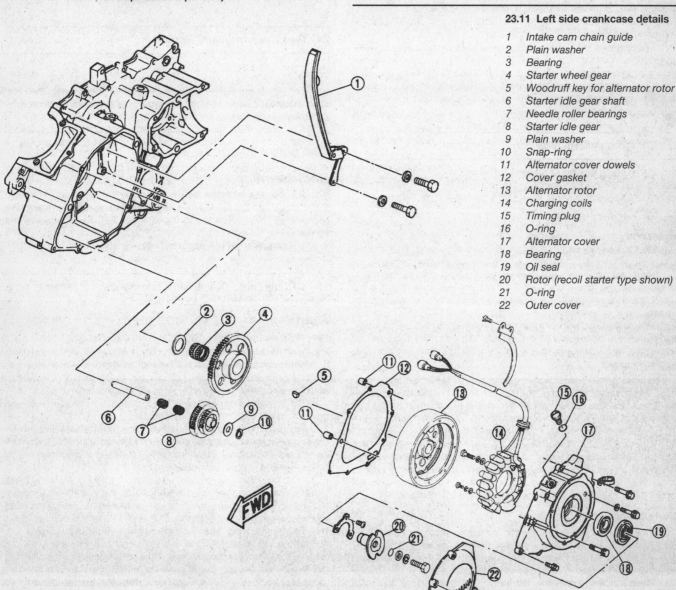

9

23.15 Thread the rotor puller onto the threaded portion of the rotor (arrow) and hold the flats (arrow) with a wrench while turning the puller bolt to free the rotor

12   Installation is the reverse of the removal steps, with the following additions:

a) *Apply non-permanent thread locking agent to the threads of the charging coil and CDI magneto screws, then tighten them to the torque listed in this Chapter's Specifications.*

b) *Remove all old gasket material from the alternator cover and crankcase. Use a new gasket on the alternator cover.*

c) *Make sure the cover dowels are in position* **(see illustration 23.11)**.

d) *Use a new sealing washer on the lower rear cover bolt* **(see illustration 23.6b)**. *Tighten the cover bolts evenly, in a criss-cross pattern, to the torque listed in this Chapter's Specifications.*

Rotor replacement

Removal

Refer to illustration 23.15

Note: *To remove the alternator rotor, the special Yamaha puller (part no. YM-01404) or an aftermarket equivalent will be required. Don't try to remove the rotor without the proper puller, as it's almost sure to be damaged. Pullers are readily available from motorcycle dealers and aftermarket tool suppliers.*

13   Remove the alternator cover as described above for access to the rotor.

14   Hold the alternator rotor with a strap wrench. If you don't have one and the engine is in the frame, the crankshaft can be held stationary by placing the transmission in gear and holding the rear brake on.

15   Thread the outer portion of the puller onto the rotor **(see illustration)**. Hold the flats of the outer portion with a wrench and turn the bolt with another wrench to separate the rotor from the crankshaft.

16   Pull the rotor off, together with the starter clutch.

17   Check the rotor Woodruff key; if it's not secure in its slot, pull it out and set it aside for safekeeping. A convenient method is to stick the Woodruff key to the magnets inside the rotor, but be certain not to forget it's there, as serious damage to the rotor and charging coils will occur if the engine is run with anything stuck to the magnets.

Installation

18   Degrease the center of the rotor and the end of the crankshaft.

19   Make sure the Woodruff key is positioned securely in its slot.

20   Align the rotor slot with the Woodruff key. Place the rotor, together with the starter clutch, on the crankshaft.

21   Take a look to make sure there isn't anything stuck to the inside of the rotor.

22   The remainder of installation is the reverse of the removal steps.

25.2a Left crankcase cover screws (Banshee)

24   Regulator/rectifier (Warrior) - check and replacement

Check

1   The regulator/rectifier is tested by process of elimination (when all other possible causes of charging system failure have been checked and eliminated, the rectifier/regulator is defective). Since it's easy to miss a problem, it's a good idea to have the charging system tested by a Yamaha dealer or substitute a known good unit before buying a new one.

Replacement

2   Remove the seat (see Chapter 8).

3   Disconnect the rectifier/regulator electrical connector (black wire, red wire and three white wires). Remove the mounting bolts and lift it off the frame.

4   Installation is the reverse of the removal steps.

25   CDI magneto (Banshee) - component replacement

Rotor

Refer to illustrations 25.2a, 25.2b, 25.3, 25.4 and 25.5

Caution: *To remove the alternator rotor, the special Yamaha puller or an aftermarket equivalent will be required. Don't try to remove the rotor without the proper puller, as it's almost sure to be damaged. Pullers are readily available from ATV dealers and aftermarket tool suppliers.*

1   Remove the shift pedal (see "External shift mechanism - removal, inspection and installation" in Chapter 2A).

2   Remove the left crankcase cover **(see illustration)**. Inspect the cover gasket for cracks and tears. If it's damaged, remove it from the cover **(see illustration)**, clean the gasket surfaces of the cover and the crankcase and install a new gasket.

3   Hold the alternator rotor with a universal holder or equivalent. You can also use a strap wrench. If you don't have one of these tools and the engine is in the frame, the rotor can be locked by placing the transmission in gear, letting out the clutch and setting the parking brake. Unscrew the rotor nut **(see illustration)** and remove the washer.

4   Thread an alternator puller into the center of the rotor and use it to remove the rotor **(see illustration)**. If the rotor doesn't come off easily, tap sharply on the end of the puller to release the rotor's grip on the tapered crankshaft end. **Caution:** *Don't strike the rotor, as the magnets will be damaged.* After pulling off the rotor, remove the Woodruff key from the crankshaft and store it in a plastic bag.

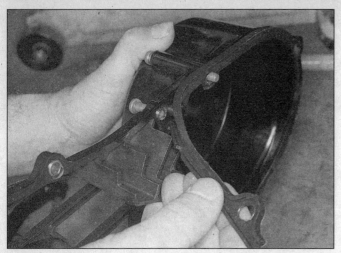

25.2b Replace the cover gasket if it's cracked, torn or deteriorated

25.3 Lock the rotor (see text) and remove the nut and washer (arrow)

5   Once the rotor has been removed, look at the inside and inspect the magnets **(see illustration)**. If a rock or stray piece of metal has made its way inside the rotor, the magnets may be damaged, which can weaken the magneto's electrical output.
6   Degrease the center of the rotor and the end of the crankshaft.
7   Install the Woodruff key in its slot in the crankshaft.
8   Align the rotor slot with the Woodruff key. Place the rotor on the crankshaft.
9   Install the rotor and washer and nut. Hold the rotor from turning with one of the methods described in Step 3 and tighten the nut to the torque listed in this Chapter's Specifications.
10   Install the left crankcase cover, making sure the gasket is seated correctly.

Stator (source coils and pick-up coil)

Refer to illustrations 25.12, 25.13 and 25.14
Note: *The stator assembly includes the source coil for the lighting system, and the source coil and pick-up coil for the ignition system. If any of these three components is defective, the stator must be replaced as a single assembly.*
11   Remove the rotor as described above.
12   Work the stator wiring harness grommet out of its hole in the crankcase **(see illustration)**.
13   Remove the stator mounting screws **(see illustration)** and remove the stator assembly.

25.4 Use a Yamaha puller (or a suitable equivalent) to remove the rotor

25.5 Serious damage can occur if the engine is run with anything stuck to the rotor magnets

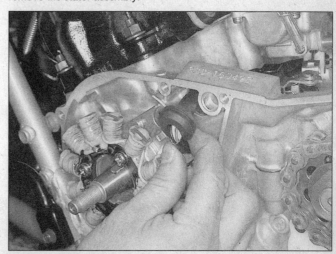

25.12 Before removing the stator, work the wiring harness grommet out of its hole in the crankcase and pull out the harness

9

**25.13 To detach the stator assembly, remove these
three screws (arrows)**

**25.14 When installing the stator, be sure to tuck the wiring
harness behind it (arrow)**

14   Installation is the reverse of removal. Make sure that the wiring
harness is tucked behind the stator assembly **(see illustration)** where
it won't be damaged by the rotor.
15   Install the rotor as described above.

26   Voltage regulator (Banshee) - replacement

Refer to illustration 26.2
Note: *To test the voltage regulator, see Section 6.*
1   Remove the seat (see Chapter 8).
2   Disconnect the regulator wiring connector and remove the
mounting screws **(see illustration)**.
3   Installation is the reverse of removal.

27   Wiring diagrams

Prior to troubleshooting a circuit, check the fuses to make sure
they're in good condition. Make sure the battery is fully charged and
check the cable connections.
When checking a circuit, make sure all connectors are clean, with
no broken or loose terminals or wires. When unplugging a connector,
don't pull on the wires - pull only on the connector housings.

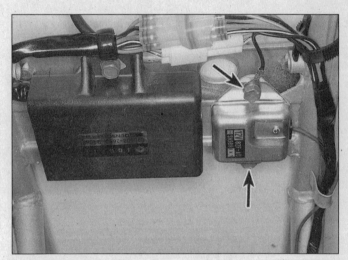

**26.2 Banshee voltage regulator mounting bolts; one bolt
secures a ground wire**

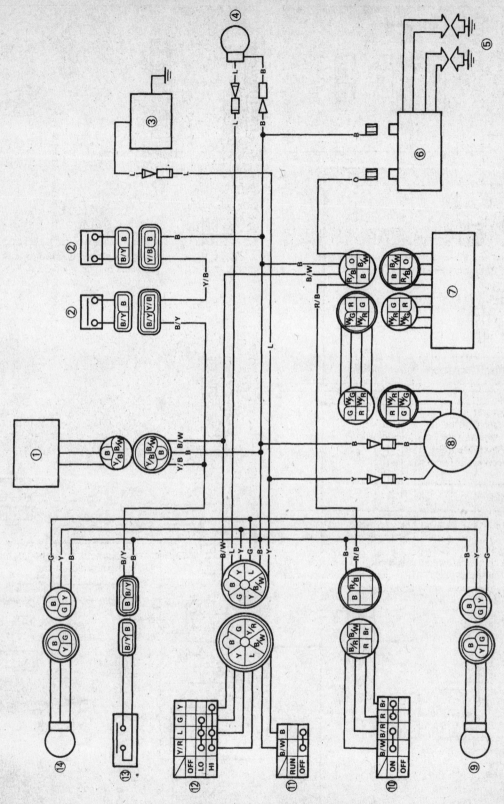

Wiring diagram (1987 through 1996 Banshee)

1	T.O.R.S. (ignition cutoff system) control unit	5	Spark plug	10	Main switch
2	Carburetor switch	6	Ignition coil	11	Engine stop (kill) switch
3	Voltage regulator	7	CDI unit	12	Dimmer switch
4	Tail light	8	CDI magneto	13	Throttle switch
		9	Headlight	14	Headlight

9

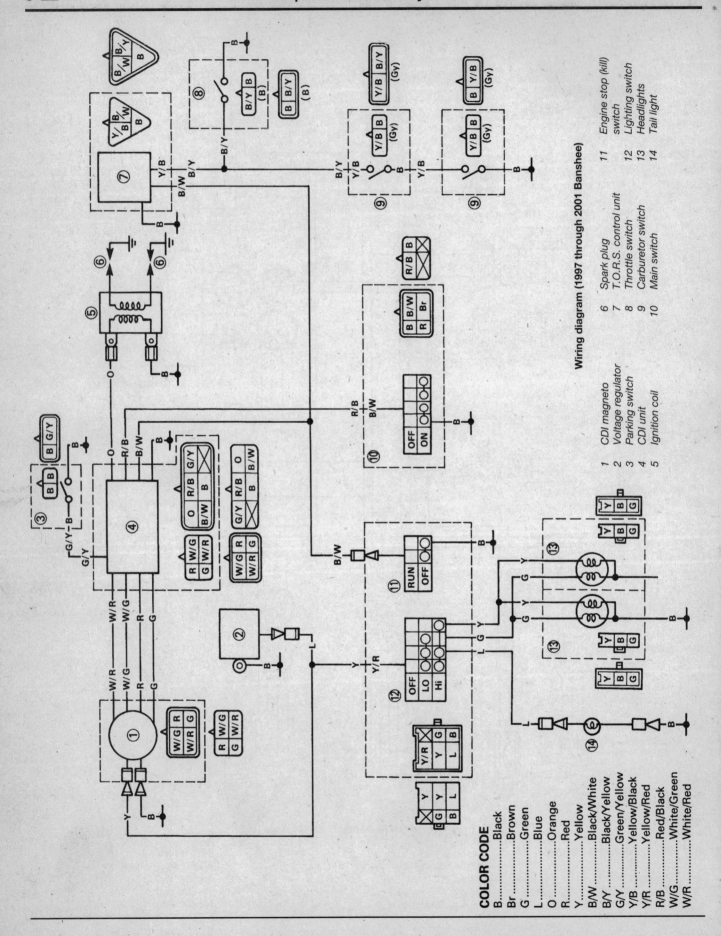

Wiring diagram (1997 through 2001 Banshee)

1   CDI magneto
2   Voltage regulator
3   Parking switch
4   CDI unit
5   Ignition coil

6   Spark plug
7   T.O.R.S. control unit
8   Throttle switch
9   Carburetor switch
10 Main switch

11 Engine stop (kill)
    switch
12 Lighting switch
13 Headlights
14 Tail light

COLOR CODE

B........Black
Br........Brown
G........Green
L........Blue
O........Orange
R........Red
Y........Yellow
B/W........Black/White
B/Y........Black/Yellow
G/Y........Green/Yellow
Y/B........Yellow/Black
Y/R........Yellow/Red
R/B........Red/Black
W/G........White/Green
W/R........White/Red

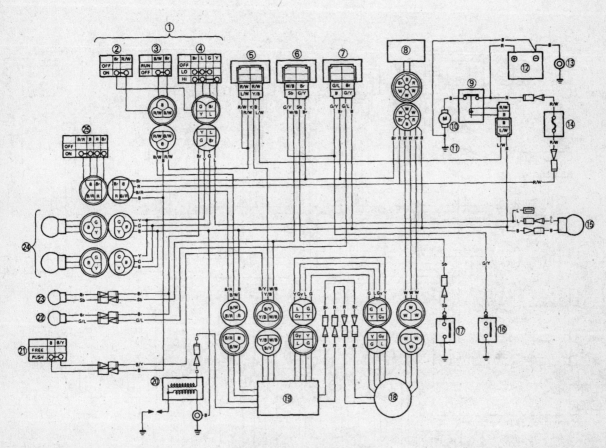

Wiring diagram (1987 Warrior)

1 Handlebar switch	10 Starter motor	19 CDI unit
2 Dimmer switch	11 Engine ground	20 Ignition coil
3 Engine stop (kill) switch	12 Battery	21 Clutch switch
4 Starter switch	13 Body ground	22 Reverse indicator light
5 Starting circuit cut-off relay	14 Fuse	23 Neutral indicator light
6 Neutral switch relay	15 Tail light	24 Headlight
7 Reverse switch relay	16 Reverse switch	25 Main switch
8 Rectifier/regulator	17 Neutral switch	
9 Starter relay	18 CDI magneto	

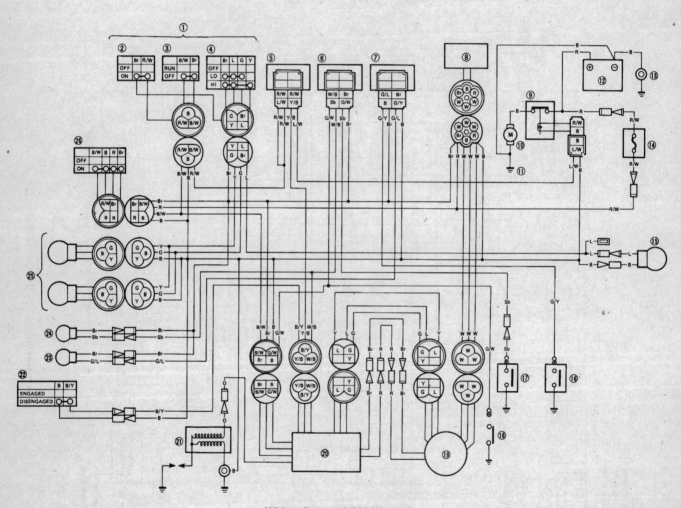

Wiring diagram (1988 Warrior)

1	Handlebar switch	10	Starter motor	19	CDI magneto
2	Dimmer switch	11	Engine ground	20	CDI unit
3	Engine stop (kill) switch	12	Battery	21	Ignition coil
4	Starter switch	13	Body ground	22	Clutch switch
5	Starting circuit cut-off relay	14	Fuse	23	Reverse indicator light
6	Neutral switch relay	15	Taillight	24	Neutral indicator light
7	Reverse switch relay	16	Reverse switch	25	Headlight
8	Rectifier/regulator	17	Neutral switch	26	Main switch
9	Starter relay	18	Reverse lever switch		

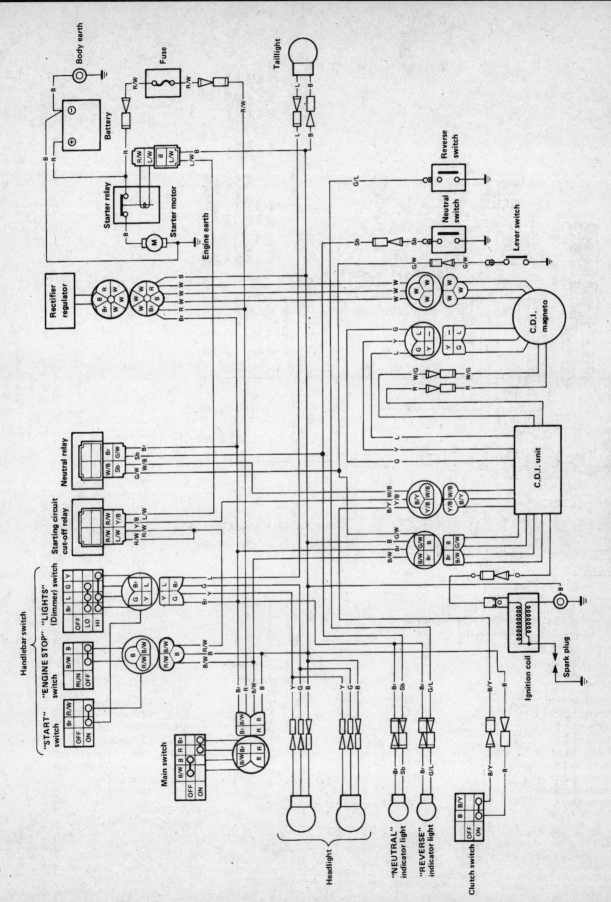

Wiring diagram (1989 through 1996 Warrior)

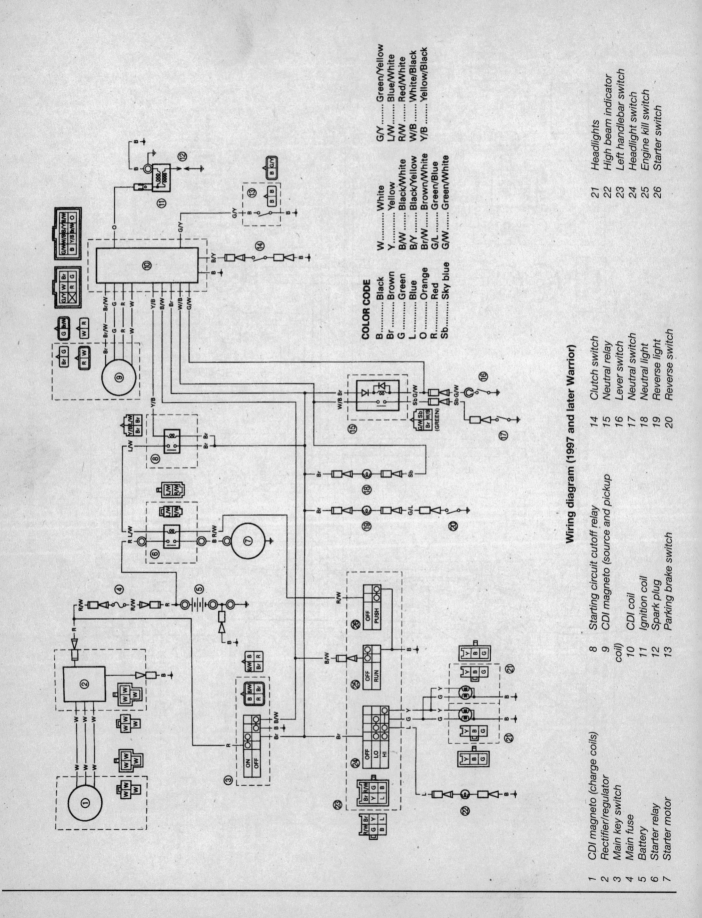

Wiring diagram (1997 and later Warrior)

COLOR CODE

B........	Black
Br.......	Brown
G........	Green
L........	Blue
O........	Orange
R........	Red
Sb.......	Sky blue

W........	White
Y........	Yellow
B/W......	Black/White
B/Y......	Black/Yellow
Br/W.....	Brown/White
G/L......	Green/Blue
G/W......	Green/White

G/Y......	Green/Yellow
L/W......	Blue/White
R/W......	Red/White
W/B......	White/Black
Y/B......	Yellow/Black

1   CDI magneto (charge coils)
2   Rectifier/regulator
3   Main key switch
4   Main fuse
5   Battery
6   Starter relay
7   Starter motor
8   Starting circuit cutoff relay
9   CDI magneto (source and pickup coil)
10   CDI coil
11   Ignition coil
12   Spark plug
13   Parking brake switch
14   Clutch switch
15   Neutral relay
16   Lever switch
17   Neutral switch
18   Neutral light
19   Reverse light
20   Reverse switch
21   Headlights
22   High beam indicator
23   Left handlebar switch
24   Headlight switch
25   Engine kill switch
26   Starter switch

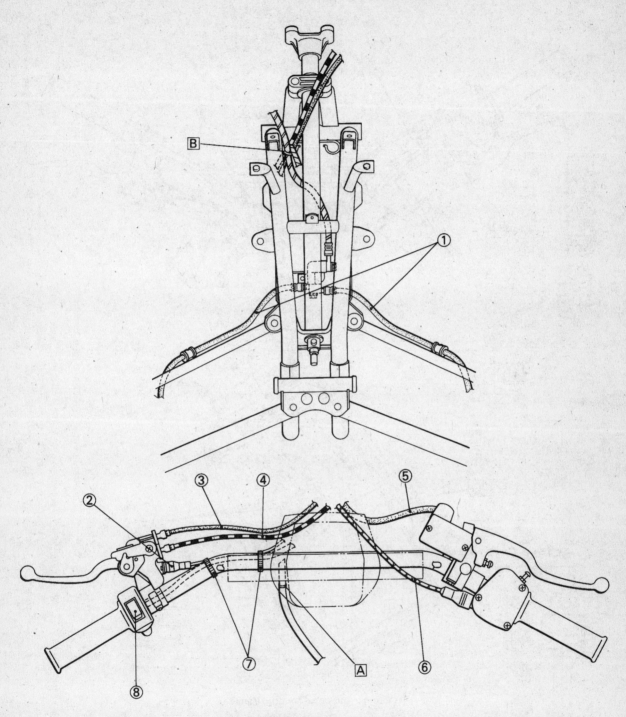

Front hose and cable routing, Warrior

1	Brake hose	4	Clutch cable
2	Clutch switch	5	Brake hose
3	Brake cable	6	Throttle cable
		7	Tie wraps
		8	Left handlebar switch

9

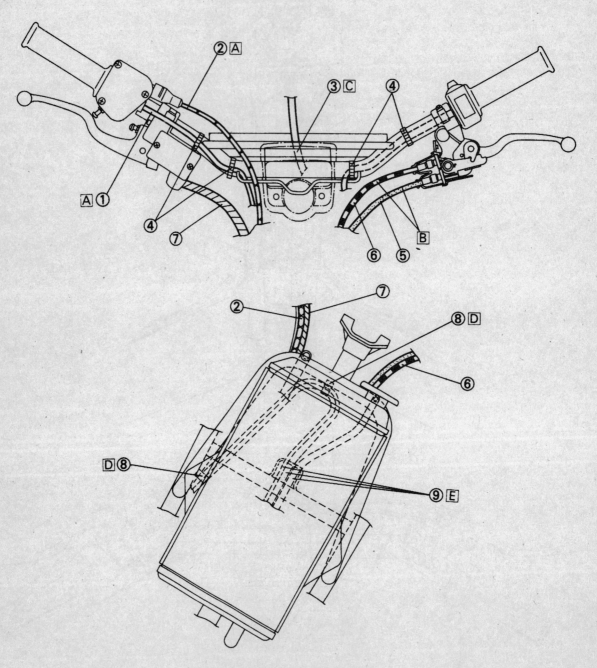

Front hose and cable routing, Banshee

1	Throttle switch harness	4	Tie wraps	7	Front brake hose
2	Throttle cable	5	Parking brake cable	8	Retainer
3	Fuel tank breather hose	6	Clutch cable	9	Breather hose

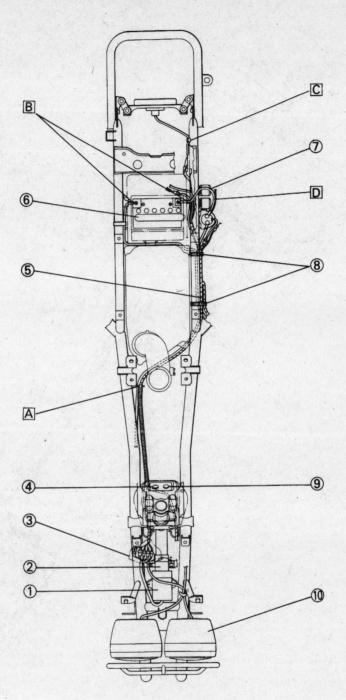

Frame hose and cable routing, Warrior

1	CDI unit	5	Wiring harness	8	Tie wraps
2	Ignition coil	6	Battery	9	Reverse lamp
3	Rubber boot	7	Positive lead	10	Headlights
4	Neutral lamp				

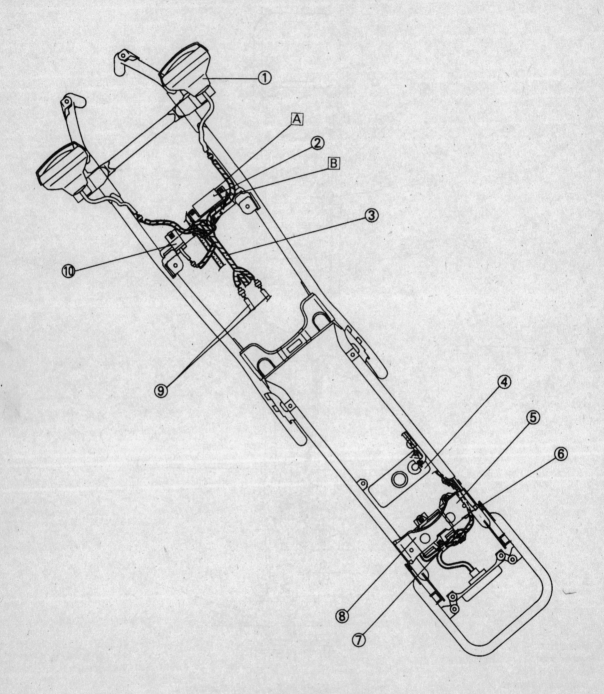

Frame hose and cable routing, Banshee

1	Headlight	5	Voltage regulator	8	CDI unit
2	Ignition coil	6	Frame ground	9	Carburetor switch harness
3	Wiring harness	7	Clamp	10	TORS control unit
4	Reserve tank				

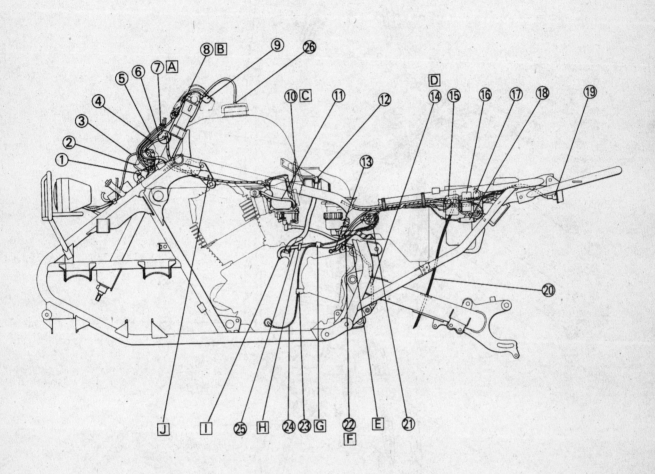

Warrior hose and cable routing, side view

1 Ground bolt	10 Air vent hose	19 Taillight
2 Rubber boot	11 Fuel hose	20 Battery vent tube
3 To right headlight	12 Crankcase breather hose	21 Rubber boot
4 Main switch harness	13 Ground lead	22 Brake hose
5 Clutch switch harness	14 Carburetor overflow hose	23 Clamp
6 Handlebar switch harness	15 Starter relay	24 Neutral switch harness
7 Retainer	16 Starting circuit cutoff relay	25 CDI magneto harness
8 Main switch	17 Neutral switch relay	26 Fuel tank breather hose
9 Indicator lamp	18 Fuse holder	

9

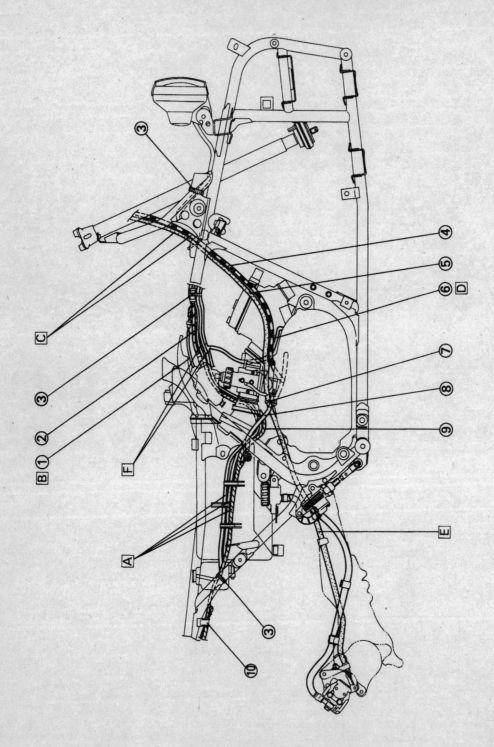

Banshee hose and cable routing, side view

1	Carburetor switch harness	5	Parking brake cable	8	CDI magneto harness
2	Throttle cable	6	Breather hose	9	Wiring harness
3	Tie wrap	7	Cable guide	10	Clamp
4	Clutch cable				

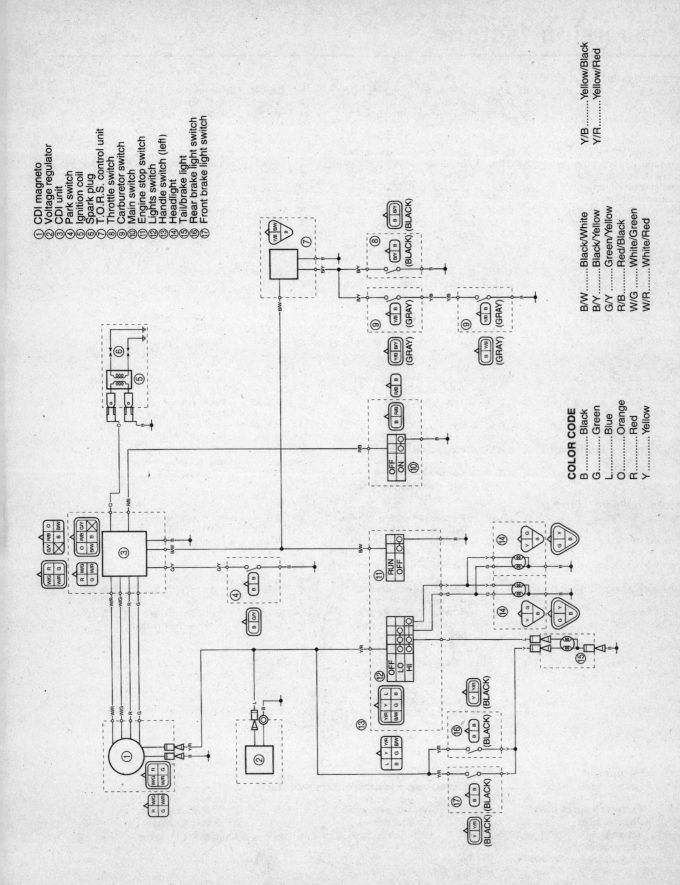

① CDI magneto
② Voltage regulator
③ CDI unit
④ Park switch
⑤ Ignition coil
⑥ Spark plug
⑦ T.O.R.S. control unit
⑧ Throttle switch
⑨ Carburetor switch
⑩ Main switch
⑪ Engine stop switch
⑫ Lights switch
⑬ Handle switch (left)
⑭ Headlight
⑮ Tail/brake light
⑯ Rear brake light switch
⑰ Front brake light switch

Y/B ....Yellow/Black
Y/R ....Yellow/Red

B/W ....Black/White
B/Y ....Black/Yellow
G/Y ....Green/Yellow
R/B ....Red/Black
W/G ....White/Green
W/R ....White/Red

COLOR CODE

B ....Black
G ....Green
L ....Blue
O ....Orange
R ....Red
Y ....Yellow

2002 and later Banshee models

9

Conversion factors

Length (distance)
Inches (in)	X	25.4	= Millimetres (mm)	X	0.0394	= Inches (in)
Feet (ft)	X	0.305	= Metres (m)	X	3.281	= Feet (ft)
Miles	X	1.609	= Kilometres (km)	X	0.621	= Miles

Volume (capacity)
Cubic inches (cu in; in³)	X	16.387	= Cubic centimetres (cc; cm³)	X	0.061	= Cubic inches (cu in; in³)
Imperial pints (Imp pt)	X	0.568	= Litres (l)	X	1.76	= Imperial pints (Imp pt)
Imperial quarts (Imp qt)	X	1.137	= Litres (l)	X	0.88	= Imperial quarts (Imp qt)
Imperial quarts (Imp qt)	X	1.201	= US quarts (US qt)	X	0.833	= Imperial quarts (Imp qt)
US quarts (US qt)	X	0.946	= Litres (l)	X	1.057	= US quarts (US qt)
Imperial gallons (Imp gal)	X	4.546	= Litres (l)	X	0.22	= Imperial gallons (Imp gal)
Imperial gallons (Imp gal)	X	1.201	= US gallons (US gal)	X	0.833	= Imperial gallons (Imp gal)
US gallons (US gal)	X	3.785	= Litres (l)	X	0.264	= US gallons (US gal)

Mass (weight)
Ounces (oz)	X	28.35	= Grams (g)	X	0.035	= Ounces (oz)
Pounds (lb)	X	0.454	= Kilograms (kg)	X	2.205	= Pounds (lb)

Force
Ounces-force (ozf; oz)	X	0.278	= Newtons (N)	X	3.6	= Ounces-force (ozf; oz)
Pounds-force (lbf; lb)	X	4.448	= Newtons (N)	X	0.225	= Pounds-force (lbf; lb)
Newtons (N)	X	0.1	= Kilograms-force (kgf; kg)	X	9.81	= Newtons (N)

Pressure
Pounds-force per square inch (psi; lbf/in²; lb/in²)	X	0.070	= Kilograms-force per square centimetre (kgf/cm²; kg/cm²)	X	14.223	= Pounds-force per square inch (psi; lbf/in²; lb/in²)
Pounds-force per square inch (psi; lbf/in²; lb/in²)	X	0.068	= Atmospheres (atm)	X	14.696	= Pounds-force per square inch (psi; lbf/in²; lb/in²)
Pounds-force per square inch (psi; lbf/in²; lb/in²)	X	0.069	= Bars	X	14.5	= Pounds-force per square inch (psi; lbf/in²; lb/in²)
Pounds-force per square inch (psi; lbf/in²; lb/in²)	X	6.895	= Kilopascals (kPa)	X	0.145	= Pounds-force per square inch (psi; lbf/in²; lb/in²)
Kilopascals (kPa)	X	0.01	= Kilograms-force per square centimetre (kgf/cm²; kg/cm²)	X	98.1	= Kilopascals (kPa)

Torque (moment of force)
Pounds-force inches (lbf in; lb in)	X	1.152	= Kilograms-force centimetre (kgf cm; kg cm)	X	0.868	= Pounds-force inches (lbf in; lb in)
Pounds-force inches (lbf in; lb in)	X	0.113	= Newton metres (Nm)	X	8.85	= Pounds-force inches (lbf in; lb in)
Pounds-force inches (lbf in; lb in)	X	0.083	= Pounds-force feet (lbf ft; lb ft)	X	12	= Pounds-force inches (lbf in; lb in)
Pounds-force feet (lbf ft; lb ft)	X	0.138	= Kilograms-force metres (kgf m; kg m)	X	7.233	= Pounds-force feet (lbf ft; lb ft)
Pounds-force feet (lbf ft; lb ft)	X	1.356	= Newton metres (Nm)	X	0.738	= Pounds-force feet (lbf ft; lb ft)
Newton metres (Nm)	X	0.102	= Kilograms-force metres (kgf m; kg m)	X	9.804	= Newton metres (Nm)

Vacuum
Inches mercury (in. Hg)	X	3.377	= Kilopascals (kPa)	X	0.2961	= Inches mercury
Inches mercury (in. Hg)	X	25.4	= Millimeters mercury (mm Hg)	X	0.0394	= Inches mercury

Power
Horsepower (hp)	X	745.7	= Watts (W)	X	0.0013	= Horsepower (hp)

Velocity (speed)
Miles per hour (miles/hr; mph)	X	1.609	= Kilometres per hour (km/hr; kph)	X	0.621	= Miles per hour (miles/hr; mph)

Fuel consumption*
Miles per gallon, Imperial (mpg)	X	0.354	= Kilometres per litre (km/l)	X	2.825	= Miles per gallon, Imperial (mpg)
Miles per gallon, US (mpg)	X	0.425	= Kilometres per litre (km/l)	X	2.352	= Miles per gallon, US (mpg)

Temperature
Degrees Fahrenheit = (°C x 1.8) + 32   Degrees Celsius (Degrees Centigrade; °C) = (°F - 32) x 0.56

*It is common practice to convert from miles per gallon (mpg) to litres/100 kilometres (l/100km), where mpg (Imperial) x l/100 km = 282 and mpg (US) x l/100 km = 235

Index